T0386068

# Desert Borderland

# Desert Borderland

*The Making of Modern Egypt and Libya*

## Matthew H. Ellis

Stanford University Press

Stanford, California

Stanford University Press
Stanford, California

Printed and bound by CPI Group (UK) Ltd, Croydon, CR0 4YY

Library of Congress Cataloging-in-Publication Data

Names: Ellis, Matthew H., author.
Title: Desert borderland : the making of modern Egypt and Libya / Matthew H.
    Ellis.
Description: Stanford, California : Stanford University Press, 2018 | Includes
    bibliographical references and index.
Identifiers: LCCN 2017038486 (print) | LCCN 2017039912 (ebook) | ISBN
    9781503605572 | ISBN 9781503605008 (cloth :alk. paper)
Subjects: LCSH: Egypt—Boundaries—Libya—History. | Libya—Boundar-
    ies—Egypt—History. | Territory, National—Egypt—History. | Territory,
    National—Libya—History. | Borderlands—Egypt—History. | Egypt—Poli-
    tics and government—19th century.
Classification: LCC DT82.5.L8 (ebook) | LCC DT82.5.L8 E44 2018 (print) |
    DDC 320.1/20620612—dc23
LC record available at https://lccn.loc.gov/2017038486

*For my parents*

It was then that I began to realize how much success the partitioning of the past had achieved. . . . I had been caught straddling a border, unaware that the writing of History had predicated its own self-fulfilment.

Amitav Ghosh, In an Antique Land

# Contents

*photo section follows page 142*

# Acknowledgments

The research for this book draws on a wide range of collections held in archives and libraries in Turkey, Egypt, Italy, and the United Kingdom. I am indebted, first of all, to the librarians, archivists, and staffs of the Prime Ministry's Ottoman Archives in Istanbul (particularly Fuat Recep); the Egyptian National Archives in Cairo (particularly Nadia Mustafa); the Egyptian Geographical Society in Cairo (particularly Dr. Muhammad Safi al-Din Abulezz); the Historical-Diplomatic Archive of the Ministry of Foreign Affairs in Rome; the Middle East Centre Archive at St. Antony's College, University of Oxford (particularly Debbie Usher); the Foyle Reading Room of the Royal Geographic Society in London; the British National Archives in Kew Gardens; and the Special Collections Library at Durham University (particularly Jane Hogan, Michael Harkness, and Francis Gotto).

This book would not have been possible without generous grants from the Social Science Research Council, as well as the American Research Council in Egypt. I also received financial support from Princeton University, Sarah Lawrence College, and the Endeavor Foundation. The Mohamed Ali Foundation granted me permission to work with the 'Abbas Hilmi II collection in Durham (all citations from that collection are reproduced by the kind permission of the Trustees of the Mohamed Ali Foundation and Durham University).

I feel tremendous gratitude for having had the support of numerous mentors, colleagues, and friends over the years I spent researching and writing this book. I thank my mentor Molly Greene for her gentle guidance, patience, and unflagging enthusiasm for this project. She continues to be a model for me as a historian and teacher. Graham Burnett introduced me to the world of spatial history and critical cartography, and his insight into the field has had a lasting impact on my thinking for this book. Eve Troutt Powell and Cyrus Schayegh offered excellent commentary on an earlier version of the manuscript, and helped me expand the scope of my argument. M. Şükrü Hanioğlu opened up new worlds to me by sharing his expertise working with nineteenth-century Ottoman documents. Khaled Fahmy embraced this project from the very start and has never ceased to be a true mentor and source of inspiration; I am also grateful for his thoughtful comments on portions of the manuscript.

Zachary Lockman, Oliver Murphey, and Edith Beerdsen each offered very helpful critiques of various chapters. Pamela Haag provided invaluable guidance as I developed the book's larger conceptual framework. Mostafa Minawi, Eileen Ryan, and Javier Puente-Valdivia graciously extended invitations for me to present my work. My steadfast research assistants, Zarka Shabir and Kitaneh Fitzpatrick, saved me precious time by attending to numerous odd jobs with their characteristic grace and efficiency.

I owe a special debt of gratitude to Aaron Jakes and Omar Cheta, both of whom pointed me to source material and offered detailed and incisive readings of the manuscript. Aaron and Omar have done more to push my thinking and writing than anyone, and I cannot imagine having completed this book without their friendship, wit, and deep insight into Egyptian history.

For the past five years, I have been quite fortunate to call Sarah Lawrence College my intellectual home. I am grateful to Jerrilynn Dodds, Kanwal Singh, Kristin Zahra Sands, Shahnaz Rouse, Glenn Dynner, Bella Brodzki, Bobbie Smolow, Lyde Sizer, Mary Porter, Suzanne Gardinier, Ellen Neskar, Griff Foulk, Joe Forte, David Castriota, and Cameron Afzal for making me feel so welcome, and for providing steady encouragement as I finished writing the book. Special thanks go to my colleagues Philipp Nielsen, Margarita Fajardo, Kevin Landdeck, Melissa Frazier, Jason Earle, James Horowitz, Fiona Wilson, and Sayuri Oyama for engaging so thoughtfully with my writing, and challenging me to think more broadly about what it could achieve; the book is undoubtedly stronger for it.

For their comradeship in the archives and at conferences, and for the numerous ways they've helped shape this project, I thank Carmen Gitre, Shana Minkin, Josh White, David Gutman, Will Smiley, Helen Pfeifer,

Tuna Artun, Liora Halperin, Louisa Lombard, Hussein Omar, Aimee Genell, Will Hanley, Junaid Quadri, Greg Hoadley, Stephanie Boyle, Michel Le Gall, Dan Stolz, Lale Can, Jennifer Pruitt, and Max Weiss.

I would like to thank Kate Wahl, editor-in-chief at Stanford University Press, for her excitement about this project from the get-go, her patience, and her gracious and steadfast stewardship as this book made its way to press. Working with her and the entire staff at Stanford has been an utter delight. I must also thank my two anonymous readers for their outstanding commentary on the manuscript.

I am eternally grateful to many dear friends for their moral support, their light, and their uplifting spirit over the years of research and writing: Isabel de Sena, Michelle Hersh, David Goodman, Amanda Croushore, Ryan Harper, Lynn Casteel Harper, Dan DiPaolo, Miriam Leviton, Phil Weitzman, Ben Roth, Lucy Rosenburgh, Andy Howard, Emma Crossen, Jeff Garland, Astrid Werner, Matt Swan, Laura Zuckerwise, Maria Siebel, Daniel Kozak, Chris Waters, Sara Schwanke-Khilji, Nick Goodbody, Peter Bohler, Mike Pinkel, Joe Gallagher, James Hollyer, Karen Bray, Dan Mandelbaum, Dov Yellin, Sameen Gauhar, Nomi Stone, Sarah Litvin, Lucas Goodbody, and the Inwood Hill Runners crew (Tamara Ewoldt, Louisa Wang, and Amy Cooper).

Above all, I thank my family. My parents, Esta and Steve, and my brother, Andy, have supported me in countless ways over the many years it has taken to complete this book. My parents have stood by me at every turn and shown their love for me to be limitless. This book is for them.

# Note on Transliteration

Throughout this book, I have adopted a system for the transliteration of Arabic and Ottoman Turkish that I hope will make the text as widely accessible as possible.

For place-names, I have used the spellings that are most common in contemporary English usage (Benghazi; Alexandria; Tobruk; Sollum). The same applies to those words of Arabic or Turkish origin that are now included in standard English dictionaries (fellah; bedouin; pasha).

Elsewhere, Arabic words and proper names are transcribed using a simplified system based on the *International Journal of Middle East Studies* (IJMES) style guidelines: this means that all diacritical markings have been omitted except for the 'ayn ('), and the hamza ('). I have made two important exceptions to this general rule, however. First, the names of Egyptian authors writing in English or French are rendered as they appear in their original publications (for example, Ahmed Hassancin, not Ahmad Hasanayn). Second, for the benefit of specialists, I have retained the full use of diacritical markings—based on the IJMES guidelines—for all translations that appear *within direct quotations*, as well as for all citations of Arabic publications in the notes and bibliography.

For the transliteration of Ottoman Turkish, I use a modified Modern Turkish orthography based on the *New Redhouse* dictionary.

Desert Borderland

# Introduction
## Rethinking Territorial Egypt

The Libyan Desert is part of our country, and it is incumbent upon
us to ascertain our borders there, so that we may better know our
country. By traversing the desert I will have established some of the
rights of our nation.

Ahmed Hassanein, *The Lost Oases* (1925)

Historians of the modern Middle East have typically treated Egypt
as a special case. Unlike the other Arabic-speaking nation-states to emerge
from the ashes of the Ottoman Empire after World War I, Egypt, so the
story goes, has maintained a continuous and stable territorial identity over
its long and dynamic history. But this narrative is belied by the curious
story of the "first modern political map" of Egypt (see Map 1).[1]

This map was a key part of the settlement that Mehmed ʿAli reached
with the Ottoman government in 1840,[2] concluding a decade-long power
struggle between the rogue Egyptian governor and his imperial suzerain.[3]
On February 13, 1841, Sultan Abdülmecid I issued a firman (decree) that
outlined the basic terms of the agreement: in exchange for withdrawing
Egyptian forces from Syria and Palestine and reducing the size of his standing army, Mehmed ʿAli would receive the right to hereditary rule over
Egypt. Often overlooked in accounts of this historic firman of investiture,
however, is the map that came with it. This is a curious oversight, considering that the text of the decree explicitly defined the scope of Mehmed ʿAli's
rule as the territory "contained within the ancient limits depicted on the
map" sent by the Grand Vezir.[4] Although the 1841 firman was an unprecedented concession by Istanbul, the map still served the important function
of circumscribing Mehmed ʿAli's ruling authority, by clarifying Egypt's position within the broader domain of Ottoman imperial sovereignty.

The image of Egypt inscribed in the 1841 map—which the Ottomans

**MAP 1.** Copy of the elusive 1841 Ottoman map of Egypt, appended to the firman of investiture sent to Mehmed 'Ali by the Ottoman Sultan. Source: Başbakanlık Osmanlı Arşivi, İ.MTZ(05) 34/2004. Reproduced with permission.

understood to represent the province's "ancient" and "known" territorial limits—differs significantly from that of the present-day nation-state. This is most apparent when we examine the map's depiction of Egypt's borders, all of which fall well short of their current location. In the south, the map's borderline intersects the Nile at around Aswan, approximately 155 miles north of the present border (which cuts across instead at Wadi Halfa). In the east, the map leaves a large portion of the Sinai Peninsula outside Egypt, marking the territory instead as part of the Hijaz (the western coastal region of present-day Saudi Arabia). Finally, in the west, the border commences from a point along the Mediterranean coastline corresponding roughly to present-day Marsa Matruh (more than 125 miles east of the current border, which lies just west of the port of Sollum).[5]

The extent to which the Ottomans' mid-nineteenth-century conception of Egypt's territorial shape diverges from the present-day Egyptian "geo-body"[6]—the standardized, infinitely reproducible mapped image of the country—is only the first of the 1841 map's surprises. Despite the Ottoman government's best intentions, the map's inclusion with the firman actually settled very little. For over three-quarters of a century, in fact, this first map of modern Egypt went missing. It was not published along with the firman,[7] and—although both the Ottoman and Egyptian governments were aware of its special significance for establishing the terms of Egypt's legal-political relationship with the Ottoman state—no one seems to have been able to locate it in Egypt prior to World War I.[8]

This was not for lack of trying. In 1892, during the initial phase of a persistent conflict between the Ottomans and the British over control of the Sinai, the Ottoman Grand Vezir lamented that the map could not be found in Cairo, since it alone could "establish the legal bounds of the [Ottoman] state."[9] A decade and a half later, during the height of the Sinai border crisis (also referred to as the Taba or Aqaba incident), the Ottomans again searched in vain for this "map showing Egypt's borders."[10] The British also called attention to the mysterious absence of this telltale map. In 1907, Lord Cromer, the consul-general of Egypt, observed that "this map is supposed to have been lost in a fire which destroyed a great part of the Egyptian Archives. The Turkish copy is occasionally alluded to by the Porte, no one has ever seen it, and its existence appears doubtful."[11]

The elusive map surfaced only in 1925, on the eve of a diplomatic settlement between Egypt and Italy, which led subsequently to the delimitation of Egypt's western border. In the course of their negotiations with the Italian government, the Egyptian authorities searched anew for the map but, once again, could not find it anywhere in Cairo. In May, the Egyptian Ministry of Foreign Affairs appealed to its ambassador in Turkey to look for the map in Istanbul's archives; several months later he finally located a copy and sent it to Egypt. This copy was then published along with the official western border treaty, signed on December 6, 1925.[12]

The inclusion of the 1841 Ottoman map with the Egyptian-Libyan border settlement of 1925 was an ironic choice, given how little the map seems to have mattered for over half a century. Ever since the emergence of the new "critical cartography" in the mid-1980s,[13] historians of nationalism have viewed maps as powerful tools, or "weapons,"[14] of nation-state formation.[15] Thongchai Winichakul—the author of a pathbreaking study of mapping's role in the making of modern Thai nationalism—has suggested that it is the presumed authenticity of cartographic knowledge that makes the inscription of mapped images of the nation so profoundly influential.[16] National maps derive much of their power from rendering invisible the messy configurations of social relations that actually exist on the ground at the time the maps are made.[17] Maps thus never merely reflect some objective spatial reality of the national community; rather, they *create* a new reality by forging a legible, panoptic image of bounded national territory. This is what made them such indispensable tools in the hands of modernizing and centralizing states throughout the nineteenth century.[18]

Egypt was different, however. Over the second half of the nineteenth century, the production of a definitive, clear-cut border map outlining the territorial shape of the nation was not a primary objective of the state. Instead, government officials were preoccupied with a very different sort of mapping. In the 1870s, the Egyptian Interior Ministry produced a series of maps to showcase various statistical data they had collected on the geographical distribution of different resources (see Map 2); the representation of all the land beyond the Nile Valley and Delta as so much white space suggests just how inconsequential the state deemed Egypt's borderlands at this time. The state's particular cartographic fixations were no different under British occupation. From 1898 to 1907, the Egyptian Survey Department worked to produce a "great land map of Egypt," intended, in the words of Timothy Mitchell, to "determine, for every square meter of the country's agricultural land the owner, the cultivator, the quality of the soil, and the proper rate of tax."[19] The sort of cartography that mattered to the colonial state, then, was specifically tailored to the twinned goals of promoting administrative efficiency and collecting revenue. The only Egyptian domains worth representing were those that were productive; the country's desert borderlands, which had little perceived value, had no place on the great land map.[20]

The lack of a precise conception of "cartographic Egypt"[21] before World War I was paralleled by the limited consideration of Egypt's territorial expanse by geographers and nationalist intellectuals. Insofar as these groups did concern themselves with the territorial contours of Egyptian identity, it was to assert an ambiguous discourse predicated on the "Unity of the Nile Valley."[22] The emergence of the "Unity of the Nile Valley" trope in the 1890s was part of a larger wave of interest in geography that burgeoned in Egyptian elite and intellectual circles over the last quarter of the

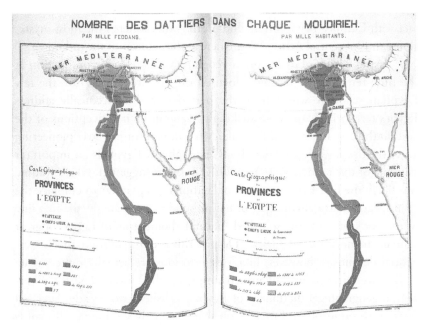

MAP 2. Egyptian Interior Ministry map from the 1870s, showing the distribution of date-palms in each province (Egypt's five western oases, all richly endowed with date-palms, are nowhere in sight). Source: Essai de statistique générale de l'Égypte. Reproduced by permission of the Hoover Institution Library.

nineteenth century. In 1875, as part of his initiative to widen the scope of Cairo's literary and cultural institutions and promote Egypt as a place of serious scientific learning, the Egyptian Khedive Isma'il (r. 1863–79) established the *Société Khédiviale de Géographie d'Égypte*—an intellectual salon for an array of explorers and amateur scholars, European and Egyptian alike.

From the outset, however, the Society's major thrust was not to re-search the geography of Egypt, which it seems to have taken largely for granted, but rather to provide a scientific foundation for Egypt's own colonial projects in Central Africa and the Sudan—most typically by sponsoring survey expeditions and ethnographic studies. In this way, the geographical knowledge produced under the Society's auspices served its members' underlying ideological aim of asserting Egypt's modernity by setting the country apart from the rest of the African continent in civiliza-tional terms.[23] As the Society's first president, German geographer George Schweinfurth, explained, "The Geographical Society of Cairo has all the advantages offered by a country which on the one hand is in intimate con-

tact with European civilization, and on the other touches the most mysterious lands of central Africa. We are here at the gateway of the unknown."[24]

If the vanguard of Egyptian geographical knowledge production at
the time remained so narrowly focused on the African interior, the few
Egyptian scholarly works from the period that did specifically address
Egypt's territorial scope were strikingly vague in their conceptions of the
land to the east and west of the Nile. Muhammad Amin Fikri's pioneering
1879 treatise *Jughrafiyat Misr* (The Geography of Egypt) is an important
example of this tendency. As Yoav Di-Capua has suggested, Fikri's volume
was likely the first Egyptian work of "national geography" to embrace the
"European territorial concept" of nationhood.[25] Accordingly, the first line
of the book presents the so-called "natural" boundaries of Egypt, "a great
state in the northeast of Africa." Despite this promise of more precise territorial definition, however, Fikri's descriptions are actually quite vague.
Egypt's western border is identified simply as "the Libyan Desert."[26] Similarly, a geographical dictionary of Egypt published two decades later fell
back on the amorphous formulation that, "properly speaking . . . Egypt is
bordered on the West by the Libyan Desert"; this led the author to conclude that "the Western frontier does not have precise limits."[27]

Egypt's path towards modern nation-statehood in the nineteenth century thus unfolded without a precise definition of a national "geo-body,"
circumscribed within clearly demarcated borders. Despite the absence of
authoritative representational practices to forge the nation, however, Egypt
began to emerge steadily as a modern territorial nation-state over the half-
century before World War I. This book seeks to explain how this came
to pass, by documenting the territorialization of the vast region I call the
"Egyptian West"—one of the desert borderlands that had been left clear
off the 1841 map.

Territoriality is a fundamental characteristic of modern nation-state formation, and yet it is often overlooked by historians, who tend to treat it
as a static background rather than a contingent historical artifact that has
had specific variations across space and time.[28] Historian Charles Maier,
whose oeuvre constitutes a noteworthy exception to this rule,[29] has defined territoriality as "the properties, including power, provided by the
control of bordered political space, which until recently at least created
the framework for national and ethnic identity."[30] According to Maier,
modern territoriality "developed alongside, indeed as a component of, the

ideas of modern sovereignty" that coalesced in Europe in the seventeenth century and were rendered more concrete with the Treaties of Westphalia. In this formative stage of modern territoriality, the onus for statesmen was on delimiting the contours of their sovereign control by drawing borders and, whenever possible, fortifying them. Over the next century, territoriality evolved so that the notion of "organizing space *within* borders"— squeezing as much revenue and resources as possible out of the lands under state control—became every bit as fundamental to prevailing conceptions of state sovereignty as boundary making had been in the earlier period.[31]

The technological advances of the industrial age ushered in a new era of what Maier calls "intensified territoriality."[32] Compelled by the period's rapid innovations in transportation, communications, and infrastructure, modernizing states around the globe embraced an ideal of territorial mastery that would have been unthinkable in an earlier age. To be a modern power in the nineteenth century meant that states needed to harness these technologies to achieve more coherent and uniform centralized control over the entirety of their domains. As Maier explains, state territoriality was now conceived as a totalizing energy field: "The center would radiate its energy outward along lines of communication (telegraphs and railroad) and implant local sources of national energy, whether schools or prefectures, throughout the territory. Every point on the map should contribute to the vitality and efficiency of the whole."[33]

This, at least, was the nineteenth-century territorial ideal. In practice, however, the territorialization projects that many states undertook in this period looked rather different. Although Maier concedes that "there are alternative concepts for claiming shares of global space and seeking territorial stability without fixed frontiers,"[34] his historical framework loses specificity when he writes about the ascendancy of bordered territoriality by 1890, after which "there was really no territory 'beyond the line' outside Antarctica" (only some "ambiguous and contested areas").[35] This formulation overlooks the range of alternate mechanisms for forging conceptions of bounded political space in the nineteenth century *beyond* the drawing of borderlines. Territoriality as practiced in the nineteenth century might have been modular, but it was not universal; as Will Hanley has recently argued for the related term *nationality*, territoriality had (and has) local particularities, which are themselves historical products that require careful contextualization and sifting.[36] If it is true that territoriality was a fundamental feature of nineteenth-century nation formation, it does not follow that modernizing states around the globe pursued only one avenue toward achieving it.

Egypt is an apt case for exploring alternate dynamics of nineteenth-century nation-state territorialization, especially considering how little Egypt's border regions seemed to matter at the time the country was first given modern political definition in 1841. In this book, I seek to explain the emergence of modern Egyptian territoriality by adopting the view from the margins—illuminating the little-known history of the Egyptian-Libyan borderland, where a range of state- and nation-making projects unfolded over the half-century before World War I. Throughout this period, a sharper sense of bounded political space—a heightened awareness of the existence of distinctive Egyptian and (Ottoman) Libyan territorial spheres—began to develop in this desert borderland despite the absence of any clear-cut boundary markers or cartographic evidence. National territoriality was not simply imposed on Egypt's western (or Ottoman Libya's eastern) domains by centralizing state power, however. Rather, it emerged only through a complex and multilayered process of negotiation with the region's predominantly bedouin and oasis-dwelling inhabitants, who were animated by their own local conceptions of space, sovereignty, and political belonging.

To advance this argument, *Desert Borderland*, drawing on some recent anthropological literature,[37] explores what I call the *lived experience of territoriality* as the conceptual lens that best enables scholars to capture the dynamic interaction between state and local actors in the forging of modern bordered political identities. Viewed this way, territoriality as it was practiced in the nineteenth century was not the sole province of state power—something that the center simply injected into the peripheries using the various administrative technologies at its disposal—but rather more of a feedback loop. Just as centralizing states were forced to adapt their territorial imperatives in light of the diversity of local spatial practices they encountered across their sovereign domains, so, too, were these various local spatial practices transformed by their encounter with modern nation-state building. The ways in which various local actors related to and inhabited space changed along with state territorialization projects; their spatial practices indeed became more self-consciously territorial.[38]

The borderland that Egypt shared with Ottoman Libya presents a particularly illuminating case study for exploring territoriality in this manner. Though sparsely populated, this vast swath of the Eastern Sahara was home to a rich tapestry of local denizens, ranging from numerous pastoralist bedouin tribes, to itinerant merchants operating along the Mediterranean coast, to sedentary agricultural communities settled for centuries in the various oases dotting the desert interior. For these populations, the desert borderland was not "marginal," as it would have been seen from the seats of state authority in Cairo or Istanbul, but rather the very locus of their spatial identity. Moreover, beginning in the mid-nineteenth century, the borderland also became the home base for the Sanusiyya—a mystical Islamic brotherhood that grew rapidly in the ensuing decades, galvanizing a striking proportion of the region's population. Through its encounter with the centripetal pull of both the Egyptian and Ottoman states, the Sanusiyya behaved increasingly like an embryonic territorial state in its own right, with its headquarters in the oasis of Jaghbub emerging by the late nineteenth century as an alternate sovereign center.

By adopting the view from the borderland, this book recasts the history of Egyptian nation-state formation as well as Ottoman re-centralization after the *Tanzimat*.[39] Territoriality as lived by the local population in the Eastern Sahara clashed repeatedly with the various centralizing projects introduced by both states during this period, but it also shaped these projects in fundamental ways. The chapters that follow document several crucial instances of this dynamic: the key role that the Sanusiyya and other local elites played in accommodating Egyptian state sovereignty in the borderland; the ways that bedouin mobility across the invisible "border" prompted both governments to reexamine the scope of their territorial definition in the region; and the competition between the Ottomans, Egyptians, and Italians to curry favor with local populations in their bid for territorial mastery in the Eastern Sahara in the decade before World War I.

Egypt's borderlands have been completely overlooked in the historiography of Egyptian nation-state formation. Particularly in light of much recent scholarship that has amply traced the discursive contours of national subjectivity in colonial Egypt,[40] the degree to which the territorial dimension of Egyptian nation-statehood has been taken for granted is rather startling.[41] This tendency has manifested in different ways. On one hand, much scholarship produced in Egypt, operating within a firmly nationalist paradigm, treats the country's territoriality as sacrosanct—a timeless essence of Egyptian identity that it is pointless, even dangerous, to question. In geographer Gamal Hamdan's multivolume study *Shakhsiyat Misr* (The Personality of Egypt), for example, Egypt's unique natural landscape—anchored by the fertile Nile Valley and Delta—molded a distinctive Egyptian national character that has endured ever since the time of the Pharaohs.[42]

On the other hand, the question of territoriality has fallen by the wayside even in much western historical scholarship on modern Egypt. It is understandable that the field's long-standing emphasis on documenting Egypt's encounter with European empire has naturally led many scholars to fix their gaze upon Cairo—the center of the colonial state, where British power was at its height, as well as the primary stage for the evolution of anti-colonial nationalism in the decades prior to World War I. This focus has had the unintended effect of obscuring much Egyptian history beyond the capital. Only in recent years have scholars begun to challenge Cairo-centric histories of modern Egypt by exploring alternate geographies within the emergent nation-state.[43] But even as Egypt's secondary cities, as well as its agricultural interior, have garnered increasing scholarly attention, the country's expansive desert borderlands are still neglected.[44]

This study's close attention to territorial dynamics in the borderland does more than merely fill a geographical lacuna, however; it also offers a unique lens through which to view Egypt's complex, multi-layered political history after 1841. Despite its concession of hereditary rule to Mehmed 'Ali at this time, the Ottoman government remained deeply invested in exercising nominal sovereignty over Egypt—now classified as a special "autonomous province" (*eyalet-i mümtaze*) within the imperial domains—even as the Egyptian state under the Khedives continued to expand and operate independently of Istanbul. The British military occupation of Egypt in 1882, which morphed seamlessly into the open-ended "Veiled Protectorate," added another layer to the composite structure of the Egyptian state. This rendered Egypt's sovereign status even more opaque:[45] henceforth, until World War I, Egypt would now have three sovereign masters—the Ottoman sultan; the Egyptian khedive (a member of the Mehmed 'Ali dynasty);[46] and the British consul-general (Lord Cromer, from 1882–1906).

Sovereignty is a fundamental premise of modern territoriality, but it would be a mistake to assume that it necessarily implies a unitary source of authority across a given state's domains.[47] James Sheehan has suggested that sovereignty "is best understood as a set of claims made by those seeking or wielding power, claims about the superiority and autonomy of their authority." Yet this sovereign claim-making never occurs in a vacuum. Rather, it is always the case that "claims imply counterclaims and contestation," so that "sovereignty involves not only asserting power but also constantly testing, extending, and sometimes accepting power's limitation."[48] Viewed in this way, sovereignty in practice has never worked according to the Westphalian ideal—the exercise of uniform centralized control over bounded state space—but rather has always been a matter of relative capability and reach, as state actors vie for ruling legitimacy in a competitive field.[49]

Adopting the view from the western borderland allows us to see the inner workings of Egypt's contested state sovereignty along these lines. Throughout the late nineteenth century, the region was transformed into a dynamic space for the articulation of overlapping sovereign claims and counterclaims by various agents of centralizing authority—the Ottoman, British-Egyptian, and (later) Italian states, but also the Khedive 'Abbas Hilmi II (r. 1892–1914), who pursued his own territorial projects across the Egyptian West in hopes of bolstering his status as the true, independent sovereign of Egypt.

Such an oblique view of the political machinations at the center of state power offers several advantages. First, it suggests a slightly alternate periodization for modern Egyptian history. From the vantage point of the borderland, Egypt's enduring Ottoman connection remains central to understanding the unfolding of events[50]—even after 1882—while the period of British colonial rule in Egypt appears more as one additional layer in a larger story of political and territorial transformation. Second, this approach recasts our understanding of colonial governance in late-nineteenth-century Egypt, by enabling us to see the delicate negotiations of power on a local level that British rule necessarily entailed. At the same time, the British appear more marginal in *Desert Borderland* than they do in most studies of late-nineteenth-century Egypt. In the story of borderland territorialization that unfolds in these pages, a multiplicity of state and non-state actors propelled events forward; accordingly, the edifice of British colonial power recedes somewhat into the background.

To reconstruct the multiple layers and meanings of territoriality in the Egyptian-Libyan borderland, this book draws from an expansive range of primary sources from the Ottoman, Egyptian, Italian, and British state archives; the personal papers of the Khedive 'Abbas Hilmi II; and a number of published memoirs, historical periodicals, and legal manuals. The objective throughout has been to read many of these disparate sources in tandem, and also against the grain, in order to hear not just from politicians and statesmen in Cairo, Istanbul, or Rome, but also from minor bureaucrats, local governors, judges, scribes, Sanusi brethren, bedouin tribesmen, and local shaykhs in the remote western oases. As the pioneering borderland historian Peter Sahlins has written in another context, "if there is a single history to the boundary and the borderland, it must take into account this multitude of voices, many of which can barely be heard."[51]

# 1

## Legal Exceptionalism in Egypt's Borderlands

Writing in 1931, retired Egyptian Coast Guard officer Andre von Dumreicher explained that "the Administration of the Nile Valley has been for years as well organized as that of any European country, but the deserts of Egypt had not been subjected to any interference by the Government until thirty-five years ago, when the Coast Guard Camel Corps was ordered to penetrate into the remotest parts of these wastes."[1] Although Dumreicher is right that Egypt's Coast Guard Administration (*Maslahat Khafr al-Sawahil*), with its celebrated Camel Corps, began to serve an important policing function in Egypt's deserts after around 1896,[2] it remains difficult to discern how these areas were governed before then. This is partly due to an acute lack of archival documentation, but it also reflects the fragmented nature of Egyptian administration beyond the Nile Valley. Before World War I, there was no single department responsible for governing the Egyptian West; rather, administration of the region was split among several discrete units, all based in the Nile Valley.

That it was necessary to carve up such a sparsely inhabited region among different governmental branches was undoubtedly a function of its vastness: today, Egyptian territory west of the Nile spans some 263,000 square miles, or more than two-thirds of the country's total land area. Given how large the Nile looms in popular perceptions of Egypt, it is easy to forget that the bulk of Egyptian soil actually comprises desert terrain. As archaeologist Ahmed Fakhry has pointed out, "the Nile Valley is, in fact, nothing but an oasis" in the extensive desert belt that runs east from

Morocco's Atlantic coast through Sinai and Arabia, continuing all the way to Central Asia.[3]

The Egyptian West's disjointed administration was also a function of the area's strikingly diverse physical and human geography. From the government's perspective, each of the region's landscapes posed distinct challenges.

First, there was the Mediterranean coastal plateau (*al-diffa*). This is a narrow strip of relatively fertile land—approximately twenty-five miles from north to south—that rises gradually from the outskirts of Alexandria all the way west to the cliffs of Sollum (located just a few miles from the Libyan border). The region has historically been inhabited by various bedouin tribes, most notably the Awlad 'Ali, who made good use of the scrubland on the southern edge of the plateau for grazing their livestock. Among the many small settlements dotting the shoreline, only Marsa Matruh—built around a picturesque harbor, approximately two hundred miles west of Alexandria—was close to being a major town, growing in the decade before World War I to become what one contemporary observer called the "commercial centre of the desert."[4]

Beyond the dramatic 640-foot escarpment marking the southern edge of the coastal plateau lies western Egypt's vast desert interior, though the broad term "desert" here, too, conceals an assortment of landscapes—ranging from the sweeping expanse of dunes known as the "Great Sand Sea" (in the far west, beginning just south of Siwa) to the dramatic mountains and rock formations of the "black" and "white" deserts outside Bahariya. This is to say nothing of the stark variations in altitude that the desert presents as one moves progressively south from the coastal plateau. The Egyptian Western Desert is striated by a series of ancient depressions that sit at or near sea level, affording access to subterranean water sources. Each of the five main western oases—Siwa, Bahariya, Farafra, Kharga, and Dakhla—lies inside one of seven major depressions, where natural springs and accessible ground water have enabled small sedentary communities to flourish.

Although these western oases are nowadays typically viewed as a single unit (not least in tourist guidebooks),[5] before World War I they fell into different administrative orbits, depending on their relative distance from the Nile Valley. Dakhla and Kharga—much closer to the Nile than Bahariya, Farafra, and especially Siwa—were more firmly tied to the social and political life of Upper Egypt (the stretch of the Nile Valley south of Cairo).[6]

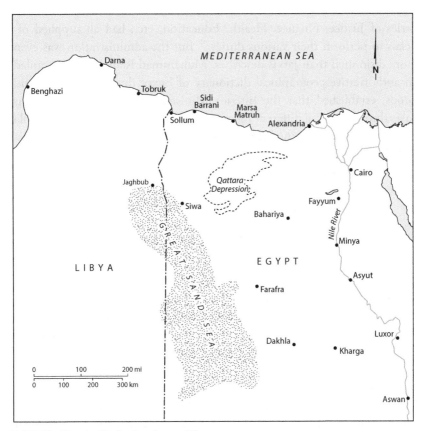

**MAP 3.** The "Egyptian West" and northeastern Libya.

But we should not presume that proximity to the Nile was historically the paramount determinant of territorial identity for the western oases—even Dakhla and Kharga. Indeed, the very names of these two oases imply that their primary orientation was not toward the Nile, but rather the desert interior: Dakhla ("inside" or "inner") is in fact further west than Kharga ("outside" or "outer"); from the perspective of one approaching the two oases from deeper inside the Sahara, the one that is closer to the Nile is the "outer" one.

Claude Jarvis, a British officer who served in a variety of desert posts during his career, alluded to the Egyptian state's fragmentary approach to governing the West: "The Coastguards had policed the Western Desert and Red Sea District; and the [Ministry of the] Interior had functioned in the oases of Kharga, Dakhla, Bahariya, and Farafra; whilst the Ministries of Justice, Finance, Health, Education, etc., had all supplied officials to perform their various duties."[7] But the administration was even more disjointed than Jarvis describes. Muhammad Ramzi, who compiled an authoritative geographical dictionary of Egypt during the 1950s and 1960s, established that the Interior Ministry administered the various oases through several different Egyptian governorates (*mudiriyyat*). Dakhla and Kharga were governed through the Asyut governorate,[8] but Bahariya and Farafra were attached to the governorate of Minya. And Siwa, which Jarvis neglected to mention—as well as Marsa Matruh and other coastal outposts, such as Sidi Barrani—would eventually be annexed to Buhayra.[9]

This patchwork system for governing the Egyptian West lasted until the First World War, when military developments along both Egypt's eastern and western frontiers compelled authorities to take immediate action. Under pressure from the Ottomans in Sinai and the Sanusiyya in the Western Desert, and citing wartime exigency, the British military in Egypt made the unilateral decision to unify Egypt's desert administration. In late 1916, British High Commissioner Reginald Wingate announced the formation of the Frontier Districts Administration (FDA), which subsumed all the administrative and police units that had formerly operated in the Western Desert and oases, including the Egyptian Coast Guard. The FDA would go on to play a crucial role in controlling Egypt's oasis and desert populations long after the conflict ended: its organization into three geographical units—the Eastern Desert, Western Desert, and Sinai divisions—formed the basis for the system of government that operates in Egypt's desert regions to this day.[10]

Jarvis became a leading figure in the FDA in the years following the war, and later praised the department's work in several publications reflecting upon his long career in Egypt. In these reflections, Jarvis echoed Dumreicher's assertion that the Egyptian government's efforts to manage its desert and oasis territories *before* the creation of the FDA had failed miserably: "The Egyptian Army looked upon service in the desert as penal servitude; the Coastguards, being hard-boiled anti-contrabandists, saw the Arabs only as potential smugglers, whilst the Interior and other Ministries used the deserts as punishment stations . . . in those days, they [the Egyptians] cared nothing about anything that happened five miles away from the River Nile."[11]

This sketch of the Egyptian state's uneven administrative geography before World War I is at odds with enduring nationalist assumptions about

Egypt's historical fixity as a bounded political community. More than this, however, it raises fundamental questions about how and why these remote desert and oasis territories beyond the Nile Valley began to matter to the Egyptian state in the first place. This chapter opens the book's investigation of territoriality in Egypt by examining how the steady expansion and centralization of the Egyptian state's governing practices and institutions in the few decades before World War I unfolded in the country's borderlands.

This analysis has implications for our understanding of Egyptian sovereignty in this period. Historian Lauren Benton has argued that "both law and geography produced ways of structuring understandings of empires as configurations of corridors and enclaves, objects of a disaggregated and uneven sovereignty."[12] In late-nineteenth-century Egypt, too, the mechanisms of state centralization yielded a "disaggregated and uneven sovereignty," whereby Egypt's borderlands emerged as enclaves of legal exceptionalism within the nascent modern nation-state. Moreover, the difficulties that the Egyptian government encountered in attempting to standardize its judicial institutions in the borderlands, with their primarily bedouin and oasis-dwelling populations, produced a discourse of otherness that would become de rigueur in local negotiations over sovereignty in this period. By highlighting the dynamic, interactive process through which Egyptian state sovereignty was introduced into the country's marginal domains, this chapter argues that the territorial imperatives of the centralizing Egyptian state ultimately worked in tandem with—and continued to rely upon—local, decentralized institutions and legal frameworks.

Siwa makes a particularly apt case study for examining Egyptian sovereignty as a process of negotiation between a tentative state and powerful local actors. Although the understanding of sovereignty that can be gained from this example would obtain for all of Egypt's marginal territories in the same period, Siwa stands out given its unique position within Egyptian nationalist historiography as well as in popular lore.

The place of Siwa in the nationalist imagination follows from its near mythical representation as Egypt's far-flung final frontier. Siwa stands out from the other western oases for having been settled by a distinctive ethnolinguistic group: Siwans are of Berber, not Arab, descent and historically spoke Siwi (a dialect of Tamazight), not Arabic; it is an open question whether most Siwans knew much if any Arabic before the 1920s.[13] Partly due to their status as a population apart, Siwans earned the reputation of being the fiercest defenders of their autonomy among Egypt's oasis-dwelling communities, and historically the most dangerous and ungovernable. Accordingly, Egyptian historians of the oasis have tended to consider Cairo's so-called "conquest" of Siwa at the end of the nineteenth century as a key turning point. For example, former army officer Rif'at Gawhari opens his detailed history of Siwa by meditating on the unique notoriety of the oasis, which had inspired "fear and mystery" throughout the ages.[14] Yet he then explains how Siwa ultimately fell under "the absolute rule of Egypt," as a result of several military campaigns dating back to Mehmed 'Ali's rule.[15]

It is this same mythology that serves as the point of departure for Baha'a Taher's celebrated historical novel, *Sunset Oasis* (*Wahat al-ghurub*), which tells the story of a fictional Egyptian officer, Mahmud 'Abd al-Zahir, who has been assigned by the Interior Ministry to become the new *ma'mur* (district governor) of Siwa in the late-1890s.[16] The central role of Siwan lore in the narrative is voiced most directly through 'Abd al-Zahir's English wife, Catherine, who accompanies her husband on his tour of duty despite the purported dangers. As she puts it, while on the long caravan journey to the oasis: "Everything about it is like a myth—the place, the people, the history, the geography . . . Its inhabitants belong to the west, not the east, to the Zenata tribe of Berbers in Morocco, and they speak a Berber dialect. Despite this, in ancient times they were part of the Egypt of the pharaohs and a centre for the worship of their great god, Amun."[17] Elsewhere, Taher invokes the conventional account of Siwan autonomy and resistance to government interference by having Catherine recount the oasis's turbulent nineteenth-century history: "I have read how they resisted Egyptian rule, ceaselessly rebelling and rising up against the soldiers and fighting them, while the Egyptians ceaselessly repressed their uprisings with a savagery that gave birth to new rebellions and new uprisings. And I know, as does Mahmoud, that the district commissioner, who is the ruler of the oasis, will always be a prize trophy for them."[18] Taher subscribes to the standard narrative of the Egyptian nation-state's successful incorporation of Siwa in this period, writing in the novel's postscript that "the customs of the nineteenth century have now disappeared and Siwa has become an *authentically Egyptian* region."[19]

In the spotty extant literature on nineteenth-century Siwan history, two overarching narratives dominate.[20] First is the ongoing conflict between Siwa's two rival factions, known as "Easterners" (*sharqiyin*) and "Westerners" (*gharbiyin*). The origins of this feud cannot be pinned down with any certainty. One Eastern shaykh named 'Umar Musallam—upon whose chronicle of the oasis various writers have purported to base their narratives—claimed that it originated with a dispute over an Eastern family's wish to enlarge its house in a way that would constrict a public thoroughfare in Shali, the inner town of Siwa.[21] Other authors contend that the conflict dates back even further, to the settlement of a pious Egyptian man, along with a mixed group of Berbers and Arabs, in the Western part of Shali.[22] Regardless of how the quarrel between Easterners and Westerners first arose, by all accounts it continued to dominate Siwan politics throughout the nineteenth century, compelling the two sides to live in separate spheres.[23]

The second prevailing narrative that emerges from the limited historiography on Siwa—and is so clearly reproduced in Taher's novel—is the Siwans' dogged resistance to the sporadic efforts of the Egyptian government to conquer it and exact an annual tribute, until the state's allegedly successful incorporation of the oasis by the turn of the century. In the earliest phase of the conflict, the Siwans succumbed to Mehmed 'Ali's forces, which were under the command of Husayn Bey Shamashurghi.[24] The consequences of defeat were severe: Shamashurghi executed sixty Siwan notables, introduced a steep annual tax, and then installed a shaykh from the oasis's Western faction named 'Ali Balli as the first government-appointed 'umda (chief or magistrate) of the oasis.[25]

Despite the Egyptian government's show of strength during this initial campaign, it lacked the power to enforce its new regime in Siwa with any consistency. The Siwans immediately flouted Balli's authority and refused to pay their taxes to Cairo. Mehmed 'Ali's response came only seven years later: in 1827, he sent Shamashurghi back to Siwa, along with a force of around eight hundred men, to reoccupy the oasis and coerce the Siwans into paying their taxes.[26] The Siwans once again countered with armed resistance, but the Egyptian force prevailed and again took extreme punitive measures against the oasis.[27]

It is difficult to discern even the most basic details of Siwa's political history in the decades following these formative events. One theme that emerges clearly from the muddled historical record, however, is that the Egyptian government's authority over the oasis was characterized by long fits of absence: the government could not, or chose not to, collect the Siwan tax with any degree of regularity. Shamashurghi's first expedition to Siwa in 1820 was only the first of four punitive tax campaigns that Mehmed ʿAli dispatched to the oasis within two decades.[28]

Given Siwa's extreme distance from Cairo, which made travel and communication between the two exceedingly time-consuming, the Egyptian government struggled to find reliable local governors. It was also challenging to ensure their safety; many Egyptian officials stationed in the oasis were in fact killed or forced into retreat. ʿAli Balli was murdered by local rivals in 1838, in what was the first of several such crimes committed against government agents in the nineteenth century. Other government officials were run out of the oasis, such as a governor named Yunus Effendi, who had been left in charge in Siwa after Mehmed ʿAli's final Siwan campaign in 1840. According to one account, Yunus's departure resulted in Siwa's being once again "left to itself and its assembly of Sheikhs" for what seems to be nearly two decades.[29] It was not until around 1857 that the Egyptian government again attempted to set its authority on firmer footing, creating the permanent post of *maʾmur* in the oasis.[30] Yet even after this reform, the government's position remained precarious, as the *maʾmur*s posted in Siwa were "totally inadequate to collect taxes or preserve order"; it is therefore unsurprising that the post of *maʾmur* continued to be deeply unpopular among Egyptian officials, considered "both by the Government and its employees as a form of banishment."[31]

That the Egyptian government remained only a distant presence in Siwa comes across clearly in the testimony of Muhammad Makki, a former qadi (shariʿa court judge) in the oasis who served in the early 1890s. In one case, according to Makki, "the Maʾmur [of Siwa] told me that he wrote at the time to the Buhayra Mudirieh (to which the oasis is attached), asking permission to sell the ground around it to natives so that both parties benefit by it; and the Mudirieh gave no answer. The people, however, do cultivate the land, but on what terms I cannot tell." Moreover, according to Makki, "there are in Siwa some 1,000 Feddans of cultivable lands which the natives are using without any benefit to the Government."[32] According to this report, the Buhayra governorate—the branch of the Egyptian government directly responsible for Siwa's administration—remained unmoved by the *maʾmur*'s attempt to flag a promising source of revenue for the state. The potential payoff was likely not worth the effort or associated costs.

The government's ongoing struggle to govern Siwa was only part of the story, however. Evidence also suggests that Siwan notables sometimes exploited the uncertain political situation in the oasis to buttress their own personal authority, or to serve their own factional interests. This dynamic can be observed in the aftermath of the murder of 'Ali Balli.

In 1838, Balli's son Yusuf petitioned the Egyptian government to appoint him as his father's successor. He then staged a ruse to curry favor with the government: he persuaded a group of Siwans to murder a hapless British traveler, James Hamilton, but then made secret arrangements for Hamilton's escape. The gambit paid off. Upon his return to Cairo, Hamilton extolled Yusuf's valor to the Egyptian Khedive, 'Abbas I (r. 1848–54), suggesting that Yusuf alone could restore order in Siwa. 'Abbas was receptive, and named Yusuf 'Ali the new *'umda* of the oasis. Yusuf's tenure would not last long, however. Two years later, on the occasion of his accession, the new Khedive Sa'id I (r. 1854–63) pardoned many prisoners of the state, including many of the Siwan shaykhs whom Yusuf 'Ali had betrayed. After a short war between the Easterners and Westerners, Yusuf 'Ali was killed, and Siwa once again entered a period of autonomy from the Egyptian government.[33]

These brief examples suggest a more complicated picture of Siwa's engagement with the Egyptian government than is typically given in standard historical accounts of the oasis. As the case of Yusuf 'Ali suggests, Siwan notables were able to harness the power and legitimacy of the state to serve their local political designs. The exercise of Egyptian territorial sovereignty in Siwa was not simply a function of the centralizing state imposing its will on the periphery, then, but rather an ongoing process of negotiation with local political actors. But Siwa was not unique in this respect. In the last quarter of the nineteenth century, a similar political dynamic was at play in many locales across Egypt's borderlands, which consequently emerged as enclaves of legal exceptionalism within the emergent Egyptian nation-state.

On November 19, 1924, a group of young Egyptian nationalists shot and killed Sir Lee Stack—the British governor-general of the Sudan, and commander (sirdar) of the Anglo-Egyptian army—as he was proceeding through the streets of Cairo. The Stack murder, one of the more notorious events in Egypt's interwar political history, has been amply documented, as has its political fallout.[34] What has typically been omitted from accounts, however, is the spatial dimension of the case.

The murder investigation came to a head far from Cairo, in the legally anomalous territory of the Egyptian West. The eight attackers had planned their getaway in advance: they would disguise themselves as bedouins, ride the Maryut Railway out to Hammam,[35] and then continue by car to Marsa Matruh and Sollum, where they could escape to Tripoli "through the help of certain Senussi Arab Sheikhs."[36] The Egyptian police, having been tipped off, assigned two undercover agents to accompany the suspects in transit. They then arranged for a Sudanese camel corps patrol to hold up the train near Hammam, at which point the police made their move and apprehended the suspects.[37]

The location of the sting operation worked in the prosecution's favor. As Thomas Russell Pasha—commandant of the Cairo City Police from 1917 to 1946—later explained, "We were particularly anxious to arrest them out West, i.e. in the Area of the Frontiers Administration where they would be outside the Parquet Jurisdiction and therefore holdable for some time without remand." Once the police brought the suspects back from the desert to the outskirts of Cairo, they were careful to leave them "with the Frontiers Administration at their Depot in Khanka, thus still keeping them out of the Parquet jurisdiction."[38] By apprehending the murder suspects and imprisoning them in territory under the special jurisdiction of the FDA, the police were able to circumvent Egyptian procedural law and handle their prisoners however they wished.[39] These agents of Egyptian justice, then, understood that a different set of legal norms prevailed even just outside Cairo, and they were keen to take advantage of the resultant discrepancies.[40]

That such unevenness in the legal regime persisted into the 1920s is particularly striking given the sweeping reorganization of the country's legal system that the government had been undertaking since the 1870s. Over the intervening decades, the Egyptian government worked to standardize its judicial institutions and practices across the country.[41] In June 1883, the government established the Native Courts (al-mahakim al-ahliyya), which became the destination for all criminal, civil, and commercial cases that did not involve any foreign litigants or property.[42] Simultaneously, it introduced a comprehensive new legal code, which outlined the jurisdiction of each court. The June decree was followed by another law, issued on December 30 of the same year, which provided more specific guidelines for defining the territorial reach of each court's jurisdiction; in some cases, the courts' jurisdiction was expanded.

Taken together, these legal reforms upended the traditional judicial order in Egypt's oases. In Siwa, a local court (*Majlis Siwa*), presided over by a quorum of shaykhs, had long overseen the administration of justice in the oasis. In February 1871, the Egyptian government had even officially recognized this local court for its role in "settling local affairs and bedouin issues."[43] The December 1883 law, however, abrogated the authority of *Majlis Siwa* by placing the oasis under the jurisdiction of Alexandria's Native Court of First Instance.[44]

But Siwa's incorporation into Egypt's new, centralized judicial regime did not go according to plan. In September 1884, the Egyptian Council of Ministers passed a special law exempting Siwa from the December 1883 jurisdiction law. As a result, Siwa was no longer under the jurisdiction of Alexandria's Native Court; instead, jurisdiction over the oasis returned to *Majlis Siwa*. Just as had been the case in 1871, the rationale given by the authors of the new law was the local court's special role in "resolving bedouin issues [*ḥall masā'il al-bedw*]."[45] A mere nine months after putting an effective end to Siwa's judicial autonomy, then, the Egyptian government reneged on its decision and restored the status quo ante.

Few documents survive to explain this curious reversal, but a letter written to the Interior Ministry by the governor (*mudir*) of Buhayra in June 1884 suggests one possible explanation. Although the governor begins his letter by establishing that Siwa is "among the dependent territories of the [Buhayra] province [*min ḍimna mulḥaqāt bilād al-mudīriyya*]," he immediately qualifies this statement by emphasizing the fundamentally distinctive character of the oasis: "The town is far from Egypt [*al-diyār al-Misriyya*] by a distance of approximately twenty days traveling by camel . . . It falls in the middle of the desert, and its people have different customs and (linguistic) conventions [*iṣṭilāḥāt*], and tastes [*mashārib*] that diverge completely from those of the Egyptians, by virtue of the fact that they are pure Arabs [*'urbān ṣirfan*]."[46] It was for these reasons, he felt, that the government had officially recognized *Majlis Siwa* in the first place, back in 1871.[47]

The governor's main impetus for writing this letter was to address a petition to the Interior Ministry from a Siwan, who complained about an unduly harsh sentence and fine he had received from *Majlis Siwa*. The governor had just happened to receive the transcript of this particular case from the authorities at Siwa (owing to the excessive distance of Siwa from the Nile Valley, *Majlis Siwa* forwarded its records to the authorities in Damanhur only once every six months). Upon examining the case, the governor concludes that *Majlis Siwa*'s ruling was just, because it was executed in a manner faithful to the customs of the Siwan people.[48]

In terms that provide remarkable insight into how Egyptian officials viewed this distant western oasis, the governor then returns to his initial invocation of Siwa's fundamental otherness—its distance from Egypt, and the distinctiveness of its people—to buttress his argument to the Interior Ministry that the government should reconsider its decision to apply the 1883 legal reforms to Siwa. Again, given the Siwans' "distance from civilization, their all being of bedouin descent, and their morals and customs being so completely different [*bu'dihim 'an al-ḥaḍāra wa kawnihim jamī'an min al-badāwa wa akhlāqihim wa 'ādātihim mukhālifatan b-il-kulliyya*]," he recommends that the Siwans should be permitted to abide by their own legal customs, for this would be the best way to promote their continued "stability, security, and obedience."[49]

At this point, the governor turns his attention to the Native Courts' jurisdiction law of December 1883, which he laments had disrupted legal tradition in Siwa. As an example, he cites the local ruling from *Majlis Siwa* that he had just recently found to be legitimate—the December 1883 law effectively annulled it. He thus argues strongly, once again, that implementing the new law in Siwa would be extremely unwise. Aside from Siwa's location "at such a distance from Egypt," the governor argues, "it is very difficult to change its customs and principles," as well as the affinity of the people for "the law of the local civil courts." The governor also cites a more practical reason for abrogating the December 1883 law: given Siwa's remoteness, it was impossible to ensure that Siwan litigants would show up in court all the way in Alexandria.[50]

The two basic arguments that lay at the heart of the governor's letter to the Interior Ministry—Siwa's excessive distance (from the Alexandria Native Court as well as from "Egypt" proper); and the fundamental otherness, or non-Egyptianness, of its inhabitants—gained wider currency around this time. Indeed, similar language would infuse debates and correspondence addressing the scope of Egypt's legal regime for decades to come.

In March 1885, the Egyptian Ministry of Justice adopted the September 1884 law (restoring the authority of *Majlis Siwa*) as a precedent for dealing with a remote desert town called al-Wajh,[51] which—like Siwa—had not been successfully incorporated into the new Native Courts system. According to Minister of Justice Boutros Ghali, al-Wajh was "equivalent to

Siwa with respect to distance" from Egypt proper. The Siwa analogy was also apt, he believed, given how the return to local jurisdiction in that oasis had served to "facilitate and execute legal cases [*tashīl wa injāz al-qaḍāyā*]," and prevent "the suffering of those liable to endure the hardships and expenses of travel." Ghali was thus advocating for the transfer of jurisdiction in both civil and criminal cases back to al-Wajh's local court—the de facto judicial institution prior to the December 1883 law—as had been done in Siwa.[52]

A similar sequence of events unfolded following the application of the 1883 Native Court jurisdiction laws in the oases of Kharga, Dakhla, and Bahariya. One crucial source for this history is the memoir of Ahmad Shafiq—a Zelig-like Egyptian official who served in a wide variety of government posts over his long career, including director-general of the FDA after World War I. According to Shafiq, Kharga's tradition of legal autonomy dated back to Roman times. Over the ensuing centuries, the implementation of justice in Kharga was entrusted to local "men who knew the customs and traditional laws [*'urf*] of the people." The Mamluks introduced an innovation when they created the position of district inspector (*kashif*) to collect fiscal taxes and oversee public order; otherwise, Kharga's ancient legal regime remained intact.[53] Even Mehmed 'Ali seemed to acknowledge the importance of preserving Kharga's legal autonomy. Shafiq interprets a decree that Mehmed 'Ali issued regarding the salaries of local judges as evidence that he "affirmed for the people of Kharga all the rights they had gained . . . which had become tantamount to custom for them."[54] For Shafiq, this decree demonstrated "the extent to which [Mehmed 'Ali] respected their customs," as well as his "utmost tolerance, and the vastness of his heart."[55]

As in the case of Siwa, the Native Court laws of 1883 disrupted Kharga's long-standing de facto judicial autonomy.[56] However, the government's attempt to incorporate the oasis into Egypt's new judicial regime played out somewhat differently than it did in Siwa, and over a longer period of time. First, the new jurisdictional legislation in 1883 stripped Kharga's shari'a representative of most of his previously wide-ranging powers and mandated that shari'a agents and judges would, from that point forward, be sent from the Nile Valley, rather than being appointed from among the residents of Kharga. The law also stripped the district inspector (now called *mu'awin al-tahsil*, instead of *kashif*) of all his judicial authority, rendering him powerless to do more than edit and sign memoranda and forward them to Kharga's new loci of power in the Nile Valley (first Girga, then Asyut).[57] In Shafiq's estimation, "it is astonishing that this district inspector was deprived even of the power to investigate crimes," a function of his exclusion from the ranks of the "judicial officers [al-ḍabṭiyya al-qaḍāʾiyya]" who had been authorized in 1883 to perform this function. The result of all these changes, according to Shafiq, was the "deterioration of security, disruption of work, and loss of rights" for all litigants in court, a circumstance that "forced the government to remedy the situation" by passing new legislation.[58]

Shafiq points to a significant new law passed in February 1890 that initiated a gradual process of rolling back the sweeping jurisdictional reforms of 1883.[59] Other evidence suggests that this process actually began in 1888, with two consecutive short laws that granted the district inspectors in both Dakhla and Kharga—as well as the superintendent (mulahidh) of Bahariya—the "privileges [ikhtiṣāṣāt] accorded to district supervisors [nudhār al-aqsām] in criminal and juristic matters [al-mawād al-jināʾiyya wa-l-mawād al-huqūqiyya]."[60] The 1890 law that Shafiq cites went even further, stipulating that these same local oasis officials would now be counted as members of the same corps of "judicial officers" from which the 1883 law had excluded them. Furthermore, the law provided these officials with the right to adjudicate minor infraction cases (mukhalafat) and the privilege of final arbitration in civil cases whose value did not exceed fifteen hundred qurush.[61] The government tweaked its oasis policy further a year later, passing yet another law that granted these same local officials in the three oases the right to final arbitration in infraction cases; Shafiq interprets this as an indication of the Egyptian government's realization that the 1890 law "had been insufficient."[62]

The most significant change, however, came in June 1900, when the government finally overturned the application of the Native Court jurisdiction laws to Kharga, Dakhla, and Bahariya. At this time, it officially sanctioned the restoration of local courts in each oasis, to be presided over by a local governing official, as well as two local notables per location, though these figures would be appointed by the Ministry of Justice and were subject to approval by the Ministry of the Interior. The law also invested the local courts with the authority of final judgment in all infraction cases, as well as jurisdiction in all punishable misdemeanor, civil, and commercial cases.[63] It was on the basis of the June 1900 law that legal scholar Henri Lamba designated these three oases, alongside Siwa, as zones of "special jurisdiction" in a compilation of Egyptian public and administrative law that he published in 1909.[64]

The jagged trajectory of judicial reform in these three oases illuminates the production of legal exceptionalism at the western margins of the Egyptian state. Shafiq's account of *why* the government felt change was needed in the case of Kharga is also significant. His explanation hinged on the notion of distance—in this case between Kharga and its corresponding administrative capital of Asyut—which created practical obstacles to the proper administration of justice in the oasis. Even after the government passed its first few amendments to the 1883 law, Shafiq writes, it still realized the prevailing system "did not serve the well-being of the people, since they still groaned from the harm done by the [initial] legislation as well as the distance of the locale" to which they needed to travel to settle their cases. The June 1900 law reestablishing the local court "relieved the people from the burden of long travel," which had previously "prevented them from obtaining their legal rights." Although Shafiq does not explicitly mention Bahariya or Dakhla, he claims that his analysis of "the stages through which legislation passed in Kharga" can similarly "be applied to the rest of the oases in the Egyptian kingdom."[65]

To be sure, there were pejorative undertones to this language of otherness that pervaded debates about jurisdiction in the western oases. What seems most critical about its invocation in this context, however, was its practical usefulness to the Egyptian government. Confronted with the basic constraints that the realities of Egyptian geography imposed on its centralizing sovereign capabilities, Egyptian lawmakers fell back on this language of otherness as a makeshift solution. Centralization and decentralization thus developed hand-in-hand: for the government to exercise greater sovereignty in these oases and extend the scope of its jurisdiction, it was necessary to allow them to continue to be *different*, by preserving their local legal practices and institutions.

Moving from the five western oases to the coastal plateau and vast desert interior of the Egyptian West, one finds that the discourse of difference also characterized the state's shifting relationship with its many bedouin tribes. This is a complex topic that warrants more attention than space allows here,[66] but it is crucial to highlight a few consequential developments from Mehmed ʿAli's reign.

In the view of successive ruling regimes, Egypt's bedouin tribes constituted an unpredictable political force. At least since Ottoman times, the tribes had often been considered a dangerous fifth column, or else a potentially useful mercenary force.[67] Mehmed 'Ali could not ignore the specter of bedouin military might—particularly after a segment of the Awlad 'Ali overwhelmed his forces at a battle near Hosh 'Isa around 1810.[68] Convinced of the need to appease the powerful Awlad 'Ali, who had de facto control over a wide swath of territory west of the Nile Delta, Mehmed 'Ali set out to unify the state's bedouin policy by reaching a series of agreements with the tribes (among whom the Awlad 'Ali would be given preferential treatment).[69]

Mehmed 'Ali's reformed bedouin policy had four main features. First, it excluded tribes from the corvée and excused all bedouins from military conscription, in exchange for their promise to serve as irregular troops in Egypt's foreign wars.[70] Second, tribes were granted tax-free usufruct rights throughout the desert territories.[71] Accordingly, they had no formal legal right to the lands they worked, and thus never owned them. Yet the flipside of this usufruct arrangement was that the bedouins were exempt from paying taxes to the state—a benefit that distinguished them from Egyptians settled in the Nile Valley.[72] Third, Mehmed 'Ali sought to co-opt tribal elites and convert them into agents of the state, often by making generous gifts of land in the Nile Valley.[73] He also offered them key administrative posts and intermediary positions created especially for them.[74] For instance, Mehmed 'Ali was instrumental in establishing a new cadre of tribal 'umdas[75]—a major innovation, given that the post of 'umda (the traditional authority figure in the Egyptian countryside) was not endemic to bedouin society.[76] Fourth, Mehmed 'Ali upheld the practice of customary tribal law ('urf) for the bedouins, thereby preserving their legal autonomy.[77]

The upshot of these reforms was that the Egyptian state's relationship with its tribal population was standardized, even as the state conceded the fundamental distinctiveness of the bedouins and devised its policy toward them accordingly. As Re'uven Aharoni—an expert on Egypt's bedouins in the nineteenth century—has suggested, Mehmed 'Ali succeeded in curbing the independent power of the tribes, while also consolidating them under the control of dominant shaykhs.[78] But we should be careful not to overstate the reforms' impact. First, it is unclear whether Mehmed 'Ali's policies reached very far, or could be enforced at all beyond the Nile Valley. As Aharoni observes, "There were several tribes with which [Mehmed

'Ali] had no contact, and their way of life within their own territory remained unchanged." This was particularly true for those tribes that dwelt in desert domains at the margins of Egyptian territory, far from the center of power.[79] Second, it was also difficult to discern where exactly those margins were located. According to Aharoni, there was a "conspicuous lack of a clear border between the 'desert' and the 'sown' regions."[80] This claim echoes historian Iman Muhammad 'Abd al-Mun'im 'Amir's assertion that "the borders between agricultural and desert (or pastoral) land were not fixed, owing to the fluctuation of the [annual Nile] flood." Over time, this led to the creation of an unstable and fluid "borderland of geographic and social intermixing between peasants and pastoral bedouins."[81]

Such demographic permeability at the desert edge made it extremely difficult to identify who was indeed a bedouin, as well as to pinpoint the precise meaning of that appellation. Some observers, such as G. W. Murray in his 1935 guide to the Egyptian tribes, defined "bedouin" as one who "travels or resides in the 'true desert' itself," rather than eking out a living on "the outskirts of civilization." He also suggested that the term bedouin connotes one's "profession or trade," and thus "has nothing to do with race, and is by no means synonymous with 'Arab.'"[82] But Murray's romantic conception of bedouin-ness was unduly crude. He ignored the fact that the Egyptian government made no semantic distinction between bedouins and "Arabs" ('arab or 'urban) in its official documentation.[83] Moreover, Murray failed to acknowledge that a significant portion of Egypt's bedouin population not only hung around the "outskirts of the cultivation," but also settled in various rural locales throughout the Delta and Nile Valley and had been mixing with the native fellahin (peasantry) for centuries.[84]

With these caveats in mind, it is worth considering a few cases, ranging across the four decades before World War I, in which various denizens of the Egyptian West exploited these ambiguities in the meaning of bedouin-ness. As was the case in Siwa, the tropes of distance and otherness could be useful to a variety of local figures, who appropriated them to register their own claims to the Egyptian government. For example, in 1887, a local notable from Maryut (the desert region lying west of Alexandria and Buhayra) named Mansur Isma'il sent petitions to four different branches of the Egyptian government, renouncing all responsibility for administering affairs in Maryut, and a nearby town called Abu Khadiga. As he explained, "These places are far from my village, I do not know them well, and they are inhabited by bedouins."[85] In this case, Isma'il felt that basing a claim on the distance of the lands, and the distinctiveness of the people beyond the edge of the Nile cultivation, would free him from unwanted administrative duties.

Another case from Maryut returns us to the theme of legal exceptionalism. In 1910, upon receiving news that the Egyptian government was about to force the local qadi, Shaykh Muhammad al-Najari, into retirement, "the *'umda*s, shaykhs, notables, and people" of Dakhila (a village in the district) sent a petition to the Egyptian Council of Ministers imploring them to reverse their decision. In doing so, they adopted the same discourse of otherness that the governor of Buhayra had used to discuss the local population of Siwa: "Maryut is one of the districts that is far from civilization [*al-'umrān*], containing people possessed of different morals and character [*al-ṭibā'*], who require someone who will provide them with the utmost refinement [*al-tahdhīb*], such as His Honor, who knew our morals and understood our character." Given how he was able to treat "each tribe, regardless of its disposition [*mashrab*] with the utmost care, zeal, trustworthiness, piety, and supreme virtue," as well as the fact that he "adhered to religious orthodoxy in all his rulings," the petitioners requested that the Council of Ministers allow him to remain in his post.[86] This document is a clear example of how non-state actors in the Egyptian West could mobilize the discourse of difference—in this case even attesting to their need for "refinement"—to serve their particular interests. Indeed, the language of otherness seems to have become common currency in the negotiations over sovereignty that arose between state and local society in the West in this period, as the state tentatively extended its centralizing reach across Egypt's marginal domains.

And yet it was not always assertions of difference that best enabled bedouins to bolster their claims to autonomy. One exceptional case suggests how tribesmen could also make appeals to the government based on their purported *sameness*, if doing so would serve their immediate interests. In 1881, several shaykhs from the Awlad 'Ali and Jumi'at tribes sent a petition to the Interior and Justice Ministries, complaining about a Khedivial decree from around 1866 that had mandated immediate exile for any bedouins posing a threat with either a firearm or sharp weapon.[87] The decree had apparently been issued after the completion of an investigation in Lower Egypt, which suggests that the tribal sections in question were those living along the edge of the cultivation. According to the petitioners, the 1866 decree had given the Egyptian authorities a free hand to persecute their tribesmen, doling out inordinate punishments even "upon the slight-est suspicion of their motives." Considering the serious harm done to their tribes because of this unjust treatment, the petitioners demanded the ab-rogation of the 1866 decree. They also claimed that their legal cases should be tried "in accordance with local laws, the same as citizens [*bi-muqtaḍā al-qawānīn al-maḥalliyya uswatan bi-l-muwāṭinīn*]."[88]

The language of the document is slippery. What did the shaykhs mean here by "local laws"? Were they referring to Egyptian law, as imple-mented throughout Lower Egypt, or something more akin to their tradi-tional law? Second, it is unclear whether their invocation of the language of citizenship constituted a claim that they themselves were citizens, or rather an articulation of their expectation of just treatment *as if* they were Egyptian citizens. Despite the fragmentary nature of the evidence, it is clear that the bedouin leaders in this case were reacting against being sin-gled out by the state for their distinctiveness, since this had led directly to their unjust treatment. Instead, to stake a claim for the equitable imple-mentation of justice, it was in their interest to argue for their *sameness*—an argument that would have been especially convincing if they were living among Egyptian fellahin in the Delta.

This example seems to have been the exception rather than the rule, however. If the bedouin tribes that lived closer to the Nile Valley were coming under increasing governmental scrutiny, those inhabiting the re-mote desert regions continued to enjoy considerable autonomy, and they accordingly played their distance to their advantage. Indeed, the govern-ment had for centuries relied upon tribes in both the Eastern and Western deserts to serve as guardsmen (*khufarā*), charged with protecting the bor-der zones.[89] One document from 1885 suggests how the Interior Ministry was reluctant to take away any local authority from the shaykhs of the tribes serving as guardsmen. In this particular case, the governor of the Suez Canal region petitioned the Interior Ministry to respond to certain deficiencies in the guardsmen system both by punishing the tribal shaykhs in charge of the guards more severely, and by standardizing the system across the country so that the shaykhs would become more subservient to the government.[90]

The ministry, in turn, formed a commission to consider the matter but ultimately decided to reject the governor's appeal. The commission reminded the governor that the bedouins are "people of the desert," with different customs and conditions than village and town dwellers; as such, they required special treatment. Additionally, the commission asserted that taking punitive measures against the shaykhs in charge would fail to deter the deficient guardsmen from wrongdoing, since they would have no problem seeing someone else punished for their own indifference. Most interesting for our purposes, the commission argued that every region in the country had its own particular circumstances that must not be tampered with; it would thus be detrimental for the guardsmen system to alter the conditions in the Suez region for the sake of one disgruntled government servant. This is another striking example of how Egyptian territoriality in the late nineteenth century was flexible enough to embrace and incorporate difference; as the officials on the commission realized, there would be no point of insisting that the state should treat every region the same. Accordingly, upon receiving the commission's recommendations, the ministry decided not to change the rules or punish the bedouin shaykhs in the region; instead, they accepted the shaykhs' continued autonomy, though they would take punitive measures against intransigent guardsmen as they saw fit.[91]

In 1895, the Egyptian government undertook a comprehensive reorganization of the Interior Ministry. As Lord Cromer, the British consul-general, would boast in his annual report the following year, the ministry succeeded in regularizing its provincial governance (in the Nile Valley, at least), creating a tight new administrative hierarchy that tied the 'umdas and shaykhs of even the smallest Egyptian villages directly to the Interior Ministry in Cairo.[92] Although the major objective of these reforms was to establish public order in the countryside, the Interior Ministry also attempted to revamp the bedouin guardsmen system—something it had been reluctant to do ten years prior. The new regulations stipulated that every town and village must have a guardsmen unit, and that guards would henceforth be chosen by government employees along with local 'umdas, and thus *not* by the tribal shaykhs. They also altered the process through which the guards were compensated, by requiring that the funds, though raised locally by village shaykhs, must pass first through the government treasury before being distributed.[93] The upshot of this intervention was to challenge the autonomy of the tribal leaders, who until that point had been largely independent in selecting and compensating the guardsmen.

A noteworthy article from the Egyptian newspaper *al-Mu'ayyad* from July 1896 richly documents the vehement opposition of a wide cross-section of tribes to this attempt by the Interior Ministry to undermine their autonomy. Although the article's author mentions that opposition to the government was widespread throughout the country, he focuses primarily on the various tribes settled in the two provinces of Gharbiyya and Sharqiyya, located in the Nile Delta. It is unclear how, precisely, the 1895 administrative reforms affected those tribal guardsmen inhabiting more remote territory in the Egyptian West, as well as the Eastern Desert and Sinai. The story reconstructed in the article nonetheless remains a fascinating example of Egypt's shifting bedouin policy.

According to the author, it was unsurprising that the bedouins resisted the Interior Ministry's reforms. After all, the nearly one million bedouins living in Egypt were "among the fiercest defenders of their customs and privileges" and had "no patience for any injustice or inequity against their personal conditions and public interests." Since the time of Mehmed 'Ali, they had enjoyed many "special privileges," having become "tantamount to guards and fortresses over the Egyptian frontiers [bi-mathābat khufarā' wa ḥuṣūn 'alā al-ḥudūd al-Miṣriyya]." The author continues by citing many instances throughout the nineteenth century when the government had failed to deprive the bedouins of these privileges, since the tribes always "fought heroically to resist [their] subservience and emerged victorious."[94]

With this narrative of resistance in mind, the bedouin leaders mobilized in opposition to the new round of government intervention. On one hand, they argued that they were best equipped to choose the individual guards and settle their salaries; they feared that if the government now stepped in to select and compensate the guards, the tribes would no longer have any guarantees of their loyalty. On the other hand, these bedouin leaders saw the intervention as an unprecedented step by the state toward their subjugation. As the author put it, the bedouin shaykhs "realized that this was a scheme by the Interior Ministry to incorporate them gradually into the body politic [silk abnā' al-bilād],"[95] and thus strip them of the "rights and privileges they had enjoyed until now."[96]

The shaykhs and 'umdas of many different tribes in Gharbiyya and Sharqiyya drafted a series of petitions. They first sent one to the "government"—the author is vague here—demanding the preservation of their traditional rights and privileges. They also sent a petition to the Interior Ministry, but received no reply. The tribal leaders then sent a third petition to the Khedive, 'Abbas Hilmi II, in which they presented an ultimatum: he must either provide them with relief, or else grant them permission to leave Egypt for another country in which they could make a living. The Khedive apparently responded to this petition with some vague promises, for which the bedouin leaders praised him, but they did not stop there. They also drafted and sealed a memorandum to the Ottoman sultan, on behalf of all the shaykhs and *'umda*s of the many tribes of the aforementioned two provinces, making a number of specific demands.

Although they ultimately decided against sending the memo to the sultan, it is still worth pausing over some of its surprising contents. The bedouin leaders asked the sultan for a hundred thousand feddans of land in the Hawran province of Syria to exploit and harvest. By their estimation, the farm (*çiftlik*) of "Bisan" had over a million feddans of fertile land, which could be cultivated with minimal hassle, since only a few local bedouin pastoralists lived in the area. They were suggesting that the Hawran could become a "second homeland." Toward the end of the petition, they underscored the seriousness of their demands: "The shaykhs and *'umda*s made a firm oath to one another that, if they did not obtain the satisfaction they were seeking, then they would leave Egypt."[97] When the article's author asked one representative how the bedouins could be serious about this proposition when they actually had property of their own and fairly good dealings with the Egyptian state, he responded by saying that they would remain determined as long as they saw that they were "being deprived of [their] rights and privileges . . . even if this costs [them] gravely." Besides, they could give their property to foreigners to manage on their behalf; and they would be close enough to Egypt in the Hawran that they could come back at any time.[98]

It is unclear how this episode was resolved. This article nonetheless remains a remarkable example of how some bedouins—albeit those settled in the Delta—negotiated with the state by threatening to leave the political community altogether. They were willing to tolerate state involvement only if they could dictate its terms and ensure they would preserve their special privileges and autonomy. This case again illustrates the limits of "Egyptianness" as a category for delineating the bounds of the state's territorial sovereignty in the nineteenth century. The government consistently resorted to a discourse of otherness in dealing with bedouins and other inhabitants of Egypt's desert peripheries; accordingly, local actors, such as the petitioners in this example, embraced their non-Egyptian status for their own benefit.

A decade after the bedouin petitions, the Egyptian government continued its efforts to streamline its authority over the country's various tribes, passing laws in 1905 and again in 1908 that outlined a comprehensive code for their administrative organization. In several respects, the new laws fleshed out some of Mehmed 'Ali's transformative bedouin policies, and recorded them in the lawbooks of the revamped state bureaucracy. Yet the new legislation can also be read as a reaction to the government's lingering inability to discern who counted as a bedouin. What made this issue particularly pressing at this moment was the discovery that many Egyptian citizens were now claiming bedouin descent in order to qualify for exemption from military service—a privilege that Mehmed 'Ali had granted to bedouin tribes only. Historian Gabriel Baer picked up on this development in his analysis of the 1897 Egyptian census: he suggests that the number of bedouins counted—an increase of over three hundred thousand, or more than twofold—was significantly inflated, due to the tendency of many fellahin to falsely claim bedouin identity to escape conscription.[99] This would explain Cromer's own acknowledgment that an inordinately large jump in the number of recorded bedouins had occurred over the fifteen years since the previous census.[100]

There is evidence to suggest that the desert edge became a dynamic space for the negotiation of identities—a liminal zone, where Egyptian peasants could mingle with tribesmen and broker special deals to be counted among the bedouins and claim military exemption. This interpretation is borne out by the testimony of German Egyptologist J. C. Ewald Falls, who gained intimate knowledge of the region during his long stint in 1905–8 working on the excavation of Abu Mina. In his memoir, Falls writes:

The circumstance that the whole of the western part of the province of Behêret [Buhayra] . . . consists of reclaimed desert land, sufficiently explains the large number of Beduins found there, some of whom are settlers and others only partly so. The insecurity of Behêret is proverbial and a great anxiety for the Government. The mixture of the two elements, the Beduins and the fellahs, by no means tends to diminish the insecurity. . . . The Arab, notwithstanding that he looks after the policing of the frontier, is a source of anxiety to the fellah, and especially to the Government, which loses greatly in prestige through carrying on the business of recruiting. The Beduin is exempt from military service and from taxation, and he extends the exemption to the children of mixed marriages. For a money bribe, responsible Government Sheikhs enter them in the lists of the tribes. Wearisome inquiries have to be made, and if the Government enlists the young men by force they flee into the desert. The fellah, who is not free, sees this with envy, but is powerless, for he dares not give information, lest he should have his Beduin competitors and the whole Kabyle against him. So in the whole of the west of the delta the Beduin is master of the situation.[101]

Similar themes emerge in the unpublished memoir of British officer Wilfred Jennings-Bramly. In a passage describing a desert journey to Siwa, he disparages a member of his caravan named ʿAbdallah, labeling him "one of those sham Bedawee [bedouin] to be met with in every village near the desert—men who have been enrolled in a tribe and pay tribute for the privilege which confers with it freedom from military service."[102] In Jennings-Bramly's view, the desert edge was a place where his trusted bedouin guide, named "Dow," could settle and blend in after squandering the fortune he had made as a merchant serving the caravan route between Kufra and Cairo. And it was where men like ʿAbdallah—though "every inch of him a fellah"—could come to know "every ʿumda of the desert country along the edge of the cultivation" and acquire "some few Bedawee habits from constantly meeting them in his wanderings."[103]

Taken together, the testimonies of Falls and Jennings-Bramly paint a picture of Egypt's desert edge as a nebulous and permeable region, where social identities often transformed and overlapped. If this is accurate, then Mehmed ʿAli's efforts to neutralize the bedouin threat by settling the tribes in and around the Nile Valley had unintended consequences. The integration of the tribes into the sedentary life of the Nile Valley made it extremely difficult to distinguish who was a bedouin, and consequently gave fellahin and tribesmen alike increased room for maneuver for negotiating their social identities.

Unsurprisingly, the Egyptian government sought to resolve this confusing situation by enacting legislation to render the country's bedouin population more legible.[104] The first decree—passed on December 28, 1905—provided a complete set of regulations for bedouin administration, seeking, according to one observer, to "organize [the tribes] in an administrative fashion approaching the organization of towns and villages."[105] The law stipulated that each tribe must have a headquarters (*markaz*) in each province or governorate, to be appointed by the minister of the interior. Additionally, the law ordered the creation within each province or governorate of a local commission for bedouin affairs, which would be presided over by the respective district governor along with an agent from the Interior Ministry, a representative from the Public Parquet, and four bedouin 'umdas. These commissions could be convened at any time by the respective governor to address matters of tribal leadership.[106]

The 1905 law also established regulations for the appointment and administrative roles of tribal notables (essentially building upon Mehmed 'Ali's strategy of converting bedouin 'umdas into state officials). In this regard, the government was simply extending its legislative reforms of 1895, which had overhauled Egypt's provincial administration by integrating village headmen into a uniform centralized state apparatus.[107] Article 2 of the law mandated that each tribe must be led by at least one 'umda who would be primarily responsible for the tribe's welfare (their appointments would be made by the local commission for bedouin affairs and approved by the Interior Ministry). Another article required that each 'umda must have a representative or deputy (wakil 'umda) in each province or governorate in which at least fifty members of his tribe resided. Additionally, state officials in each governorate would appoint local shaykhs to serve under the 'umdas, thus completing the tribal hierarchy. The primary duty of the tribal leaders would be to arrest any tribesman wanted by the authorities, and to turn him over within a reasonable time frame. The law even went so far as to lay out regulations for where the 'umdas and their agents could reside: 'umdas were free to live wherever they pleased, but deputy 'umdas were required to live within the domains of the province or governorate to which they were attached.[108]

Whereas the 1905 law laid out the basic administrative organization of the bedouin tribes, a second law, passed three years later, addressed the issue of military evasion more directly, by establishing a new system for bedouin registration.[109] The initiative for the new legislation at this time seems to have come from the minister of war, who argued that "since the bedouin ['urbān] census carried out in 1264 A.H. [1848] has become obsolete, it no longer serves its purpose and cannot be relied upon for implementing military conscription."[110]

Again, however, the government was forced to cede considerable authority to the local tribal leaders in enforcing the new legislation. The 1908 law required a register to be kept at the Ministry of War of "all persons of bedouin extraction in the male line of descent, resident or settled in any part of Egypt in which recruiting operations are carried on," yet stipulated that the register would be kept primarily by the tribes themselves, rather than the governorates. The language of this clause is somewhat vague in its delineation of enforceable territory: would the law pertain only to settled bedouins around the Nile Valley, or would recruiting operations extend further into the desert?

Additionally, the new law responded to the minister of war's charge by establishing a new bedouin census, though this, too, would be undertaken by a commission composed of eight 'umdas. Despite the state authorities' continued reliance on local bedouin leadership, the intent of the new law was clear: to aid the recruitment effort by clamping down on bedouin impostors. The law thus mandated that, upon the completion of the new census, "no person shall be exempt from military service . . . unless his name is entered in the said register." At the same time, however, the law included a sort of grandfather clause for the earlier census from 1264 A.H., no matter how imperfect or obsolete the authorities found it: "Every person who is descended in the male line from some person whose name is included in the Beduin Census of 1264 A.H. or who proves that he is of Beduin extraction shall be treated as if he were of Beduin extraction in the male line."[111] Due to the law's underlying ambiguity, it is unclear to what extent it achieved its goal of increasing the legibility of the population around the Nile Valley by clarifying who was a true bedouin.

The law made some impact, however, since key representatives of the bedouin population, construing it as a threat to their autonomy, strongly opposed its implementation. Leaders of twelve separate tribes sent a petition to the Khedive, once again complaining that the new legislation was "detrimental to bedouin privileges," and they demanded the formation of a special council to meet with the bedouin 'umdas to discuss the law's most problematic provisions.[112] Additionally, according to Isma'il Abaza Pasha—president of the special commission formed to draft the bedouin law—several bedouin 'umdas explicitly demanded that the law be amended to remove all references to slavery, so that it would "consider their slaves as bedouin [ 'itibār raqīqihim min dimna al-'urbān]."[113]

This chapter has demonstrated that the Egyptian borderlands emerged as enclaves of legal exceptionalism *within* the emergent modern nation-state of Egypt in the decades before the First World War. As the centralizing mechanisms of the Egyptian state confronted the challenges of difference and distance in the desert and oasis peripheries, the government necessarily relied upon established local institutions and legal frameworks for the exercise of nominal territorial sovereignty. Indeed, the government's swift decision to overturn the application of the country's sweeping judicial reforms in each of the western oases was just one example of a strategic and pragmatic response to the state's incapacity to project uniform territoriality on a nation-wide scale. In this way, Egyptian state centralization in the late nineteenth century went hand-in-hand with decentralization: in the case of the remote borderlands, it was far easier for the government to continue to devolve sovereign authority to local non-state actors and institutions it did not consider truly Egyptian, even as it strove to renegotiate the terms of its relationships with them.

This analysis of Egyptian state centralization is at odds with more conventional accounts of nation-state territoriality in the nineteenth century, for which western Europe is still typically assumed to be normative. Eugen Weber's classic study *Peasants into Frenchmen* remains a touchstone for conceptualizing how modern centralizing states worked to incorporate their own "savage" peripheries in this period.[114] In several key respects, Weber's characterization of France at the dawn of the Third Republic parallels this chapter's portrait of Egypt in roughly the same period: in both nations, endowed with a historically strong center, a taken-for-granted myth of "essential unity" masked the basic underlying diversity of the nation-state. The story that Weber then proceeds to tell is how the French state responded when a new set of territorial imperatives rendered the diversity of its national citizenry tantamount to "imperfection, injustice, failure, something to be noted and to be remedied."[115]

But it is worth considering whether it is the Egyptian case, with the fragmentation of its sovereignty across different legal enclaves, or the French case, with its strong, top-down assertion of a national civilizing mission, which represents the real aberration in how territoriality was practiced throughout the nineteenth century. Unlike the French Third Republic, the Egyptian government adapted to the particular challenges posed by its uneven geography by working through local society, and accommodating the diversity of its population—even if this meant conceding a great deal of autonomy to a variety of non-Egyptian authorities and institutions. The idea of imposing large-scale projects to bring Egyptian national culture and civilization to these regions would come only much later.[116] The Egyptian government's consistent articulation of a policy of legal exceptionalism and otherness across the country's borderlands thus reflected a phase of modern territorialization in which the fundamental diversity of its population had not yet become a measure of imperfection, or a source of national embarrassment.

# 2

## Accommodating Egyptian Sovereignty in Siwa

In February 1897, Wilfred Scawen Blunt—poet, traveler, and notorious critic of the British occupation of Egypt—journeyed across the Western Desert to the oasis of Siwa. Shortly after Blunt's arrival, a force of two to three hundred Siwans attacked his camp. They were commanded by a powerful shaykh named 'Uthman Habun, who was also the local agent of the Sanusiyya Brotherhood. The attackers pillaged much of Blunt's property, and he was fortunate to escape without serious injury.[1]

Back in Cairo, Blunt lobbied the British consul-general, Lord Cromer, to mobilize the Egyptian government to apprehend his Siwan assailants and bring them to justice. He also expected the authorities to recover his looted property. Cromer, though not unsympathetic, explained that the government could not comply with Blunt's demands, lest such an endeavor "incur a possible quarrel with the Senussia brotherhood."[2] Instead, Cromer simply dispatched a new *ma'mur* to Siwa that summer, along with some extra police.

A year after the incident in Siwa, having grown increasingly incensed over the Egyptian government's inaction, Blunt wrote a scathing letter to Cromer laying out what he felt was his fundamental right, as a British subject, to government protection and justice. After all, as he chided Cromer, "Siwah [*sic*] is an Egyptian town, paying its taxes to the Government, and the Egyptian Government is responsible there as elsewhere for law and order. These may be difficult to enforce, but the responsibility remains."[3] Cromer's patience ran out at this point. In a pointed response to Blunt, he retorted, "You started for this remote region, which is notoriously inhabited by a very turbulent and fanatical population, and over which the Egyptian Government has, for a long time past, exercised little more than a nominal control, without, so far as I am aware, warning any one in Egypt of your intentions."[4] Cromer also challenged Blunt's assertion that Siwa was a bona fide "Government Town":[5] "To any one who has been so long acquainted with this country as yourself, I need not insist on the point that, for the purposes of the argument, Siwa cannot, with any degree of reason, be assimilated to the rest of Egypt."[6]

Cromer's exchange with Blunt over the latter's ill-fated journey to Siwa, much like the story of the Stack murder case discussed in Chapter 1, offers another window into the underlying unevenness of Egypt's political geography and the contested nature of Egyptian sovereignty in the West. What did it mean for Cromer to assert that the state had only "nominal control" of Siwa, or that it could not be "assimilated" into Egypt? The fallout from the Blunt episode also sheds light on how the Egyptian government viewed the inhabitants of this remote territory. What was the political significance of the "fanatical" Sanusiyya,[7] represented locally by Blunt's attacker 'Uthman Habun, and why was Cromer so loath to antagonize them?

This chapter explores the implications of Cromer's suggestion that powerful local actors played a key role in mediating the Egyptian government's exercise of sovereignty over Siwa in the 1890s, the period in which the state intensified its efforts to unify practices of rule across the country.[8] Foremost among these notable Siwan actors were local leaders of the Sanusiyya Brotherhood, who receive special attention here. Although Cairo managed to secure a firmer foothold in Siwa by 1900, it achieved this only by relying upon local intermediaries such as the Sanusiyya to carry out the most basic functions of government—collecting taxes, administering justice, and enforcing law and order. In the process, Sanusi and other Siwan elites successfully harnessed the new political opportunities opened up by the government's reinvigorated presence in the oasis to arrogate more power and formalize their customary authority.

The local negotiations of power between state and non-state actors in Siwa were a defining feature of territorialization in Egypt's western borderland more broadly. Historians Michiel Baud and Willem van Schendel have argued that historians must pay special attention to borderlands for what they "can teach us about ways of conceptualizing social space and local identity, and the roles these have played in promoting or thwarting the development of modern states."[9] In a similar spirit, this chapter views the dynamics of Egyptian state centralization through a *regional* lens, focusing on the complex interplay between the state's territorial imperatives and the spatial practices of the local population, over which an alternate sovereign center held sway. Egyptian sovereignty was not simply imposed on Siwa by Cairo, but rather emerged as government officials deferred to local political forces, which operated within the Sanusiyya's own nascent territorial framework, based in the nearby oasis of Jaghbub.

According to Charles Dalrymple Belgrave—a British officer serving in Egypt's Frontier Districts Administration, briefly posted in command of Siwa after World War I—the Sanusiyya emerged over the last quarter of the nineteenth century to become the "ultimate arbitrators in any disputes which arose among the people" of Siwa.[10] Having first established a presence in the vast Libyan Desert in the mid-nineteenth century, the Sanusiyya managed over a mere half-century to become the predominant power brokers in the region, counting among their ranks the vast majority of bedouin tribesmen and oasis dwellers inhabiting the Egyptian-Libyan borderland. Despite this extensive reach of the Sanusiyya beyond Libya, however, the Egyptian dimension of the Brotherhood's history has been overlooked in much scholarship—perhaps because the Sanusiyya practiced a "cross-border" authority that challenged the very concept of national territoriality in Egypt and Libya alike.[11]

The Sanusiyya Brotherhood was founded by Muhammad bin 'Ali al-Sanusi, an Algerian-born religious scholar who traveled widely across the Arab world, studying the Islamic sciences under prominent teachers in Fez, Cairo, and Mecca.[12] Al-Sanusi initially took much inspiration from the Sufi mystical traditions prevalent in his home milieu in North Africa, but in Mecca he came under the spell of the *salafi* movement—particularly the teachings of jurist and Shadhili disciple Sayyid Ahmad bin Idris al-Fasi. Al-Sanusi established his own religious order in 1837 and galvanized a group of Hijaz bedouins into becoming his first followers. Around 1840,[13] al-Sanusi headed back west, across Egypt, to Siwa, where he stayed for several months and attracted a sizeable following.[14] He ultimately settled in northeastern Libya (the region historically known as Cyrenaica, under Ottoman rule at the time), after being invited by the shaykhs of several different tribes in the region to settle among them. In 1843, al-Sanusi and his followers completed the construction of the Brotherhood's first *zawiya* (plural: *zawaya*; "lodge" is an approximate translation), on the central Cyrenaican plateau in the Jabal al-Akhdar region. This became known as the "White Lodge" (*al-zawiya al-bayda*). A decade later, al-Sanusi set up a headquarters for the Brotherhood, as well as a university complex, in the uninhabited oasis of Jaghbub, approximately one hundred miles from the Mediterranean coast and only sixty miles west of Siwa. Jaghbub would remain both the spiritual and administrative center of the Brotherhood for over four decades.[15]

The *zawiya* was the fundamental building block of the Sanusi system in the borderland. In its formative years, the Sanusiyya was primarily a missionary organization, and the construction of new *zawaya*—typically at the behest of tribal leaders who sought out the religious guidance of al-Sanusi—was the primary means of spreading the word and solidifying new outposts of Sanusi allegiance. Though *zawaya* across the Sanusi sphere were by no means identical—those in very remote villages could be quite rudimentary, for example—they all shared certain unifying features, including a school room for the instruction of local children; a guesthouse where travelers could rest for up to three days, free of charge; living quarters for the shaykh of the *zawiya*, as well as the other brethren who served as full-time teachers and administrators; and a mosque.[16] The central *zawiya* in Jaghbub was built on a grander scale, and included a mosque that could hold up to six hundred worshipers; a large library with over eight thousand volumes; and, interesting for our purposes, a special boarding room for students from Siwa.[17]

In the decade and a half between the founding of the White Lodge and the death of Muhammad bin ʿAli al-Sanusi in Jaghbub in 1859, the Brotherhood had already grown considerably. According to one scholar, around sixty lodges were built during the lifetime of the founder.[18] Yet under al-Sanusi's successor—his son, Muhammad al-Mahdi bin Sayyid Muhammad al-Sanusi—the Brotherhood continued its prodigious expansion. According to renowned ethnographer E. E. Evans-Pritchard, by the time Muhammad al-Mahdi died in 1902, the Sanusi order had grown to encompass approximately 150 *zawaya* spread across North Africa and the Hijaz, of which thirty-one were on Egyptian soil (with seventeen of those alone belonging to tribal sections of the Awlad ʿAli).[19] French explorer Henri Duveyrier estimated that the Sanusi order comprised some three million followers.[20] Egyptian desert explorer Ahmed Hassanein cited a similar figure: between one-and-a-half and three million people who owed spiritual allegiance to the Sanusiyya during Muhammad al-Mahdi's lifetime.[21] The scope of Sanusi authority did not fail to impress the British authorities. In 1902, for example, the author of an intelligence report stated that "practically the whole of the oases and the nomad population between Egypt and the Sudan on the east and the Tuareg country on the west are Senussites to a man."[22] And as Arthur Silva White, a British traveler who visited Siwa in the late-1890s, put it, "The Senussi rule the Sahara, and no power can touch them there."[23]

In his classic ethnography of the Sanusiyya, Evans-Pritchard noted that the Brotherhood thrived because it carefully grafted itself to the preexisting tribal system in Cyrenaica and western Egypt. The *zawaya* were fundamentally "tribal institutions," actively sought, built, and maintained by the leaders of each of the many tribes and subtribes in the region.[24] The *zawaya* were built on lands specially allocated by each tribe, and bedouins were expected to pay a tithe to their respective *zawiya* at harvest time. The Brotherhood also strategically "seeded itself in the crevasses between tribes and between tribal sections."[25] The monumental White Lodge, for example, was built at the intersection of four tribal zones, thereby setting a precedent of tribal cooperation and equality.[26] Similarly, Jaghbub was chosen to be the Brotherhood's headquarters due in part to its prime location as the main locus for tribes located throughout the Sanusi sphere; it also fell along a major north-south caravan route, as well as the main Hajj route from the west.[27] The Brotherhood operated as a federal system of sorts: even as all *zawaya* managed their own revenues and typically arbitrated local disputes without recourse to Jaghbub, each *zawiya* shaykh was appointed by, and responsible to, the local Sanusi leader. In fact, all the Sanusi shaykhs in the region normally convened each year in Jaghbub for a "council of the order," where they were required to report on their respective *zawaya*.[28] Each *zawiya* was also expected to pay annual tribute (often payments in kind) to Jaghbub.

The *zawaya* additionally served as internal channels of long-distance communication. Those operating this information network carefully vetted any pilgrims intending to visit the Sanusi leader in Jaghbub, in order to identify and weed out impostors and thereby preserve the sanctity and secrecy of the Brotherhood. Any pilgrims traveling from the east had to pass through a chain of *zawaya* along the Mediterranean coast west of Alexandria, spaced about one day apart by camel. After asking each traveler a series of questions about his background, loyalties to the Brotherhood, and reasons for the journey, the officials at each *zawiya* would then send a report to the next lodge along the route ahead of the traveler's arrival there.[29] In this way, all visitors making their way through Sanusi territory would be "cross-examined," to ensure their narrative never wavered. Reports would also be forwarded to Jaghbub: according to a Sanusi follower from Sudan, visitors arriving at the Brotherhood's headquarters would be carefully vetted yet again before they gained access to Muhammad al-Mahdi.[30] The Sanusi *zawaya*, in their capacity as guesthouses and caravanserais, also became the most efficient means for merchants to exchange news and information about conditions along several expansive caravan routes. In the case of the route running from Wadai (in modern-day Chad) to the port of Benghazi, the Sanusiyya even established a regular postal system.[31]

The elaborate grid of Sanusi *zawaya* that proliferated across the Eastern Sahara during the second half of the nineteenth century, and provided so many social functions—from courts of law, to storehouses, to information hubs—steadily emerged as the defining territorial framework of the Egyptian-Libyan borderland, indeed laying the foundation for an embryonic Sanusi state structure. In the mid-1890s, the widespread authority of the Sanusiyya throughout the borderland would prove pivotal in the unfolding of the Egyptian government's sovereign claims over Siwa.

In February 1896, tensions between Siwa's two main factions—the Easterners and Westerners—once again erupted into protracted violence.[32] Raids on crops and cattle occurred daily, and the situation deteriorated to the point that no shaykh would leave his house unarmed or unattended. As one observer put it, the "administration of justice was at a standstill." Eighteen ninety-six was also the third consecutive year that the Siwans had neglected to pay their state taxes; their arrears now totaled 4,970 pounds.[33] By September, the Egyptian government was unable to ignore the chaotic situation in Siwa any longer, and it dispatched the governor of Buhayra, Mustafa Maher Bey, to the oasis. The objective of Maher and his men was to investigate the roots of this latest upsurge of violence, restore law and order, and resume the collection of taxes.[34]

The work of the Maher commission began inauspiciously. According to an important Interior Ministry report on Siwan affairs, written by T. B. Hohler and published in 1900, "Mustafa Bey was received with considerable distrust. Neither by his assurances, nor by the smallness of his escort, was he able to impress upon the people the peaceful nature of his mission."[35] At the same time, many men from Maher's military entourage fell ill.[36]

The brief publications and unpublished diaries of British officer Wilfred Jennings-Bramly underscore Maher's tenuous position.[37] Shortly after Maher's work began, Jennings-Bramly arrived in the oasis on a private expedition accompanied only by his bedouin guide, Dow, and his servant 'Abdallah (whom Jennings-Bramly denigrated as one of the "sham bedouins" mentioned in Chapter 1).[38] Upon entering Siwa's main square, where he saw "some dozen Egyptian police . . . strolling about," Jennings-Bramly came upon "a grave assemblage of sheiks, sitting in conclave," at the center of which "sat a man in European clothes," whom he recognized instantly to be Maher.[39] After speaking briefly with Jennings-Bramly, Maher decided that the traveler's fortuitous arrival in Siwa "might be turned to some use"—that Jennings-Bramly could be passed off as a military official on government business. Jennings-Bramly played his part well, handing his passport over to Maher and the Siwan shaykhs for inspection.

Later that evening, Maher offered Jennings-Bramly a fuller explanation of his ruse:

> He told me afterwards it had struck him then what to say about me . . . [he] informed me that I had become a colonel in the British army. The Government, he had told the sheikhs, tired of waiting for the payment of the taxes, three years overdue, had sent me to see what answer they were giving to his demands. I had hurried along alone, not wishing, unless absolutely forced to do so, to alarm Siwa by bringing my armed escort with me.[40]

As Jennings-Bramly recalls, "Maha Bey [sic] was not slow to make what capital he could out of the military romance he had wound around me by pointing out now and then that the Government would not leave him unaided, and that they had best decide and pay, and not force me to return with an army."[41] According to Jennings-Bramly, his participation in this act of deception—performing the role of a special government envoy bent on revenue collection—produced the desired results: "It all passed off satisfactorily. They decided the taxes should be paid if time were given them."[42]

Jennings-Bramly's narrative of his assistance to the Maher commission accords with the account included in Hohler's Interior Ministry report, which provides much of the best evidence from this critical period. Around October 3, the Siwan shaykhs—having awaited the return of several Sanusi elders from Jaghbub—promised to pay a portion of their back taxes within a week.[43] On October 10, they presented Maher with approximately 220 Egyptian pounds, claiming they could not pay their arrears in full, "on the ground that the crops were not yet gathered, the merchants had not yet arrived, and that the harvest was indifferent." The Sanusi leadership in Jaghbub also wrote letters to their respective constituencies in Siwa, urging them to obey the government's orders.[44] At the same time, Maher managed to gain approval for a new criminal law, which he had previously read aloud to Siwa's traditional governing assembly of shaykhs (*Majlis al-Shuyukh*) for approval. Two provisions stand out from the penal code contained within this new law: first, the government had the right to punish by death any Siwan who took up arms to "fight the Government, fight against other inhabitants, or destroy part of the town";[45] second, government officials reserved the right to inspect the houses of any suspects for weapons, upon news of any murder, attack, or theft.[46] Of course, recording these provisions in the lawbooks did not guarantee that the local government had the means to enforce them.

Maher's assertion of authority at this juncture elicited fierce opposition, spearheaded by a shaykh of the Westerners named Hassuna Mansur. Refusing to go along with Maher's efforts to collect taxes, Mansur sequestered himself, along with an armed force of slaves and supporters, in his fortress-like compound on the outskirts of town. He forcibly resisted all attempts at arrest, and rejected his family's attempts to appease him. Some Siwans who were sent to apprehend him ended up joining his ranks. According to Hohler, "the whole town was in an uproar."[47]

Maher, finding himself completely powerless in the face of Mansur's armed opposition, gave in to the entreaties of shaykhs from both Siwa's Eastern and Western factions to summon the Sanusi brethren from Jaghbub. Within ten days, a close relative of Muhammad al-Mahdi arrived in Siwa, and Mansur and his followers "at once surrendered to him."[48] Maher would later describe this abrupt turn of events as "a striking instance of the implicit trust and absolute obedience rendered to the authority of the [Sanusiyya]."[49]

Maher's deference to the Sanusiyya for the preservation of order was not without precedent. According to former Siwan qadi Muhammad Makki, the Sanusiyya had often played a chief intermediary role for the Egyptian government:

When a Government official goes to Siwa, he is supposed to go to Jaghbub and make a visit to the Senussi, especially if he were the Qadi, so as to be able to live peacefully and respectably with the Senussis of Siwa. Ahmad Abdullah, the late Mamur of Siwa, could not live peacefully with the Senussis there as he refused to make a visit to the Se-nussi; and they repeatedly accused him to the Buhayra Mudiriyeh for misgovernment until they succeeded in changing him.[50]

Visiting Siwa in 1898, Arthur Silva White also marveled at the authority the Sanusiyya commanded in the oasis. White observed that many Si-wan notables took extreme measures to protect the routes to Jaghbub in order to keep unwanted travelers from trespassing: "Six of the chiefs in Siwa town are held responsible for the protection of the northern road; and on the southern road there are people . . . whose special duty is to keep watch and ward over the caravans."[51] White was particularly aston-ished to learn that the freedom of movement of Siwa's ma'mur at the time, Mahmud 'Azmi, was similarly at the mercy of Sanusi authorities: "Here are you, the Mamur of Siwa, with 25 policemen; and you cannot go for more than a day's excursion [westward] without permission of the Senussi."[52] Moreover, White made it clear in his memoir that 'Uthman Habun—the "dominant sheikh" of the Westerners who had led Blunt's assailants a year prior—was really in charge. In White's eyes, Habun, "the representative of Senussi-ism," was "the *imperium in imperio* of Siwa . . . the autocrat who gave [him] permission to go everywhere, without let or hindrance." Ac-cordingly, Habun enjoyed "absolute and uncontrolled authority."[53]

From the time of Maher's arrival in Siwa until the First World War, Egyptian officials in the oasis could not govern effectively without the aid of the Sanusiyya, who were prominent among Siwa's traditional shaykhs. Take, for instance, a new tax law that Maher introduced on April 20, 1897. Maher knew that the matter of tax collection needed to be handled with utmost caution, and not just due to Siwa's long history of armed resistance to state encroachment. It was also the case that the Siwans had long ob-jected, ever since one comprehensive tree census conducted around 1871, to any new official count of the oasis's date and olive trees, so that the government might assess Siwa's tax burden more accurately.[54] There is evi-dence that Egyptian officials were still relying upon the 1871 tree census more than forty years later, even though the total number of fruiting trees had increased by around 25 percent during that period.[55] It was the opin-ion of Siwa's ma'mur in 1895, on the eve of Maher's arrival, that any new inventory of the oasis's date and olive trees would be impossible to imple-ment "except by great force."[56]

Maher thus introduced the new law by first reading it aloud to Siwa's assembly of shaykhs, in order to gain their approval. He then leaned on the Sanusiyya to assist with the implementation of the government's new tax regulations. Again, this was nothing new. As Muhammad Makki (the former qadi) pointed out, the Sanusiyya had been a reliable partner for the government on the issue of tax collection in Siwa since well before Maher's arrival on the scene: "The Senussi wishes to be in peace with the Egyptian as well as with the Turkish [sic] Government. He stays quiet in his Zawia and avoids all that displeased either Government. When his followers refused to pay Government taxes at Siwa, he wrote to them as soon as he knew it officially to obey the Government and pay up the taxes, the same as he did with the Bara'sa for the Turkish Government."[57] It would be no different under Maher's watch. Hohler's description of the tax-collection protocol that was implemented after 1897 reflects the outsize role that Siwa's notable shaykhs—many of whom were Sanusi brethren—continued to play:

The method adopted by the Sheikhs for the distribution of taxation is to hold, from time to time, a public examination into the ownership of taxed trees; they enter the changes effected by sale or succession against the entries in the original register made on the occasion of the census of 1871. The revised list is read out to the assembled people, so that complaints may be presented and examined; and the Sheikhs apportion to each family, in accordance with the new register, the share of taxation for which they are liable. Trees planted since 1871 do not appear in the old register, and so escape payment; they are consequently of a higher value. The time would almost seem to have come when it would be desirable to effect a new census. Each family hands the amount for which it is responsible to its Sheikh, and when all have done so, the Sheikhs proceed in a body to the Maamourieh [sic], and deliver the money to the Maamour [sic] in exchange for a receipt.[58]

Siwa's elites thus fared rather well with the tax regime ushered in by Maher in April 1897. The new law, issued by Egypt's Finance Ministry, contained four basic provisions. First, the tax burden for Siwa was reduced from 1,998 to 1,750 Egyptian pounds annually.[59] Second, the head Sanusi shaykh was granted a yearly allowance in exchange for his "support for the government,"[60] while other Siwan shaykhs would be given a small yearly bonus for their assistance in collecting taxes.[61] Third, tax collection would now occur in three installments throughout the year, based on the harvest of the three taxable date varieties. And fourth, Siwans were given a full reprieve for their unpaid taxes from 1896, "out of consideration for their condition of poverty."[62]

Along with restoring order and amending Siwa's chaotic tax situation, a third objective of the Maher commission was to modify the administration of justice in the oasis by redefining the jurisdiction of the local court, *Majlis Siwa,* through a series of new laws. Some nationalist historians have interpreted this legislation as a decisive step toward the Egyptian state's ultimate incorporation of the oasis by 1900.[63] Yet this view is not borne out by the historical record. More careful attention to the individual provisions of these three laws reveals a subtler process at play.[64] Though intended to reinforce the state's sovereign reach in the western borderland, these new jurisdiction laws of 1897 actually enhanced the traditional authority of the Siwan elites.

The Khedivial Decree #25 of May 25, 1897—which legal scholar Henri Lamba designated as the Siwan counterpart to the laws of "special jurisdiction" passed in 1900 for the other western oases[65]—was the most straightforward of the new laws. The first articles of the decree spelled out the geographical scope of the court's jurisdiction—comprising the whole town of Siwa, including Aghurmi, and the neighboring oasis of Qara—as well as some basic requirements (such as minimum age) for the eight shaykhs who would serve as members of the court. The Egyptian government made it very clear who was in charge: for example, the decree stated that members of the *Majlis* were required to take an oath before the Egyptian *ma'mur,*[66] and that the language of the court must be Arabic, not Siwi.[67]

But the matter of sovereign authority was left much vaguer in the law's description of the Siwan court's specific functions and procedures. For instance, the decree stipulated that *Majlis Siwa* would have jurisdiction in all levels of criminal cases—felonies (*jinayat*), misdemeanors (*mukhalafat*), and infractions (*junah*)—but that it must "rule in accordance with customs and norms followed in that locale." The ensuing clause was equally ambiguous: all civil and commercial claims would continue to be resolved through a process called "arbitration" (*tahkim*), and cases of this type should be judged "according to norms of justice, in accordance with the customs of that region."[68] This invocation of local custom as the basis for legal decisions indicates that Egyptian officials were still inclined to treat Siwa as an anomalous legal enclave, just as the governor of Buhayra had done a decade prior, with his insistence on the fundamental otherness of the Siwan and bedouin population.[69]

Other provisions of the May 1897 law are noteworthy for the wide-ranging powers they gave the traditional Siwan elite. For example, it stipulated that Siwan shaykhs would be held responsible not only for locating and arresting perpetrators of crimes, but also for collecting evidence, performing preliminary investigations, and detaining perpetrators. The decree also established that the shaykhs were primarily responsible for entering suspects' homes to search for weapons.[70]

The law's list of prerogatives (*ikhtisasat*) granted to the Siwan shaykhs struck a similarly balanced tone. For example, it clarified that all shaykhs appointed to Siwa's traditional governing assembly must be approved by the Interior Ministry in order for the selections to become final.[71] It also gave the *ma'mur* the power to review any ruling issued by a shaykh,[72] and required the shaykhs to implement any orders from the government that came to the oasis via the *ma'mur*.[73] At the same time, the shaykhs were given wide-reaching authority to oversee the day-to-day administration of law and order in the oasis. Siwan shaykhs retained the power to punish criminals in minor offenses and impose fines; to deal with "all the tasks pertaining to public security"; and to help arrange the guardsmen.[74] Moreover, the law maintained that "the shaykhs of Siwa are to be given the same treatment as employees of the government," in terms of the "respect shown them by the people," and the right to bring to trial "those who challenge them in the fulfillment of their job."[75]

On the whole, these laws reveal the exercise of sovereignty in Siwa to have been a balancing act between the nominal authority of the Egyptian government, on one hand, and the specific political and judicial powers of the shaykhs, on the other. The traditional Siwan shaykhs were essentially being coerced into accepting the very responsibilities for governing and administering justice in the oasis they already had prior to the Maher commission. The upshot of these reforms, then, was not the ultimate imposition of centralized Egyptian state power, but rather the state's legal formalization of the customary authority that the Siwan shaykhs had historically wielded in the oasis.

Peter Sahlins has argued that nation-state territoriality in the French-Spanish borderland "appeared less as a result of state intentions than from the local process of adopting and appropriating the nation without abandoning local interests, a local sense of place, or a local identity. At once opposing and using the state for its own ends, local society brought the nation into the village."[76] This framework parallels the work of an earlier generation of colonial historians who argued that the implementation of "indirect rule" by British and French colonial officials in Africa enabled local notables to appropriate the trappings of legitimacy and authority provided by the imperial states, and in turn to entrench their power base at home.[77]

Similar political processes were at play in Siwa in the late 1890s. Rather than exhibiting all-out resistance to rule by outsiders, savvy Siwan elites adapted to the new conditions created by the Egyptian government's territorialization project in the oasis, and consequently brought the state into Siwa on their own terms. At the same time, they tethered the new mechanisms of governance in the oasis to their customary social and legal practices, which operated within the alternate territorial framework of the Sanusiyya. In contrast to straightforward models of local resistance to centralizing state encroachment,[78] then, the Egyptian state's territorial imperatives in Siwa were willingly accommodated by the Sanusiyya and other local notables, who stood to win significant political gains by working with the government and tolerating its nominal territorial sovereignty.

The new legislation of exceptionalism introduced in Siwa in 1897 was another makeshift solution by the central government to address the problem of Egypt's uneven political and legal geography, which frustrated efforts to unify the exercise of sovereignty over the variegated territorial domains of the state. But to what extent did the character of governance in Siwa actually change?

It is undeniable that the Egyptian government finally established itself as a permanent fixture in Siwa by 1900. First, government institutions were now much more visible in the oasis's built environment: Siwa boasted a new government office on the central square of the town—providing accommodation for the *ma'mur*, qadi, two police officers, and the clerk of the *markaz*—as well as a prison, dispensary, and post office.[79] All this new infrastructure supported an augmented police and military presence.[80] Additionally, to facilitate the administration of the oasis, the population of Siwa was officially counted, for the first time, in the Egyptian census of 1897.[81]

On the surface, then, Siwa had finally succumbed to government intervention and forfeited its autonomy, the spirited defense of which had made it legendary for much of its history. Yet this does not mean that the conventional nationalist narrative of the state's ultimate triumph over Siwa is vindicated. Contemporary accounts from the turn of the century paint a more complicated picture of Egyptian sovereignty in Siwa, even after the seminal events of 1896–97 recounted in this chapter.

In his Interior Ministry report, Hohler suggested that the Egyptian *ma'mur*'s authority in Siwa remained tenuous at best, even despite the modest improvements in the spheres of law and public order achieved by the Maher commission: "The power of the Government is very much curtailed by the fact that, although a law court, a Mehkemeh Shari'a, a dispensary, &c., exist, for the most part the people refuse to have anything to do with them." In Hohler's view, this demonstrated "sufficiently to how great an extent Siwa is *autonomous*; it has been administered for centuries past by the head men of its component tribes, and its people are extremely jealous of interference from outside."[82] Arthur Silva White's account of his visit to Siwa in 1898 also complicates the picture of Egyptian sovereignty in Siwa after Maher's intervention. White credited the Egyptian *ma'mur* at the time of the visit, Mahmud 'Azmi, for pursuing a "conciliatory and wise policy" toward the Siwans, to the extent that his visit to Siwa could go so smoothly (unlike for so many travelers before him, who could not take their safety in Siwa for granted):[83]

The efforts of the Mamur appear to be meeting with success. He informed me that he had largely succeeded in inducing the men to go about the oasis unarmed. Up to a year or so ago, no man was ever seen without a gun. . . . The tribes having been pacified, at least for a period of time, many families are building houses for themselves in the oasis. Though savage and fanatical, they submit to the overlordship of Egypt, and even pay their taxes . . . altogether, the Mamur . . . is doing a lot of good.[84]

In White's view, Siwa was now "becoming more and more subject to Egypt," even if "the Mamur presides over the deliberations of the council [of shaykhs]," only "within certain limits."[85]

Despite his acknowledgment of these noteworthy improvements, White still felt the Egyptian government's presence in Siwa was tooth-less: "The mere handful of Egyptian police that occupies the oasis, as a symbol of sovereignty, cannot be expected to afford travelers any adequate assistance against the fanaticism of a turbulent and warlike population," since "law and order in the oasis are upheld by prestige rather than police protection."[86] White made clear that the local elites were still in charge of the oasis. With twenty or twenty-five Siwan shaykhs in possession of "full administrative powers," White could only conclude that "The Siwans enjoy Home Rule."[87]

There were also limits to the institutions that the Egyptian government was able to provide at this time. Most Siwans did not receive their education under the auspices of the state, for example. The local qadi ran only one of the five schools in the oasis, whereas the Sanusiyya operated three, and the Madaniyya—a rival order with a much smaller following among some of the Easterners—operated one.[88] The government also did little to bolster Siwa's transportation infrastructure in the pre–World War I period; in fact, the first paved road to the oasis was completed only in the early 1980s.

Just as the triumphal nationalist narrative of Siwa's incorporation must be revised, so, too, must conventional accounts of the cessation of factional violence in the oasis by 1900. As much of the extant literature on Siwa would have it, the resolution of the Hassuna Mansur incident marked a new dawn in the oasis. According to former officer and historian Rif'at Gawhari, for example, after the events of 1897, "the situation has become stable and has gone from good to even better."[89] Western Desert archaeologist and historian Ahmed Fakhry goes further, arguing that "the authority of the *Ma'mur* had increased and the oasis was essentially as secure as any place of its size in Upper Egypt at the time. . . . Thereafter Siwa remained quiet, and the wars between the Westerners and Easterners became stories of the past."[90]

This interpretation is incomplete. Once again, a closer look at the available evidence from the period leads to some very different conclusions regarding the putative docility of Siwans after 1896.

Shortly after Maher introduced the legal reforms of 1897, the oasis erupted into a new, particularly fierce round of factional violence that, over a two-year period, left somewhere between 80 and 180 Siwans dead—including Hassuna Mansur and several other notables.[91] Although it is difficult to reconcile the contradictory historical accounts of this turbulent period, it appears that two separate conflicts broke out in quick succession in the spring of 1897. The first began as a minor dispute over some goats, yet quickly escalated into an all-out war between Easterners and Westerners; it was during this first conflict that Mansur was killed. The latter conflict—what Belgrave calls the "Widow's War"—broke out several months later, when the young widow of an Eastern shaykh declared her intention to marry someone from the rival Western faction. The situation intensified when she sought refuge with 'Uthman Habun, who then led the Westerners into a daylong battle that ensnared the entire oasis and resulted in more casualties on both sides. According to local legend, Habun only narrowly escaped being captured, and possibly executed, by absconding to the tomb of Sidi Sulayman disguised as a woman.[92]

The effect of these turbulent events was twofold. First, the hapless Egyptian authorities needed to call for backup, summoning a larger force of around a hundred soldiers to maintain order.[93] Second, the Egyptian authorities again deferred to the Sanusiyya for assistance in resolving the conflict. Brethren from Jaghbub returned to Siwa to mediate between the two factions.[94] There is some evidence indicating that the Sanusiyya managed to achieve a conclusive peace settlement at this juncture, in part by embracing a strategy of arranged marriages between the two factions.[95] The Egyptian government and police thus had very little to do with settling Siwa's factional violence; rather, it was the Sanusiyya who kept the peace. The resolution thus came on very local terms, once again underscoring the deep-seated authority and influence of the Sanusiyya in the oasis.

At the same time, the resolution was far from perfect. Even after the Sanusi-brokered peace settlement, the Easterners and Westerners remained in a sort of cold war. According to Hohler, each of the town's factions maintained separate facilities (markets, wells, and storehouses, for example), and they also refused to live among (or sell property to) one another.[96] Hohler also cautioned the Interior Ministry that, henceforth, any officials stationed in the oasis would need to take special care to remain a neutral party vis-à-vis the two factions:

The task of Maamour, supported by his force of some twenty police who are weakened by the local fever, is no light one. He must exercise the greatest tact to hold the balance evenly between the contending factions, using his escort only as a preponderating weight in critical moments; and, while taking advantage of every opportunity to assert the authority, and to heighten the prestige of the Government, he must be scrupulously careful to show no trace whether of hostility or favour to either party. Thus the Maamour for the past year never witnessed a dance of the Westerns without being present on the next occasion when the Easterns performed: he and the other Egyptian officials made their prayer in the mosque of the Sanusi and in that of the Madani on alternate Fridays.[97]

The deep-seated tensions between the Easterners and Westerners, therefore, did not subside so easily. Indeed, as I discuss in Chapter 3, Siwa's age-old factionalism would continue to roil the oasis in the following decade, playing a key underlying role in a series of events culminating in the murder of a Siwan *ma'mur* in 1909.

This revised account of Siwa's political and legal history at the end of the

nineteenth century is at odds with the typical narrative of Siwa's incorporation provided by nationalist authors such as Fakhry and Gawhari, who
argue that the Maher commission finally subdued the unruly Siwans once
and for all and ushered in a new period of subservience to the Egyptian
government. Egyptian sovereignty in practice was much more complex
than these scholars suggest. In Siwa, it was inextricably bound up with the
continued primacy of local and regional politics, including the factionalism that had always played such a key role in the construction of customary authority in the oasis.

Lord Cromer knew all this, but so did his old adversary Blunt. Both
men understood that Egyptian sovereignty in Siwa in this period was
chiefly a negotiation with traditional shaykhs who still ran the oasis's affairs
more or less as they always had. Where Blunt and Cromer disagreed was
in their attitude toward what, if anything, ought to be done about such a
state of affairs. Blunt simply could not abide, as Cromer apparently could,
the fact that the masterminds of the plot against him were also his de facto
protectors—the same traditional shaykhs empowered by the 1897 legislation to administer "Egyptian" law and justice. "The attack made upon me
was not made by a few hotheaded or suspicious men," Blunt lamented,
"but by the whole armed force of Siwa deliberately brought out and led by
the recognized Sheikhs of the town, the same that the Egyptian Government had entrusted and still entrusts with judicial authority there."[98]

But the story does not end there. A closer look at the evidence reveals
yet another dimension to this curious episode, which underscores the extent to which the exercise of Egyptian sovereignty in Siwa intersected with
the intricacies of local politics.

It turns out that Blunt's claim that the raid was "the most outrageous
case of violence offered to a European traveller in Egypt during the last sixty
years" was grossly exaggerated.[99] Blunt might have had cause to fear mo-
mentarily that his assailants intended to murder him; he did take a beating
in his tent, after all. But the attack came to an abrupt halt when, according
to Blunt's own published diaries, "half-a-dozen sheikhs on horseback"—
several of whom had visited him in his tent the previous night, to make
introductions over coffee—arrived at his campsite and dragged him to the
local *Majlis*, presided over by shaykhs of Siwa's Western faction. At this
point, the shaykhs summoned Siwa's sergeant of police (*mu'awin*), Husayn
Effendi, who instantly put Blunt at ease and pledged to help restore his
plundered property. By Blunt's own admission, the episode turned out to

be a tempest in a teacup: "After all the trouble nothing serious has really happened. Only it is clear our onward journey is stopped. Our money and our arms are gone . . . None of us is hurt, and for the small losses I shall make the Egyptian Government responsible. They should either give up holding Siwah or keep order here."[100]

What upset Blunt so much, then, was not the violence he experienced at the hands of the Siwans; he was in fact escorted out of the oasis by four Western shaykhs, including Habun, with whom he shared an amicable farewell.[101] Rather, the source of Blunt's lingering resentment toward Cromer was the latter's apparent willingness to allow what ought to have been a straightforward matter of Egyptian justice to be hijacked by local intrigue and factional politics.

Despite his exhortation to Cromer, however, Blunt was entirely at fault for this turn of events. With hindsight, it is clear that Blunt had made a couple of fateful mistakes upon his arrival in Siwa, which played directly into Siwa's factional strife. First, he came disguised as a Syrian Muslim merchant, claiming that the ultimate purpose of his journey was to continue west, to visit relatives in Darna and Benghazi. This raised the suspicion among Siwa's Sanusi brethren that he secretly wished to visit the sacred oasis of Jaghbub, which was indeed the case.[102] Second, Blunt set up camp outside the Eastern half of the town and immediately proceeded to deliver a letter of introduction to the leading Eastern shaykh, Muhammad Sa'id.[103] This certainly did not help his cause with the Western notables, all Sanusi followers, who were already wary of Blunt's larger designs. Blunt himself later acknowledged that the Sanusiyya orchestrated the raid: "There is little doubt that the prime movers in the affair were the Akhwan [Brethren]. . . . The Sheikh of the Western town led the *ghazu* [raid], but the men who first attacked me were, I am sure, slaves of the Akhwan. . . . Indeed, it was all done in the name of Sidi el Mahdi [al-Sanusi]."[104] Rather than admit that the suspicions of the Sanusi brethren were legitimate, however, Blunt dismissed their actions as a mere instance of opportunistic plunder and "fanaticism," made worse by the "recklessness which Ramadan brings."[105]

This is not how Cromer saw things. In Cromer's view, the Siwans' hostile reception of Blunt was entirely understandable, given Blunt's poor planning and inept conduct upon entering the oasis. After all, not only did Blunt come to Siwa without any authoritative documents to establish his identity or explain the purpose of his visit, he also brought "a letter addressed to the leader of the anti-Senussi party by a follower of one . . . of the Constantinople Palace Sheikhs." Seen in this light, Cromer's rationale for faulting Blunt seems fairly convincing: "It is difficult to imagine any conduct more calculated to excite the suspicions of an ignorant and suspicious people. I really do not think it is any matter for surprise that, in your own words, they should have supposed you were a 'secret agent from the Egyptian or the Ottoman Government.'"[106]

Although Blunt made his case to Cromer by grandstanding against Sanusi fanaticism in the name of Egyptian justice, he was not himself above the local political fray. What Blunt neglected to tell Cromer was that he had implicated himself in the intricate web of local Siwan politics—only to become exasperated later on when things did not go his way.

A couple of days after the attack, Blunt sat down with all the shaykhs of Siwa's Western faction, including Habun, who repaid him the money that had been seized. As Blunt wrote in his diary, the Western leaders were "now polite enough and anxious their quarrel with me should be settled"; Blunt in turn "used a little *siasa* [*siyasa,* or "politics"] with them," agreeing to pin the blame for the raid on Hassuna Mansur, rather than the powerful Habun. Mansur, it turns out, had alienated his fellow Western shaykhs for being "in rebellion" ever since his defiant stand against the Maher commission almost a year prior—behavior that risked provoking a broader Egyptian military response. Accordingly, they asked if Blunt might be able to "get him removed by the Government as a mischief maker."[107]

Blunt's descent into local political intrigue did not stop there. On his way out of Siwa, Blunt had a brief exchange with Muhammad Sa'id, the leading Eastern shaykh, who handed him a list of notable Western Siwans who had been involved in the attack; it seems clear that this was a ploy on Sa'id's part to incriminate his Western adversaries, so as to gain an upper hand in the local political arena. Blunt also sat down one last time with Husayn Effendi, the police sergeant, and promised that he would use his influence in Cairo to "get him named Mamur." At the same time, Blunt disagreed with the sergeant's attitude toward the Sanusiyya. Blunt felt that Husayn Effendi would only be able to establish his authority in Siwa if he got rid of Habun—"the only dangerous one of the lot, as he is intelligent, unscrupulous, and bold."[108] But Husayn Effendi was "anxious not to compromise the Senussia with the Government" and in turn endorsed the Western shaykhs' plan to peg Hassuna Mansur "as the dangerous man, making him scapegoat" in the place of Habun.[109]

In sum, by the time Blunt left Siwa—four days after he arrived—he seems to have made countervailing promises to three different parties about the message he was to deliver to officials back in Cairo. Despite his overtures to the Western Sanusi shaykhs, he seemed poised to betray them and side instead with Husayn Effendi, as well as the Easterners. But Blunt never got the chance to continue playing *siyasa* as he might have wished. Several weeks after his return to Cairo, Blunt heard the news about Hassuna Mansur's death in a new round of factional violence in Siwa; it was at this point that he realized he had been deceived, possibly even used, by Siwan shaykhs as well as the police sergeant.

It was this realization that compelled Blunt to renew his crusade against Cromer on behalf of Egyptian law and order. In a letter to Cromer roughly a year after the attack, Blunt condemned the Egyptian government for not prosecuting Husayn Effendi, his erstwhile ally, whom he now firmly believed "must have connived in the subsequent intrigue" leading to Hassuna Mansur's death, and the Sanusiyya's subsequent reassertion of authority in the oasis.[110] Blunt felt duped by Husayn Effendi, whom he accused of "doing his best to screen" the Western Sanusi shaykhs (most notably Habun), with whom he had strategically allied following Blunt's visit. Livid that his hapless expedition to Siwa had been manipulated in this way, Blunt could only resort to wild conspiracy theory, concluding that Mansur's murder was an utter fabrication invented by Husayn Effendi and the Western shaykhs to forestall any formal government inquiry, and thus to protect Habun (and, by extension, Sanusi interests in the oasis).[111]

Ultimately, in Blunt's eyes, the Egyptian government's unforgiveable sin in its handling of the Siwan affair was its apparent complicity in what he called "sham justice."[112] It was not only that the government "ignored the one central fact of the situation, namely the temporary but complete collapse of the Egyptian authority at Siwa" at the time of Blunt's visit. More egregious, in his view, was how the jurisdiction laws of 1897 underpinned the legal authority of the oasis's local tribunal, *Majlis Siwa*. Blunt knew that the "the real leaders of the attack could hardly be brought to justice" so long as the tribunal was dominated by Western Sanusi shaykhs.[113] And yet the coup de grâce came when Blunt discovered that Husayn Effendi, ostensibly a government man, had colluded with the shaykhs of the tribunal to protect Habun and the other Sanusi leaders, by scapegoating Mansur.

The real "sham," then, was the government's willingness to overlook how the devolution of jurisdiction to *Majlis Siwa* had created ample room for local notables to bolster their own local authority—in this instance, by exploiting Blunt's visit to protect their leader and enshrine Sanusi power in the oasis. As far as Blunt was concerned, this series of events made a complete mockery of the Egyptian justice system. But Cromer remained unmoved by such arguments. Cromer seemed to understand something fundamental that Blunt absolutely could not: this was all quite ordinary as far as the government's dealings with Siwa were concerned. It was simply politics as usual.

Even after the efforts of the Maher commission in 1896–97 to establish new, permanent government institutions in Siwa, the oasis continued to operate as an anomalous legal enclave. Whatever territorial sovereignty the Egyptian government claimed over Siwa in 1900 was, in practice, contingent upon the traditional political role of local intermediaries—a coterie of shaykhs, dominated by the Jaghbub-based Sanusiyya Brotherhood, who performed the most basic tasks of governance, including the administration of justice. Accordingly, these shaykhs managed to convert this moment of intensified Egyptian territorialization into an opportunity to formalize their customary authority and bolster their traditional ruling legitimacy in the oasis.

The fluid model of local borderland politics presented in this chapter lies in stark contrast to the more rigid, one-dimensional models of local resistance to government authority that have become typical of the limited historiography on Siwa, but which are also reproduced more broadly in many historical studies of state centralization. In the case of Egypt's western borderland, centralization worked in tandem with the entrenchment of the alternate, noncentralizing marks of sovereignty wielded by the Sanusiyya and other traditional authority figures in the region. The layered political field in Siwa would only become further complicated by the onset of a new era of Khedivial interest and investment in the oasis and surrounding region, as the next two chapters highlight.

# 3

## 'Abbas Hilmi II and the Anatomy
## of a Siwan Murder

On August 5, 1907, Husayn Effendi Fahmi, the *ma'mur* of Siwa, drafted a detailed report summarizing some noteworthy news from the oasis. One of the main issues he discussed was the curious local fallout of Lord Cromer's resignation as consul-general that past April. By Fahmi's account, local authorities had taken advantage of the long information lag between Cairo and Siwa to aggrandize the prestige of the Khedive, 'Abbas Hilmi II: "We spread the rumor that His Excellency the Khedive, having witnessed the poor behavior of the Lord, actually had dismissed him, [and] that it was not a resignation." Not everyone accepted this specious account of politics in the distant capital, however. Siwa's qadi defied Fahmi and his men by demonstrating "in front of the people his strong regret for the Lord's resignation." But Fahmi's version of events ultimately won the day: "By virtue of good planning, Shaykh [Sa'ud] returned from Alexandria and informed the Siwans that the Lord had been dismissed,[1] and all the people believed our rumor [*'umūm al-ahālī ṣadaqū ishā'atna*]."[2]

In his report, Fahmi also described a separate incident in which the Khedive's personal authority in Siwa had been on the line. While Fahmi was out strolling with the town doctor and scribe, he found himself harassed yet again by the meddlesome qadi. The tension was only defused by a "fortuitous" encounter with two prominent Siwan elites: the aforementioned Shaykh Sa'ud and 'Uthman Habun (Siwa's local Sanusi representative), who proceeded to invite the entire ensemble to his home.

Over the course of what one can only imagine were several rounds of sweet Siwan tea, the conversation turned to the Khedive's role in the oasis's affairs. Habun and Saʿud expressed their hope that their "town would be blessed with peace," to which Fahmi responded by assuring the group that "the Khedive gives generously to the loyal and the upright." But the qadi took umbrage at this line: "Fine, you get [his] gifts, and what do I get? It would have been appropriate for him to give me a cashmere scarf or clothing!" The qadi's outburst then prompted a lengthy discussion about whether a decorative watch the Khedive had given Habun was made of silver or gold. It turns out this was a pet topic of the qadi, who had been chiding Habun for some time that it was silver. But examining them up close that day in Habun's home, the men concurred that the watch was indisputably made of gold—and of very fine quality, to boot. Thus emboldened, Habun reproached the qadi: "You are always telling me that the watch is silver; but does it befit someone like His Excellency the Khedive to give something of so little value, like you say?" The game was up at this point, and the qadi fell silent. Although this might seem like a trivial episode, Fahmi ascribed genuine political significance to it in his report. In his view, the qadi's "disparagement" of ʿAbbas Hilmi's gifts was part of a larger, more dangerous pattern of attempts to undermine the Khedive's local authority in the oasis.[3]

Just as striking as Fahmi's close attention to local political intrigue was his choice of audience. The recipient of his report was not, as might be expected, an advisor at the Interior Ministry (*Nizarat al-Dakhiliyya*)— the government branch that oversaw Egypt's provincial administration, including the appointment of district *maʾmurs* such as Fahmi—but rather a senior agent of the Khedive's *Daʾira Khassa*.

The Khedivial *Daʾira Khassa* has not received much attention by historians of colonial Egypt. This is understandable, given its steady eclipse as a political institution over the last quarter of the nineteenth century. The *Daʾira Khassa* was a holdover of the *Daʾira Saniyya*, which emerged in the 1840s under Mehmed ʿAli as a distinct administrative unit encompassing the Pasha's vast holdings in private estates.[4] After its steady expansion under Mehmed ʿAli's successors, the *Daʾira Saniyya* shrunk considerably, beginning in 1875, when Khedive Ismaʿil (ʿAbbas Hilmi's grandfather) sold off a large portion of his properties to alleviate his personal debt in the wake of Egypt's declaration of bankruptcy. In 1878, for example, Ismaʿil ceded 425,729 acres of *Daʾira Saniyya* and domain lands to the state.[5] Between 1888—when the Egyptian government under the British began to sell erstwhile *Daʾira Saniyya* lands to private interests—and 1914, the bulk of Egypt's large estates fell into the hands of either individual landowners (European as well as Egyptian) or foreign companies, such as *Credit Foncier Égyptien* and the Land Development Company of Egypt.[6]

In short, after the period of land transfers that began in the mid-1870s, the *Da'ira Khassa* came to denote all that was left of the Khedivial properties, as well as the administrative apparatus that oversaw them. Why, then, was the Siwan *ma'mur* reporting directly to one of the *Da'ira Khassa*'s senior agents? And why, in turn, would an administrator of the Khedive's private properties have been interested in the minutiae of local politics in remote Siwa?

To answer these questions, this and the following chapter develop an alternate interpretation of the Khedivial *Da'ira Khassa* under 'Abbas Hilmi. I argue that the *Da'ira Khassa* gave cover to a network of political operatives loyal to the Khedive, and that this network constituted a shadow institution that he utilized to bolster his political power across Egypt. Although the Khedive's agents sometimes worked or even overlapped with Egyptian officials—Interior Ministry bureaucrats, provincial governors, local law enforcement officers—the *Da'ira Khassa* also developed alongside the Egyptian government as a parallel, and sometimes rival, channel for the projection of territorial sovereignty outside Cairo.

That 'Abbas Hilmi—technically the "sovereign" of Egypt—pursued his own political designs largely outside the purview of the Egyptian government has important implications for our understanding of Egypt's contested sovereignty during the period of British colonial rule. By examining how the political machinations at the center of the colonial state played out well beyond Cairo, it becomes clear that Egyptian sovereignty in this period was exercised as a series of competing claims and counterclaims—or "marks" that different agents of centralizing power wielded to gain ruling legitimacy. Accordingly, the political network operating through the *Da'ira Khassa* was instrumental in establishing 'Abbas Hilmi as the paramount sovereign figure in a region where, as we saw in the last two chapters, the institutional capacity of the Egyptian government was still quite weak. At the same time, the Khedive's consistent investment in cultivating intricate networks of loyal supporters not just in the Egyptian West, but wherever he owned property around the country, played a significant role in Egypt's emergence as a more cohesive territorial domain over the two decades before World War I.

From the earliest years of his reign, 'Abbas Hilmi found himself caught in a relentless power struggle with the British Residency. In 1893—only one year after his accession, at age seventeen—Lord Cromer blocked his bid to replace the standing Council of Ministers (headed by the pro-British Mustafa Fahmi) with a new slate of officials more in line with his political outlook.[7] As 'Abbas Hilmi would later note in his memoir, he was deeply dismayed by his discovery that "the Khedive could scarcely choose his Prime Minister without the approval of the English resident!" He felt he should be able to rule without paying "heed to Lord Cromer, whom [he] did not think [he] needed to consult regarding the composition of the Government." In his view, "the choice of ministers appeared to be left to the Sovereign alone."[8]

The young Khedive never forgot this early object lesson in British colonial power. Determined not to become a hapless puppet of the Residency like his father, Tawfiq, had been, 'Abbas Hilmi cast his lot with the nascent Egyptian nationalist movement. Around 1894, the Khedive formed a close partnership with popular nationalist hero Mustafa Kamil. The Khedive then worked closely with the nationalists for over a decade,[9] supporting the efforts of Kamil's National Party (*Hizb al-Watani*) to secure financial backing around Europe, while simultaneously promoting its political agenda through the anti-British newspaper *al-Mu'ayyad*, run by stalwart Khedivial loyalist Shaykh 'Ali Yusuf.[10] Additionally, to the great consternation of the Residency, the Khedive helped fan the flames of nationalist sentiment across the Egyptian countryside by appointing staunchly anti-British figures to numerous local posts in the provincial government.[11]

To counter the rising tide of popular Egyptian nationalism that the Khedive's activities had in part provoked, the British introduced a series of reforms that culminated in the complete restructuring of the Egyptian Interior Ministry. By the end of 1895, the Khedive had been stripped of his authority to appoint government officials; in his place, a new "Provincial Commission," operated by the Interior Ministry, now had control over all government appointments at the provincial, district, and village levels.[12]

As the British tightened their grip on the reins of the Egyptian government, the Khedive pursued alternate channels to circumvent the Residency and realize what he maintained was his rightful ambition to rule as an independent sovereign. It was with this lofty goal in mind that the Khedive assembled a private network of informants and spies. Headed by an Interior Ministry bureaucrat named Muhammad Sa'id Shimi Bey, this

network contained individuals from a variety of posts and institutions—
including the Khedivial *Da'ira Khassa*. As Aaron Jakes has argued, the Khedive's private intelligence network served to "furnish the young Khedive
with an ominous tableau of the institutions his family had worked for almost a century to erect . . . institutions [that] now appeared as the strong-
holds from which the British and their lackeys were launching a relentless
barrage of assaults upon the country's moral and material well-being."[13]

The Khedive's political and financial options grew ever more limited
the longer the British occupation wore on. Accordingly, he relied increasingly upon his network of informants, as well as the *Da'ira Khassa*, for
these were two vital resources over which he continued to exercise exclu-
sive control. With its extensive holdings in private estates all around Egypt,
the *Da'ira Khassa* was an ideal locus for the Khedive and his agents to pursue political projects outside the purview of the Egyptian government—
particularly after the British takeover of the Interior Ministry in 1895. As
the vast collection of the Khedive's private papers reveal, his agents were
active all over Egypt during the two decades before World War I.[14] This
chapter illuminates the relationship between 'Abbas Hilmi's *Da'ira Khassa*,
his network of informants, and broader currents in the exercise of sovereignty in Egypt by focusing on just one locale: Siwa.[15] The story unfolds
with the Khedive's monumental journey to the oasis in the winter of 1906.

By all accounts, the Khedivial expedition was a transformative moment
in Siwa's history. 'Abbas Hilmi was, after all, ostensibly the first Egyptian
ruler to visit the oasis since Alexander the Great made the long voyage to
consult the legendary oracle of Amun. The picture of the Khedive's Siwan
sojourn that emerges from the extant sources reveals that it was a grand
affair, clearly designed to make a lasting impression.[16]

The journey was split into two separate legs: first, the Khedive and
his entourage traveled by train to Garawla (the terminus of the Khedive's
Maryut Railway at that time), and then by automobile to Marsa Matruh.
From there, they proceeded through the desert in an expansive royal caravan, led by a vanguard of sixty-two camel-borne bedouins in addition to
twenty soldiers on horseback.[17] The main division of the caravan, which
contained the Khedive's unwieldy horse-drawn coach, comprised 288
camels, 22 horses, and 28 mounted guardsmen.[18] The caravan toted 120
iron tanks and 200 jugs in order to transport water from Cairo, as well
as 19 tents.[19] In the evenings, the Khedive liked to entertain his guests—

including the noted German Egyptologist J. C. Ewald Falls, whose published memoir provides invaluable information on the Khedivial expedition—in his tent with meals served on fine china, along with wine, spirits, and tobacco.[20]

The significance of the Khedive's decision to remove himself from Cairo and spend an entire month trekking through the Western Desert was not lost on the Ottoman or Italian authorities, who grew anxious that the trip signaled the Khedive's grander territorial designs in the region. The Ottoman government sent a unit of gendarmes from Benghazi to investigate the progression of the Khedive's caravan;[21] they would later report back that the Khedive undertook the journey "accompanied by a great number of tribal shaykhs and notables," and that he had stopped by Sollum en route to Siwa.[22]

The Italians, for their part, were principally concerned with the prospect that the Khedive might head from Siwa—an indisputably Egyptian locality, in their view—across the "border" to Jaghbub, which they contended was within the coveted domain of Ottoman Benghazi. In May 1906, an official at the Ministry of Foreign Affairs in Rome ordered a diplomat at the Italian embassy in Cairo to "collect accurate information on these events, in order to establish whether or not they correspond[ed] to reality, and if they [were] connected—as [was] supposed—to a well-determined project of the Egyptian Government relative to the regions located on the other side of the Western frontier of Egypt."[23] Once it was ascertained that the Khedive never made it further west than Siwa, the Italians felt satisfied that "for now, any political aim [of the Khedive] on the other side of the border can be ruled out," since the expedition's objective was merely "to reclaim [*mettere in valore*] the region considered desert, which he [the Khedive] believes can be developed for his own personal financial gain."[24]

On the seventh day of its journey, the caravan arrived in Siwa.[25] The Khedive rode out front on horseback, and was received by the Siwan *ma'mur* along with some notable shaykhs, including representatives of the Sanusiyya. The procession then wended its way into the center of town, where crowds of Siwans had gathered to welcome the Khedive with a musical and visual display.[26] Yet the reception was not entirely warm. Despite many trappings of an enthusiastic welcome, a prominent group of Sanusiyya—"the men in fluttering white burnous and narrow turbans, the bronze-colored monks," according to Falls—met the Khedive "in silence and with ceremonious coldness. On their faces might be read curiosity and compulsion mingled with hatred, unconcealed hatred of the descendant of the plunderer [Mehmed 'Ali] whom no real native of Siwa unreservedly recognizes as master."[27] The Khedive's prestige and sovereign legitimacy in Siwa were thus by no means a given; they would have to be gradually earned.

For the duration of his four-day stay, the Khedive set up camp in the northern outskirts of the oasis, in an area known as 'Ayn Radi (approximately two miles from Siwa's town center). This became the caravan's home base, from which the Khedive undertook several local excursions. Perhaps the most significant of these was his visit, accompanied by some fifty Siwan shaykhs, to the tomb of Sidi Sulayman.[28]

The wooing of Siwan elites was one of the Khedive's top priorities during his visit. The same group of fifty shaykhs who joined the Khedive at the tomb of Sidi Sulayman would accompany him on most of his business around the oasis. Additionally, the Khedive gave several of them generous gifts: cashmere shawls to six Siwan shaykhs; gold watches and chains to 'Uthman Habun, 'Umar Musallam, Muhammad Sa'id, and Shaykh Sa'ud (all of whom were members of *Majlis Siwa*); and calico garments to the shaykhs of what one author refers to as the *turuq* (likely referring to the heads of Sanusi and Madani *zawaya*). The Khedive also hosted a sumptuous lunch banquet for the shaykhs of Siwa, and organized a series of celebrations and games that were open to all of the oasis's inhabitants.[29]

The Khedive's other main priority during his visit was to survey various sites around Siwa that might be suitable for agricultural development. Immediately following the lunch banquet, the Khedive asked Shaykh Sa'ud to accompany him during his meals and evening activities. The next day, Shaykh Sa'ud served as the Khedive's personal guide, bringing him to various springs around the oasis, some bountiful olive gardens, as well as some of Siwa's storied archaeological sites.[30]

On the following day, Shaykh Sa'ud and the Khedive made a special visit to 'Ayn Qurayshat, the oasis's largest spring, located approximately seventeen miles southeast of Siwa proper, near the small village of Zaytun. According to Ahmad Shafiq (now a member of the 'Abbas Hilmi's entourage), the Khedive "became very pleased" upon seeing the spring and the lands adjacent to it, and hastened to appoint Shaykh Sa'ud as his *Da'ira Khassa* representative (*wakil*) in charge of agriculture there. The Khedive proceeded to pay the "necessary expenses," and then gave Shaykh

Sa'ud fifty Egyptian pounds to cover the cost of dredging the spring.[31] In Shafiq's telling, the Khedive—realizing the obvious potential of a particularly plum piece of real estate—spontaneously marked it off as his own, and then made the necessary financial arrangements to secure it as *Da'ira Khassa* property, under the personal supervision of a key local notable, Shaykh Sa'ud.[32]

Beyond tapping the network of Siwa's prominent local figures, above all Shaykh Sa'ud, to work for the *Da'ira Khassa*, the Khedive's land dealings in Siwa also ended up implicating the *ma'mur*, Khalil Effendi Hafiz. On June 21, 1906, Hafiz received a letter from the governor of Buhayra ordering him to travel to Cairo for an important meeting at the Ministry of the Interior. A month later, Hafiz met with an advisor at the ministry, who began the conversation by asking for the *ma'mur's* opinion why the Khedive might have given explicit orders for Hafiz to remain in his post for another year. Hafiz responded by referring to a petition he had encouraged several Siwan shaykhs to write in his favor: "I think that the people—on account of their contentedness with my plans for them—requested this of the Khedive." The advisor confirmed the receipt of this petition, which had been placed in a special file.[33]

The advisor then steered the conversation toward the matter of the Khedive's property dealings in the oasis. As Hafiz recalled, "He asked me if the Khedive is buying land. I told him yes." The advisor pressed the *ma'mur* for more details. Hafiz responded by confirming that the Khedive had purchased approximately three thousand feddans of land—located within an hour and a half to three hours from the center of Siwa—ever since the Khedivial expedition. Upon hearing this news, the advisor grew quiet, so Hafiz returned to the topic of his remaining in Siwa: "As long as the Khedive wants it, I would happily accept another year in Siwa." The advisor, still agitated, continued to sit in silence and merely "rapped his hand on the table" for awhile. Eventually the two men came to terms: Hafiz accepted a salary of eighteen Egyptian pounds and was ordered to take a two-month leave before reassuming his post for another year.[34]

Hafiz's testimony—written up the very next day in a report to an upper-level official of the Khedivial *Diwan*, Muhammad 'Uthman—confirms that the Khedive wasted no time securing large swaths of Siwan land for the *Da'ira Khassa* during and after his visit to the oasis.[35] More centrally, however, it raises intriguing questions about the relationship between the Khedive and the Siwan *ma'mur*. Why was the Khedive so keen to keep Hafiz in office, to the extent that the Interior Ministry had become suspicious of his loyalty to the government? To what extent were the Khedive and his local *Da'ira Khassa* agents actively seeking to attract Siwan *ma'murs* as willing partners in their own political gambit? That Hafiz immediately offered such a detailed account of his meeting at the Interior Ministry to a high-up Khedivial agent certainly lends credence to the notion that Hafiz was on the side of the Khedive, rather than the British-controlled Interior Ministry.

Indeed, several months later, Hafiz helped the Khedive secure new Siwan properties for the *Da'ira Khassa*. In December 1906, Hafiz—now back in Siwa, serving a new term as *ma'mur*—wrote to a *Da'ira Khassa* representative named Muhammad Bey Rashid, notifying him of the successful acquisition of some new lands in and around Siwa that the Khedive had requested for purchase (including two large springs: 'Ayn Kibrit and 'Ayn Shamsin). Hafiz had been instrumental in completing the deal. After first inspecting the springs with the Siwan police superintendent, Mitwalli Effendi Hilmi (who would later become *ma'mur*), and a local shaykh, 'Umar Musallam,[36] Hafiz gave his authorization to buy them for the *Da'ira Khassa*. He then took fifty-five Egyptian pounds from Shaykh Sa'ud and distributed this sum—"in accordance with Khedivial orders"—to the poor and needy. Hafiz concluded his report to Rashid by assuring the *Da'ira Khassa* agent that "we are indeed ready for all the tasks required of us in the service of our Khedive."[37]

The available evidence from the *Da'ira Khassa*'s files reveals that the administration of the Khedive's new properties in Siwa entailed sustained collaboration between several local shaykhs, on one hand, and a succession of Siwan *ma'murs*, on the other. In April 1908, for instance, Hafiz's successor as *ma'mur*, Husayn Fahmi, reported to Ahmad Sadiq (the aforementioned senior *Da'ira Khassa* official) on the progress that had been made at 'Ayn Qurayshat, the Khedive's prize possession in Siwa. His letter provides a unique glimpse of how the Khedivial properties in the oasis were managed. According to Fahmi, the *Da'ira Khassa* hired several key local notables besides Shaykh Sa'ud to supervise agricultural work at the spring: "I received your entire response on the issue of agriculture in Qurayshat. In accordance with its contents, the shaykhs 'Uthman Isma'il Habun, 'Umar Musallam, Muhammad Sa'id, and Sa'ud Muhammad Sa'ud Tawiya were put in charge." Moreover, on the *Da'ira Khassa*'s orders, Fahmi authorized one Western and two Eastern shaykhs to help out at the spring, "on account of their being well-known in the science of agriculture in Siwa." But it was not just the elite shaykhs who oversaw the project of agricultural development at Qurayshat. They also worked with an engineer employed by the Khedive named Hassan Effendi Labib, and—arguing that "the only effective way of farming this land is the Siwan way" (meaning, without plowing)—they hired a Siwan farmer named Ahmad Hamid to work the spring on a full-time basis.[38]

There is no doubt that the work of developing the Khedivial lands at 'Ayn Qurayshat often remained in the hands of the local elites. In July 1913, for instance, Shaykh Sa'ud reported to the *Da'ira Khassa* that he and a team of several shaykhs—'Abdallah Hamid Muhammad, 'Abd al-Rahman Mu'arrif, and Muhammad Sa'id—had camped in 'Ayn Qurayshat for four days and did all the work of opening up the spring and improving its irrigation system.[39] Yet at other moments, it is clear that the *Da'ira Khassa* relied extensively on local labor to assist with the Khedivial properties.[40] In June 1909, for example, Shaykh Sa'ud hired 160 Siwans to help with important repairs at the spring; the workers each received ten Egyptian pounds for their efforts, "in the personal presence of the *ma'mur*."[41] Around the same time, the new Siwan *ma'mur*, Mitwalli Effendi Hilmi, distributed clothing on behalf of the Khedive in order to entice several Siwans to do the job of cleaning out the spring.[42] Over time, the Khedive's development projects at 'Ayn Qurayshat began to flourish. In October 1912, the *ma'mur* blithely reported to the Khedive that the nearly six hundred date-palms in the area around 'Ayn Qurayshat were thriving, and that the clover found around the spring was "in extremely good condition—the best found in all the lands of Siwa" and thus suitable to bring to market twice a week.[43]

As these documents reporting on the progress of 'Ayn Qurayshat reveal, the development of the Khedivial properties in Siwa was an involved, collaborative endeavor that brought together local labor as well as key figures from Siwa's political landscape: Shaykh Sa'ud and other notable shaykhs, including members of the oasis's Eastern and Western factions; and a series of *ma'mur*s who played a central role overseeing the works at 'Ayn Qurayshat and other Khedivial properties in the oasis.

The Khedive's acquisition of substantial property in Siwa for the *Da'ira Khassa* constituted one important facet of his project of cultivating personal sovereignty. Beginning with his historic expedition in 1906, the Khedive—by carving out his own private territorial domain in the oasis and then cultivating a network of important local political figures to administer it—steadily inserted himself into the traditional power structure in this distant locale.

Another means that the Khedive adopted to establish himself as the paramount sovereign figure in Siwa was the undertaking of a major building project: a new central mosque. The story of the mosque's construction goes even further in revealing the extent to which the Khedive staked his sovereignty in Siwa on both personal relationships and private largesse. It also demonstrates the extreme measures that the Khedive and his agents would take to challenge anyone standing in their way—notably, in this case, a hapless Siwan *ma'mur* named Sayyid Effendi Muhammad.

The Mosque of Sidi Sulayman, dedicated to one of the most revered figures in Siwan history, is still the largest mosque in the oasis. The Khedive introduced the idea of building a new mosque during his stay in Siwa in 1906. According to Shafiq, "When the Khedive visited Siwa, he won over the hearts of the people with the order to build a great mosque," the total area of which would comprise over three thousand square meters.[44] Due to a shortage of funds,[45] the mosque was not finished during 'Abbas Hilmi's reign. It is the Khedive's uncle, King Fu'ad I, who is credited today with seeing the building project through to completion, following his own royal visit to Siwa in 1928.

In December 1907, the Khedive gave the order for construction to begin. Upon receiving word, Husayn Fahmi, the *ma'mur* at the time, assembled all the Siwan shaykhs to discuss how the work should proceed. They decided to employ the entire Siwan population, and they organized a labor rotation to minimize the chance of any factional strife. On the first Saturday, for instance, the Easterners were charged with the task of transporting gravel to the building site, whereas Westerners were responsible for collecting sand. But on the ensuing workday, the two sides swapped: Westerners were now in charge of gravel, and Easterners took over sand collection. Fahmi supervised the labor from a seat overlooking the construction site and was pleased to report that the project "brought together all the workers," who frequently prayed for the long life of the Khedive.

The *Da'ira Khassa* covered all the costs of building materials and labor for the mosque project. Accordingly, Shaykh Sa'ud, along with another Khedivial agent—Muhammad Effendi Tawfiq Shawqi, a member of 'Abbas Hilmi's entourage—oversaw the work and reported frequently back to the Khedive. Although the Siwan *ma'mur* helped supervise the project, he still took a backseat to the Khedive's personal representatives. Detailed records have survived that demonstrate the tremendous care with which the *Da'ira Khassa* managed the project. For instance, Shawqi regularly sent the Khedive itemized expense reports that carefully laid out how much of the *Da'ira Khassa*'s money was spent each day on supplies and labor over a two-week period.[46]

Given the Khedive's personal investment in the mosque, the *Da'ira Khassa* representatives took great pains to ensure that Siwans understood it as a symbol of the Khedive's personal largesse, as well as his respect for Siwa's most cherished customs (that the mosque was dedicated to Sidi Sulayman was no accident). Reminders of the Khedive's personal involvement could be fairly unsubtle: in January 1909, for example, Shawqi gave the workers a week-long holiday in honor of the Khedive's birthday.[47] For the most part, work on the mosque went smoothly: in April 1910, for instance, Shawqi blithely informed the Khedive that the building had finally reached the mandated height of three levels of columns.[48] Yet one deceptively trivial episode that disrupted work on the mosque for at least a week in March 1909 reveals how the Khedive and his agents considered this building project primarily as a means for projecting the Khedive's sovereign authority in the oasis.

On March 13, 1909, it was discovered that a substantial quantity of cement had gone missing from a barrel located among the *Da'ira Khassa*'s supplies allocated for the construction. In Shawqi's view, this "strange incident" marked the culmination of a most unwelcome development in the oasis, since "from the time that the building of the Siwa mosque was started until now, all the supplies, tools, and materials" could be safely left in place without being guarded, because none of the Siwans would "dare to take anything . . . out of fear and dread" of the punishment that would befall them. The *Da'ira Khassa* agents had also typically counted on previous *ma'murs* to safeguard its property.[49] This began to change, however, with the arrival of a new *ma'mur* in town: Sayyid Effendi Muhammad.

When Shawqi first came to Siwa to begin work on the mosque, Shaykh Sa'ud had warned him that Sayyid Effendi Muhammad was different than previous *ma'murs*—that he was consistently unwilling to assist with any *Da'ira Khassa* affairs. Shawqi found this extremely hard to believe: "I initially doubted Shaykh Sa'ud's words, owing to my arrogant failure to imagine it possible for an official not to help and serve the [*Da'ira*] *Khassa* to the best of his abilities." Yet the cement theft finally convinced Shawqi that Shaykh Saʿud was right to have been wary: the *maʾmur* was an obstacle to the *Daʾira Khassa*'s interests and could not be trusted.[50]

Unsurprisingly, Shawqi was quick to suspect that Sayyid Effendi Muhammad was partly to blame for the cement theft; it was not every day, after all, that someone stole from the Khedive. Shawqi's memo included a litany of complaints against the *maʾmur*: he did not show up when summoned to a meeting; he neglected to arrange an assembly of shaykhs in order to solicit their help with the investigation; and he refused to conduct searches in the homes of five merchants living in Siwa. Considering the *maʾmur*'s inaction, Shawqi took decisive action to intimidate the Siwans, so that "they would not dare to take anything else belonging to the [*Daʾira*] *Khassa*, as was the case during the time of the previous two *maʾmurs*." On the second day after the theft, Shawqi assembled all the Siwan shaykhs and "informed them that if Our Lord [the Khedive] . . . got wind of this affair, he would be incredibly angry" and would hold them accountable. Shawqi's warning had the desired effect: the shaykhs agreed to do all they could to aid the investigation.[51]

Although the outcome of the theft case is unclear,[52] the Khedive's agents refused to let it pass lightly. Shawqi continued to harass the *maʾmur* even after his tour of duty in the oasis had ended, ultimately lodging a formal complaint against him with both the Governorate of Buhayra and the Interior Ministry, the latter of which subsequently launched an official inquiry.[53] Sayyid Effendi Muhammad pleaded his innocence in a long report to the governor of Buhayra. In sharp contrast to Shawqi's allegations, he claimed that he had actively pursued the case; not only had he authorized Siwan shaykhs to carry out investigations on his behalf, he even secretly recruited a woman to conduct numerous house searches.[54] Sayyid Effendi Muhammad agreed with Shawqi on only one point: "no one would be reckless enough to take anything from the possessions of the *Daʾira Khassa*."[55]

The Interior Ministry dispatched an investigatory commission to Siwa. The commission interviewed six witnesses, the first of whom was Shaykh Saʿud, who parroted everything Shawqi had alleged. Muhammad Saʿid—one of the notables whom we have seen was also involved in some of the Khedive's affairs—also corroborated Shawqi's story. But the other four witnesses denied having had any interactions with Sayyid Effendi Muhammad along the lines of what Shawqi had described. After weighing the conflicting testimonies, the Interior Ministry investigators concluded that the accusations leveled against Sayyid Muhammad were groundless.[56]

The Interior Ministry appointees eventually decided to wipe their hands clean of the affair—"the stolen item was not important," after all—but not before considering some possible reasons why Shawqi, Shaykh Saʿud, and Muhammad Saʿid would have sought to "frame [Sayyid Muhammad] and remove him from his position in Siwa."[57] Some of the reasons were decidedly personal. For instance, Muhammad Saʿid's son had recently been charged with a crime that his father could not bribe his way out of. But the commission also surmised that Shaykh Saʿud and Muhammad Saʿid had made a secret pact to oust the *maʾmur*.[58] In other words, Shawqi and several notable Siwan shaykhs harnessed the cement incident as a political maneuver. It was, in effect, a ploy to protect the local authority of the Khedive against the threat they associated with Sayyid Effendi Muhammad, the Egyptian government's man on the spot.

The stakes of this seemingly minor incident were thus quite high, at least for the Khedive and his agents. Indeed, the rationale behind the mosque construction had been to cement the Khedive's sovereign status in Siwa, and to deepen the perceived connection between his personal largesse and his claim to legitimate rule. The capacity to deliver on a major building project—one that honored a revered local figure, while also employing the entire oasis—thus constituted another mark of sovereignty that the Khedive marshaled to entrench his personal authority in a distant locale, over which the Egyptian government still exercised only limited control.

None of this would have been possible without the Khedivial network's cultivation of close relationships with key figures in Siwa's intricate political landscape. As the Khedive quickly deduced, politics in Siwa was bound up in a web of personal relationships, and agents of the *Daʾira Khassa*, such as Shawqi, pegged the Khedive's sovereign legitimacy on their ability to penetrate and control this web. Over the years following the Khedivial expedition, the recruitment of figures such as Shaykh Saʿud— whose social and political status received a significant boost once the Khedive tapped him to be his main representative in the oasis[59]—was essential to the project of entrenching Khedivial sovereignty in the westernmost reaches of Egypt. Even the high-profile murder of a Siwan *maʾmur* cannot be understood without considering the Khedivial network's successful integration into Siwa's traditional power structure.

On the evening of October 2, 1909, Siwan *ma'mur* Mitwalli Effendi Hilmi
(Sayyid Effendi Muhammad's successor) made a move to arrest 'Uthman
Habun. The pretext for the *ma'mur's* decision was a rumor that Habun had
been hiding a large cache of smuggled weapons and ammunition.[60] At first,
Hilmi tried to coax Habun into turning himself in at the *markaz* (district
headquarters). Yet Habun, "fearing that the *ma'mur* would betray him,"[61]
refused to comply, essentially forcing Hilmi's hand. Later that night, Hilmi
led a force of sixteen policemen and soldiers to Habun's compound. What
Hilmi did not know, however, was that Habun had been tipped off about
the impending raid, giving him time to mobilize his family and servants to
defend their home turf.[62]

At around two-thirty in the morning,[63] Hilmi and his men arrived at
the foot of Habun's hilltop compound. The story of what ensued depends
on who is telling it, but the essential details are as follows. Hilmi and six
of his men forcibly entered the compound and encountered Habun's son
Muhammad 'Uthman Habun (also known as Hamadu). Hamadu claimed
that his father was absent, even though, by one account, Habun could be
seen hiding on an upper story of the house. A melee broke out shortly
thereafter, and several rounds of shots rained down upon Hilmi and his
men from different vantage points. According to an eyewitness, one assail-
ant (likely Habun) yelled out, "Shoot the *ma'mur*, Hamadu!"[64] Hilmi and
five other men were severely wounded while they tried to flee; Hilmi later
succumbed to his injuries back at the *markaz*. Two others of the wounded
men—a coast guard sergeant named Surur Musa, and a soldier named
'Abd al-'Aziz—also died from their wounds (the other three would eventually make full recoveries).[65]

Muhammad Kamil Muhammad, Siwa's superintendent (*mulahidh*)
and Hilmi's second-in-command, took over the investigation after the
*ma'mur's* death. As he would later report to his authorities in Cairo, he
began by meeting with the leading shaykhs of the Eastern faction—'Umar
Musallam, Muhammad Sa'id, and Muhammad Mu'arrif—who told him
that they "were ready to fight the Westerners." What Kamil Muhammad
left out of his account, however, is the key role that Shaykh Sa'ud played
in pushing the Easterners to adopt this position. Indeed, as Shaykh Sa'ud
would later explain to the Khedive, he was the one who had initially "assembled all the Eastern shaykhs and informed them about the incident,"
and urged them that "it was incumbent upon [them] now to assist the
government" in arresting the murderers. It was at this point, Shaykh Sa'ud

continues, that "we—all the Eastern shaykhs—agreed that we would alert our families to prepare their weapons and go to Habun's house to resist him and attack" those responsible for the crimes.[66] When the Eastern shaykhs arrived at the *markaz* to inform Kamil Muhammad of their plans, the superintendent talked them down—out of consideration for "public security"[67]—and urged them instead to create a blockade around the town to prevent Habun from escaping the oasis.

A short time later, Muhammad Sa'id confessed to Kamil Muhammad that he had been giving refuge to Habun in his home since the night of the murder, when Habun had escaped to the other side of town disguised in women's clothing.[68] He also informed Kamil Muhammad that Habun soon intended to flee the oasis, possibly to Jaghbub.[69] The superintendent immediately dispatched a soldier to make the arrest: Habun was duly apprehended and brought to the *markaz* in chains.[70] Likewise, Hamadu was arrested at a friend's house, where he had been hiding.[71] Kamil Muhammad then ordered the remaining suspects to come to the *markaz*, and issued a proclamation that suggests his sensitivity to the factional undertones of the Habun affair: "The obedient man to the East, the rebel stays in his place."[72] Accordingly, the Westerners completely vacated their section of town, save for a few who were still holding out in Habun's compound. The other suspects were arrested soon thereafter ("with great ease," according to Shaykh Sa'ud) and locked up in the *markaz* along with Habun and Hamadu.[73]

The next order of business for Kamil Muhammad was to round up as many of Habun's smuggled weapons as possible, including those used against Mitwalli Hilmi and his men. Although the details are a bit murky, it appears that Kamil Muhammad—aided once again by Shaykh Sa'ud, Muhammad Sa'id, 'Umar Musallam, and Muhammad Mu'arrif[74]—managed to organize systematic weapons inspections around town. Ultimately, many weapons (including several Martini rifles) were recovered from Habun's storehouses.[75]

Similar to their reaction to the Blunt episode, more than a decade prior, the British authorities were extremely reluctant to become entangled in Siwan affairs. According to one Foreign Office official, "The more we, I mean the British, keep out of the matter, the better. . . . It must be remembered that the Siwa Bedouins are nearly all Senussites and a very wild lot over whom the Government have no real hold at all."[76] Consul-General Gorst, for his part, felt that it would be imprudent to "interfere with the decision," particularly "since the remoteness of the scene of the murder and the somewhat shadowy and purely informal nature of the control exercised by the small Egyptian police force posted there render[ed] it very necessary to afford adequate protection to the representatives of Government."[77]

Meanwhile, the Egyptian press was fanning the flames of this anti-Sanusi paranoia. Several newspapers warned that the Sanusi brethren in the oasis would violently resist government intervention.[78] The *Egyptian Gazette*, for instance, ran a piece declaring that "the expedition of the Egyptian Government to the Oasis of Siwa is far more serious than it looks, as the circumstances connected with the tragedy of the Mamour's death are of a complicated character and are rendered very grave owing to the enormous influence wielded by the agent of the Senoussi, Sheikh Osman Haboun."[79]

Once it became clear that Habun and his accomplices, already in custody, would have to be brought to justice, it was not immediately obvious to the authorities in Cairo how best to proceed with the case. At issue was whether such a heinous crime—the murder of the highest Egyptian official in Siwa—should be tried by the local court, dominated as it was by traditional shaykhs. As Gorst noted, "The Oasis of Siwa is not under the ordinary jurisdiction, but enjoys under an old decree a Bedouin Court of its own, composed of shaykhs elected by the inhabitants. . . . In regular course this court should try the case, but some doubt was expressed as to whether it could be relied upon to award a just and adequate sentence for so grave a crime."[80] Kamil Muhammad shared Gorst's concerns: "The most important issue is the courts (and implementation). The courts adhere to the law that pertains in Siwa."[81]

To address these concerns, the government appointed a former Siwan *ma'mur*,[82] Mahmud 'Azmi Bey—now the chief of police (*hikimdar*) in Gharbiyya province—as a special envoy to oversee the murder investigation. Government officials felt they needed a seasoned veteran such as 'Azmi, who possessed a "thorough knowledge of the place, its inhabitants and their customs," to assess the situation objectively and determine the feasibility of trying the Habun case locally.[83]

On October 16, after receiving his orders from the Khedive via telegraph, 'Azmi set off for Siwa accompanied by around one hundred police and coast guard officers.[84] The 'Azmi expedition proceeded first by train, then by a series of coaches "belonging to the Khedivial [*Da'ira*] *Khassa*."[85]

In Garawla, they camped in tents which the Khedive had given to 'Azmi and his men (among other gifts). They continued via camel caravan, stopping for a day in the oasis of Qara.[86] According to 'Azmi, his men took extra care to carry out their duties with "complete orderliness and care," given the "fire of grief and sadness in their hearts" that arose "due to the murder of this officer [the *ma'mur*] and his men."[87]

On October 27, 'Azmi met with the shaykhs of *Majlis Siwa* at 'Ayn al-Baqr, a spring located about two hours from Siwa. As the ensemble proceeded together to Siwa's *markaz*, 'Azmi took the opportunity to reprimand the Siwan shaykhs, letting them know how angry the recent murders had made the Khedive. When 'Azmi arrived at the *markaz*, he immediately inspected the thirty-one prisoners being held there and decided to tighten security. The next morning, 'Azmi visited Mitwalli Hilmi's gravesite and fired several honorary rounds. According to Shaykh Sa'ud, this salute was another means by which "fear of the Government has entered into the hearts of the people," so that they now "recognized the value of the Government and particularly His Excellency the Khedive."[88]

On October 30, 'Azmi and his men began their official investigation by questioning twenty-one witnesses who were *not* suspected of any wrongdoing. This lasted a few days. Then, for the better part of a week, 'Azmi interrogated each of the thirty-one men who had been implicated in the murders. At the end of the investigation, 'Azmi determined that Habun was "the leader of the gang," even though he had not actually inflicted any of the fatal wounds. Habun's son Hamadu would be charged as the *ma'mur's* actual murderer, whereas a Siwan named Ahmad Rumi would be charged with killing the coast guard sergeant, and a notorious local troublemaker named Mansur Hassuna—whom 'Azmi described as "one of those brigands who inherited nastiness from his parents and suckled the blood of corruption"— was charged with the murder of the soldier 'Abd al-'Aziz.[89]

'Azmi scheduled the trial in *Majlis Siwa* for the morning of November 9. He also made special arrangements to send the court's ruling to the Khedive via a "special messenger," to expedite the communication of any news requiring his immediate action.[90] The Siwan court, under 'Azmi's supervision, did its job efficiently, handing out various rulings to the thirty-one accused individuals: Habun, Hamadu, Rumi, and Hassuna received death sentences; eleven suspects were acquitted, including three of Habun's other sons. The remaining guilty parties were given prison terms of varying lengths.[91]

The swift implementation of justice in the Habun murder trial marks a clear departure from the government's laissez-faire conduct during the Blunt affair, during which officials in Cairo had chosen to drop the case largely out of fear of antagonizing the Sanusiyya. Clearly, much had changed in the intervening twelve years. That the most powerful Sanusi shaykh in Siwa was now being condemned to death was a surefire sign of a government more confident in its abilities to preserve law and order, even as it disrupted the traditional power structure in the oasis.

Moreover, if we can believe a remarkable report that 'Azmi sent to the governor of Buhayra soon after the murder trial, the recent turmoil had finally compelled Siwan notables to resolve the age-old factionalism in the oasis. What stands out in 'Azmi's testimony is his narrative of how the Siwan shaykhs responded so positively to his initiative "for the town to become one—no East and no West—in accordance with the wishes of Our Lord the Khedive." 'Azmi first assembled groups of representatives from each side to lecture them on the unsavory consequences of disunity. The shaykhs, in turn, presented 'Azmi with a petition—to be presented to the authorities in Cairo—to "make the two towns one town, without distinction—no East, and no West." This decision was subsequently upheld through a ruling from *Majlis Siwa*. 'Azmi considered all of this "a great step in the reform of the public security situation in this oasis," and consequently asked the authorities to move swiftly in ratifying the court's decisions.[92] On the surface, then, this momentous sequence of events following the murder trial seems to signal the Egyptian government's ultimate victory in its longstanding struggle to rule this notoriously recalcitrant oasis.

Yet if we look deeper into the case, a different interpretation of the murders and their aftermath emerges. The Siwa murders and ensuing trial of 'Uthman Habun and his accomplices cannot be understood apart from the intricacies of the Siwan political milieu, in which the oasis's affairs operated through an intricate web of personal connections. Moreover, a more thorough postmortem of the Siwan murders reveals the subtle underlying role that the Khedive, backed by his local *Da'ira Khassa* agents, played in navigating the complex political fallout of this critical event.

The key to unlocking some of the lingering mysteries of the murder case lies in reexamining the nature of the relationships between Habun, the ill-fated *ma'mur*, and several key shaykhs from *Majlis Siwa*. As discussed in the last chapter, Habun had wielded inordinate influence in Siwa for quite some time, to the extent that previous *ma'murs* found themselves at his mercy.[93] Habun also maintained connections to the Khedivial network: he was related to Shaykh Saʿud through marriage,[94] and he was also allegedly an active agent for the *Daʾira Khassa*, buying up properties for Shaykh Saʿud and the Khedive by "tricking the old owners." There seems little doubt that Habun's relationship with the Khedive's network of political operatives is partly what had enabled him to become such a "little despot" in the eyes of several *ma'murs*.[95]

Yet Habun's firm grip on power in the oasis had come under threat in the year or two before the murders. According to Egyptian Coast Guard officer Andre von Dumreicher, Habun's dominance over Siwa's economic life had started to wane once a pioneering Siwan police sergeant "admitted some merchants from Alexandria who traded with the Siwi and reduced Habun's business."[96] This development had prompted Habun to intensify his smuggling activities (particularly of firearms), dealing with several local bedouin tribes. Dumreicher also suggests that the same police sergeant had started to take over some of Habun's responsibilities for settling local disputes.[97]

Yet it was not the government authorities who were ultimately responsible for Habun's downfall. Rather, the coup de grâce was a conspiracy masterminded by rival Siwan shaykhs, which only comes into focus through a startling report that ʿAzmi sent to the governor of Buhayra. Approximately two months before the murders, Habun had persuaded a team of shaykhs to assist Mitwalli Hilmi on a campaign against a bedouin tribe (the Hassuna) that had recently pillaged a local encampment of Awlad ʿAli tribesmen. The mission was unsuccessful, and Hilmi held Habun personally responsible for his failure, claiming that Habun had "willfully impeded the expedition's movements" by commanding his fellow shaykhs not to pursue the Hassuna tribesmen across the border. Hilmi thus felt that Habun was "in league with the Hassoun [*sic*] who had given him a present of three camels, a slave, and two hundred pounds."[98] As a punishment, Hilmi suspended Habun from *Majlis Siwa*.[99]

Yet ʿAzmi's testimony allows us to go even deeper into this story. By his account, a group of Eastern shaykhs—ʿUmar Musallam, Muhammad Saʿid, and Muhammad Muʿarrif, namely, the same three shaykhs whom we know would later help Kamil Muhammad collect Habun's weapons after the murders—"joined together to bring down [*tahālafa ʿalā al-īqāʿ*] ʿUthman Habun," agreeing unanimously to testify against him by telling the *ma'mur* that it had been Habun's fault that all the shaykhs abandoned the *ma'mur* on the mission against the Hassuna tribesmen. To ensure that the plan remained secret, the three shaykhs assembled all the Siwans who had come along on the Hassuna campaign, making each of them "swear an oath that they would be one hand, and that none of them would go to the *ma'mur* on his own even if he summoned them." The three shaykhs then offered the *ma'mur* another "false report," urging him that "Habun was determined to flee the town" and therefore must be apprehended before daybreak. Finally, once they gave the *ma'mur* this false information, the three shaykhs sent a messenger to Habun, informing him that the *ma'mur* was on his way to besiege his compound, all but ensuring that a violent confrontation would ensue.[100]

'Azmi claims to have investigated the local accusations of conspiracy, and brought the case against the three leading shaykhs to trial. The local Siwan court found all three guilty of being complicit in uniting as "one hand" against the *ma'mur*, although only Mu'arrif was indicted for the apparent setup. Each of the shaykhs was punished with a fine and dismissed from *Majlis Siwa*. According to 'Azmi, the verdicts provoked feelings of great "joy in the town . . . for these three were the most powerful troublemakers in it," and he considered their "dismissal [to be] among the most important factors strengthening security in Siwa."[101]

But can we take 'Azmi at his word? Another remarkable document—a long personal letter to the Khedive from a merchant named 'Abd al-'Aziz Ghani Karam, who had long resided in Siwa—presents a contradictory interpretation of 'Azmi's treatment of these shaykhs. For Karam, it was necessary to revisit the immediate aftermath of the murders. First, he claimed that 'Azmi had accepted a "bribe" from Habun's wife, through "the mediation of her relative, Shaykh Sa'ud Tawiya," to acquit three of her sons from the murder charges.[102] Again, it is clear from the official list of the thirty-one sentences that—while Habun and his son Hamadu were beyond saving—Habun's other three sons had been exonerated by the 'Azmi-led court.[103] Karam's charge of bribery is therefore plausible.

Second, Karam provides a backstory for why 'Azmi would have harbored particular ill will against the shaykhs he ended up indicting for conspiracy related to the abortive bedouin campaign. After 'Azmi's service in Siwa ended, he brought five Siwan shaykhs to Cairo "in order to provide testimony in front of the authorities" of his virtuous conduct during the expedition. Unsurprisingly, these five are some of the usual suspects in the local political scene. All of them played regular roles in the affairs of the *Da'ira Khassa*: Shaykh Sa'ud (whom Karam reminded the Khedive was related to Habun); Shaykh 'Abd al-Hamid (the father of Habun's wife); Shaykh Muhammad Rajih (Habun's cousin); Shaykh Muhammad Sa'id; and Shaykh 'Umar Musallam. 'Azmi expected all five to testify on his behalf, even though, according to Karam, "testimony to the virtue of His Excellency would be a lie."[104]

Shaykh Sa'ud, 'Abd al-Hamid, and Muhammad Rajih were the "three primary witnesses," and Karam said they were with 'Azmi Bey "for the long haul"; after all, "they [were] the ones who presented 'Azmi with the big bribe." Karam also explained why they all found themselves at 'Azmi's mercy: "How could they not testify for the man who had acquitted their children, first of all, and acquitted Shaykh Muhammad Rajih, second of all? It was he [Rajih] who had held onto the weapons of 'Uthman Habun and concealed them in his home, after pretending not to have anything to do with it." Shaykh 'Abd al-Hamid was similarly beholden to 'Azmi for the acquittal of his daughter, whereas Shaykh Sa'ud—aside from being Habun's son-in-law—had also been "acquitted from a big charge" connected to the murder case.[105]

Muhammad Sa'id and 'Umar Musallam, however, demonstrated a "lack of bias" toward 'Azmi and made it clear that they were "not beholden to him"; this made 'Azmi anxious that they would incriminate him during their testimony. Consequently, 'Azmi "brought extreme measures to bear" against these two shaykhs: he imprisoned them for three days, charged them with crimes he could not prove they committed, and then—as we saw above—hit them with fines and dismissed them from *Majlis Siwa* (along with Mu'arrif, the third conspirator).[106]

Karam's powerful testimony forces us to revise our understanding of the political fallout of the Siwan murders. Contrary to the narrative he fed his superiors at the Interior Ministry, 'Azmi does not appear to have been such a dutiful servant of the Egyptian government—a crusader for justice, who had succeeded in restoring state authority in the notoriously unruly oasis. On the contrary, 'Azmi played the game of local Siwan politics extremely well, striking deals with key shaykhs, accepting a bribe from Habun's people to secure their personal loyalty, and even exploiting Siwa's age-old factional discord to brandish his achievements back in Cairo. More than serving the interests of the government, then, 'Azmi leveraged his unique position and intimate knowledge of the Siwan political landscape to bolster his own personal power, both in Siwa and back in Cairo.

The final piece of the puzzle is the role that the Khedive played in the aftermath of the murders. According to the British authorities in Cairo, the Khedive was taking much personal "interest in the present case and [had] himself superintended the police measures adopted."[107] It should also be remembered that the Khedive had given direct orders to 'Azmi and was personally responsible for outfitting his expedition to Siwa. Though it can only be the subject of speculation for now, this evidence raises the suspicion that 'Azmi might in fact have been working closely with the Khedive (perhaps as a member of his spy network).[108] Additionally, once the Siwa court issued its verdict, 'Azmi ensured that "the sentences in this special case" could not be implemented "without the approval of the Khedive";[109] this is presumably why, as we saw above, 'Azmi designated a special courier to bring the verdict directly to the Palace. Indeed, the Khedive took advantage of his special authority in the case to review the Siwan murder verdicts: he commuted three of the four death sentences (only Habun would hang, in the end),[110] pardoned three other suspects, and reduced the jail time for all other accused individuals.[111] Between the actions of 'Azmi and the Khedive, the Habun family came off as well as it could have considering the circumstances: three of 'Uthman's sons were acquitted, and Hamadu—Mitwalli Hilmi's convicted murderer—ended up avoiding execution.[112]

Yet there is even more to be said about the Khedive's personal involvement in this episode. Shortly after 'Azmi's arrival in Siwa, Shaykh Sa'ud sent a frantic letter to 'Abbas Hilmi, having recently learned that the Khedive was "very angry" with him on account of "the incident . . . of 'Uthman Habun in the murder of the deceased *ma'mur*." Shaykh Sa'ud was so distraught by the prospect of a rift with the Khedive that he exclaimed, "I would have to throw myself into the sea . . . if His Excellency the Khedive were angry with me."[113] Although it is not entirely clear why Shaykh Sa'ud was so terrified of the Khedive's wrath, his letter offers at least a clue.

What is particularly striking about Shaykh Sa'ud's letter is not so much his desperate plea for the Khedive's pardon, but rather his fervent explanation of how he had actually tried to prevent the *ma'mur*'s siege on the Habun compound from happening in the first place. According to Shaykh Sa'ud, he had reacted immediately once he heard noise coming from "the direction of 'Uthman Habun's house," and went to "inquire as to what was really happening." Sa'ud continues: "When I approached the house, I found some police officers in front of me, and they told me to go back, because the *ma'mur* had forbidden any of the people [of Siwa] from being there." Sa'ud persisted, however, demanding to be let through so that he could talk directly to the *ma'mur*, but he was held back a second time, at which point he claims it was futile to resist.[114] At this point, according to Sa'ud, there was nothing left to do but rally the shaykhs to assist with the investigation. Sa'ud concluded his letter by promising that, "God willing, what goes on after today in all matters will be pleasing" to the Khedive, and that he was "now always in the *markaz* ready for requests from the Bey [Kamil Muhammad], and . . . under the command of the Khedive."[115]

Shaykh Sa'ud's dogged effort to prove to the Khedive how he first sought to prevent the *ma'mur* from carrying out his siege on Habun's compound, and then subsequently intervened at various moments afterwards, brings us back, full circle, to the nature of the Khedive's interests in Siwa. Why was the Khedive so upset about these murders in such a remote locale? The loss of a powerful *Da'ira Khassa* ally in 'Uthman Habun was certainly part of it; even if the Khedive had been able to step in and help Habun's family, 'Uthman himself was beyond saving. Yet this is not the full story. Much more alarming to the Khedive was the prospect of intensified British interference in Siwa in the wake of the violence. This anxiety was echoed by one of the Khedive's relatives, Prince Muhammad 'Ali, who claimed that "the inquest for the murder of the *ma'mur* [was] merely a pretext for concealing [the] political motives of the Egyptian government, and perhaps for the territorial aggrandizement in those regions."[116] It is thus plausible that the real issue for the Khedive at this critical juncture was his fear that the British-led Egyptian government's newfound interventionism would severely disrupt his project of cultivating sovereignty in Siwa. This would certainly explain why the Khedive would, in turn, unleash his fury on Shaykh Sa'ud, whom he blamed for allowing local political intrigue to get so out of hand that the government had no choice but to interfere.

How should we characterize the Khedive's intensive involvement in Siwan affairs, beginning with his historic expedition to the oasis in 1906, and culminating in his significant behind-the-scenes role negotiating the political fallout of Mitwalli Hilmi's murder?

If we are to believe J. C. Ewald Falls, 'Abbas Hilmi's travel companion on his maiden voyage to Siwa,[117] the real appeal of the oasis for the

Khedive lay solely in its potential for profitable investment. The trip, in Falls's view, had been "dictated chiefly by *commercial* interests. Two questions occupied the chief place: first, is there in the region of that desert oasis land capable of cultivation; and, second, would it be worth while to construct a branch line of railway from the Marmarika port, Mirsa Matru [*sic*], to Siwa."[118] Falls, lamenting that the Khedive did not share his own interest in Siwa's archaeological treasures, concluded that 'Abbas Hilmi was merely a "tradesman" rather than a "patron of science," in "direct contrast to his predecessor, Ismail Pasha."[119]

This interpretation of the Khedive's motivations leaves much to be explained. As this chapter has argued, even the Khedive's commercial ventures in Siwa must be understood as part of a much larger political project: the projection of Khedivial sovereignty throughout the western borderland. On one hand, the Khedive's acquisition of lucrative Siwan properties, such as 'Ayn Qurayshat, was never detached from his broader objective of embedding the *Da'ira Khassa* within Siwa's intricate political landscape, in order to win the loyalty of the oasis's major powerbrokers. On the other hand, the Khedive sought to bolster his sovereign legitimacy by including the Siwan populace in a range of development projects—first hiring local labor for his private agricultural properties, and then employing the entire oasis to help build the Sidi Sulayman mosque, which he personally financed. Through these various means, the Khedive forged an important symbolic link between political power, economic progress, and his own personal largesse, so that Siwans would ultimately come to see him as a benevolent patron of change—and, consequently, as the literal personification of centralizing sovereignty. It was the Khedive's considerable achievement in realizing these goals that was on display—even as it was under threat—during the great Siwan murder case of 1909.

The evidence examined in this chapter serves to deepen our understanding of how territorial sovereignty was exercised in Egypt in the decades before World War I. If sovereignty is only ever expressed in relative terms—as a competitive field in which different actors harness particular capabilities in order to pursue authority over a given territory's population and resources—then it is essential to examine how the Khedive managed to garner sovereign legitimacy in Siwa, where the Egyptian government—represented by a succession of hapless *ma'mur*s, a small police force, and a handful of Interior Ministry bureaucrats—could not. The key difference lies in the specific "marks of sovereignty" the Khedive was able to marshal once the *Da'ira Khassa* effectively integrated itself into the local political order: lavish ceremonial displays; gift exchanges; the demarcation of distinct, privately run territorial domains; the construction of a new mosque imbued with local customary significance; and the capacity to protect notable families by commuting death and prison sentences. These were the political resources that enabled the Khedive to succeed, over a relatively short period, in cementing himself as the locus of centralizing power in a region where state sovereignty was experienced as fundamentally truncated, uneven, and contingent.

# 4

## Cultivating Territorial Sovereignty in the Western Desert

On September 2, 1910 (a Friday), the Egyptian government opened a new mosque in Marsa Matruh. At this time, Marsa Matruh (literally, "remote anchorage")—located on the Mediterranean coastline 180 miles west of Alexandria, and approximately 140 miles from today's border with Libya—was still a relatively small outpost settlement. Although its population swelled each summer with the arrival of around a thousand Greek sponge fishermen, the town only had 398 full-time residents at the time of the 1907 Egyptian census.[1] Yet for a fleeting moment in 1910, the official inauguration of the Sidi 'Awam Mosque transformed Marsa Matruh into the site of an impressive ceremonial display.[2]

Taking center stage in the drama was the ubiquitous Khedivial agent Ahmad Shafiq, whom 'Abbas Hilmi had recently appointed as public director of Egypt's *Diwan al-Awqaf* (General Administration of Pious Endowments). The festivities commenced early in the morning with a ceremonial procession: Shafiq, escorted by several coast guard officials as well as a Camel Corps brigade, marched over a mile from the harbor toward the mosque. Once they arrived, Shafiq was greeted warmly by an assembly of bedouin shaykhs, who cheered vociferously for "His Excellency, the Khedive." Over the next couple of hours, Shafiq received more local elites—*'umdas*, shaykhs, Greek merchants—in a large pavilion that had been erected next to the mosque for the occasion. This was followed by a bedouin arms display, as well as a rollicking camel race between four coast guard officers.[3]

Just before the noon prayer, Shafiq addressed the substantial crowd gathered in the pavilion. He opened his remarks by highlighting the Khe-dive's largesse toward the local inhabitants: "[The Khedive] extended the railroad lines for your benefit, and paved the roads, and established mar-kets for the sake of your livelihood. And he initiated the improvement of this district in order to restore security among you, and then he ordered the construction of this mosque in order for you to cultivate your religious feelings." Just before ceding the pulpit to Shaykh Muhammad Bakhit (the president of Alexandria's Shari'a Court; he would later become the mufti of Egypt) to lead the prayer and deliver the Friday sermon (*khutba*),[4] Shafiq again emphasized the Khedive's unique role in transforming the local land-scape: "I ask God, high and mighty, to extend the life of Our Great Lord, so that we see these arid desert lands become green and verdant with the attentive care of His Excellency and his government. . . . In the Name of God, and with my Master's [the Khedive's] permission, I proclaim the in-auguration of the mosque."[5] With this last line, wild cheers erupted from the crowd, while the coast guard troops saluted the Khedive by calling out in Turkish three times, "Long live our master [*Effendimiz çok yaşa*]."[6]

The wider significance of Shafiq's remarks lies in his effort to connect the mosque opening to a much larger narrative of Egyptian territoriality. The erection of a mosque to satisfy the local population's religious sensi-bilities in what was still a peripheral backwater became, in Shafiq's telling, the capstone of the Khedive's grand vision for fostering development and civilization throughout the Egyptian West—a vision that was being real-ized through the establishment of new railway lines, modern roads, and a network of commercial markets. Thanks to the Khedive's progressive thinking and personal largesse, Marsa Matruh and the surrounding coastal region would be reclaimed and transformed into a prosperous, "verdant" swath of Egyptian soil.

There is some anecdotal evidence to suggest that the underlying mes-sage of Shafiq's speech would have lasting resonance with the local popu-lation. In the mid- to late 1990s, Western Desert ethnographers Donald Cole and Soraya Altorki discovered that elders from the Awlad 'Ali—the largest tribe in the region, then as now—actively recalled the Khedive's personal role in the development of the Egyptian West. In fact, they virtu-ally echoed the language of Shafiq's speech to recount the history of their ancestral homeland's modern transformation. According to one, "Yes, we like Abbas very much. . . . He was the first to open the desert. He made maps and brought schools and started the '*amar* ['building'; 'development']. He came to visit us and went to Siwa and visited the border. He also introduced police stations [*marakiz*]." Another tribal elder recalled that "Abbas brought the railroad. He was the one who opened up the desert," adding that tribal leaders in their grandfathers' generation had responded to an alleged British plot to annex the Western Desert to Libya by saying, "No. We are Egyptians. We are with Abbas Pasha."[7]

This chapter advances the book's analysis of territoriality by examining the Khedive's paramount role in the early development of the Egyptian West. I argue that a particular discourse of economic development was a central feature of 'Abbas Hilmi's broader political project of expanding his personal authority throughout the Egyptian West. By emphasizing his *own* unique role in ushering in economic progress and prosperity throughout the region, the Khedive strove to be perceived as the literal embodiment of Egyptian territorial sovereignty as it emanated out from the capital, into the Western Desert and northwest coast. Just like in the case of Siwa, then, the Khedive sought to ensure that he, and not the British-controlled Egyptian government, would represent "Cairo" in the eyes of the local population.

'Abbas Hilmi pursued this objective by steadily investing in an array of development projects during the first decade of the twentieth century, drawing almost exclusively from his own private coffers. Foremost among these projects was the construction of a new railway line, which he intended to run from Alexandria all the way to Ottoman Libya. The Maryut Railway (or Khedivial Railway, as it was sometimes called) ultimately fell short of this goal during 'Abbas Hilmi's reign, only reaching the eastern outskirts of Marsa Matruh. In its first decade of operation, however, the Maryut Railway successfully fostered the development of several key commercial nodes along the coastline, while also serving to connect the Khedive's private estates across the region.

In staking his sovereign legitimacy on the success of the Maryut Railway and other related development projects, including a series of agricultural experiments on his private estates, the Khedive was following the logic of what, in the French colonial context, became known as *mise en valeur*—the reclamation of lands that were unproductive and thus devoid of commensurable economic value. According to historian Alice Conklin, the concept of *mise en valeur* first gained currency in France in the 1890s. It was at this moment, Conklin suggests, that colonial interest groups and policy makers alike began to downplay further conquest in favor of constructively exploiting "territories already acquired." Furthermore, this new mode of "exploitation" would depart from France's old ethos of colonial plunder, serving instead as an engine of "rationality, progress, and conservation," and heralding the beginning of a new era of sustainable development that would benefit colonizer and colonized alike.[8]

*Mise en valeur* was not limited to colonial domains such as French West Africa, but rather emerged as a defining feature of modern territoriality around the globe by the end of the nineteenth century. Egypt was no exception. From the mid-1890s, Egypt witnessed a raft of *mise en valeur* projects, as various state and non-state actors began to pour large sums of capital into the "progressive development," or "reclamation," of Egyptian territory. This was the wider context for the Khedive's bid to use economic development as a means for cultivating territorial sovereignty in the Egyptian West.

Before turning to the Khedive's own development schemes, however, it is first necessary to consider the broad scope of *mise en valeur* projects in the Egyptian West, and their role in ushering in a new phase in the formation of territorial Egypt beginning in the 1890s.

In the opening pages of his book *The Redemption of Egypt*, published in 1899, English barrister W. Basil Worsfold alighted on the fundamental problem that has chronically plagued *mise en valeur* projects beyond the Nile Valley (then as now): the lack of sustainable water sources. According to Worsfold, "where the waters of the Nile can be laid upon the earth, there, and there only, does Egypt cease to be the desert. . . . Egypt, then, is so much of the area of the desert of North-East Africa as is either flooded or irrigated by the waters of the Nile." Although Worsfold applauded the efforts of the Egyptian government "to extend and perfect the irrigation system, first of the Delta, and then of Upper Egypt,"[9] he overlooked the possibility that such irrigation projects could also "redeem" Egyptian territory beyond the fertile Nile Valley.

For instance, it had been the decades-long dream of an American engineer named Frederick Cope Whitehouse to revitalize Egyptian irrigation by first locating and then rebuilding a storied ancient reservoir in the Western Desert. In 1882, Whitehouse discovered a basin he claimed to be the ancient Lake Moeris in Wadi Rayyan, a large desert depression located just southwest of Fayyum. He then persistently lobbied the Egyptian government, to no avail, that a system of water storage centered around this basin, rather than a new dam at Aswan, would be the panacea for Egypt's irrigation troubles. In Whitehouse's view, this ancient reservoir was "seemingly waiting to be used in the reclamation of vast areas of arid land." Whitehouse's ambition to make Egypt's deserts "bloom again" was nothing short of a utopian dream for the regeneration of Egypt's storied biblical prosperity. As he told a reporter, "I want to give a new country to the world, a garden of perfect conditions and complete the work of Joseph the Jew. I'm a sort of reincarnation of Joseph, who made Egypt a great nation and made money for his people."[10]

Whitehouse was not alone in envisioning Egypt's modern redemption as a grand return to the halcyon days of agricultural bounty it had known in antiquity. In the first decade of the twentieth century, the northwest coast—comprising the once prosperous Roman provinces of Marea (present-day Maryut) and Marmarica (the territory west of Marsa Matruh)—garnered increasing attention as a region ripe for *mise en valeur*. This was driven partly by archaeological evidence discovered during the excavation of Abu Mina between 1905 and 1907. According to the project's lead archaeologist, Monsignor Carl Maria Kaufmann, "the whole of the northern Auladali Desert could today be restored to its ancient flourishing condition . . . indeed, by employing the ancient foundations."[11]

Central to this vision of redemption was the presumption that the northwest, having reached its agricultural zenith under the Romans, had been gradually sullied by centuries of Arab-Muslim rule. This account of the region's *longue durée* degradation comes through clearly in British official Anthony De Cosson's book *Mareotis*, published in 1935. According to De Cosson, after the Muslim conquest, "the decline must have set in, for with the Arabs came the wild Beduin [*sic*] and the disappearance of the Roman master farmers. The land must have suffered progressively with increase of the lawlessness of the Beduin, farms and villages would have become deserted, and wells and cisterns neglected, as security was less and less guaranteed."[12]

De Cosson's interpretation of Maryut's steady environmental decline mirrored contemporary European accounts produced in other colonial settings. As historian Diana Davis has shown, a narrative of steady environmental degradation in "what was once the apparently fertile 'granary of Rome' in North Africa" was a mainstay of French colonial discourse, useful for justifying France's own *mise en valeur* projects across North Africa.[13] Similarly, the representation of Palestine as barren and uncultivated—

due to the native Arab population's allegedly neglectful stewardship of the land—was a fundamental underpinning of Zionist ideology, similar to other forms of settler colonialism in the late nineteenth century.[14]

It was not only utopian dreamers like Whitehouse and De Cosson who were animated by the promise of desert reclamation projects. Egypt's new epoch of *mise en valeur* around the turn of the century also owed much to the efforts of the government, which sponsored various explorations of Egyptian territory beyond the Nile, beginning in the mid-1890s. The bulk of this work fell to the Egyptian Geological Survey, established in 1896. Over the ensuing two decades, the Egyptian Geological Survey sponsored an array of projects to map Egypt's deserts and oases, and to investigate the mineral deposits, water sources, and agricultural potential of each locale. The career of British geologist Hugh J. Llewelyn Beadnell was exemplary in this regard. In addition to his noteworthy studies of upper Egypt and the Sudan, Beadnell published detailed scholarly works on the geology and topography of Farafra, Bahariya, the Fayyum, and Kharga.[15]

In the first decade of the twentieth century, the western oasis of Kharga became the key testing ground for *mise en valeur* in Egypt's desert domains. Early in 1904, a company known as the "Oases Syndicate, Limited" began to experiment with camel-borne carriages in the desert territory between Kharga and Nile Valley, with hopes of "ascertaining the possibilities of trading in the oases." This project was apparently "being watched with keen interest in many quarters," for—if it succeeded—it would "solve a difficulty which nearly every company working at any distance from the railway [had] to encounter."[16] Lord Cromer, for his part, was one of those keeping an eye on the work of the Oases Syndicate. In his annual report from 1904, he intimated that "possibly something may eventually be done . . . in the oases of the Libyan Desert."[17] Although this was hardly a ringing endorsement of *mise en valeur* in the Western Desert, his remarks were alluded to a couple of years later in an article in the *Egyptian Gazette* (a daily tabloid that represented the interests of Egypt's foreign capitalist class): "Certainly judging by the boring of wells, building of railways, export of fruit, and some other projects contemplated, this looks very much like something being done, and Lord Cromer's prophecies are already being gradually fulfilled."[18]

By this time, the development work around Kharga was in the hands of another British firm known as the "Corporation of Western Egypt," which had taken over the Oases Syndicate's concessions in 1904. The

Egyptian government's terms were extremely generous. According to the Corporation of Western Egypt's prospectus, the government had granted them "concessions dealing with land, water, railways, and earthy and precious minerals in the Oases of Khargeh . . . Dakhla, Farafra, and Bahara [*sic*]."[19] The land grant alone—600,000 feddans (over 622,000 acres), given pro rata for thirty years—was said to be "one of the most valuable land concessions yet granted by the Egyptian Government."[20]

To facilitate its development works in Kharga, the Corporation of Western Egypt hired Beadnell, who resigned from the Egyptian Geological Survey after nine years of service. As the Corporation's "manager" in the oases for the next three years, Beadnell oversaw the Corporation's "extensive boring and land-reclamation operations in Kharga."[21] In Beadnell's view, Kharga and Dakhla were ideally situated to become the epicenter of *mise en valeur* in the Western Desert. Although Kharga's water supply "had diminished over the years from neglect," forcing a large portion of the oasis's population to migrate to the Nile Valley,[22] it was his expert opinion that "the underground artesian supply in the oases was practically inexhaustible." Moreover, as Beadnell was keen to point out, "the oases lands have one great advantage over those of the Nile Valley in that they are not dependent on the time, volume, and duration of the Nile flood." The prospects for Egyptian mining in the oases were no less sunny, in his view. He declared Dakhla's deposits of phosphates to be "the very best in Egypt," and, like the water supply, "practically inexhaustible."[23]

The Corporation devoted the bulk of its resources towards two major projects. First, it desperately needed to increase the oasis's artesian water supply. In February 1906, the Corporation imported several new steam boring machines into Kharga, so that "more rapid progress will now be made" with tapping the oasis's artesian water reserves.[24] Second, the Corporation constructed a light rail that would connect the western oases to the Nile Valley, in part to facilitate a lucrative commercial trade in dates and other agricultural produce.[25] Believing that "the future of the company was mainly wrapped up with the provision of railway facilities," the Corporation's leadership spared no expense in pushing the Kharga light rail forward.[26] The railway was finally completed early in 1908:[27] it ran for 122 miles from Kharga to a new station ("Kharga Junction"), built along Egyptian State Railways's Upper Egypt line, near the town of Farshut.

The Corporation's activities in Kharga offer a compelling window into the nature of colonial "economism" in Egypt at the fin-de-siècle.

Aaron Jakes has defined economism as an overarching logic of colonial rule based on the premise that "political legitimacy . . . would be a direct function of [the regime's] economic achievements." For Jakes, the state's "overt economism" was the "defining feature" of British rule in Egypt after 1882: the Veiled Protectorate could only uphold its claim to political legitimacy by consistently delivering palpable material benefits to Egyptians, whom Cromer and his colleagues felt were just rational enough to recognize their own material self-interest.[28]

*Mise en valeur* projects such as the Corporation of Western Egypt's reclamation work in Kharga represented one typical instantiation of Egyptian economism under the British occupation. Jakes, in fact, alternately refers to the Egyptian state's "fundamentally economistic 'construction' of colonial state-building as *isti'mar*"—a term derived from an Arabic root that denotes civilization, cultivation, and prosperity, but which began to assume its distinctly negative meaning of exploitative colonialism only at the end of the nineteenth century.[29] Indeed, the *mise en valeur* projects undertaken by the Corporation of Western Egypt at this time are significant precisely for how they dwelt in the gray area between the negative and positive connotations of *isti'mar*.

On one hand, the Corporation was yet another foreign capitalist enterprise maneuvering within the crowded Egyptian marketplace, seeking to buy up cheap available land and ultimately sell it for a huge profit. According to an article in *The Statist* ("A Journal of Practical Finance and Trade"), after reclamation, the oasis lands would "be sold either immediately or after holding for a period for enhancement in value, and the entire purchase moneys [would] be received by the Corporation. Taking a very conservative estimate an average profit of at least £10 per feddan . . . [was] to be anticipated."[30] On the other hand, the Corporation's interests were closely aligned with those of the Egyptian government, which gave its "assurance that they [would] do all they reasonably [could] to assist the Corporation in its various operations."[31] For instance, the government pledged to facilitate the Corporation's development work by taking on the "responsibility of policing and public order" in the oases.[32]

This, in a nutshell, was the logic of a colonial "development regime" at work.[33] What was essentially a speculative land scheme on the part of a foreign capitalist firm was warmly embraced by the Egyptian government, given the promise it heralded for expanding the country's overall revenue base. At the same time, the Corporation championed its *mise en valeur* work as another progressive achievement of British rule in Egypt: by reclaiming the remote western oases on behalf of the government, it would transform the region into "a province which would participate in the general conditions of prosperity which Anglo-Egyptian beneficent rule had so abundantly brought to Egypt at large." Additionally, so this line of thinking went, the recent spike in land prices in the Nile Valley would even compel the *"fellaheen* to rent or purchase buildings in the oases, and thus be instrumental in transforming these once thickly populated tracts into a busy province again."[34]

There was an important territorial dynamic implicit in such economistic justifications for desert reclamation. Beyond increasing the general prosperity of the colonial state, as well as filling the pockets of the Corporation's shareholders, *mise en valeur* in the Western Desert would also engender a more expansive conception of Egyptian territory. The oases would now become a "province" of Egypt, more closely tethered to the economic life of the Nile Valley than ever before, and subject to the same market forces. Egyptian territoriality thus developed hand in hand with speculative land development in this period. This dynamic did not escape the Corporation's leadership or shareholders. Indeed, at its first general meeting (held in London in December 1905), the audience erupted into boisterous applause upon hearing the Corporation's chairman proclaim that their reclamation efforts in Kharga had proven that "Lord Rosebery's saying that 'Egypt is the Nile and the Nile is Egypt' no longer completely held good."[35]

It was not long before the Corporation of Western Egypt garnered attention in Europe. Early in 1906, the French newspaper *Progrès* published an article offering a detailed analysis of a report by Beadnell, which showed "evidence of the great future reserved for the Company, which is occupied in the *mise en valeur* of the Western oases." In the estimation of the article's author, the Corporation had become "one of the safest and most profitable investments in Europe."[36] This article from *Progrès* was, in turn, clipped by an Italian official and forwarded to the minister of foreign affairs in Rome, along with a warning that the Corporation's ambitions "to reclaim the western oases of Egypt" had possibly given cover to an "English mission towards the Western limits of Egypt."[37]

Several months later, another Italian official voiced his suspicions about the Corporation's role in fostering the "progressive development of English interests in the Western Egyptian oases, and the danger that this could render Lord Cromer and the British Government less deferential" to Italian interests in Cyrenaica. This prospect was particularly alarming to the Italian government considering its own *mise en valeur* projects in Cyrenaica at the time, which it pursued through an outfit known as the "Italian Society of Commercial Exploration."[38] In the eyes of the report's author, the activities of the Corporation—particularly the construction of its light rail—raised troubling political questions regarding the extent of the Egyptian government's territorial claims in the Western Desert. He therefore recommended that the minister of foreign affairs should ascertain whether the company "restricts its activities only to those oases which are undoubtedly in Egyptian territory, without pushing its aspirations . . . to Giarabub [Jaghbub] and Kufra."[39] Months later, an official at the embassy in Cairo reported back that, through a "happy accident, for now (at least), the organization has not been granted a concession to extend a branch of this railroad up to Jaghbub, but has assured that it will do this in time."[40]

The Italians' anxieties about the Corporation of Western Egypt's political designs turned out to be for naught. By spring 1908, the Corporation was running into serious financial trouble. The construction of the railway—which took nearly four years to complete—had been a huge financial drain, costing shareholders around a quarter million pounds sterling, even though it had been "built as cheaply as possible"; and the balance of the Corporation's holdings had "gone exclusively to the development in the oases." In short, the Corporation had run out of capital.[41]

At the Corporation's annual meeting in London in April 1908, the chairman tried to reassure the shareholders:

We are possessed of an important and valuable railway. We have made financial arrangements to keep the work of land development going, and we trust that the general conditions will soon be more favourable for the completion of arrangements for carrying into effect on a large scale an important programme of land development, the results of which will be calculated to give you a return in dividends. That the lands can be readily disposed of when brought into cultivation there is no reasonable doubt. You will be glad to know that more intimate acquaintance with the possibilities of the oases has not only justified every statement in our prospectus, but has shown that our concessions are of more intrinsic value than we had anticipated.[42]

But this was wishful thinking. A year later, as shares of the Corporation of Western Egypt plummeted on the London stock exchange, the Egyptian government agreed to take the Kharga light rail off the Corporation's hands, purchasing it for £128,200. The idea was to relieve the Corporation of the "burden of keeping up the railway during the unproductive stage," thereby freeing it up to expend its resources solely on land reclamation and agriculture.[43]

The activities of the Corporation plodded on for another few years. By 1914, the Corporation had sunk about forty artesian wells and reclaimed one thousand acres from the desert.[44] But a few years later, the Corporation of Western Egypt finally went belly up. According to William H. Hobbs, an American geologist who traveled in the Egyptian Western Desert during World War I, "After two and a half millions of dollars had been spent in development, it was established beyond doubt that valuable minerals were wanting [in Kharga], and the exploitation of the agricultural possibilities developed such difficulties that the project ended in complete failure."[45]

Other *mise en valeur* projects in the West were more successful, however. In the late 1880s, for instance, the government granted a British company a concession for the reclamation of Lake Abuqir, six miles west of Alexandria. The company hired Scottish engineer James Abernathy to devise a comprehensive drainage system. Lake Abuqir was completely dry by April 1888, giving way to a plum new stretch of fertile land—what Abernathy later described as "a waving sea of green crop." By 1892, the "Egyptian Lakes Reclamation Company" had already "reclaimed and sold 781 feddans" of land where the lake used to fill each winter and with every Nile flood.[46]

The government also made great strides with the reclamation of land along the desert edge of the Nile Delta, in the western outskirts of Buhayra. As J. C. Ewald Falls—the German archaeologist who traveled to Siwa with the Khedive in 1906—observed, given that the stretch of desert "on the western borders of the delta of the Nile" was "extremely flat, there is a greater chance of rendering it once again capable of cultivation. It was only a question of getting a drop of the source of all blessing in Egypt, the Bahr al-Nil [the Nile]."[47] Here, the problem of water was readily solved by building a series of smaller irrigation canals that connected with the numerous branch canals flowing through the Nile Delta. At the same time, the government began, in the early twentieth century, to impose taxes on lands in Buhayra and Maryut that had been outside the cadaster and exempt for nearly two decades.[48]

Yet given the breakneck pace of transformation in the region, it was not long before "a perfectly organized land speculation had set in." According to Falls:

One day the Hukuma appears on unenclosed ground, hattje, or desert; the authorities intervene and make the owner's title safe. Such and such a Beduin tribe can perhaps prove certain ancient rights, and is then compensated with money. Until then the land had no value. For a feddan, or Egyptian acre, £3, £4, or £5 is paid, an enormous sum for worthless land. A year later the drainage of the ground is begun by making little trenches, the network of which is drawn closer and closer. The Bey or the company that bought the land has only to wait for the connection with the neighbouring canal to be made for the gold to flow in streams. The company itself cultivates half of it; cotton, rice, durrha are planted and attended to by fellahs, who obtain cattle and implements and a fifth of the harvest by way of wages. The rest is offered for sale, at £15 to £40 and more an acre, according to its quality and its propinquity to water. The owner, supposing that he is no poor speculator, is a millionaire pasha in ten years, but the fellahs toil and moil as before for their Bey or their "compania," and the Beduins see with astonishment what is lured forth out of the land.[49]

Here too, then, the successful reclamation of desert land went hand in hand with the seamy underside of *isti'mar*: the new space opened up for profiteering and the exploitation of local labor.

The cornerstone of the government's vision for transforming the northwest coast was the progressive development of Marsa Matruh (Paraetonium, in Roman times). In early 1895, a captain in the Egyptian Coast Guard Administration named W. F. Caborne surveyed Marsa Matruh on behalf of the government. He found the town to be in a sorry state: "As there is no sea-transport to Alexandria its shores are now practically deserted, although a few Arabs are to be found encamped in the vicinity, and the harbor is resorted to during the season by the Greek sponge fishers." But Caborne—animated, like Whitehouse had been, by fantasies of ancient Egypt's prosperity—argued that "should a fair supply of water be discovered, there is no reason in the world why dead and gone Paraetonium, after the lapse of centuries, should not return into being."[50]

Caborne proposed several practical measures the government might adopt to revive the ancient town: taxation of the sponge trade; the development of a fishing industry and a regional shipping fleet; and the digging of "Abyssinian wells" (which the French had recently introduced into the Sahara with "very satisfactory results"), so that "an encampment of Arabs would soon spring up, forming the nucleus of a town." He also insisted that regular transport be established between Marsa Matruh and Alexandria, which would have the added benefit of facilitating trade in agricultural produce with Siwa. Caborne was realistic: "Rome was not built in a day, and it would be unreasonable to suppose that this ancient town could be fully resuscitated and brought to life again without some years of anxious and watchful care." But ultimately Caborne made a firm if measured pitch for undertaking *mise en valeur* in Marsa Matruh: "Any new or neglected industry or trade brought into activity, although it may not directly contribute largely to the revenue of the country, cannot fail to add alike to the prosperity of the government and the people."[51]

Over the decade following Caborne's survey, the Egyptian government took important steps to foster the development of Marsa Matruh. Its top priority was tackling the problem of procuring a steady water supply. To inspect for subterranean water sources and undertake the work of boring new artesian wells, the government awarded free concessions to two engineering outfits: the Mersa Matrooh [*sic*] Syndicate, which received a grant of ten thousand feddans between Marsa Matruh and Sollum; and the Artesian Boring and Prospecting Company, which received five thousand feddans within the same swath of territory.[52]

In a memo to the Egyptian Council of Ministers, Ahmad Mazlum Pasha, the minister of finance, employed standard "development discourse" to rationalize the two concessions.[53] In his view, Marsa Matruh was the key to unlocking the entire region. If Marsa Matruh, which had recently "entered an era of relative prosperity," could be made to flourish, then the "development" or "reclamation" of the entire "uncultivated" region out to Sollum would follow,[54] to the "benefit of the rural population of this part of the country as [much as] for the interest of commerce in general." Yet Mazlum also admitted that serious challenges still loomed. Aside from the vexing matter of irrigation, it would also be difficult to find agricultural labor since "the majority of the inhabitants of this region [was] composed of nomadic bedouins."[55]

Several other public works projects were implemented in Marsa Matruh in the first years of the twentieth century. An Italian syndicate won a government concession to deepen a five-hundred-meter channel in the Bay of Marsa Matruh, as well as to dredge the mouth of Marsa Matruh's inner harbor.[56] This work facilitated the transport of large steamers, while simultaneously reducing the number of accidents in port. As Dumreicher recalled, "Great was the rejoicing when for the first time the cruiser *Abdel*

*Moneim . . .* felt her way, dead-slow, by soundings into the inner harbor and made fast at the new buoy."[57] The government also enhanced Marsa Matruh's communications infrastructure by extending a telegraph line out from Alexandria; this was completed in June 1907.[58]

At the same time, the Egyptian government normalized Marsa Matruh's status within the provincial administration, declaring it a *markaz* on March 16, 1903. According to the Khedivial decree that functioned like a sort of town charter for Marsa Matruh, the new *markaz* would extend westward all the way out to the "frontier of Tripoli," though the location of this frontier was left ambiguous.[59] Three years later, apparently in response to the region's recent population growth, the terms of the charter were revised so that *markaz* Marsa Matruh was split into two—a new *markaz*, based in al-Dab'a, would now encompass the region east of *markaz* Marsa Matruh as far as al-'Umayyid.[60] Both decrees gave a great deal of governing authority to the Egyptian Coast Guard Administration. The 1903 charter, for instance, stipulated that the governor (*muhafidh*) of Marsa Matruh would be the local senior officer of the coast guard. Additionally, coast guard officials in the district were given wide powers of judicial arrest.[61]

Indeed, the coast guard's institutional capacity expanded in tandem with the development of Marsa Matruh. From its humble roots as a branch of the Egyptian Customs Administration, based in Alexandria, the coast guard grew rapidly in the first decade of the twentieth century, taking over responsibility for the port police in all of the country's harbors. After the renovation of Marsa Matruh's inner harbor to permit safe, direct access for the *Abdel Moneim* (the coast guard's prized cruiser), the town became the new home base of the coast guard's Western Desert branch.[62] Additionally, members of the coast guard were instrumental in establishing much of the new administrative infrastructure in Marsa Matruh's burgeoning town center, including a police station, prison, school, post office, and hospital.[63]

The Italian government reacted to the news of Marsa Matruh's development and conversion into an Egyptian *markaz* with its characteristic dose of suspicion. One official, lamenting in 1904 that the government's "project to create a new Governornate in Marsa Matruh" was now a *"fait accompli [fatto compiuto]*," warned that the Egyptian administration might undertake "colonization projects along the littoral from Alexandria to the Tripoli border."[64] A few years later, an anonymous Italian informant who managed to hitch a ride to Marsa Matruh on the *Abdel Moneim* reported back on the remarkable growth of the town in only a few years, as well as the government's successful efforts in coaxing "Arab fellahs" to settle there.

But this informant's testimony reveals some possible confusion about what he meant by "the government." For what he found most alarming about Marsa Matruh's future prospects was "the intention of the government to tie Siwa and Marsa Matruh together via railroad, and Marsa Matruh with Alexandria"—an endeavor that would divert the Eastern Sahara's traditional caravan trade away from Benghazi. Yet what he described here was not the ambition of "the government," strictly speaking; rather, this was the particular vision of 'Abbas Hilmi. The Khedive, not the Egyptian government, was responsible for the course of railroad construction throughout Egypt's northwest.

Indeed, a closer look at the development projects around Marsa Matruh reveals ample evidence of the Khedive's handiwork. In the terms of the concessions granted to the Mersa Matrooh Syndicate and Artesian Boring and Prospecting Company, for example, a provision was inserted to make special allowances for "The State Railway Administration *or any private Company or person duly authorized to make a railway* through any land leased to or acquired by the lessees."[65] Despite the direct reference to Egyptian State Railways, the "private Company or person" with the capacity to bring a railroad to Marsa Matruh at this time was clearly the Khedive.

It is also worth looking more closely at how the Khedive financed the construction of Marsa Matruh's Sidi 'Awam Mosque, opened with such fanfare in 1910. The branch of "government" that funded the construction of the mosque was the *Diwan al-Awqaf* (General Administration of Pious Endowments). Given its status not as a "ministry" (*nizara*) but rather as a "general administration" (*diwan*), the *Diwan al-Awqaf* was outside the political and financial control of the British Residency.[66] As the author of an op-ed in the *Egyptian Gazette* put it, "the Director General of the Wakfs is the most powerful post a native can attain to in Egypt, for he can act to a great extent independently of the Council of Ministers."[67]

The *Diwan al-Awqaf* was thus another resource that 'Abbas Hilmi could marshal independently of the British. This naturally made the British wary of it. Cromer consistently fulminated against the *Diwan al-Awqaf* for its corruption, for which he blamed the Khedive:

The peculiar nature of those institutions which are essentially indigenous [the *Diwan al-Awqaf*, and the Shari'a Courts] afforded great facilities to the Khedive for opportunities to add to his private fortune. . . . The revenues at the disposal of the [*Awqaf*] Administration are very large. They have for a long time past been grossly mismanaged. Of late years, the abuses have been singularly flagrant, the Khedive having practically taken the Administration into his own hands.[68]

In sum, the Khedive seems to have been personally involved in key aspects of Marsa Matruh's expansion throughout the first decade of the twentieth century. A special allowance for his railway was included in two key documents underwriting the region's development; the Khedive seemed to be moving forward with plans to extend his railroad from Marsa Matruh as far as Siwa; and, through his personal control over the *Diwan al-Awqaf,* the Khedive constructed what would become the most significant religious building in the area. In light of these findings, it does not seem far-fetched to accept Falls's claim that "Marsa Matruh . . . [was] a creation of Abbas Hilmi."[69] But, as the remainder of this chapter will demonstrate, the growth of Marsa Matruh was just one part of 'Abbas Hilmi's comprehensive vision for developing Egypt's entire northwest coast and transforming it into an enclave of Khedivial sovereignty.

'Abbas Hilmi first contemplated the region's revitalization in the mid- to late 1890s. As he would later explain to Amédée Baillot de Guerville, the noted French war correspondent and travel writer:

The country which extends to the west of Alexandria towards Tripoli is quite unknown to travelers. It is generally thought to be an immense desert. . . . I decided one day to make a long trip on horseback through this unknown land. To my great surprise, instead of finding a sandy desert as I had expected, I found a rich soil excellently suited to cultivation. The soil is not as dark in colour as that watered by the Nile, but it is evident that it has, under the Romans, supported a large population. Everywhere we saw the remains of towns, villages, and farms, occupied at one time by the Romans.[70]

Having discovered the region's tremendous agricultural potential during his travels, the Khedive swiftly purchased considerable land holdings all along the coast, from Alexandria to Marsa Matruh. He then set about converting these properties into agricultural estates, for which he utilized experimental irrigation techniques. As he told Guerville, "suddenly an idea struck me. You know how it is only necessary to bring the Nile water on to the sand of the Desert to make it fertile. I thought then, that in filling up these marshes, in levelling them and covering them with sand brought from the Desert, and finally making the necessary irrigation works, I could obtain excellent land." Although the Khedive was initially ridiculed for these experiments with lift irrigation, the results spoke for themselves. Within a few years, the Khedive had reclaimed twenty-five hundred feddans of valuable land—a "miracle" that he achieved merely by harnessing "the waters of the Nile and the sunshine of Egypt." The profitability of his *mise en valeur* schemes was not what he said truly animated him, however. As he was keen to point out, "my satisfaction comes less, I can assure you, from my success as a financier than from the pleasure I have gained in seeing these dead lands brought back to life."[71]

By the time of the Marsa Matruh Mosque opening in 1910, the Khedive already held properties in many of the key locales along the coast: beyond his oft-visited Maryut villa, the Khedive owned estates in Edfina and 'Amriyya; vineyards at Ikingi Maryut; quarries in Sidi 'Abd al-Rahman; a large farm in al-Dab'a, where he stationed a number of camels and automobiles; and a cattle ranch at Garawla. He also spearheaded agricultural experiments on properties in Hammam as well as in Qattara, a small desert oasis he discovered on his return trip from Siwa in 1906.[72] The Khedive was quite fond of his abundant northwestern properties, which enabled him to "live the life of a gentleman farmer,"[73] and he visited them often.[74]

Once his agricultural projects were underway, 'Abbas Hilmi commenced the next phase of his vision for the development of the northwest coast: the establishment of a regional transportation network. In the Khedive's own telling, at least, the inspiration for what would become the Maryut Railway came during one of his early sojourns in the barren northwest:

One evening I pitched my camp by the side of the great [caravan] track. I had not a wink of sleep. The whole night through an uninterrupted procession of caravans passed. So, whilst listening through the long hours to the heavy, slow tread of the camels, and the shrill whistle of their drivers, I thought of the hours, days, weeks, even months which these Bedouins spent on the journey, and I said to myself: "Since there are so many of them why not make a railway? It will be a good thing for them, and very likely, a good thing for the makers."

When later on, far away towards Tripoli, I saw the rich oases whose products were tied up, the cattle which could not be sold, the animals fed on figs and dates for which there was no market, my mind was soon made up, I set to work immediately and began the construction of the line.[75]

Aside from his goal of transforming the region's economy along these lines, the Khedive also hoped the railway would revolutionize travel from Eu-

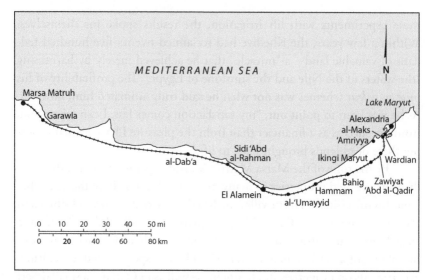

**MAP 4.** The route of the Maryut Railway, along Egypt's northwest Mediterranean coastline.

rope. 'Abbas Hilmi ultimately planned to extend the Maryut line into Ottoman Benghazi, where tourists could arrive by sea from Brindisi, Messina, or Marseilles in a fraction of the time it took them to reach Alexandria. He also hoped this speedy new overland route from Benghazi to Alexandria would attract the business of the Indian and Australasian mail services.[76]

The Maryut Railway was officially launched on July 4, 1899, when W. E. Garstin—Egypt's undersecretary of state for public works—approved the *Da'ira Khassa*'s request to construct a narrow-gauge railway from the western outskirts of Alexandria to Maryut. The government's letter of authorization stated that the railway's main function would be to "serve the *Da'ira Khassa*'s properties" in the region, and stipulated that all expenses for its construction would be borne by the *Da'ira Khassa*.[77] Four years later, the *Da'ira Khassa* gained the government's approval to upgrade the railway from narrow to standard gauge, and to extend the line out to Sollum.[78]

The Khedive appointed a German named Gustav Kayser to serve as the railway's chief engineer and oversee the critical work of surveying the railroad's route and devising a construction plan.[79] The *Da'ira Khassa* purchased many of the necessary tools for building the Maryut line from the Egyptian State Railways, and—at least initially—used prisoners on loan from the Interior Ministry as labor.[80] In 1906, arrangements were made with Egyptian State Railways to exchange traffic between the Maryut line and the burgeoning national network.[81]

From its flagship station at Wardian, on the western outskirts of Al-exandria, the railway proceeded through al-Maks and then across Lake Maryut on a narrow three-mile-long embankment (see Map 4). From there, the railway stopped at the bedouin village of Zawiyat ʿAbd al-Qadir before continuing on to ʿAmriyya—the official seat of *markaz* Maryut, located thirteen miles down the line from Alexandria.[82] From ʿAmriyya, it proceeded along the coastline toward Marsa Matruh, maintaining a dis-tance of around six to nine miles from the sea, while passing through many towns the Khedive was actively working to develop—most notably Ikingi Maryut, Bahig, Hammam, and Sidi ʿAbd al-Rahman. By 1907, 108 miles of track had been laid down. And by the time construction was halted, in late 1912 or early 1913, the Maryut Railway spanned 145 miles: a hundred miles of standard-gauge track reached as far as al-Dabʿa, and then another forty-five miles of narrow-gauge track extended the line to the small out-post of Garawla, twelve miles east of Marsa Matruh.

The Maryut Railway operated several different services.[83] Train 1—"composed of a locomotive, almost entirely covered with brass, bril-liantly polished, whilst the latter part was formed by a glass-paneled *salon*"[84]—was reserved for the Khedive's personal travel. Two trains han-dled the transport of commercial goods and livestock, while another two were used exclusively for passenger travel. The railway also ran two express trains between Alexandria and al-ʿUmayyid.[85] Passenger trains would run between Wardian and al-ʿUmayyid three times a day, whereas service be-yond al-ʿUmayyid to al-Dabʿa was offered only every other day.[86]

Since the *Daʾira Khassa* was responsible for all of the railway's ex-penses,[87] the British generally gave the Khedive a free hand in its construc-tion and administration. Moreover, they did not feel obliged to interfere, given their view that the railway was merely "a toy with which he [the Khedive] would amuse himself, and that he had no serious intention of making a proper Railway."[88] The Ottoman authorities took the railway project far more seriously, however. The Ottoman sultan, Abdülhamid II, was reputedly "not very enthusiastic about this railroad, which could . . . arrive at the frontiers of his African possessions," and he was already "fear-ing the consequences."[89]

The Ottomans were right to be wary. The Maryut Railway was ini-tially very successful, proving it to be anything but a mere amusement for the Khedive. ʿAbbas Hilmi boasted to Guerville that he was "delighted" with the project in its early stages:

Already, in goods alone and for the first year, we have carried 1,000 tons, this year we shall reach 6,000 and more . . . As we proceed towards the oases, traffic will become more and more important. Lately I was present at a large market held at the terminus of the line. Caravans had come in from Tripoli itself, and, to give you an idea of the importance of the meeting, I can tell you that there were no less than 22,000 sheep there.[90]

The railway continued to grow more lucrative as the decade wore on. Among its most important functions was the regular transport of barley, as well as bountiful gypsum lodes, from the Khedive's properties along the coastline. The railway carried some five hundred thousand tons of goods yearly, on average, and conveyed an estimated two hundred thousand passengers each year. In 1907, the railway yielded profits of 10 to 12 percent, with its revenues having steadily increased each year (except for 1906, due to a bad barley harvest).[91]

The Khedive and his agents in the *Da'ira Khassa* carefully monitored the progress of the railway, as well as the volume of commercial traffic through the market towns it served. From around 1900, the Khedive received weekly updates on the region's development from engineers, police officers, and the *ma'mur* of Maryut himself. One report from Hammam in June 1905, for example, focused on the activities of local "agricultural bedouins [*al-'urbān al-muzāri'īn*]" bringing produce to market, while also giving a specific count of the livestock traded on the most recent market day (320 camels and 3,270 sheep).[92] The authors of these dispatches were keen to ascribe broader progressive values to the Khedive's *mise en valeur* schemes. In a weekly report to the *Da'ira Khassa* from June 1902, for instance, an officer stationed at Ikingi Maryut concluded by asserting that "Maryut is in a state of continuous development and progress [*bi-hālat irtiqā' wa taqaddum mustamirr*]."[93]

If the British Residency treated the Khedive's railway with indifference, Egypt's foreign business community was quick to celebrate its successes. Summarizing the railway's business prospects in July 1907, a writer for the *Egyptian Gazette* suggested that "the success of the line as a financial venture is already assured and every year it will realize greater profits, owing to the progress of the country." This sort of argument was typical of the logic of colonial development thinking—again, a lucrative private capital investment was ultimately justified by its contribution to Egypt's general prosperity.

Moreover, beyond bringing the Khedive a very favorable return on his investment, the Maryut Railway was celebrated for achieving a larger territorial objective, catalyzing the *mise en valeur* of the entire northwest coast. Another article in the *Gazette*, from July 1907, suggested that the railway "had been of great benefit in developing the Mariout district," primarily by facilitating trade within four new commercial markets that the Khedive had established along with the railway stations: in Hammam (on Mondays), Bahig (Tuesdays), 'Amriyya (Wednesdays) and Sidi 'Abd al-Rahman (Saturdays).[94] And in a separate feature on the railway, the *Gazette* proclaimed that "Now that the railway secures easy communication with Alexandria there is every reason to believe that the ancient prosperity of Mariout will return, and the first who recognized the potentialities of this renaissance was the Khedive, whose labours are now beginning to bear fruit."[95] The author was especially keen to emphasize 'Abbas Hilmi's unique individual role in fostering the region's development: "The credit of the idea of opening up this hitherto secluded part of Egypt is due to him alone, and we are not aware of any railway in the world of such an extent, which is solely due for its inception, outlay, and upkeep to the initiative of an individual capitalist."[96]

The Maryut Railway also had a transformative social impact on the local population, particularly the region's bedouin tribes. According to the *Gazette*, the bedouins of the northwest benefited directly from the new employment opportunities afforded by the railway:

One of the most significant characteristics of the line is the fact that, although there are about a thousand persons employed on it, yet it is found to work quite easily with the assistance of only a single European. Another interesting social feature of this railway is the attraction it has for the Bedouin population of the district, who are gradually becoming alive to the advantages of permanent work at fixed wages, and are found to become in most cases satisfactory railway men. This is one of the many civilizing influences which the line is exercising over the tent-dwelling nomads. . . . Everywhere there are signs that the Bedouin are waxing prosperous.[97]

Guerville, for his part, also emphasized the salutary effect of the railway on the local tribes, particularly insofar as it fostered their sedentarization and incorporation into Egyptian economic life:

Far from being opposed to the railway, [the bedouins] are intensely interested in it. Many of them work on the line as well as on the construction of the telephone, of which over one hundred miles were then complete. Business is brisk, and the trains which we pass, carrying men, animals, and goods, are crowded. Charming little villages, constructed by His Highness, replace here and there the wretched tents in which the Bedouins lived; and there is no doubt that the inhabitants of this lost and forgotten land are only too pleased that the Khedive has come to call them to another and a better existence. . . . and they await with impatience the time when the line shall be completed, and a regular and paying trade established between the rich country of Tripoli and the markets of Alexandria and Cairo.[98]

In addition to providing ample employment opportunities through his railway, the Khedive also strove to strengthen his bond with the local population by actively demonstrating his respect for their religious sensibilities. In Hammam and Bahig, the Khedive implemented a new "religious ceremony," dispatching an imam on each town's market day to deliver a special sermon, during which all commerce was temporarily halted.[99] Moreover, the Khedive consistently made a show of his loyalty to the Sanusiyya. According to a Sanusi shaykh named Sidi Musa—who oversaw the Brotherhood's *zawaya* in several locations throughout the region—the Khedive made sure to stop at a Sanusi *zawiya* "each time he head[ed] to his properties and passe[d] on camel at Sidi 'Abd al-Rahman."[100] The Sanusiyya in fact operated *zawaya* in each of the four market towns served by the Khedivial railway,[101] and it appears that the Khedive collaborated with Sidi Musa in launching the agricultural development of "a great deal of land" in these locales.[102]

The Ottoman authorities, too, were aware that the Maryut Railway was earning the Khedive the loyalty of the Awlad 'Ali, the region's largest tribe. According to a bedouin informant working for the governor *mutasarrıf* of Benghazi, the Awlad 'Ali "expressed [their] satisfaction [*beyan-ı memnuniyet*]" when the Khedive told them he would be extending the railway from Sidi 'Abd al-Rahman to Marsa Matruh and Siwa. Their gratitude to the Khedive was apparently so great that they came to recognize his complete sovereign authority over them. On one occasion, for instance, in response to an incident at the frontier outpost of Sollum, the Khedive threatened the Awlad 'Ali—"scolding them by urging them to 'recognize [*malûmunuz olsun ki*] that I, as the Khedive of Egypt, and being in command, am ready to sacrifice life along with the people of Egypt and its surrounding lands for the sake of the Ottoman state.'" This apparently "made such an impression that the aforementioned tribe and other tribes along the border with the *sancak* of Benghazi [began] to coexist peacefully with the people."[103]

In short, the prosperity of the Khedive's various development initiatives across the northwest seems to have succeeded in solidifying his sovereign legitimacy among the local population. There is in fact some evidence to suggest that the region's bedouins began to perceive 'Abbas Hilmi's personal rule as a bulwark against British colonial power, and thus actively worked on his behalf. According to Falls, the Khedive, eager to prevent outside interference with the railway, operated a network of bedouin spies to inform on the activities of the Europeans at the Abu Mina excavation site.[104] Moreover, 'Abbas Hilmi hired bedouin shaykhs to promote the message that "the land of the Nile belonged to the Effendi, *i.e.,* the Khedive; that the English were the enemies of the Khedive, and the foreigners were intruders." Falls even disguised himself to attend a speech in Bahig by a notorious anti-British bedouin shaykh named 'Ali Abu al-Nur al-Gharbi. Falls was alarmed to hear this shaykh declare in a fiery speech that "This earth here, this land, belongs to Effendine; no one except Effendine is master here. The Khedive is our master." Al-Gharbi apparently traveled all throughout the "Bedouin districts," with the use of a free railway pass, at the Khedive's personal expense.[105]

In light of the foregoing analysis, it is striking that 'Abbas Hilmi consistently denied that he harbored any ulterior political motives with his various *mise en valeur* projects in the northwest. As he insisted to Guerville, the Maryut Railway "had not, and could not have, any political purpose." Only "certain people, who have now awakened to the commercial importance of the scheme," sought to "create trouble" by suggesting that the Khedive had political designs in the west.[106] Yet the Khedive's insistence upon the fundamentally apolitical nature of his development vision would come under question in the final years of his reign, once the British got wind of his plan to sell the Maryut Railway to a foreign syndicate.[107]

Things came to a head in January 1913, when Lord Kitchener first heard that one of the Khedive's lawyers was in Rome, looking to sell the railway to an Italian firm.[108] Two months later, the Khedive agreed to a deal to sell the Maryut line—along with the rights to the Sollum extension—to an Italian businessman living in Alexandria named M. Aldon Ambron, who represented the "Italian North Africa Railway Syndicate."[109]

News of the deal left the British Foreign Office in a state of panic. The British were unsurprisingly distressed by the prospect that an entire coastal railway, stretching from beyond the western border of Egypt all the way to Alexandria, "should fall into alien hands." Kitchener suspected that the deal was illegal, however: "as this line is built on Government property, [the] Khedive cannot sell."[110] Consequently, the British resolved that the Khedive should "be severely taken to task"; as one official put it, "he hasn't had a good wigging for years, and it's the only thing that keeps him temporarily straight."[111] First, however, the British Residency scrambled to find proof that the Khedive had indeed overstepped his legal bounds.

The evidence was inconclusive. Although the British claimed not to find proof of any formal "concession" for the extension to Sollum, the Khedive did have "various authorizations from individual ministers." As Kitchener observed wistfully, "Both sides sold what was not theirs, for the syndicate is to pay the Khedive one quarter of profits of a concession for a line through Cyrenaica which . . . they do not hold. The Khedive sold on the authorisations he held, which the syndicate accepted as sufficient."[112] Despite their tenuous legal standing, the British continued to assert that "the Khedive has exceeded his rights in granting an option, as the Mariout line is built on Government property."[113] As another official put it, "The Khedive has overstepped all bounds . . . for pecuniary advantage to himself, [he] was selling to foreigners a means of penetrating his country."[114]

In an intense confrontation with the Khedive, Kitchener argued that ʿAbbas Hilmi had "put himself in a very tight spot because he sold land that he does not own."[115] The Khedive responded that he would only back out of the deal with the Italian syndicate if the Egyptian government agreed to purchase the Maryut Railway, instead—a position that Foreign Secretary Grey likened to "blackmail."[116] At first, the British adamantly refused to buy the railway for the government. According to Lord Cecil, a Foreign Office official, "There is no financial justification whatever for the purchase of this line," given that it "runs through a country to a great extent devoid of cultivation, and sparsely inhabited by Arab tribes. . . . The railway connects no population centers, nor does it open up any district of either mineral or great agricultural wealth." Cecil also balked at the railway's sticker price, given the delicate state of the country's finances; after all, the Egyptian government needed to shore up the confidence of those who had invested "large sums of foreign capital in this country."[117] Sir James Rennell Rodd, the British ambassador to Italy, agreed: "What British capitalists are going to look at 'The Khedive's toy' as a commercial proposition?"[118]

The Egyptian government's insistence upon the Maryut line's worthlessness at this moment clashed strongly with the auspicious projections that had coursed through the pages of the *Egyptian Gazette*, as well as Guerville's memoir, just six years prior. At that time, as we have seen, both the *Gazette* and Guerville had portrayed the Khedive as the darling of capitalist development in Egypt. What had changed in the intervening years was a fundamental shift in British thinking, in response to a deep and enduring financial crisis that unfolded toward the end of 1907 and would last through the war years.[119] Before the crisis, during a period of prolonged financial boom, land reclamation schemes in the barren Egyptian West were widely celebrated—as one author put it, "the prosperity of the country [was] returning" through the Khedive's visionary efforts. Yet once the crisis began and a mindset of austerity set in among British officials, all land reclamation projects in the region were dismissed as intrinsically wasteful. It was as if the heady period of *mise en valeur* boosterism at the beginning of the decade had never happened. Instead, the prospect of development in the region was consistently approached with stolid skepticism: in the words of architectural historian and traveler Martin Shaw Briggs, "to anybody who knows this part of Western Egypt—its sparse population, its inhospitable soil, and its great waterless areas—it is difficult to believe that any such scheme could be financially successful."[120]

Lord Grey, the British foreign secretary, instructed Kitchener not to purchase the Maryut line. Instead, he hoped to defeat the sale by applying pressure on the Italian syndicate. He also suggested that the Khedive—unlike the Corporation of Western Egypt, which the government had bailed out by purchasing the Kharga light rail back in 1908—should be allowed to fail: "I realize that the consequences of this decision may be serious to the Khedive, whose financial position . . . appears to be most precarious. . . . It will be better to let the crash come, and we shall then be able to take the Khedive's affairs out of his hands."[121] Grey also ordered Kitchener to pass on a threatening memo to the Khedive:

His Majesty's Government considers with grave concern the decision taken by Your Highness concerning the Mariout railway, according to which, part of the railway communications on Egyptian territory has been put under the influence of a foreign power. . . . The position of the Egyptian Government is that it will not acquire the Mariout line. . . . I take this opportunity to warn Your Highness against concluding the agreement, and against entering into negotiations with any other Government or foreign syndicate for the sale of this line.[122]

The Khedive proved defiant in the face of the foreign secretary's threat. In his response to Kitchener, he merely pointed out he was "deeply grieved that a political character which had never entered his mind should have been given to negotiations relative to an act of purely financial interest.[123] Agents of the *Da'ira Khassa* also appealed to the Egyptian government, arguing, for example, that "the establishment of the line up until Sollum has a definitive and indivisible character" based on the authorizations granted in 1903, and that the *Da'ira Khassa* had every right to do as it liked with the railroad—especially since the Egyptian government had not bothered to interfere with it for over ten years.[124] Agents of the *Da'ira Khassa* also played down British exhortations to rethink the syndicate deal in light of the outbreak of the Ottoman-Italian war in 1911.[125] The director-general of the Maryut Railway did not agree that the looming prospect of Italian sovereignty on the other side of the border changed anything, and he refused to renege on what he called the *Da'ira Khassa's* "natural and legitimate rights."[126]

The British begrudgingly realized that buying the Maryut line from the Khedive was unavoidable. After weeks of intense discussions, Ambassador Rodd received "full and frank admissions as to [the Italian government's] position with regard to the Khedive's railway": the Italian government's backing of the syndicate stemmed from its desire to curb Khedivial support for the Sanusi-led resistance movement in Benghazi. Accordingly, the "Italians had hoped to be able to influence the Khedive through his pocket," viewing the "railway scheme . . . as a means of holding His Highness and checking his further intrigues by prospect of financial advantage which they could neutralise if he did not desist."[127] Moreover, the Italian government informed Rodd that if it was going to force the syndicate to back down from the deal, then the British would have to do more to ensure that the Khedive did not deepen his involvement with anti-Italian forces in Benghazi.[128]

Lord Grey was annoyed that "the Italian Government should have entered into direct negotiations with [the] Khedive in a matter affecting [the] security of Egypt without informing either [the] British or Egyptian Governments."[129] Yet at this point, his hands were tied. The British thus agreed to purchase the Maryut Railway, primarily as a security measure, in exchange for a guarantee from the Italian government that it would remove its backing for the syndicate. In early April, the Khedive agreed to the terms of a forced renunciation of the syndicate deal. In early February 1914, Kitchener agreed to buy the Maryut Railway from the Khedive on behalf of the Egyptian government, for a sum of 376,000 Egyptian pounds.[130] Upon the conclusion of the deal, one Foreign Office agent remarked that "It is well that this Railway has been got out of the Khedive's hands. The price paid can hardly be regarded as remunerative expenditure, but it is under half of what the Khedive originally wanted."[131]

At the center of the conflict over the Maryut Railway sale was a disagreement about the Khedive's underlying intent in dealing with the Italians. For the British, there was "little doubt that the transaction had from the first a political rather than a strictly commercial character."[132] The Khedive rejected this interpretation outright, however. As he would explain in his memoir, published over two decades later: "[The British] tried to find a political purpose in the transactions I undertook for the sale of the Mariout Railway, but it was merely a financial operation. I hoped to connect Alexandria to the frontier with Cyrenaica in order to serve the vast region of Maryut, where I had undertaken important agricultural enterprises."[133]

The very terms of this debate over the character of the railway are misleading, however. As this chapter has demonstrated, it is impossible to parse the commercial from the political motives in assessing the significance of the Maryut Railway, or any of the Khedive's grand development projects. The logic of *mise en valeur* in this period fundamentally blurred the boundary between politics and profit. The reclamation of territory for commercial gain was always intrinsically part of a wider bid to cultivate sovereign legitimacy in an ever-expansive Egyptian national landscape.

By privately funding an array of development projects in the Egyptian northwest (of which the Maryut Railway was the centerpiece), 'Abbas Hilmi was essentially mimicking British economism. For the Khedive, *mise en valeur* was the paramount mark of sovereignty that would enable him to achieve political power and ultimately circumvent the authority of the Egyptian government. We can glimpse the Khedive's fundamentally economistic approach to development in the Egyptian West in a couple of key passages in his memoir: "A profound joy still grips me at the recollection of my first attempts to fertilize the desert and drain the swamps. The Mariout railway represented for me the trigger that led to the beneficial development of uncultivated land and the settlement of a group of scattered and indigent nomadic Bedouin tribes. (Both my country and the occupying power had come to possess a strategic line as a result.)."[134]

*Mise en valeur* in the region was therefore justified not by its benefit to 'Abbas Hilmi's financial interests, then, but by its role in advancing the general prosperity of the entire country: "In Egypt, the metamorphosis of the uncultivated and muddy soil into orchards, the enrichment of the savannah where herds could multiply, the extension of communications and irrigation and the growth in the population represented a substantial economic gain for the nation."[135]

That the Khedive sought to outplay the British at their own game of economism—justifying his sovereignty by delivering economic prosperity—is deeply ironic. After all, Britain's claim to ruling legitimacy had always hinged on positing a clear dichotomy between Egypt before the occupation—a time of Oriental despotism—and the ordered, lawful regime of the British residency, which transformed the state into a finely calibrated "instrument" or "machine" for maximizing the general prosperity of the country.[136] Cromer never stopped seeing the rule of 'Abbas Hilmi as an unfortunate reversion to the old Khedivial despotism and corruption: "I felt very strongly that, if he were allowed to pursue his way unchecked, the civilising work which Great Britain had undertaken in Egypt would be gradually undermined, that corruption of various sorts would again become rampant, and that there was even some risk that, as in the days of Ismail Pasha, Egypt would again degenerate into being the happy hunting-ground of the political and financial adventurer."[137]

What Cromer and other British officials generally overlooked, however, is that the Khedive, too, was working toward the public utility and general prosperity of Egypt. But unlike the British, he would deliver it in a way that allowed him to pose as an authentic Egyptian leader who also honored the political, not just the material, interests of those living under his sovereignty.[138] The fact that the Khedive could brandish his image as the foremost builder and agent of progressive development in the West only enhanced his sovereign legitimacy among the region's native population. When the Awlad 'Ali interlocutors in Cole and Altorki's study looked back so fondly on how the Khedive "started the *'amar*" and "opened up the desert," they were speaking to the lasting significance of the sovereign authority 'Abbas Hilmi had succeeded in cultivating within one short decade, through the dogged pursuit of the region's development, which had created manifold economic opportunities for the local population.

After World War I, the relationships that 'Abbas Hilmi had forged with the bedouin communities of the northwest would be squandered, even as the Egyptian government continued to invest in developing the region. British and Egyptian government officials paid no attention to the extensive experience in agriculture that the region's bedouins had gained through employment on the Khedivial properties all along the coast. In the 1930s, for instance, De Cosson lamented that "if ever the Maryut is to be developed with lift irrigation, supplementary labour will have to be brought from the Delta, as the present scanty Bedouin population in the interior is not sufficient nor would it appreciate regular employment on the land throughout the year."[139]

As this chapter has demonstrated, however, bedouins working for the Maryut Railway (or in agricultural projects alongside it) in the first decade of the twentieth century had been keen to settle down into routines of regular employment. The stark disregard for bedouin labor potential—a function of what Cole and Altorki label "Nile Valley ethnocentrism"— would remain a constant theme in the history of the western Mediterranean coastline's modern development throughout the twentieth century. As Cole and Altorki argue, regarding the Nasser era: "Bedouin living in and around land reclamation projects in the desert at this time were excluded from participation in the projects on the basis that they had no or little previous experience in agriculture. Thirty to forty years later in the 1990s, their exclusion from projects on what they consider ancestral land still rankles among at least some of the old desert dwellers."[140]

If the legacy of bedouin labor on the Khedive's northwestern development projects was ultimately tossed aside by the Egyptian state after World War I, 'Abbas Hilmi's dramatic push for the region's *mise en valeur* in the decade prior to the war still had an enduring impact on conceptions of Egyptian territoriality. The first decade of the twentieth century was in fact the critical period in which the Egyptian government's prevailing doctrine of colonial economism gained currency beyond the Nile Valley, including the deserts and coastal plateau of the Egyptian West. For the Khedive, as for the British, political authority and legitimacy naturally followed from the successful advancement of a given territory's economic prosperity. And so by practicing Khedivial economism from Alexandria to Marsa Matruh (and ultimately, it was hoped, into Ottoman Benghazi)— being the first to invest significantly in a region over which the British had previously exerted little if any sovereign control—'Abbas Hilmi sought to ensure that the northwest would become his own sovereign domain within Egyptian territory. In the process, prevailing notions of Egypt's expanse as a connected and cohesive political and economic space were fundamentally transformed.

# 5

## The Limits of Ottoman Sovereignty in the Eastern Sahara

On July 9, 1902, the Egyptian Coast Guard learned that an Ottoman flag had been raised at Sollum—a remote outpost on the Mediterranean, some 320 miles west of Alexandria.[1] This news, once it finally reached Cairo, provoked a flurry of correspondence among British officials, who sought to ascertain whether the Ottoman government had any rightful claim to a locale they had assumed was Egyptian territory. One Foreign Office agent went straight to the notorious 1841 firman for evidence, but discovered upon close examination that there was "nothing . . . to throw light upon the precise line of frontier between Egypt and Tripoli"—only some vague gestures toward the "ancient limits of Egypt as laid down in a map" that "has never been forthcoming."[2] Another official consulted the map collection at the British Museum in London, to "determine what frontier was shown as the 'ancient limit' of Egypt in the map attached to the Firman of 1841." After perusing every map of Egypt printed between 1770 and 1860, he determined that "very few maps . . . show a western frontier to Egypt" at all. In the end, he found only a French map from 1827 that indicated a clear borderline, running from Sollum in a south-westerly direction.[3]

Amid all the confusion, the British proconsul in Benghazi, Justin Alvarez, emerged as a voice of reason. Alvarez had been suspecting an Ottoman advance on Sollum for several months. Back in May, he had made a futile attempt to urge Cromer to occupy Sollum as a precautionary measure, in light of news that the Ottoman *kaymakam* (district governor) in Darna had recently been ordered to proceed to "the Turco-Egyptian frontier, with an escort of 100 men."[4] A month later, the emergence of new intelligence concerning Ottoman designs on Sollum prompted Alvarez to meet with the Ottoman governor of Benghazi.[5] At the meeting, Alvarez argued stridently that Sollum was on Egyptian soil, and that the Egyptian government already exercised its sovereignty there through periodic coast guard patrols. The Ottoman governor strongly disagreed, however, claiming that "ancient official maps" held in Istanbul proved that the western limits of Egypt lay no further west than Ras 'Alam Rum, a point close to Marsa Matruh (about 130 miles east of Sollum). Alvarez, unfazed by this argument, retorted that Sollum was the point of departure for Egypt's western border in every European map he had seen, ancient as well as modern.

By Alvarez's account, the Ottoman governor reluctantly accepted the British viewpoint regarding the border, and "readily promised" not to advance Ottoman troops beyond any point not already under their firm control.[6] But this turned out to be a blatant lie: within two weeks, the Ottoman occupation of Sollum proceeded as planned.

In this and the following chapter, I trace the emergence of the Eastern Sahara as a contested borderland linking two territorial abstractions: the Ottoman province of Benghazi, and Egypt, which gained special status as an "autonomous province" (eyalet-i mümtaze) within the Ottoman Empire in 1841, when the sultan conceded hereditary rule to Mehmed 'Ali.[7] As this chapter's opening vignette illustrates, the Ottoman occupation of Sollum in 1902 was a critical moment in this process, setting in motion a period of diplomatic turmoil that witnessed both the Ottoman and Egyptian states scrambling to assert territorial claims at the fuzzy margins of their respective sovereign domains in the Eastern Sahara. This story is carried forward in the next chapter, which documents how, after 1902, the increasingly fraught competition between the Egyptians and Ottomans over control of the local bedouin population engendered a decade-long inter-imperial border crisis.

In this chapter, by contrast, I focus on an earlier, more inchoate phase of borderland formation. During the second half of the nineteenth century, an abstract sense of bounded political space began to develop in the Eastern Sahara despite the absence of any clear-cut territorial markers or cartographic evidence. This argument follows the approach to historical borderland formation developed by Jeremy Adelman and Stephen Aron for nineteenth-century North America. Adelman and Aron argue that the term *borderland* should not be conflated with *frontier*, but rather must be reserved for zones of "intense imperial rivalry" that afforded indigenous populations "room to maneuver and preserve some element of autonomy." In other words, *frontiers*—which Adelman and Aron define simply as "borderless" zones of cultural and geographic intermixing—emerged as *borderlands* when the interactivity between various imperial powers transformed the region into one of open political contestation.[8]

Adelman and Aron go a step further in their analysis, accounting for the eventual transformation of fluid North American "borderlands" into ossified "bordered lands."[9] Although the Eastern Sahara never reached this stage before World War I, Adelman and Aron's framework remains useful for understanding the evolution of the borderland between western Egypt and Ottoman Libya, given that it was precisely the increasing contestation between two opposing, expansive states—as well as their ongoing interaction with the local population—that gave the region more territorial definition. If Egypt and Benghazi had not yet crystallized as "bordered lands" by 1902, or 1911 (when Italy invaded the Ottoman Libyan provinces), the trajectory of inter-imperial competition in the preceding decades nonetheless served to inscribe a sense of territorial distinctiveness, or "borderedness," in the region.

At the same time, the spatial practices of the region's bedouin tribes were central to the story of borderland formation in the Eastern Sahara. Although both the Egyptian and Ottoman states acted upon similar centralizing impulses in the final decades of the nineteenth century, it was actually bedouin mobility across the putative "border" that prompted both governments to examine the scope of their territorial sovereignty in the region, even before the Ottoman occupation of Sollum. As both the Ottomans and Egyptians responded to the vexing problem of bedouin mobility, each side developed a keener awareness of the region as a zone of contested state sovereignty, in which the deeper ambiguities inherent in their legal-political relationship since 1841 were thrown into high relief.

The emergence of the Egypt-Benghazi borderland is at once a larger Ottoman story—illuminating some common features shared by *internal* borderlands across the empire[10]—as well as a unique lens through which to view the peculiar nature of Ottoman sovereignty in Egypt after 1841. For centuries, it had been the standard practice of the Ottoman authorities not to delineate any formal boundaries between provinces within the empire. As such, from the time of the Ottoman conquest of much of North

Africa in the sixteenth century until the end of World War I, the frontier between Benghazi and Egypt merely represented a transitional zone between two provinces lying within the broader sphere of Ottoman imperial sovereignty. Once Egypt became an autonomous province in 1841, the Ottoman government still refused to acknowledge the legitimacy of any formal border marking off a distinctive Egyptian sphere of territorial sovereignty. The Ottomans chose instead to refer to both Egypt's western and eastern borders as a *hatt-ı imtiyaz* (line of distinction) or *hatt-ı fasl* (line of separation), and thus not as a boundary line as such.[11]

The upshot of this ambiguous situation was the gradual emergence of the Egypt-Benghazi borderland as a zone of overlapping Egyptian and Ottoman sovereignty, where the parallel territorialization projects of the Egyptian state and its imperial suzerain came into uneasy contact. This chapter's analysis of borderland formation thus serves to highlight the continued salience of Egypt's Ottoman imperial context, even after the onset of the British occupation, by developing two key claims. First, the Ottomans sought to exploit the ambiguity of their legal-political relationship with Egypt, as it manifested in the borderland, in order to assert their sovereign claims in this key province—a central policy objective of both the Hamidian and CUP regimes.[12] Second, national territorialization in Egypt's western domains was actually driven by broader regional developments—most importantly, the ramifications of Ottoman state re-centralization in the Libyan provinces since the dawn of the *Tanzimat* era.

In 1835, the Ottoman military reconquered Tripoli and Benghazi from the Qaramanli dynasty, which had exercised de facto autonomous rule in both provinces since 1711. The reestablishment of direct Ottoman rule in Libya was part of a broader imperial policy of state re-centralization that was first articulated during the *Tanzimat* period and then expanded during the Hamidian era. During the latter half of the nineteenth century—as Istanbul grew increasingly fearful of European interference in its foreign affairs, and was perpetually preoccupied with preserving its territorial integrity—the Ottoman government sought to reassert its central control over many formerly recalcitrant, largely tribal zones along the empire's frontiers.[13] As was the case for other marginal regions with substantial tribal populations, such as Yemen or Transjordan, state re-centralization in the Libyan provinces posed a particular set of challenges to the Ottoman government.[14] The main issue was how to reestablish their ruling legitimacy and provide effective administration over an underpopulated region that comprised a vast, inhospitable desert interior beyond the Mediterranean coastal plateau.

Historians have debated the ultimate efficacy of the *Tanzimat* and Hamidian reforms in the Libyan provinces.[15] It seems clear, however, that the Ottoman government grew far more concerned about the fate of its North African possessions after the French conquest of Tunisia in 1881, and then the British occupation of Egypt the following year. Over the ensuing two decades, Istanbul devoted significant energy and resources toward its re-centralization project in the Libyan provinces; by 1902, this remote southern frontier of the empire was undoubtedly far better administered than it had been during the first few decades after the 1835 reconquest.[16] This was also the period in which the Ottomans tried their hand at the European diplomatic game by invoking Bismarck's "hinterland doctrine," first spelled out at the Berlin Africa Conference of 1884, to claim sovereignty over regions to the south of Tripoli and Benghazi, around the Lake Chad basin; these efforts did not amount to much, however.[17]

What has often been overlooked in prevailing accounts of Ottoman re-centralization in the Libyan provinces in the late nineteenth century is the fact that Tripoli and Benghazi experienced the period quite differently. In the case of Tripoli, the Ottomans managed to establish a competent bureaucracy, raise ample revenues, and usher in a series of public works projects. Benghazi was an entirely different story, however. It remained a relatively poor, underdeveloped backwater that officials typically considered a place of "honorable exile."[18]

The crux of the issue for the Ottoman government was the nature of Benghazi's population. In the late nineteenth century, the entire province only had around 200,000 to 250,000 inhabitants, the vast majority of whom were nomadic bedouins. The province also had no large population centers to speak of: the town of Benghazi, by far the most populous, grew from around 5,000 inhabitants at mid-century to 13,000 by 1884 or, by another estimate, 19,000 by 1900.[19] The province of Tripoli, by contrast, had 570,000 inhabitants in 1911.[20]

Given Benghazi's relative lack of importance to the Ottoman center, the presence of troops in the province was relatively light. Likewise, Benghazi suffered from inadequate building and communications infrastructure. This naturally exacerbated the province's extreme sense of isolation and poverty.[21] For most of the nineteenth century, there was no telegraph line connecting Benghazi to Tripoli (a distance of 620 miles); the nearest telegraph office was actually in Crete. Ottoman ships called on the port of Benghazi extremely infrequently—once a month at most—and the port infrastructure was extremely shoddy.[22] The British proconsul stationed in Benghazi was duly appalled: in a report on the state of the province in 1879, he suggested that the failings of Ottoman administration in Benghazi and the consequent "isolation of this province from the rest of the Turkish Empire, and commercial centres" were "calamities greatly to be deplored in this age of progress."[23]

The most persistent problem plaguing the administration of Benghazi was a chronic lack of funds. Local officials often failed to make regular salary payments to troops and local bureaucratic employees, for instance. In this regard, Benghazi was not alone: many provinces struggled to balance their budgets after the Ottoman government declared bankruptcy in 1875, since they could no longer count on financial assistance from Istanbul.[24] Ottoman officials in Tripoli actually fared much better than their counterparts in Benghazi when it came to raising revenues, however. This was due to Tripoli's relative number of sizeable and prosperous towns, the largesse of local merchants and notables, and its more centralized bureaucratic structure.[25] Beyond the local ramifications of imperial bankruptcy, Benghazi's fiscal situation was aggravated by the suppression and decline of the slave trade, which at its height had been a boon for the region, as well as Istanbul's decision to establish Benghazi as an independent province (*vilayet*) in 1878, which required the local administration to finance bureaucratic and military salaries, and purchase military supplies, from its own budget.[26]

Around 1880, it became clear to Ottoman officials in Istanbul that drastic measures were required to fix Benghazi's finances.[27] The only recourse was to go after the bedouins—the bulk of the province's population, and predominantly Sanusi followers[28]—who had managed in most cases to avoid paying any direct taxes to the state. This was a dramatic departure from previous policy. For the first forty years after the Libyan reconquest, local officials had left many of the unsettled tribes in the interior to their own devices. Moreover, the Ottomans never completed a comprehensive land survey in Benghazi,[29] as they had done in other frontier zones such as Transjordan.[30] By around 1880, however, the Ottoman government could no longer tolerate this situation. As historian Michel Le Gall puts it: "The conclusions to be drawn by the Ottoman authorities were obvious: indirect taxes—customs dues and some municipal taxes—were insufficient sources of revenue. New measures to enlarge the tax rolls were needed. This meant more, and effective direct taxation of the bedouin."[31]

In 1882, the Ottomans took decisive action by appointing Haci Reşid Paşa—notorious for his harsh repression of unruly bedouin tribes in the Hijaz in the mid-1850s, as well as Transjordan in the late-1860s[32]—as the new governor of Benghazi. Within a few months of his arrival, Reşid embarked upon the first of what would be three lengthy tax campaigns into the province's desert hinterland, to bring the bedouins under effective Ottoman sovereignty.[33] The first few months of the campaign were a complete failure. Even though Reşid tried to conciliate the bedouins by offering them ceremonial gifts and making a show of converting to the Sanusi faith,[34] the tribes refused to pay their taxes to the state. Moreover, Reşid's campaign compelled a large number of tribesmen to flee toward the Egyptian side of the border, beyond his reach.[35] This opening salvo against the bedouins yielded only a tenth of the intended sum in back taxes,[36] and rumors that Reşid had actually squandered more cash than he had managed to recover led to his temporary removal from his post, as well as an investigation into his conduct.[37]

Apparently cleared of all charges, Reşid returned to Benghazi in late 1888 and immediately mounted a second campaign into the province's interior. This time he was more successful: his battalion defeated the Zuwayya tribesmen and coerced them into paying six years of back taxes.[38] Reşid launched a third tax campaign against the backdrop of an extreme famine and drought that had beset the province in 1892. Acting on the assumption that such hardship offered the government a unique opportunity to subdue the province's tribal population once and for all, Reşid doubled the tax burden on the bedouins in the first year of the drought, while they were already beholden to the provincial government for food relief.[39] The results of this ruthless policy were mixed: while the government did succeed in raising revenues, it also drove many tribesmen to resist or, once again, to flee to Egypt or locales further south. By 1893 or 1894, the tax campaigns appear to have failed to net any lasting financial gains for the government.[40] Ottoman officials in Benghazi were in fact still scrambling to raise tax revenues from the province's numerous tribes well into the first decade of the twentieth century.[41]

Most significant for our purposes, however, is the impetus that Reşid Paşa's tax campaigns—the centerpiece of the Ottoman state's re-centralization efforts in Benghazi—gave to many bedouin tribes to flee to Egypt. But such tribal traffic between the two provinces was actually nothing new, even if Reşid's campaigns ushered in a new, more intense phase. Bedouin mobility across the internal Ottoman "border" between Benghazi and Egypt was in fact a long-standing spatial practice that local authorities had already been struggling to manage for decades.

Less than a decade after their reconquest of Tripoli and Benghazi—and three years after granting Mehmed 'Ali the historic firman of investiture—the Ottomans were forced to address the fluidity of the internal border between Benghazi (then still a subprovince of Tripoli) and the autonomous province of Egypt.[42] In January 1844, a local Ottoman official named Amin Efendi received a series of letters from shaykhs of two bedouin groups: one comprising tribesmen originally from an area known as Zil al-Tayn, in Tripoli; the other comprising bedouin from the western part of Benghazi. Fourteen years prior, these bedouin groups had "left their homelands and moved to and settled in Egypt [terk-i evtan ile, Mısır tarafına nakil ve iskân eylemişler]." Now, however—"choosing to return to their homelands"—they petitioned the sultan for official pardon, as well as for permission to resettle in the hinterlands of Tripoli and Benghazi.[43]

Faced with a nearly identical situation a decade later, the Ottomans responded with a similar degree of careful deliberation. That the tribes were freely crossing the border was not what was at issue, however. Rather, the Ottomans were happy to permit the tribes to return to their homelands, so long as they could harness this migration as an opportunity to implement a more robust and legible bedouin policy in both Tripoli and Benghazi.[44]

In 1856, approximately three thousand bedouins from several different Benghazi tribes—having crossed into Egypt and settled there approximately thirty or thirty-five years prior[45]—decided to return to their original homelands.[46] The tribes moved back across the border and came to rest at a location approximately thirty hours away from the town of Benghazi. As a gesture of good will, they also paid their taxes "like the rest of the population."[47]

This latest wave of bedouin migration compelled the local Ottoman authorities to seek guidance from the central government. Istanbul's response was twofold. First, the Ottomans appealed to the Egyptian governor, Sa'id Pasha, to inquire whether the Egyptian government would have any objection to the resettlement of the tribes. The answer was no. In fact, the Egyptians were only too happy to be rid of the unruly tribes, which had openly revolted when the government—once it realized the tribesmen had "been on Egyptian soil for a considerable length of time"—attempted to settle them.[48] It was, in fact, the Egyptian military's violent repression of this tribal revolt that had driven a large number of bedouins to seek refuge in their original homelands in Benghazi in the first place.[49]

Second, the Ottomans turned the matter over to the highest legal authority in the empire, the *Meclis-i Vâlâ* (High Council of Justice). Upon reviewing the details of the case, the *Meclis* stipulated that the Ottomans would pardon the tribes and permit them to resettle in Benghazi, provided they continue to pay their taxes, promise never to return to Egypt, and "concern themselves strictly with their own affairs and customs." The *Meclis* also requested the institutionalization of population registers (*nüfus defterleri*) in order to keep track of the resettled bedouins. The Ottomans ultimately responded favorably to the Egyptian governor, informing him of the decision of the *Meclis-i Vâlâ*, and assuring him that the tribes would never again "set foot in Egypt."[50]

There is evidence to suggest that the Ottomans were successful in resettling at least some of these bedouin groups in Benghazi, and keeping closer track of their activities. In 1864, the Grand Vezir wrote a memorandum reporting on an official tour of inspection in the easternmost parts of the subprovince, which had recently been commissioned in order to "investigate the conditions of the country, and to safeguard and reform the ideas of the bedouins [*teftiş-i ahval-i büldan ve temin ve teslih-i efkâr-ı urban için*]." According to the Grand Vezir, the sultan was very pleased with the results of the measures taken in Benghazi toward "classifying the bedouins and tribes, and resettling the tribes, which had [formerly] migrated to Egypt, in their old homes."[51] Ostensibly emboldened by these successes, the sultan even asked the governor to select some bedouin notables from the province to form a new special ceremonial honor guard in Istanbul.[52]

In most other cases, however, the free movement of various bedouin tribes across the unmarked internal border consistently confounded the local Ottoman authorities, posing two main challenges to their efforts to govern the Libyan provinces more soundly. First, Ottoman officials realized that the ease with which local tribes slipped back and forth across the border significantly impaired their ability to collect taxes—a major problem, given the chronic financial woes of Benghazi's administration. Second, the

Ottomans struggled to deal effectively with the matter of internecine conflict between groups of Benghazi or Tripoli bedouins, and tribes living in Egypt, which typically took the form of cross-border raiding.

One case, which highlights both of these problems, began with the activities of approximately seven hundred Magharba bedouins from the environs of Sirte. Around 1854, these tribesmen were forced to abandon their homes due to crushing scarcity in the Sirte region; they retreated all the way to the Sudan. As a consequence of their departure, the arrears from their unpaid taxes exceeded six thousand *keyses*,[53] a sum the Ottoman authorities in Tripoli certainly wished to collect. To remedy the situation, the governor of Tripoli, Osman Paşa, managed to achieve a sort of reconciliation and convinced a group of the tribesmen to return to Sirte.[54]

But the Magharba were not compliant once they were back in their home turf. Shortly after their return, they crossed into Egypt and raided four tribes, stealing approximately twenty-five hundred camels. Making matters worse, ever since this wanton act of plunder, the Magharba had been living in what Ottoman officials called "a state of nomadism, and [following] a path of savagery and brigandage [*hal-i bedeviyette ve meslek-i vahşet ve şekavette*]."[55]

It took several years for the Tripoli authorities to take decisive action against the Magharba, however. Tripoli's local administrative council cited two main reasons for its eventual decision to act: first, the fact that "the bedouins of both sides are subjects of the imperial Sultanate, under the shadow of the sultan's protection [*iki taraf urbanı saye-yi şahanede müstazıll tebaa-yı saltanat-ı seniyeden bulundukları*]"; and second, the fear that the Magharba's hostile activities were "causing damage to the security of their neighbors."[56] The local council's contention here that the Ottoman government had a responsibility toward the security and well-being of bedouin tribes on the Egyptian side of the border is particularly striking given the unstated political subtext: although Egypt was still technically an Ottoman province (albeit a semi-autonomous one), the Ottomans were finding it difficult to exercise their sovereignty across the invisible internal borderline.

To set matters straight, the governor of Tripoli and one local council member named Haci Ahmed Kumudu accompanied the shaykhs of the four aggrieved tribes from the Egyptian side of the border to Sirte. Once there, with the assistance of some local notables, the appointed messengers delivered the "necessary warnings" to Magharba leader Ali Latboş and other prominent shaykhs in the Sirte region. The situation took a danger-ous turn, however, when it came to the issue of recovering the camels for the Egyptian tribesmen. Seventy-six camels deemed to be originally from their herds—"recognizable by their distinguishing marks [*nişanlarından tanıyarak*]"—were given back to them. But as recompense for the vast re-mainder of the animals owed to them, the shaykhs from Egypt actually took a large number of camels from the Ottoman authorities and swiftly withdrew with their tribes into the desert.[57]

The theft of government-owned camels inevitably drew the local Ottoman authorities deeper into the conflict, and they began to weigh a suitable military response. Several factors complicated the issue, however. First, it was going to be particularly difficult to pursue these bedouins given that they had "no place or home" and were "roaming around no-madically inside a vast desert—exceeding four hundred hours in terms of latitude and longitude—and reaching as far as the Sudan." Moreover, the local council members felt that the bedouins would merely retreat further into the desert at "the moment they heard of any plans to send troops" from Benghazi. Consequently, there "would be no use" pursuing them from only one direction. Instead, the mission required an all-out "three-pronged" siege—coordinated from "Benghazi to the east; Fezzan to the south; Khoms from the west"—until the bedouins could be "cornered in one place."[58]

The local authorities were also concerned about allocating the requi-site funds to cover what they expected to be an unusually expensive mis-sion. Since a campaign against the tribes would take place in "a vast desert devoid of water and cultivation [*su ve şenlikten hâli badiye-yi vâsi'ye*]," it would be particularly difficult and costly to transport food and drink, or to supply other necessary provisions to the troops. Ultimately, the local authorities—aware they would receive no financial assistance from the central government—decided not to undertake the large-scale military campaign they had initially envisaged, on the grounds that it would be unduly expensive. Instead, they opted to pursue a course alternating "be-tween threat and reconciliation"; failing that, it was their hope that they could trap the Magharba at the moment they returned to their home turf. The matter was still unresolved at the time the local council sent its final report to Istanbul, although the governor of Tripoli—Ahmet İzzet Paşa—assured the Grand Vezir that "serious attention and effort will be given to recovery of the stolen camels and state [*mîrî*] funds."[59]

Reading between the lines of this case, it appears that the ambiguity of Ottoman jurisdiction in Egypt was a tacit underlying factor. Even though Tripoli's local administrative council initially felt the Ottoman government was responsible for the bedouins living on the Egyptian side of the border—they were still subjects of the sultan, after all—the military action they designed, but were unable to finance, was always contingent on their pursuing the disobedient bedouins within the bounds of the Benghazi or Tripoli hinterlands—in short, before they effectively crossed over into Sudan or Egypt. Moreover, once the officials abandoned the military option, their only recourse was to wait until the tribesmen in question returned to Tripoli or Benghazi. Although İzzet and other officials do not come out and say it, what is implicit in the course of action they adopted was their inability to pursue the bedouin thieves across the internal border. Once the bedouins were safely in Egypt, the Ottoman authorities lost their sovereign authority over them.

Another episode of cross-border tribal violence that occurred three years after the Magharba incident underscores the fundamental limitations of Ottoman sovereign jurisdiction across the border in Egypt. At the same time, it illuminates the degree to which the free movement of bedouins in both directions across the border—as well as the various social networks linking many of these tribal groups together—posed unique challenges to Ottoman efforts to achieve robust state re-centralization in Benghazi.

In 1857, a group of Awlad 'Ali bedouins crossed into Benghazi from Egypt and staged several raids against the local population throughout the province;[60] they also attacked a postal delivery convoy somewhere on the road between Benghazi and Tripoli. By all accounts, the damage done by these Awlad 'Ali "brigands" was severe, "unleashing a state of total destruction on the local inhabitants [ahaliye iş'al-i dest-i hasar etmekte]." When the attackers learned of the Ottoman authorities' plans to arrest and prosecute them, however, they slipped back across the border to Egypt and consequently avoided punishment.[61]

This situation put the local government in Benghazi in a serious bind. On one hand, as the governor of Tripoli warned, the local population in Benghazi "would fall into a state of devastation" if no action were taken against the Awlad 'Ali brigands.[62] On the other hand, the local authorities were fully aware they had no de facto jurisdiction in Egyptian territory, where a different set of legal conditions prevailed, and therefore could not pursue the Awlad 'Ali across the border and attempt to arrest them there. The Ottoman officials thus found themselves powerless to prosecute a series of crimes committed inside the sovereign territory of the empire, for the simple reason that the brigands had taken full advantage of the legal authority vacuum that had emerged in the borderland once Egypt became an autonomous province after 1841. Fully aware of the strategic advantages of invoking the internal border between two distinct realms, the Awlad 'Ali cleverly sought refuge back in Egypt, where they knew the arms of Ottoman justice could not reach them.

Determined to take action, however, local officials in Benghazi and Tripoli turned to the Egyptian government for assistance. Osman Paşa—the same governor of Tripoli who had dealt with the Magharba a few years prior—sent two different letters to Sa'id Pasha (still governor of Egypt), imploring him to take punitive measures against the Awlad 'Ali brigands on the Ottomans' behalf.[63] In other words, the last resort of the officials in Benghazi was to hope the Egyptians would arrest and sentence the criminals for them. The matter was passed on to the office of the Grand Vezir, who—apparently uncertain whether the Egyptians would comply with Osman Paşa's request—requested a sultanic decree that would legally require Sa'id to take disciplinary action against the brigands.[64]

The Awlad 'Ali episode also highlights another major implication of the de facto authority vacuum that prevailed along the internal border between Benghazi and Egypt—and a situation that the bedouin tribesmen knew precisely how to exploit to their advantage. In a second report to the Grand Vezir, Osman Paşa lamented that the Awlad 'Ali—who were exempt from paying fiscal taxes under Egyptian law—had managed to provoke their kinsmen on the Benghazi side not to pay the taxes they owed to the Ottoman government. Consequently, when it came time to collect the taxes that year, many of the Awlad 'Ali in Benghazi fled across the border and took up residence with their fellow tribesmen living within Egyptian territory. The coffers of the Benghazi government took a direct hit as a result, and officials watched with dismay as the fiscal deficit rose to dangerous heights.[65] Once again, it seems, the Awlad 'Ali had proven to the Ottoman authorities that they knew how to manipulate the system. When it was in their interest to do so, the bedouins tacitly invoked—and thus effectively reified—the border, by crossing over it into the safe haven that was autonomous Egypt, where they knew an entirely different tax code and justice system now prevailed.

But this would not be the last time that the Ottomans appealed to the Egyptians for help in response to Awlad ʿAli brigandage. Three decades later, in July 1888, Awlad ʿAli tribesmen in Egypt stole a number of animals that had been transported across the border by a Benghazi-based merchant. In response, the Ottoman Interior Ministry drafted a memo to its equivalent institution in Egypt, requesting that the Egyptian authorities work to restore the plundered animals, and also take the necessary steps so that similar incidences of theft would not reoccur.[66] Again, the Ottomans could not effectively provide justice and security for their subjects in Benghazi so long as the perpetrators of the crimes against them were safely ensconced on the Egyptian side of the border. They needed the Egyptian authorities to step in on their behalf, though there is no evidence that this ever happened to a satisfactory degree.

Brigandage was not the only problem that the local bedouins consistently posed for the Ottomans in this emergent borderland. In the last two decades of the nineteenth century, many tribes—including those that had, in the 1840s and 1850s, resettled in their original "homelands" in Benghazi—fled back in the other direction, toward Egypt, seeking to escape Haci Reşid Paşa's brutal tax campaigns deep inside Benghazi's hinterland. The Ottomans' response to this problem, illustrated with a few examples below, once again demonstrates how bedouin mobility in the face of Ottoman state re-centralization served to instruct the Ottomans about the limits of their sovereign reach in Egypt.

In one case, brigandage and tax evasion were linked together. In 1896, several bedouin tribes from the districts of Tobruk and Bomba (both subsumed within the administrative subdivision, or *kaza*, of Darna) crossed into Egypt to avoid paying their taxes to the Ottoman state. Along the way, they attacked some tribes living close to the border on the Benghazi side. Benghazi officials immediately sent a team of officials to the border to arrest the assailants and collect the substantial tax arrears the tribesmen owed to the local government.[67]

This episode also generated a lengthy discussion between Ottoman government officials at various levels concerning the revenues they so sorely needed to raise in Benghazi due to the substantially reduced bedouin tax base. In a letter to the Ottoman Interior Ministry, for example, the Benghazi administrative council explained that a careful perusal of the bedouin tax registers for the *sancak* revealed that "more than one third of the bedouins from the district" were currently residing in Egypt.[68] In light of this alarming number, local officials decided to consider different strategies for managing the financial shortfall. The arguments adduced by different officials during the ensuing deliberations not only reveal a great deal about how the Ottomans perceived the limitations of their own authority over the tribes even within Benghazi, but also—yet again—underscore the powerlessness they felt in the face of bedouin flight to Egypt.

The Ottomans made a clear distinction between two types of bedouins from among those currently based in Egypt: there were "those who had left behind land and property [*arazi ve emlâka munsarif olanlar*]," who henceforth would be considered "tantamount to settled [*meskûn hükmünde*]"; and then there were those "unsettled" bedouins who were "not obliged" to pay state taxes.[69] According to one revealing report sent by the Grand Vezir to the Interior Ministry, this second group of "unsettled" bedouins had never been required to pay the state tax, but rather had only ever paid a 9 percent duty on the proceeds from their trade in animal products.[70] Consequently, it was impossible to pursue them for their arrears. Instead, the Ottomans targeted the group of so-called "settled" bedouins, threatening to confiscate and sell the property they had left behind upon crossing into Egypt, as compensation for the taxes they owed.[71] This was the only real recourse for the Ottomans, given that these tribesmen had once again managed to slip into the cross-border authority vacuum. After all, as the Grand Vezir lamented, "the Egyptian government would not be able to do anything," since there was no present Egyptian law giving officials the authority to collect taxes from any bedouin tribes. Moreover, it was not clear if the Egyptian authorities could even help the Ottomans bring the perpetrators of the recent bedouin attacks to justice. The Egyptian high commissioner told the Grand Vezir that it would be necessary first to have the names of all the attackers in order to arrest them in accordance with Egyptian law, and it seems clear from the evidence that the Ottoman authorities were unable to provide this information.

Almost a year later, the Ottoman authorities began to advocate a very different response to the fiscal crisis that the cross-border tax evasion of so many tribesmen had engendered. The officials still upheld the general principle that they should implement a de facto absentee property tax—and, accordingly, that they had the right to sell any lands and property that the more prosperous of the tribesmen now resident in Egypt had abandoned. But now they argued that a sounder basis for tax collection—one that actually "was possible to implement"—needed to be established, "in order to prevent a set of harmful occurrences" from besetting the province.

Ultimately, the Ottomans had to find a way to "bring the aforementioned bedouins all back to their homelands." There was, in their view, "no other measure that could be envisaged": to make up for the large fiscal deficit, they needed to force the bedouins back to Benghazi, where they would once again be under unequivocal Ottoman sovereignty. By making such arguments, Ottoman officials once again acknowledged implicitly that they had no legal authority to pursue the guilty parties, or even to force the Egyptians to collect taxes from the bedouins on their behalf, so long as the tribes remained on the eastern side of the border.[72]

Try as they might, the Ottomans could never escape the vicious cycle that their tax policy in Benghazi had initiated. Desperate to raise revenues for this habitually underfunded province, successive Ottoman governors sought to force the largely tribal population to pay its fair share, which in turn spurred many tribes to cross the border to evade taxation. But seeking to make up for this lost revenue, the government attempted to exact inordinately steep taxes on those tribes it could reach, which only had the unintended consequence of driving even more tribesmen across the border.

In 1899, for instance, many tribes from the Tobruk region migrated to the Egyptian side after learning of the Benghazi government's intention to make them pay the same taxes as the sedentary population.[73] Similarly, a section of the 'Abaydat tribe near Darna set off for Egyptian soil in protest of renewed "pressure of taxation," as well as the purported abuses of some tax collectors; they decided to move to Egypt after hearing "favorable accounts" from the Awlad 'Ali in Egypt concerning "their present position and their satisfaction with the Egyptian government."[74] According to British officials monitoring the affair, the Benghazi governor sent two pious Muslims to the 'Abaydat in order to persuade them not to resettle in Egypt, but they only "partly succeeded."[75]

Bedouin flight to Egypt as a way to avoid taxation continued to plague Ottoman authorities in Benghazi into the first decade of the twentieth century. In 1902, the Ottoman finance minister in Istanbul weighed in on this chronic problem. According to a lengthy report he sent to the Grand Vezir, a fixed tax had been levied *in principle* on the various tribes of different districts in Benghazi for the past thirty-five years, without the policy ever being amended. This had not meant that the taxes could actually be collected, however: "some of these tribes were dispersed," whereas others were too impoverished to pay. As the finance minister saw it, the problem of unpaid taxes could be broken down into four different scenarios: some Benghazi tribes had "joined up with other tribes in the sub-province" (ostensibly making themselves difficult to locate and thus leading to key omissions in the tax registers); some had "migrated to other places" or else were simply "unaccounted for" (cross-border tax evasion to Egypt seems implied here); some were "unable to settle their debts on account of their being in a state of poverty"; and, finally, some tribes had "claimed that they were exempt from taxation."[76]

In the remainder of his report, the finance minister outlined various proposals for handling each of these scenarios. Those bedouins who had joined or latched onto other tribes within Benghazi should still be required to pay their share of the "tribe tax [*kabileye ait vergi*]" to the shaykhs of their original tribes (who were then responsible for turning the sums over to the Ottoman authorities). The bedouins who had moved to other regions, including Egypt, should pay taxes based on the land and property they left behind. This stipulation echoed the discussion from five years prior of how to raise revenue from the so-called "settled" or propertied bedouins, though it stopped short of recommending the forcible sale of these tribes' abandoned lands and property. Those bedouins who were too poor to pay—and who owned no land or property—would have their share of the debt waived. Finally, those bedouins who claimed complete tax exemption were required to adduce documentation to prove their case.[77]

Whether or not the Benghazi officials ever successfully implemented the finance minister's recommendations, the report remains a striking testament to how seriously bedouin mobility—most typically, flight to the autonomous province of Egypt—damaged the financial situation of the province and, consequently, hindered the larger project of state recentralization along the empire's Eastern Saharan frontier.

In one important respect, however, the porousness of the Egypt-Benghazi border could be effectively harnessed for the benefit of the local Ottoman administration. For years, local authorities had been enforcing an informal customs tax on all livestock transported by land from Benghazi into Egypt, where tribes and merchants from Benghazi did a robust business (particularly in Alexandria). This was known as the *Derbend-i Defne Parası*, named for a mountain pass located at the small coastal town of Defne.[78] As far as the Ottomans were concerned, the Defne duty—set at three or four *kuruş* per animal[79]—was merely the latest instantiation of the long-standing tax on animal husbandry in the region, officially replacing the Ottoman "livestock tax" (*ağnam resmi*) in Benghazi and Tripoli in the early-1860s.[80] Ever since, local officials had seized upon the opportunity to levy this tax on the lucrative cross-border traffic in animals,[81] although not without controversy.

In March 1883, the Ottoman authorities in Benghazi informed the European consular corps there that, henceforth, the *Derbend-i Defne* tax would be expanded to include all non-Ottoman subjects engaged in the local animal trade. Moreover, a new commission would be formed to issue mandatory transit permits (*tezkere*), the neglect of which would result in a substantial fine. The British proconsul in Benghazi at the time, Cecil Wood, adamantly refused to accept this new tax policy, arguing that it contravened an Ottoman-European commercial treaty signed at Kanlıca on April 29, 1861, "wherein it is declared that all such taxes and monopolies on the transit by land of goods and animals [on Ottoman territory] are abolished."[82]

Moreover, Wood claimed that the *Derbend-i Defne* tax had actually been "declared both arbitrary and illegal in 1878" by two former governors of Benghazi, on the basis that the tax had never fulfilled its stated objective. According to Wood, the tax dated "from the time of the abolition of inland custom houses during the Mutasarrifship of Halil Pasha, who recommended to the Sublime Porte the establishment of a fort and garrison at Defne to protect the exporters of cattle (etc.) on their way to Egypt, who would pay a certain amount in return for the protection thus afforded to them." But, in light of the fact that "neither fort nor garrison have ever existed at Defne," according to Wood, the levy had no legal basis: "The Arabs have been forced to pay the tax for the protection" that the Ottomans failed to provide them.[83] Ultimately, after mounting "united pressure" on the Sublime Porte, the European consular corps in Benghazi succeeded in compelling the Ottoman government to condemn the actions of the local authorities as illegal, and thereby discontinue the duty.[84]

But it was not long before local officials defied Istanbul's orders. Within a few years at most, the *Derbend-i Defne* tax was reestablished. Justin Alvarez, who took over as British proconsul in Benghazi in 1890, blamed this on the persistence of "vested interests in corruption";[85] an official in the Foreign Office also noted that the duty had now been reimposed "apparently on the sole authority of the local governor."[86] Alvarez later hinted at another possible explanation for the bad behavior of the local officials: the Ottoman governor of Benghazi had "practically abdicated from the cares of Government in favour of the Muhassebejy [*sic*], or Provincial

Accountant."[87] In other words, seen from the perspective of the province's chief financial officer, there was a perfectly reasonable explanation for why officials in Benghazi would have ignored Istanbul's orders and resumed collection of the *Derbend-i Defne* tax: it was an extremely lucrative revenue source in a province habitually strapped for cash.[88] It did not matter to local officials that Benghazi's animal merchants were extremely dissatisfied with the duty, or that the local population had "for a long time groaned under the [duty's] illegal imposition" to the point that they had even telegraphed the sultan and the Porte several times "begging for its removal."[89] The Ottoman officials understood that they would always be able to raise substantial revenue from the *Derbend-i Defne* duty, legal or not. The cross-border trade in animals was such a vital part of the livelihood of Benghazi's population that they really had no choice but to pay the tax, however reluctantly.

The issue of the *Derbend-i Defne* duty's legality came up again following several incidents in 1902. Around this time, due to the increased freight costs for animals,[90] as well as a new quarantine for vessels due to arrive in Alexandria,[91] European merchants had to abandon the sea option for transporting animals—which they had vastly preferred, given that the sea route was not taxed[92]—and take the overland route to Egypt, instead. In one case, a British subject was charged four piasters per sheep and three per goat at Defne as he sought to move 1,874 animals overland for sale in Alexandria; the *Derbend-i Defne* tax was also similarly levied on Italian and French merchants making the same journey.[93]

Subsequently, in late February, the Ottoman *memur* (district supervisor) of Defne stopped a caravan consisting of some sixteen hundred sheep being led overland by the chief shepherd working for a Benghazi-based merchant named Joseph Abuharoun—a British subject. When the shepherd was unable to produce a permit proving his authorization to cross the border, the *memur* declared him a smuggler, seized three hundred of the animals, and demanded the payment of a steep fine. Abuharoun later filed an official complaint alleging that—in addition to the three hundred cattle confiscated as a penalty—another 140 sheep had been lost en route, due to "robbery in consequence of the confusion produced by the seizure and the detention of three shepherds out of the eight in charge of the flock."[94] Abuharoun, seeking to sue for damages, argued defiantly that "any contention on the part of the Benghazi local authority that I have broken any law or regulation by sending my animals from this province into Egypt is fundamentally incorrect."[95] Like Wood and Alvarez before him, Abuharoun argued, on the basis of the 1861 Kanlıca treaty, that the *Derbend-i Defne* tax was "an arbitrary and illegal impost levied without the sanction of His Imperial Majesty the Sultan."[96]

In light of these episodes, the European consular corps in Benghazi again took the local governor to task over the *Derbend-i Defne* tax, which they considered to be a violation of international treaty law. Over the course of a three-hour meeting with the governor, Alvarez and his counterparts from Italy, France, and Austria-Hungary made an impassioned argument for the tax's illegality, and "obtained from him with the greatest difficulty a promise that orders should be given to the Mamur of Defne . . . to allow all flocks belonging to foreigners to pass freely," so long as they carried a certificate declaring the number of animals and names of their owners. The governor did not follow through on his promise, however.[97] In the meantime, while European ambassadors and Porte officials once again debated the legality of the *Derbend-i Defne* tax in Istanbul, Benghazi officials pressed Abuharoun to pay the money he owed the government "in settlement of any just claim which the Local Authority might have upon him . . . in the event of the decision that this imposition was a legal tax."[98]

There was arguably much more at stake with the *Derbend-i Defne* tax than the question of its legality, however. What the tax's European critics seemed to overlook was that it had become a vital means for the local Ottoman authorities to exercise sovereignty in the emergent Egypt-Benghazi borderland in the late nineteenth century. The coastal caravan route was, after all, the lifeblood of the lucrative regional livestock trade. Consequently, making a strong show of authority at Defne—regulating the mobility of local merchants, whose most important markets were in Egypt, and transforming it into a key revenue base—was an ideal solution for the cash-strapped Ottomans. In this case, then, territoriality was not being conceived or practiced by the local government as uniform control over bounded political space—which was well beyond its sovereign capabilities at this time—but rather as the means to control one key node along a well-trodden commercial pathway.[99] At the same time, by carefully administering this vector toward Egypt, the Ottomans reified a sharper sense of territorial distinctiveness at the margins of two provinces where no official boundary line yet existed (in fact, Defne was much further west than any locale that either the Ottomans or Egyptians would ever cite as the starting point for an official border).

It is therefore unsurprising that the Ottomans were so loath to give up the tax, the significance of which transcended the much-needed revenue it provided. The Porte and the European embassies were still fighting over the legality of the *Derbend-i Defne* tax in the summer of 1902, but by this time the issue was practically moot. The politics of the Egypt-Benghazi borderland were already escalating into a new, more acute phase.

The Ottoman occupation of Sollum marked a clear turning point in the evolution of the Egypt-Benghazi borderland, catching the British completely off-guard and drawing them into what would become a protracted dispute with Istanbul over the location of a supposed border. At the same time, however, the Sollum occupation can be seen as the logical culmination of the underlying forces governing borderland formation that have been the main subject of this chapter thus far. By 1902, after decades of mounting contestation with an ever-expansive Egyptian state over the exercise of sovereign authority over the local population, the Ottomans had become sufficiently unnerved by the creeping sense of Egyptian territoriality in the region that they felt compelled to stake a more ambitious territorial claim of their own.

The Ottoman government had in fact been considering such a move for over a year, as part of a broader initiative to solidify its military presence along the Benghazi coastline. Unbeknownst to proconsul Alvarez and other British officials, however, the Ottoman decision was prompted less by outward aggression than by a sense of confusion and defensiveness. In the spring of 1901, the sultan ordered a special meeting of the Ottoman Cabinet (*Meclis-i Vükelâ*), after receiving intelligence that an Egyptian military brigade had orders to establish an outpost at the mouth of Sollum's harbor.[100] The sultan was particularly horrified to discover that previous instructions to transfer funds to Benghazi, in order to erect new garrisons along the coast, had never been implemented. In order to thwart the anticipated Egyptian advance, he ordered the Cabinet to allocate the necessary funds and troops in order to establish a small military station (*karakolhane*) in Sollum, which various officials agreed was at the "extreme limit of the border [*münteha-yı hudud*]."[101]

The Ottomans' resolve to fortify key positions along the Egypt-Benghazi borderland intensified in the first months of 1902, when the sultan learned from Gazi Ahmed Muhtar Paşa, the Ottoman high commissioner in Egypt, that the British had claimed the port of Marsa Matruh as Egyptian territory, and were embarking on new settlement and construction projects there. In response, the sultan ordered his military staff officers (*erkân-ı harbiye*) to ascertain the correct location of Marsa Matruh. Based on the map they consulted—presumably a copy of the original 1841 map—they affirmed that Marsa Matruh was in fact "inside the Sancak of Benghazi," a finding that contradicted the decision of the Cabinet just several months prior. The sultan then issued a decree (*irade*) that, in effect, chastized various branches of the imperial bureaucracy for not having been better informed about the political situation along the disputed stretch of Mediterranean coastline.[102] The decree provoked swift action among the Ottoman Cabinet members. They immediately appealed to the *mutasarrıf* of Benghazi for information regarding the administrative and police apparatus at Marsa Matruh. They also wrote to the Interior and Naval Ministries for precise details concerning the names of civil officials in Marsa Matruh, the number of gendarmes stationed there, and the name of the port director.[103]

The Ottomans' decision to occupy Sollum was thus the product of more than a year of deliberation at various levels of the bureaucracy. By the summer of 1902, at the behest of the sultan, the government had managed to organize the establishment of a small but permanent garrison at Sollum. Additionally, officials had now reached a consensus that the 1841 map actually showed the eastern limits of Benghazi to extend well beyond Sollum, up to the area around Marsa Matruh—the very same spot that the Egyptian Coast Guard was just beginning to develop. Ironically, then, if the flurry of activity by British officials to address the situation at the border was a direct reaction to the Ottoman presence at Sollum—as we saw in the opening of the chapter—then the Ottomans, too, only mobilized in the borderland as a reaction to a perceived British-Egyptian threat. In this way, through mutual suspicion and mutual ignorance of the facts on the ground, the Ottoman-Egyptian border conflict began to escalate into a new, more acute phase.

British officials were, on the whole, far less confident than Alvarez about how to respond to the new territorial claims put forth by the Ottomans. One official questioned Alvarez's contention that Jaghbub could possibly be Egyptian territory, suggesting instead that it was legally Sanusi territory by Ottoman decree.[104] The same official also took serious issue with the Ottoman claim to Marsa Matruh—"the most important point on the Egyptian coast line west of Alexandria"—though he lamented that so long as "the only known copy of the map annexed to the Firman" was in Istanbul, Egypt's western boundary would remain shrouded in doubt.[105] Lord Cromer also weighed in. In his view, although it had "always been fully understood that Sollum is Egyptian territory," he was not "aware of any document having the formal law that lays down the frontier." Finally, an intelligence memo from the Egyptian War Office similarly conceded that it was merely "consensus of opinion" that established Sollum as the border's starting point, since—again—the only map ever to define the border was no longer extant.[106]

This lack of certainty compelled some officials to argue that the British government should immediately appoint a commission to delimit the border. The British decided against such a move, however, for a couple of different reasons. First, a coast guard reconnaissance mission revealed that the Ottoman post was actually perched on a ridge overlooking Sollum Bay and consequently appeared "to be on, and not over, the generally accepted frontier line."[107] Second, the coast guard men determined that the garrison was extremely small, consisting of only four men (though twenty more were stationed further west along the coast at Port Sulayman). Even though one coast guard officer heard a rumor that the purpose of the occupation was for the Ottomans to begin collecting taxes in the environs of Sollum,[108] which would be unacceptable to the British, they let the matter slide for the time being. A border crisis had been temporarily averted.

But not for very long. On the morning of October 5, 1904, Shalabi Mustafa—a coast guard officer who had recently been appointed ma'mur of Marsa Matruh—had only just anchored his steamer at Sollum when two bedouins swam out to the ship asking to have a look around. Shalabi Mustafa let them on board, but—suspicious of some ulterior motives on their part—went ashore to investigate. Speaking directly to the Ottoman commanding officer at Sollum, Shalabi Mustafa learned that the bedouins were actually Ottoman spies who had been sent to snoop around for evidence whether the Egyptian Coast Guard intended to build a new military base by the harbor. At the same time, Shalabi Mustafa saw firsthand that the Ottoman *karakolhane* at Sollum was no longer the tiny, innocuous outpost that had been observed two years prior. In the intervening period, the Ottomans had erected two permanent stone structures at different strategic vantage points, and were in the process of constructing what was to be a "big station" on top of the hill that could quarter around a hundred men. This was evidently part of a grander scheme to reorganize the administrative infrastructure at Sollum so that it would function like other Ottoman coastal garrisons, with a customs house as well as a regular "port office." Moreover, the Ottoman officer informed Shalabi Mustafa that he had received strict orders to "prevent the Egyptians from building at Salloom [*sic*] as they [had] no rights in the harbor or any part of Salloom, which are within the limits of Tripoli."[109]

The disturbing results of Shalabi Mustafa's fact-finding mission in Sollum slowly made their way up the chain of command. Andre von Dumreicher—at that time the staff inspector of the coast guard's Western Directorate—feared that the Ottomans' renewed claim to territory around Marsa Matruh would disrupt the stream of revenue the Egyptian government had been collecting from sponge-fishing licenses, and also have a negative impact "on the minds of Bedouins" in the region. He thus made a strong recommendation to the coast guard's acting director-general, George Purvis Bey, that a survey commission should be assembled to delimit the boundary at once.[110] Purvis, in turn, forwarded all the pertinent information about Shalabi Mustafa's voyage to Cromer.[111]

In light of Cromer's professed uncertainty about the location of the western boundary back in 1902—as well as the persistence of voices within the British Foreign Office maintaining that "the only apparent reason for fixing Sollum as the boundary is tradition"[112]—his reaction to this recent episode was strikingly cocksure. He now argued that "the western frontier of Egypt has always been considered as beginning at Ras Jebel Sollum . . . to follow the crest of the ridge, and then to run in a south southwesterly direction, including the oases of Siwa and Jerhboub [*sic*]"; therefore, the construction of buildings by the Ottomans on the southern end of the ridge constituted a surefire act of "encroachment on the part of the Turkish troops in Tripoli." Moreover, Cromer asserted that the Ottoman claim to territory as far east as Marsa Matruh was "quite inadmissible," and that the Ottomans must be called upon "to immediately withdraw the detachment which has been sent to Sollum . . . which is attempting to exercise jurisdiction over what has always been regarded as Egyptian territory." Cromer ultimately decided that the British ambassador in Istanbul should file a formal complaint with the Sublime Porte, though he stipulated that no "allusion should be made" to the telltale 1841 map, which might provide evidence that was "more favorable to the claims of the Ottoman Government."[113]

Meanwhile, the Egyptian Coast Guard was taking matters into its own hands. On October 20, coast guard officer Sheehan Bey led a commission to Sollum. Sheehan first handed the Ottoman commanding officer a formal document of protest spelling out the British position that the Ottoman construction projects currently underway were illegal, since they were "on territory which was regarded as belonging to Egypt." Sheehan also accompanied the Ottoman officers to the top of the ridge in order to point out where the British thought the border commenced. Finally, Sheehan conducted more reconnaissance around the augmented Ottoman garrison, ultimately confirming Shalabi Mustafa's observation that the new buildings were much more formidable than the ones initially erected back in 1902, and that the Ottomans now enjoyed sweeping command over both Sollum's inner and outer harbors.[114]

Unsurprisingly, the Ottoman government took umbrage at Sheehan's presumptuous attempt to compel Ottoman forces to cease construction of their *karakolhane* and withdraw from Sollum. After learning of Sheehan's visit, officials at the Ottoman Interior Ministry underscored that Sollum was in fact within the bounds of the province of Benghazi. Moreover, the Ottomans used the Sheehan declaration as an opportunity to chastise the Egyptians for subverting the proper chain of command—dealing with this border issue as anything other than strictly an Ottoman imperial one, which ought to be handled internally, without British interference. After all, one official wrote, "Egypt is among the domains of the Imperial Sultan"; even if the Egyptian administration wanted to complain about the presence of the Ottoman *karakolhane* in the "border region [*hudud civarında*]," it was still necessary to take it up with the Sublime Porte, not with the British Residency.[115]

The British ambassador, Walter Townley, received similar censure from the Grand Vezir in Istanbul. According to Townley, the Grand Vezir opened the meeting by expressing his dismay that "an English officer in the service of the Egyptian Government should have been selected to convey the protest," since Egypt was still effectively under Ottoman sovereignty. The Grand Vezir then "proceeded to explain that he could not understand the contention that there had been an encroachment on Egyptian territory," since an Ottoman garrison had in fact been posted at Sollum for several years,[116] and reminded Townley that "Sollum was clearly marked in the map attached to the Firman" as belonging to the Sancak of Benghazi.[117] Not only were the Ottomans unwilling to back down, then, but now the sultan—in light of these new British protests against Ottoman activities in Sollum—also issued orders to complete the construction work there "as hastily as possible."[118]

A few months later, on February 13, 1905, Townley passed on another official declaration to the Ottoman minister of foreign affairs, ordering the Ottomans to "step down and stop with their pretention to exercise jurisdiction over territory that was always recognized as part of Egypt."[119] Cromer was willing to concede that the Ottomans could "occupy the ridge overlooking the harbor . . . this ridge having always been regarded as the frontier," but he remained adamant that the Egyptian government would "not recognize the right of the Turks to construct buildings on the beach," nor their claim to administer the harbor.[120]

The two sides were clearly at loggerheads, but the question of whether to delimit the border was once again tabled[121]—this time on account of a new round of bedouin hostilities that will be explored in depth in Chapter 6.

In this chapter, I have demonstrated how an amorphous desert frontier region, linking two territorially abstract Ottoman provinces, began to evolve into a contested borderland, marked by the emergence of a newfound sense of bounded political space on the part of both Egyptian and Ottoman state officials, as well as the local bedouin population. Over the second half of the nineteenth century, all of these parties gained an increasing awareness that claiming to be either in Egypt or Benghazi *mattered*, insofar as each side offered its own unique legal or economic advantages at particular historical moments.

Likewise, I have argued that bedouin mobility was perhaps the key catalyst forcing the Ottoman government to confront the limits of its own sovereign jurisdiction vis-à-vis Egypt, which came to represent an entirely different legal-political climate to the local inhabitants of the region at this time, as a function of its status as an autonomous province after 1841. Even if it is true that Ottoman taxation policies initiated a cyclic pattern of antagonistic relations between the state and the local Benghazi population, driving many tribesmen across the border to Egypt, it remains the case that it was the consequences of such bedouin mobility that, for the Ottomans, helped cement the idea of Egypt as a rival political entity in an emergent contested borderland. It was with this burgeoning sense of political rivalry in mind—based on a newfound understanding that sovereignty in this region, where Ottoman and Egyptian territorial claims overlapped, could only be exercised in *relational* terms—that the Ottomans decided to occupy Sollum in 1902.

The story of how this swath of the Eastern Sahara was territorialized as a contested borderland is therefore the story of the Ottoman and Egyptian states' increasing level of engagement with spatial practices on the local level. This was the mechanism that arguably governed the process of Ottoman state territorialization in marginal zones and internal borderlands throughout the empire in roughly the same period. Historian Reşat Kasaba, in his study of the key role that tribes played in late-Ottoman state making, has argued that the "institutionalization of the Ottoman state" must be seen as a "process unfolding in continuous relationship with other groups and elements of society." Kasaba in fact calls direct attention to how the ambiguous nature of Ottoman internal borderlands facilitated the constant movement of local populations that, in his view, defined the empire for most of its history: "There was always movement of people, goods, and ideas . . . that cut across internal divides as well as the borders of the Ottoman Empire. Consequently, both the imperial center and the modern state that emerged from it were deeply embedded in local practices, making it impossible to talk about centralization as having clear starting and end points."[122]

Seen in this light, the study of internal borderlands within the Ottoman Empire enables us to view Ottoman peripheral zones not as the final frontiers of a unidirectional process of state re-centralization, but rather as complex meeting points, where divergent social and spatial practices came into uneasy contact and compelled new sorts of responses from state and non-state actors alike. In the case of Benghazi, Ottoman re-centralization played out not only between two poles—center and periphery—but rather had a crucial regional dimension, ultimately spilling over into Egypt and contributing to the process of borderland territorialization in Egypt's western domains.

This process reached a fever pitch in the decade following the Ottoman occupation of Sollum. The border crisis that emerged as a result will be the subject of the next and final chapter.

FIGURE 1. The acting *ma'mur* of Siwa (seated center), surrounded by local shaykhs (Nov. 1911). Source: G. G. Hunter Collection. Reproduced by permission of Durham University Library.

FIGURE 2. The Mosque of Sidi Sulayman in Siwa (also referred to as the "Khedivial Mosque") under construction (Nov. 1911). Source: G. G. Hunter Collection. Reproduced by permission of Durham University Library.

**FIGURE 3.** Ahmad Shafiq and his entourage proceeding to the new Sidi ʿAwam Mosque in Marsa Matruh. Source: *Iftitāḥ Masjid Marsa Matruh*, 1910.

**FIGURE 4.** The Sidi ʿAwam Mosque in Marsa Matruh, on the day of its inauguration. Source: *Iftitāḥ Masjid Marsa Matruh*, 1910.

**FIGURE 5.** Ahmad Shafiq, members of his entourage, and local shaykhs outside the Sidi
'Awam Mosque on the day of its inauguration. Source: *Iftitāḥ Masjid Marsa Matruh*, 1910.

**FIGURE 6.** Group of Egyptian officials and an Ottoman
customs officer, in front of a telegraph office in Sidi Barrani
(Dec. 1911). Source: G .G. Hunter Collection. Reproduced
by permission of Durham University Library.

**FIGURE 7.** G. G. Hunter Pasha, director-general of the Egyptian Coast Guard Administration, outside a coast guard encampment in the Western Desert (Dec. 1911). Source: G. G. Hunter Collection. Reproduced by permission of Durham University Library.

**FIGURE 8.** Egyptian Coast Guard personnel on the shore at Sollum, prior to embarking (Dec. 1911). Source: G. G. Hunter Collection. Reproduced by permission of Durham University Library.

# 6

## The Emergence of Egypt's Western Border Conflict

On December 21, 1911, the small Ottoman garrison at Sollum—established with so much fanfare back in July 1902—abandoned its post. By this time, the Ottoman-Italian War had been raging for two months. The Italian naval blockade in the Eastern Mediterranean was fully operational, and, on October 3, Italian forces began to bombard and occupy several key towns along the Libyan coast, including Tripoli, Benghazi, Darna, and Tobruk. On October 10, Italian warships arrived at Sollum and began to take soundings around the harbor.[1] Despite Ottoman objections, two Italian destroyers patrolled the Bay of Sollum daily.[2]

The Ottoman commanding officer at Sollum was cavalier in the face of the impending Italian siege. He claimed that "he was not afraid of the Italians," and boasted that his men would "hold the post at all costs."[3] Nevertheless, the Ottoman government decided to cede provisional custodianship of Sollum to the Egyptian government, and move the troops further west.[4] Despite these orders from on high, the Ottoman officer was extremely reluctant to retreat from Sollum. George Hunter Pasha, the director-general of the Egyptian Coast Guard Administration, wrote that "it was the funniest procession he had ever seen—a long-legged Coast Guard Officer pacing while the Turkish Officer stopped every 100 yards to protest that he would die sooner than give up more territory" to the Egyptians.[5]

Within a month of the Ottoman withdrawal from Sollum, Lord Kitchener—the British consul-general of Egypt since July 1911—seized upon the uncertain political climate in the borderland to devise a new western border policy for the Egyptian government. After making a short visit to Sollum,[6] Kitchener ordered the Survey Department to issue a special reprint of an old "school map" of Egypt with all boundary lines purposely left blank, so that new ones could be drawn by hand.[7]

Kitchener then sketched two hypothetical boundary lines on the map. The first (Line A) represented a more maximalist territorial claim, commencing approximately six miles west of Sollum, and thereby including the oasis of Jaghbub as part of Egypt. The second (Line B), by contrast, was more conventional: originating from the heights of Sollum, it outlined a more limited swath of territory for Egypt. This map, filled in by Kitchener, became the basis for what the British authorities in the Egyptian government began to refer to as the "latest Western Frontier of Egypt." By the end of 1911, the so-called "Kitchener lines" had become a key British talking point in all diplomatic discussions concerning Egypt's western border.[8]

Taken together, the Ottoman evacuation of Sollum and the cartographic inscription of the Kitchener lines heralded a new phase in the formation of Egypt's western border. Although the Ottomans could not have known it when they handed Sollum over to the Egyptians, this was the beginning of the end of their sovereign rule in the Eastern Sahara. After the war, the British would now deal exclusively with the Italians, not the Ottomans, in negotiations over Egypt's western border. At the same time, once the Kitchener lines were sketched, the British became firmly committed to the idea of a formal border settlement—a radical departure from their official policy up to that point. Although the outbreak of the First World War would prolong the diplomatic process for another decade,[9] an agreement with Italy over the delimitation of the border was inevitable once Kitchener drew his lines in the sand.

Political geographers typically identify three distinct phases of border formation: allocation, delimitation, and demarcation.[10] According to J. R. V. Prescott, *allocation* refers to the first, most tentative stage of border definition, in which the interested parties settle upon loose, often arbitrary dividing lines in regions that are still relatively unknown. *Delimitation* strives "to eliminate this inconvenient uncertainty" of allocation, and often entails the dispatching of a survey commission to map a specific border trajectory.[11] Contending political actors typically agree to delimit an official border when the borderland in question is mutually understood to have acquired some palpable economic or strategic value; accordingly, most border disputes occur during this phase. Finally, *demarcation* is the act of inscribing, on the ground, the final borderline that was agreed upon during the delimitation process. Techniques of demarcation have ranged from the erection of security fences to the simple placement of cairns at regular intervals along a designated border route. Once demarcation occurs, the border is effectively settled. At this point, it is up to the states sharing the border to administer their respective territory on each side of it.[12]

Much social science scholarship on border formation has focused on the significance of borderlines only *after* they have been delimited and demarcated.[13] Historians of borderlands, by contrast, have tended to focus more on the messy process of delimitation. Some studies have emphasized the fraught diplomacy that preceded the signing of border-delimitation treaties; others have adduced evidence left behind by geographic explorers and border-survey commissions to destabilize the tidy mapped images that ultimately come to represent the contours of modern nation-states.[14]

The story I tell in this chapter is rather different. Over the decade before the Italian invasion of Libya in 1911, the formation of Egypt's western border never evolved beyond the abstract allocation phase. Even the proposed Kitchener lines, which nudged Egypt down the inexorable path toward signing a western border treaty, left the picture extremely fuzzy, merely foreshadowing a delimitation stage that was still far in the future.

What we see instead throughout this period are multiple, countervailing attempts at what Prescott terms "definition in principle"—one of two approaches to border allocation, whereby political actors assert territorial claims in an abstract, haphazard manner, typically without any meaningful knowledge of "the exact distribution or location of the physical features or cultural attributes" of the region in question.[15] In the case of Egypt's western borderland, what this meant in practice was that an array of political contenders—the Italians, the Ottomans, the British, and the local Egyptian authorities (the coast guard, most notably)—each began to contemplate the relative merits and disadvantages of transforming an indeterminate Ottoman "line of distinction" (*hatt-ı imtiyaz*), adjoining two territorially amorphous Ottoman provinces, into a de facto international border.

This chapter documents how an abstract sense of bounded political space within Egypt's western borderland continued to crystallize despite a prolonged and messy allocation process that never actually resolved any territorial questions. The decade prior to the Italian invasion was the critical period for advancing the dynamics of contestation—both between rival states, and between state and non-state actors—that governed borderland territorialization in this part of the Eastern Sahara. In what follows, then, I offer a comprehensive portrait of the emergence and intensification of a modern border conflict within Egypt's western borderland, culminating with the outbreak of the Ottoman-Italian War.

Some common threads run throughout the narrative. First, the Egyptian authorities proved far better equipped than their Ottoman counterparts to capitalize on the political space opened up by the bedouin unrest that erupted consistently throughout the decade. Consequently, the Ottomans grew increasingly desperate to reverse the tide of their waning authority vis-à-vis Egypt, which was now behaving increasingly like an independent nation-state outside the Ottoman imperial fold. The patent differences in how both states were exercising sovereignty in the region were not lost on the local bedouin population, which responded by making frequent appeals to the Egyptian government for protection and justice.

Second, the period witnessed a growing tension between disparate approaches to territoriality in the borderland. On one hand, the Italians consistently pushed for a formal diplomatic settlement that would mandate the delimitation and demarcation of an official borderline, thereby slicing the region into clear, cartographically precise territorial spheres. The Ottoman and Egyptian governments, on the other hand, remained extremely reluctant to delimit a border, opting instead to uphold an ambiguous status quo whereby each side tiptoed around the other's vague territorial claims. In this way, both governments could pursue their strategic interests and project their sovereign reach among the region's population without provoking a major diplomatic dispute—one they knew would expose uncomfortable tensions within the Egyptian-Ottoman relationship.

Although the events recounted in this chapter never yielded a definitive, universally agreed upon understanding of the border's true location—in fact, precisely *because of* this lingering territorial ambiguity—the strange brew of borderland politics came to a slow boil over the course of the decade. As a result, by the time of the Italian occupation, the basic contours of a modern political border separating two distinct territorial spheres had already crystallized, even if that dividing line was still impossible to draw on a map.

The Italian invasion of Libya in 1911 was actually a long time in the making. After the French occupation of Tunisia in 1881, the Italian government began to focus on Ottoman Libya as a potential fourth shore for its expansive imperial state. To clear the way for its strategic designs in the Eastern Sahara, the Italian government sought the assurance of various European powers that they would maintain a hands-off policy in the event of an Italian colonial occupation. Italy thus signed a *rapprochement politique* with France in December 1899, through which it gained the blessing of the French to do as it pleased in the Libyan provinces; in return, the Italians promised not to interfere with France's colonial project in Tunisia.

When the Italians turned to the British in order to gain similar assurance, however, the situation proved more complicated. In January 1902, Italy requested a formal declaration from the British, specifying that they had absolutely no designs on territory beyond Egypt's western border.[16] The Italians were particularly adamant due to their anxiety over the Anglo-French Convention, signed in 1899, which neglected to take Italy's African interests under consideration.

The British were reluctant to make any such promise. On one hand, they maintained that it was beyond their legal authority to make diplomatic decisions with regard to Ottoman sovereign territory.[17] On the other hand, the Italian demand alerted the British to just how poor a grasp they had of the political situation in the Egypt-Benghazi borderland. Cromer noted that the "Western frontier of Egypt has never been very clearly defined," and that the Anglo-French Convention of 1899 had settled "nothing . . . respecting the frontier North of the Tropic of Cancer."[18] The British were in fact so ignorant about the geography of the borderland that—when the Italians insisted on referring to the contested territory as "Cyrenaic Tripoli," rather than the "Province of Tripoli"[19]—the Intelligence Office in Cairo launched a special investigation to establish that "Cyrenaica and Tripoli are two different things."[20]

In light of all this confusion, the British decided that it was "inadvisable" to stake any specific claims as to the "exact frontier between Cyrenaica and Egypt," or to the "amount of hinterland to be accorded to Tripoli and Cyrenaica."[21] The Foreign Office thus refused to give Italy the official declaration it so urgently demanded, opting instead to make an informal "positive assurance" that the British had "no aggressive or ambitious designs" on the Libyan provinces.[22]

Even without an official British declaration, the Italians did not hesitate to stake out their position in the coveted Ottoman Libyan provinces.

In February 1902, Justin Alvarez (the British proconsul in Benghazi) reported on the arrival of an Italian steamer to take soundings in the harbors of Darna and Bomba.[23] In May, according to Alvarez, several Italian government agents arrived in Benghazi "for the purpose of setting on foot various enterprises of more or less public utility," including "a distillery; stores or warehouses; the dredging of the harbor and completion of the breakwater; [and] the construction of a railway along the coast from Benghazi to Derna."[24] A few months later, an Italian admiral visited with the European consulates in Benghazi, and Alvarez noted several officers taking measurements and surveying the port there.[25] At the same time, various Italian schemes to acquire large tracts of land in Tripoli and Benghazi got underway in this period, despite Ottoman restrictions on European landownership.[26]

The impending threat of an Italian colonial occupation was not lost on the local population. In June 1902, Alvarez learned that five hundred merchants from Tripoli had sent a petition to the Egyptian Khedive 'Abbas Hilmi requesting him to annex their country to Egypt. The impetus for this bold step was apparently the "great hatred of the Italians freely expressed" in both Libyan provinces, "on account of their [the Italians] making no secret of their designs on this country."[27] A few months later, another group of local notables declared that the annexation of Benghazi and Tripoli by the Egyptian Khedive was the best solution to the Italian menace: Ottoman and Muslim "susceptibilities would be thereby spared" if the Libyan provinces were prevented from falling into the hands of a European power.[28]

This short-lived annexation movement illustrates that certain segments of the local population saw the writing on the wall, anticipating that their lands were "going to be swallowed up" by Italy in the near future.[29] In turn, they began to envisage alternative territorial arrangements that would enable them to preserve Muslim, and indeed Ottoman, rule. But they were right to be wary of Italian designs: in 1904, when a new round of bedouin hostilities erupted throughout the Egypt-Benghazi borderland, the Italians were already firmly rooted in the region, and poised to emerge as a key player in the nascent inter-imperial border conflict.

The bitter conflict that broke out between the Benghazi-based 'Awaqir and Shihabat tribes in 1904 marked a turning point in the politics of the Egypt-Benghazi borderland. Its origins are not clear, however.[30] According to the testimony of various Shihabat tribesmen, a notorious

'Awaqir shaykh named 'Abd al-Qadir al-Kazza instigated the feud when he commanded the Shihabat to vacate their ancestral territory in the region around Wadi al-Bab. When the Shihabat refused, 'Abd al-Qadir al-Kazza led four hundred tribesmen in a violent attack that resulted in the murder of five Shihabat, as well as the death of his own son.[31] By contrast, the Ottoman governor (*mutasarrif*) of Benghazi suggested that it was the Shihabat who were responsible for igniting the blood feud, and that 'Abd al-Qadir al-Kazza's campaign at Wadi al-Bab was actually an act of retaliation.[32]

Whoever was to blame, the 'Awaqir quickly gained the upper hand. Within a few weeks, 'Abd al-Qadir al-Kazza led another attack, killing thirty-four Shihabat tribesmen and plundering four hundred camels and one thousand *ardeb*s of barley.[33] This second siege was intended to punish the Shihabat for their decision to appeal to the Ottoman authorities for protection.[34] The Shihabat had in fact pleaded their case to the Ottoman governor in Benghazi, but they were told that they should turn instead to the Sanusi leadership for assistance. The Sanusiyya, too, proved unable or unwilling to deal with 'Abd al-Qadir al-Kazza and his men.[35] Clearly running out of options—and understanding fully that "they were relatively weak compared to their adversaries"[36]—the Shihabat decided to seek refuge across the border with the Awlad 'Ali.

The Shihabat's flight only served to widen the conflict, implicating the Awlad 'Ali in what had begun as a smaller affair between two neighboring Benghazi tribes. Soon afterward, 'Abd al-Qadir al-Kazza led a raid on a group of Awlad 'Ali who were pasturing in Benghazi; he and his men seized eighty-five of the Awlad 'Ali's camels. This sent a strong message to the Awlad 'Ali: the 'Awaqir would not make any meaningful distinction between the Shihabat and their Awlad 'Ali protectors. Alarmed by this prospect, the Awlad 'Ali sent a group of shaykhs to Benghazi to appeal to the Ottoman authorities for recompense. As was the case with the Shihabat, however, the Ottomans could not offer any assistance.[37] The Awlad 'Ali retorted by threatening to raid any livestock caravans from Benghazi that passed through their territory en route to Egypt.[38] In the meantime, 'Abd al-Qadir al-Kazza amassed a force of three thousand men to continue the war against the Shihabat and Awlad 'Ali.[39] By mid-January 1905, bedouin tribes throughout the borderland were bracing for an imminent raid from the west.[40]

It was at this point that the Egyptian authorities stepped in to defuse the situation. In late January, Shalabi Mustafa—the same coast guard officer who had investigated the Ottoman occupation of Sollum back in 1902—arrived at a small Awlad 'Ali village near Sidi Barrani called al-Khur, where many of the Shihabat had settled. It was here that Shalabi Mustafa learned about the tremendous violence of the preceding months, as well as the impending threat from 'Abd al-Qadir al-Kazza's forces.

During his stay in town, Shalabi Mustafa received petitions from two separate groups of Awlad 'Ali tribesmen. The first enumerated the tribe's grievances against the 'Awaqir, and complained about the Benghazi government's inability to help them recover their stolen camels. The main objective of this petition was to implore Shalabi Mustafa—who, in the authors' words, represented "our Government"—to compel the Egyptians to represent their interests to the Ottoman authorities. They concluded with a warning that "if this cannot be done, we are prepared to take revenge ourselves and carry away a number of their camels equal to that taken from us."[41] The other petition was even more demonstrative in its show of allegiance to the Egyptian government, asserting that the victims of 'Abd al-Qadir al-Kazza's impending depredation would be those "bedouins living at the boundaries of Egypt and *belonging to the Egyptian Government*."[42]

Shalabi Mustafa's response was swift. First, he convened all of the Awlad 'Ali family heads and "explained to them that the Egyptian Government is taking steps with the authorities of Benghazi for the recovery of the camels" plundered by 'Abd al-Qadir al-Kazza. Shalabi Mustafa then "deputized" various tribal shaykhs, "holding them responsible for any disorder in their respective beats." Additionally, upon hearing that Ottoman officials from Benghazi recently had tried to collect taxes from tribes residing in Egypt, Shalabi Mustafa instructed the shaykhs not to cooperate with the Ottomans; instead, they were to "inform such collectors that if they [had] any claim to make they [were] to communicate with the Egyptian Government."[43] Finally, Shalabi Mustafa successfully lobbied for the construction of a permanent coast guard station at Sidi Barrani, which would house around fifty men. In Shalabi Mustafa's view, the new station would ensure that the "Bedouins will see the influence of the Government." At the same time, it would better enable the Egyptians to block the "interference of the Turkish authorities with Bedouins of Egyptian territory."[44]

Shalabi Mustafa's actions in response to the bedouin unrest constituted a robust new approach toward local governance in the western borderland. Capitalizing on the Ottomans' reluctance to intervene, Shalabi Mustafa stepped into the fray and promoted the idea that the coast guard—

the local administrative arm of the Egyptian government—would be a staunch ally for those "Bedouins belonging to us."[45] In turn, the Awlad ʿAli and their neighbors were keen to consider themselves Egyptian subjects, at least temporarily. This was a key turning point in how the bedouins related to the local Egyptian administration: as a result of Shalabi Mustafa's bold and innovative decision making on the spot, the Egyptian authorities managed to bolster their sovereign reach and legitimacy in the borderland.

The British Residency, ignorant of developments in the borderland until Shalabi Mustafa's reports made their way to Cairo, had no choice but to follow his lead and adopt the language he used to identify particular bedouin tribes. In a memo responding to the tribal hostilities, Cromer spoke openly about exercising control over "our Bedawin [*sic*]" (or "Egyptian Bedouins"), as well as the need to resolve the disputes "between Bedouin tribes belonging respectively to Turkey and to Egypt."[46] Moreover, by conflating the recent bedouin strife with other grievances against the Ottomans, Cromer framed recent developments in the West as if there was one overarching border conflict between the Egyptian and Ottoman governments. The new coast guard post at Sidi Barrani would therefore serve the dual purpose of bolstering Egyptian authority over the bedouins *and* "preventing encroachments on the part of the Turks." These were now seen as two discrete but related "questions involved in the dispute with the Turkish Government respecting the Western frontier of Egypt in the neighborhood of Sollum."[47]

In response to Shalabi Mustafa's recommendations, the British applied more pressure on the Ottoman government to prevent another raid by ʿAbd al-Qadir al-Kazza.[48] In their view, the entire "dangerous situation" had erupted due to "the license permitted to Bedouin on the Tripoli side of the frontier to raid Egyptian Bedouin with impunity."[49] At the same time, Ottoman officials in Benghazi were under fire from local merchants who were unable to move their livestock overland to Egypt on account of ongoing threats from the Awlad ʿAli.[50] When the Ottomans appealed to the Egyptian government to guarantee the safe passage of their merchants' flocks and herds, the Egyptians replied that they would "be happy to do so" if the Ottomans could ensure that the eighty-five plundered camels would be returned to their rightful owners in Egypt. But if the Ottomans were "unable to keep order among the Bedouin on their own side of the frontier," then the Egyptian government would not "shield them from the reprisals which are usual among Bedouin in such cases."[51]

The Ottomans took the Egyptian government at its word. Around mid-March, news arrived in Cairo that the 'Awaqir had finally returned the eighty-five plundered camels to the Awlad 'Ali, and that the three feuding tribes had reconciled.[52] With the crisis ostensibly defused, some British officials began to ponder the efficacy of an official border delimitation at this time. Yet this was quickly vetoed on the grounds that a clear territorial resolution to the question of contested Egyptian and Ottoman sovereignty in the borderland would be far more trouble than it was worth. As the British ambassador in Istanbul put it: "the direct intervention of His Majesty's Embassy in affairs touching the sovereignty of Egypt is always a delicate matter, and does not fail to arouse the susceptibilities of the Porte."[53] Despite having taken some concrete steps toward more effective administration in the western borderland, then, the Egyptian government still balked at the idea of defining a border and settling the territorial dispute with the Ottomans once and for all.

The cessation of bedouin hostilities in March 1905 ushered in a period of relative calm in the borderland. A few political developments kept tensions between the contesting state actors at a simmer, however.

First, the British dispatched a bedouin 'umda named Lamlum Bey al-Sa'adi to Benghazi to help mediate between several tribes. They felt that Lamlum, 'Abd al-Qadir al-Kazza's brother-in-law, would be a particularly "trustworthy emissary" to the 'Awaqir;[54] the local Ottoman authorities, too, were eager to have Lamlum's assistance.[55] British proconsul Alvarez noted that the Lamlum mission was "proceeding very satisfactorily,"[56] but Dumreicher interpreted it as a "failure" for the Egyptian government, since Lamlum "seemed to have been more anxious to smooth out the many differences between the Awagir and the Turkish Government than to occupy himself with the object of his mission." By Dumreicher's estimate, Lamlum managed to convince the Ottomans to pardon around 150 'Awaqir tribesmen who had been recently apprehended.[57] Indeed, as the Ottoman governor observed, Lamlum seemed to be "profiting" from his role as mediator while serving Ottoman interests.[58]

News of the Lamlum mission came to Italian officials in Benghazi on the heels of two other events they found similarly confounding. The first was the Khedive's visit to Siwa in winter 1906, which gave the Italians the false suspicion that the Khedive also visited Jaghbub, in what they felt was indisputably Cyrenaican territory.[59] The second was a small, "almost unobserved" event from the previous year that the vice-consul in Benghazi could only interpret as evidence of some diabolical Egyptian scheme. For the first time in memory, he wrote, "one of the usual large caravans" from Wadai had deviated from its typical route north through the Cyrenaican oases of Kufra, Jalo, and Awjila, opting instead to travel through Upper Egypt, via the western Egyptian oases. The vice-consul worried that "a new route has been inaugurated between Wadai and the Mediterranean that cuts outside of Cyrenaica."[60]

By linking together "the significance of these three facts, now associated with one another"—the Lamlum mission, the Khedive's western voyage, and the re-routing of the Wadai-Benghazi caravan route—the vice-consul concluded that the British must be taking measures to incorporate Cyrenaica into their sphere of influence, in violation of their agreement from 1902.[61] Like the British, then, Italian officials were connecting the dots between several discrete developments in the borderland, viewing them as different facets of one comprehensive border conflict that threatened their vital interests in the region.

In the meantime, the Ottoman and Egyptian governments continued to squabble over the location of their respective administrative outposts in the borderland. In spring 1905, the Ottoman government learned that the construction of the new Egyptian Coast Guard station at Sidi Barrani (known locally as "Bamba") was underway.[62] The Ottomans were also distressed by a report that segments of "the local population" were saying that "the area between Marsa Matruh and Sollum has been abandoned [metruk] to the Egyptians."[63] This all caused various Ottoman officials to fear that the Egyptian government intended to seize even more territory that did not "belong" to it.[64] In response, the Ottoman government allocated the necessary funds and manpower to bolster its military outposts at Sollum, Tobruk, and Darna.[65] At the same time, the Ottoman Cabinet resolved that Egypt should not be permitted to build or station military detachments in Bamba or Sollum. The Cabinet based its argument on the 1841 map, which it felt clarified beyond any doubt that the Egyptian government's latest advances were unacceptable.[66]

The Egyptian administration, baffled by this claim, retorted that the "aforementioned Port of Bamba is inside the Province of Benghazi, and is located a considerable distance to the West of the Port of Sollum," so that "there has not been any act of encroachment."[67] In this way, the Egyptian government betrayed its ignorance of the geography of the borderland region, by conflating "Bamba" (the alternate local name for Sidi Barrani, which the Egyptian Coast Guard was in fact occupying) with "Bomba," a town in Benghazi indisputably under Ottoman sovereignty. The Egyptian government also made the paradoxical claim that Sollum was at once "*inside* the bounds of Egypt [*dākhil al-ḥudūd al-Misriyya*]," while also "being the line of demarcation between Egypt and Benghazi" [*huwwa al-khaṭṭ al-fāṣil bayna Binghazi wa Misr*]."[68]

Against this backdrop of mounting diplomatic tensions, it would not take much to reignite the nascent border conflict. The fateful spark came in 1906, with the flare-up of more bedouin hostilities.

In January 1906, the ʿAwaqir launched a series of small-scale livestock raids, targeting various tribes on both sides of the border. Later that year, the ʿAwaqir plundered around a hundred camels from three different tribes.[69] The *maʾmur* of Marsa Matruh warned of the potentially grave consequences of the tribe's "insistent attacks made upon Bedouins living in Egyptian territory and under Egyptian protection."[70] At the same time, a completely separate cross-border feud—between the Awlad ʿAli and the Baraʿsa—was starting to heat up.[71] By the end of the year, a dangerous climate of tribal warfare had once again beset the borderland.

One episode in particular caught the attention of the Italian authorities in Benghazi. In the final days of 1906, the Benghazi vice-consul learned from a bedouin informant that six Egyptian soldiers, accompanied by six "Arab-Egyptians" of the Awlad ʿAli tribe, had recently crossed into Cyrenaican territory (meaning, Ottoman Benghazi) to pursue a group of Magharba tribesmen who had allegedly stolen a large number of camels from the Awlad ʿAli. The Egyptian team pursued the Magharba "all across the Cyrenaican hinterland" before they finally caught up with the thieves and managed to apprehend them.[72]

The Italians were concerned less with the fate of these tribesmen than with what this episode revealed about the flimsiness of Ottoman sovereignty in Benghazi. That an Egyptian military unit could cross over into Benghazi territory and carry out such an operation—a "veritable incursion," not more "trespassing"—"on their own devices, without the Ottoman authorities," was a clear indication of the striking "impotence" that had befallen the Ottoman government in the Libyan provinces.[73]

As was the case before, the Italians did not view this episode in isolation, but rather connected it with other developments in a way that suggested a broader political pattern emerging in the borderland. By "bringing together . . . this circumstance" with the Khedive's purported visit to Jaghbub as well as recent news about the progress of the Maryut Railway, the Italians could only conclude that the Egyptian government was pursuing its "proposed expansion of Egypt towards Cyrenaica." Gravely alarmed by this prospect, the Italians urged the British to agree to a definitive border settlement once and for all.[74] The British response was noncommittal, however. Cromer reminded the Italian consul-general in Tripoli that "any delimitation to which the Turkish Government was not a party would not be of very much value."[75]

By early 1907, the feud between the 'Awaqir and Shihabat reached a fever pitch. In February, the Egyptian and Ottoman governments agreed to convene a joint commission that would bring the warring tribes together for peace negotiations.[76] On February 10, an Egyptian Coast Guard steamer left Alexandria for Benghazi, carrying on board a delegation of Awlad 'Ali and Shihabat shaykhs under the command of the sub-*mudir* of Buhayra (Sa'id Bey Fahmi) and the *ma'mur* of Marsa Matruh (Muhammad Effendi Na'im).

There was much at stake with the joint bedouin commission. Both the Egyptian and Ottoman governments hoped it might pave the way for the "repatriation" of the Shihabat, as well as other Benghazi tribesmen who had been residing on the Egyptian side of the border. Since the Shihabat refused "to leave Egyptian territory, or to return to their old homes, until satisfactory guarantees" of their safety had been obtained, it was necessary to convince the 'Awaqir to return to the negotiating table in good faith.[77] In short, both governments agreed that such a step was crucial for restoring "public security" to the region. By adopting this position, they were essentially reaffirming the nascent notion, first introduced during the 1904–5 conflict, of distinct bedouin political membership in the borderland: peace and security were contingent upon the two governments' ability to keep the tribes on their respective sides of the border.

To the chagrin of the Ottomans and Egyptians alike, the joint commission was a huge failure. Soon after the arrival of the Egyptian delegation, the Benghazi governor sent a local 'Awaqir shaykh and Ottoman official to induce 'Abd al-Qadir al-Kazza to participate in the commission. When 'Abd al-Qadir al-Kazza refused, the governor dispatched six gendarmes to bring him forcibly to Benghazi, but this also came to nothing.[78] In the end, the Ottomans could not compel 'Abd al-Qadir al-Kazza to come to Benghazi, even though he resided only ten hours away.[79] The joint commission was dissolved soon thereafter, and the Egyptian delegation returned by ship to Alexandria, having nothing to show for their weeks-long mission.[80]

In the meantime, while the Egyptian delegation was waiting for 'Abd al-Qadir al-Kazza to show up in Benghazi, the other bedouin feud—between the Awlad 'Ali and Bara'sa—was intensifying. In March 1907, the Egyptian government received a petition from an Awlad 'Ali tribesman complaining of a recent raid by the Bara'sa: he was asking the government to secure the return of around three hundred plundered sheep, as well as a cache of weapons. Upon further investigation, the British discovered that the hostilities had begun with a murder the Awlad 'Ali committed against a Bara'sa tribesman by mistake.[81] Ever since, the two sides had been staging several raids back-and-forth across the border; by early spring 1907, these were growing increasingly violent.[82]

The Egyptian government, deeply alarmed by the prospect of an on-going, multipronged tribal war, began to consider a vigorous new adminis-trative approach in the western borderland. Cromer again invoked a sense of duty to those tribes dwelling on the Egyptian side of the border. This time, Cromer was so adamant that the Egyptian government was "morally bound to protect the Awlad 'Ali" that he warned it might be necessary to risk a diplomatic confrontation with the Ottomans by insisting on the delimitation of the western border. Even though "nothing could be further from the wishes of the Egyptian Government," in Cromer's view, "the duty of the Government to defend its subjects from attack in Egyptian territory is clear."[83]

Before taking such a drastic step, however, Cromer issued an ultima-tum to the Ottomans, giving them one last chance to pacify the unruly tribes on their side of the border. Cromer hoped the ultimatum would forestall a border delimitation: "The question of the western frontier is one which I am most anxious not to see raised, but, if this contingency is to be avoided, the Turkish Government must of necessity exert themselves seriously to put an end to the raids now being made by Turkish Bedouins on those dwelling on the Egyptian side of the frontier."[84] But if the Otto-mans could not take "vigorous steps to restore order among the Bedouins of Tripoli," and prevent the "chaos now existing" there, then the Egyptian government would consider itself "bound to protect" the Awlad 'Ali by any means possible,[85] and "the question of the Western frontier must almost inevitably arise."[86]

On March 23, the British ambassador in Istanbul delivered Cromer's ultimatum to the Grand Vezir, who took the threat to heart. Pinning the government's ongoing struggles on the personal "incompetency" of the former governor of Benghazi,[87] who had overseen the abortive joint bedouin commission, the Grand Vezir assured the British that the Ottoman government had just instructed the new governor to implement all necessary measures to prevent such disturbances between the tribes, which are a "result of their ignorance."[88]

In the meantime, the Egyptian Coast Guard took steps to elicit a lasting reconciliation between the Baraʿsa and Awlad ʿAli. Most notably, Yuzbashi Ahmad Effendi Fahmi (the new maʾmur of Marsa Matruh) dispatched a delegation to the Sanusi zawiya in Baraʿsa territory in Benghazi, "inducing [the Baraʿsa] to make and accept peace." Fahmi preferred the Sanusi option to the prospect of "entering in long and futile correspondence with [the Ottomans at] Benghazi."[89] Sanguine about a possible end to this long-standing feud, Cromer cited Fahmi's efforts as an example of how "the influence of the Egyptian Government over these tribes is due to moral and not to physical force," in stark contrast to the Ottomans, whose "influence over their tribes" was "practically non-existent."[90]

The Egyptian government took another important measure to bolster its sovereign capabilities in the borderland in the wake of the recent bedouin warfare. This was the establishment of a new coast guard camel corps, comprising around one hundred men, "for the sole purpose of keeping the peace between the two sets of Bedouins."[91] As Cromer noted, "the want of such a camel corps was greatly felt" the year before, "during the acute phase of the Sinai Peninsula question." This was an important upgrade to the coast guard's policing authority: in this way, a "regular force" would be "ready for service without withdrawing the Coast Guard from their regular work, for which their numbers [were] no more than adequate."[92]

Meanwhile, the Italians kept close watch over developments in the borderland. Once the Italian government discovered that an Egyptian delegation had landed at Benghazi, it grew more anxious about a potential British occupation of Cyrenaica. Although Italian intelligence reports maintained that the delegation had been sent solely to address the cross-border bedouin feuds, local officials did not seem to believe them. Instead, the Italians insisted that "the real reasons"[93] for the delegation revolved around a delimitation treaty they were not privy to.[94] At the same time, the Italian press was publishing frequent "unfounded reports that Egypt was going to occupy some oasis or other," which only compounded the Italian government's sense of panic.[95]

In response, the Italian government once again lobbied the British to authorize a joint border-delimitation commission—one that would completely exclude the Ottomans. The Italians also pitched a proposal for the location of the border, marking a line that commenced from a point east of Sollum and included both Jaghbub and Kufra as part of Cyrenaica.[96] The proposed border reflected the centrality of the lucrative Benghazi-Wadai caravan route in their thinking. As the Italian consul-general in Tripoli explained, only a border originating east of Sollum would ensure that all of the key nodes along the caravan route were incorporated "into Cyrenaican territory," while preventing the Egyptian government from using Siwa to "divert—in Egypt's favor—all the caravans that now come from Darfur and Wadai to Benghazi."[97]

The Italians' border proposal represents a case in which their conception of territoriality clashed with more local ones. In the Italian mindset, administration of the caravan trade required total control over the territory they intended to occupy, and this territory in turn had to be circumscribed with cartographic precision. But this was a fundamentally different approach to the governance of overland commercial traffic through the borderland than what the Ottomans pursued with their *Derbend-i Defne* tax (see Chapter 5). In the latter case, territorial sovereignty was not derived from comprehensive control over bounded political space, but rather from the regulation of movement across one key node of the commercial pathway.

The British found the Italian attempt at border allocation to be completely unacceptable. Not only were they unwilling to cede Sollum, but they also took issue with how the proposed line reached too far south into their sphere of influence as outlined in the 1899 Anglo-French declaration. As one Foreign Office official suggested, "The Italians are now claiming . . . more than is claimed even by the Turks."[98] Although the British wanted to "allay the feeling of unrest and suspicion" the Italians had been harboring,[99] they could not possibly accept such a brazen territorial claim from a power that as yet had no official status in the region.

Moreover, the British were still reluctant to undertake any diplomatic measures that might provoke a serious political dispute with the Ottomans—especially considering the drawn-out conflict a year prior, over the delimitation of Egypt's eastern boundary in the Sinai. As Foreign

Secretary Lord Grey put it, "for a year and a half it had been my endeavor to prevent the question of the Western frontier of Egypt being raised with the Turkish Government."[100] In marked contrast to Italian thinking, then, this was essentially a policy of upholding ambiguity as a key strategic principle. Based on the firm belief that an official border settlement would jeopardize their relationship with the Ottoman government, the British sought to avoid delimitation and demarcation at almost any cost.

After temporizing for several months, Grey informed the Italian minister of foreign affairs (the Marquis di San Giuliano) that the British rejected the Italian border proposal, on account of "the peculiar position in which Egypt stands with regard to Turkey, and of the existing sensitiveness shown by the Turkish Government last year respecting any definition of the frontier between Egypt and portions of the Turkish Empire." Grey merely offered his "general assurances" that the British would not encroach upon Cyrenaican territory, referring the Marquis to former Ambassador Walter Townley's official memo to the Ottomans from November 1904, which he argued was the definitive statement on the matter (see Chapter 5).[101] The Italians responded by urging the British to cede at least Jaghbub and, especially, Kufra to some future hypothetical Italian colony; as long as the Italians could be "reassured about Kufra," they were "willing to let the [border] question drop."[102] In late December, Grey informed the marquis that the British government would "regard Kufra as being in Turkish territory, and that the Egyptian government have never claimed it as belonging to them."[103]

While the British were hashing out their border policy toward the Italians, the Ottomans periodically challenged the Egyptian Coast Guard's sovereign claims along the coastline east of Sollum. In late May, the Ottoman commanding officer at Sollum led a small force to the settlement of Baqbaq (approximately twenty miles to the east). When the Egyptian Coast Guard officer stationed at Sidi Barrani, 'Ali Effendi Shahin, went to inquire about the purpose of this mission, the Ottoman officer told him he was investigating a rumor that the Egyptians intended to erect permanent barracks at Baqbaq.[104] The Ottoman officer also informed Shahin that he intended to press a number of bedouin tribes into paying their back taxes, which they had evaded on account of being outside the limits of the province. Shahin responded that, since "these Bedouins were now living in Egyptian territory . . . of course they should not pay."[105]

The Ottoman troops returned to Sollum a week or two later, but their short expedition to Baqbaq had a lasting impact. Some bedouins in the area soon complained to Egyptian Coast Guard officials and asked Dumreicher to prevent the Ottomans from returning "to Egyptian territory."[106] Ultimately, the Khedive intervened on behalf of the bedouins: in a letter to the Ottoman sultan, 'Abbas Hilmi argued that the recent Ottoman mission disturbed "the spirit of the bedouins who live in this locality, and [drew] attention to the security and public order that the Egyptian government strives to maintain there." The Khedive concluded by asserting that "it is necessary to prevent, in the future, the Egyptian frontier line from being crossed" by local Ottoman officials.[107]

But the Ottomans were back within a month. In late July, a force of around twenty men occupied 'Alam Tagdida, a settlement located fifteen miles east of Sollum. This time around, the Ottomans were more aggressive in pursuing the bedouins who had run away from their tax burden. According to the Egyptian officer sent to investigate, Ahmad Abu Shadi, the Ottomans had been "frightening the Bedouins by saying that forces are coming by sea and land" to collect what they could in arrears." Additionally, the Ottoman officer at 'Alam Tagdida ordered the Egyptian Coast Guard to stay away from the Ottoman camp, as "the Bedouins living there belong to the Turkish Government."[108]

The situation quickly devolved into a game of chicken between the Ottoman and Egyptian local authorities over each state's respective sovereign claims in the borderland. So long as the Ottomans remained at 'Alam Tagdida, the Egyptian Coast Guard refused to leave Baqbaq; but if the Ottomans agreed to withdraw the garrison, then the Egyptians would let go of Baqbaq.[109] The Ottoman government again argued that the Egyptians were occupying and building on territory that was west of the true boundary, which was clearly laid out on the 1841 map.[110] Once again, however, both sides backed down before a more serious crisis arose. The Ottomans, for their part, explained they were "most anxious to avoid the possibility of creating a political question in regard to the Turco-Egyptian frontier," given that "'they had not forgotten the Akaba incident.'"[111]

In other words, the Ottomans—like the British—shrewdly adopted ambiguity as a key political strategy with respect to Egypt's territorial limits in the western borderland. The lesson of the previous year's Sinai debacle was clear: to delimit and demarcate an autonomous province's contested internal boundary, or *hatt-ı imtiyaz*, was to risk losing whatever flexibility and freedom of action the Ottoman government still enjoyed there. For the government to agree to delimitation would mean to forfeit its capacity to project its sovereign reach among its inhabitants, just as it was trying to do by chasing the bedouins into Egypt and pressuring them to pay their arrears.

Just as this skirmish between the local Ottoman and Egyptian authorities was wrapping up, another outbreak of tribal violence shook the borderland. In August 1907, a group of Shihabat staged two separate raids against 'Awaqir tribesmen in Benghazi, thus breaching the supposed reconciliation between the two tribes that had been negotiated mere months earlier.[112] The crimes committed in this case were grave: in addition to a substantial amount of livestock being plundered, two 'Awaqir tribesmen were murdered.

Once the guilty parties were apprehended, government officials had to figure out the best course of action for bringing them to justice. The answer was not immediately obvious. Officials considered three different options: the offenders could be brought to Alexandria for trial in an Egyptian government court; they could be tried by a special tribunal of tribal shaykhs, under the supervision of a coast guard officer; or they could be handed over to the Ottoman authorities in Benghazi.[113]

To adopt the most suitable option, it was necessary first to determine the legal-political status of the Shihabat. One official thought the Alexandria option might be desirable, "assuming that they [were] 'Egyptians, *sujets locaux*,'" but worried that the location of the incidents, outside of Egypt, might complicate matters.[114] After further investigation, the Egyptian authorities concluded that the "men accused were 'Turkish Bedouins'" who had "migrated from Turkish into Egyptian territory" three years prior.[115] Consequently, they turned the Shihabat captives over to the Ottomans, convinced that "such administrative action . . . might forestall reprisals or an exaggerated importance being attached to the incident," and also that "a proceeding so unwelcome to the delinquents would act as a powerful deterrent" to other belligerent tribes.[116] On September 15, coast guard officers loaded the suspects (as well as the recovered livestock) onto a steamer and sailed to Tobruk, at which point they wiped their hands clean of the matter.[117]

The decision to hand the Shihabat criminals over to the Ottomans was met with some criticism. One Foreign Office agent warned against "relying on the Turkish authorities to keep the peace of *your* border" and suggested that the incident exposed the Ottoman government's lack of "adequate powers" for controlling the border on its own.[118] Ultimately, however, the officials' eagerness for the criminals to be "dealt with according to law," rather than being left to the vagaries of traditional bedouin justice, won the day.[119] It was a revealing moment. Despite their clear lack of faith in the local Ottoman authorities, Egyptian officials ultimately agreed that the Shihabat tribesmen's status as Ottoman subjects—"Turkish bedouins" who had merely been interloping on Egyptian soil—was the decisive factor. Extending the rule of law into the borderland, in their view, meant honoring such nascent (and often imprecise) territorial distinctions among the region's bedouin population. Accordingly, the Benghazi government would be left to deal with the Shihabat assailants however they liked.

After the year of protracted tumult that had beset the borderland beginning at the end of 1906, a short period of relative calm once again prevailed throughout the region. This enabled the various contenders in the burgeoning border conflict to regroup and pursue their respective interests as per usual.

The Italians redoubled their efforts to sidestep Ottoman restrictions and buy up large swaths of land (as well as livestock) in the Libyan provinces. These activities got a huge boost when the Banco di Roma opened branches in Benghazi and Tripoli in 1907.[120] The Italian vice-consulate in Benghazi also oversaw the establishment of three different schools—one of which offered free Italian language classes in the evenings, often attended by local merchants—as well as a new Catholic mission. The local population in Benghazi continued to interpret these initiatives as a sign of an impending Italian colonial occupation.[121]

The Ottomans, for their part, took new steps to bolster their sovereign authority in the borderland—including territory the Egyptians had claimed. First, the Ottomans increased their troop levels in eastern Benghazi, dispatching four hundred men toward the Egyptian border.[122] Second, they established another small outpost in the disputed territory east of Sollum, with the aim of preventing tribes from their side of the border from "evading the payment of customs dues on the export of sheep to Egypt." When the British asked the Ottomans to withdraw from the post, the Ottoman commandant refused. But the matter was soon tabled, as others had been in the past. Instead of confronting the Ottomans directly and risking a broader diplomatic dispute, the British simply set up a small outpost of their own nearby, in order to keep watch over Ottoman activities in the area.[123]

The Ottomans redoubled their efforts to pursue Benghazi tribes that they claimed were hiding out in Egypt to avoid taxation. In May 1908, the Ottoman commandant at Sollum sent five men into "Egyptian territory" to collect taxes from Shihabat tribesmen residing there. When questioned by Shalabi Mustafa, the commandant replied that he should "not ignore the habit that the bedouins have of always moving around from once place to another." The Ottoman commandant assured Shalabi Mustafa that he would "denounce them [the bedouins] to the requisite authorities," and there the matter seemed to end.[124]

These Ottoman efforts to extend and fortify their authority across the borderland came at a time of particular sensitivity in Istanbul with respect to the Egyptian government's increasing sovereign capabilities, which the Ottomans felt were gravely out of step with Egypt's status as an autonomous province. Indeed, in early 1909, according to a report from Yıldız Palace, the Ottomans were actively reconsidering their long-standing policy of devolution to the Egyptian military in certain areas. Whereas in the past, the Ottomans had allowed Egyptian gendarmes to protect Hajj caravans traveling through Sinai, and to administer other regions "not shown as Egypt" on the original 1841 map, the situation had changed completely now that the British Army was in control of Egypt, rendering the province "not fully independent." It was now far too risky to leave the Egyptian gendarmes to their own devices, since the country was no longer "under the full control of the Khedive."[125]

At stake was the very future of Egypt as an Ottoman autonomous province. The authors of the Yıldız report therefore took great pains to affirm that Egypt remained "an integral part of the Ottoman Empire [*Devlet-i Aliye'nin ecza-yı mütemmimesindendir*]," despite the de facto autonomy that had been granted to Mehmed 'Ali with the 1841 firman. They also addressed the potential consequences of delimiting the border now that the British were in charge of the Egyptian government. Particularly considering what had transpired in the former Ottoman-Egyptian provinces of Suakin and Massawa,[126] the lesson to be learned was that the determination of fixed boundaries within the Ottoman domains inevitably led to serious misunderstandings between the "sovereign and vassal state." In the case of Egypt, then, a boundary treaty "would be tantamount to recognizing Egypt as a foreign country," and therefore could only have "disastrous consequences."[127]

In short, the Ottoman government was clearly anxious that Egypt, under the auspices of the British, was in the process of breaking away from Istanbul and starting to assert itself as an independent nation-state. It was therefore necessary for the Ottomans to do everything in their power to reverse this trend. This included upholding their staunch commitment to scotching any move toward border delimitation. Once again, border ambiguity emerged as a vital tactic to avoid any major diplomatic disputes that would bring the imprimatur of international law to bear on the limits of the empire's territorial claims. Only by resisting delimitation could the Ottomans preserve whatever freedom of action they still had in Egypt's western borderland.

It was with this set of concerns in mind that, in the spring of 1909, the Ottomans tried to resolve the long-standing feud between the 'Awaqir and the Shihabat once and for all. Although officials were under no illusions about the failures of past Ottoman-Egyptian tribal commissions, the new CUP-led government placed the blame for these on the administrative shortcomings of the old prerevolutionary regime. The Ottomans convinced the Egyptian government that convening a new commission was still the best means to "safeguard public security, and to resolve the hostilities that [had] been ongoing for a long time between the bedouins of Benghazi and the bedouins of Egypt." The two governments agreed to assemble leading bedouin shaykhs from both sides at a summit in Sollum.

In setting up the summit, the Ottoman government knew there were much larger political questions at stake than the resolution of some lingering bedouin disputes. As noted by the *kaymakam* (subgovernor) of Darna, who was put in charge of the Ottoman delegation, the Egyptians had capitalized on the local bedouin feuds three years prior, by "annexing a section of territory from the eastern part of Darna, which is twice as large and more valuable than Belgium." The *kaymakam* was referring here to the Egyptian Coast Guard's advance as far as Baqbaq, which, being well to the west of Marsa Matruh, the Ottomans maintained was firmly within Ottoman sovereign territory by virtue of the 1841 map. Likewise, the *kaymakam* lamented that Egypt also now controlled a swath of territory that put them within forty-five miles of the oasis of Jalo, a pivotal crossroads for the Benghazi-Wadai caravan route. It was therefore imperative that this latest bedouin commission succeed where others before it had failed; Ottoman imperial sovereignty in the borderland depended on it.[128]

Much to the *kaymakam*'s horror, however, the commission was an unmitigated disaster for the Ottomans. The Porte had promised the Egyptian government that a number of notable 'Awaqir shaykhs would be in attendance, yet the local Ottoman authorities once again could not impel them to turn up. Moreover, as the *kaymakam* complained indignantly, he waited around in Sollum for an entire week without receiving so much as a word about whether the 'Awaqir were coming. Beyond the Ottoman authorities' inability to uphold their end of the bargain by producing the bedouins in question, the event also turned into something of a public relations debacle for the empire. The *kaymakam* noted sardonically that, while he and the other Ottoman officials had been made to look like the poor relations, waiting in vain for an entire week, the Egyptian delegation—"being governed according to the British rules of punctuality [*İngiliz usûlünce dakikası dakikasına idare edilmekte*]"—arrived precisely "on time at the right place." In addition, whereas the Ottoman delegation had traveled to Sollum on foot, the Egyptian delegation—"not wasting a moment"—had been outfitted with an impressive coast guard ship.[129]

In arguing his case to the Benghazi governor, the Darna *kaymakam*'s tone was remarkably strident. In his view, the Ottomans had already paid a serious political price in the past, losing territory around their borders because of poor administration in the face of the region's unyielding bedouin troubles. He reminded the governor that the conflict between the 'Awaqir and the Shihabat was "not the only issue that was the impetus for convening the commission"; countless other tribes—including the Egyptian-protected Awlad 'Ali—were embroiled in ongoing hostilities,[130] all of which would "yield serious consequences" for the political situation in the borderland. After all, he went on, "even if the current Egyptian administration is not [closely] following" all these troublesome events, "for us it is a matter of life and death [*bizim için bir mesele-yi hayatîye olduğuna*]."[131]

At the same time, the *kaymakam* implored his government to mobilize to help the Ottoman delegation save face in the eyes of their Egyptian counterparts, and thereby contain the damage already done to Ottoman prestige. Miraculously enough, the Ottomans would be given one more opportunity in which to do so: the Egyptians tentatively agreed to convene yet another bedouin commission at the beginning of the month of Şaban (around mid-August), even as they warned the *kaymakam* that "it would not be possible any more for their time to be wasted for no reason [*daha beyhüde izaa-yı vakit etmesi mümkün olamayacağı*]." The *kaymakam* wanted the next meeting to be held in Darna, but his own intelligence sources informed him that the Egyptian government would insist on holding it again in Sollum, "as if Sollum were actually the border between the two governments [*gûya ki Sollum, iki hükümetin hududu imiş*]." The *kaymakam* persistently urged his government to take adequate measures to ensure the commission's success. After all, he argued, "major problems" would ensue if "Egyptian officials once again came and went in vain."[132]

Taking the *kaymakam*'s desperate plea to heart, the Benghazi governor appealed to the Interior Ministry in Istanbul for assistance. The ability to assemble the ʿAwaqir shaykhs and transport them efficiently to Sollum was, according to the governor, a fundamental matter of "protecting the authority of the government." If the Ottoman authorities failed to bring about a settlement this time around, the Egyptian bedouins were threatening to "take matters into their own hands," which would only exacerbate the conflict.

More than anything, however, the governor expressed concern over the transportation situation in advance of the rescheduled summit. He argued that it would be impossible to reach Sollum by land by the beginning of Şaban—a serious problem, since it would be impossible to postpone the summit yet again. He also suggested that it would be damaging to "the government's honor" if their officials arrived by camel, since the Egyptian delegation would again be arriving in a special coast guard vessel. It was therefore necessary to procure an Ottoman ship for the occasion (which he felt was long overdue—he had been requesting a surveillance ship from the Naval Ministry ever since he assumed his post).[133] Ultimately, however, the governor was told that a ship was unlikely to be ready by the designated date, and that "it was necessary to find other means to transport" the delegation to Sollum.[134]

The Ottomans were clearly losing the public relations battle with the Egyptians, who once again demonstrated their superior sovereign capabilities toward the borderland's tribes.

As the decade wore on, it seemed as if the Ottoman and Egyptian governments could go on indefinitely dodging and parrying each other's advances in the borderland, without ever bothering to delimit an actual boundary. Again, both governments consistently articulated a clear preference *not* to delineate a clear-cut border. Instead, after weathering the crises brought on by the escalating bedouin tensions in 1904–5 and then again in 1906–7, the two sides seemed more or less content to monitor each other's activities in the borderland, only stepping in periodically to raise some cavils. This was the state of the border conflict in the summer of 1911, when the Egyptians and Ottomans began to squabble once more.

The issue of the day was the Ottoman government's wish to extend a telegraph line east of Sollum, to the outpost at 'Alam Tagdida which it had maintained ever since 1907. Although the coast guard had always tolerated this Ottoman garrison, the news that the Ottomans now wished to connect it to their network in Benghazi was distressing. As one official put it: "If the Turks continue their telegraph line . . . without any protest from us we should be giving away the principle that the Egyptian frontier starts from Sollum."[135] The British thus went through the usual motions, making an appeal through their embassy at Istanbul, and reminding the Porte of Britain's "1904 attitude" vis-à-vis the border question, stated most clearly in the Townley memo that the Ottomans had, of course, consistently ignored from the outset.[136]

In the end, it was only the Italians' unilateral decision to occupy the Ottoman Libyan provinces that fundamentally altered the political dynamics of the borderland, breaking the cycle by which the border crisis—the contours of which were by now fairly well defined—had periodically been invoked and debated, but never actually resolved. It was clear from the beginning of the Ottoman-Italian War that the rules of the game had suddenly changed. The Italians alarmed the British by establishing their naval blockade of the Mediterranean coast as far east as Ras al-Kana'is—the point near Marsa Matruh that the Ottomans had always claimed, on the basis of the 1841 map, to represent the actual border. The British felt this action marked off a swath of territory as "Turkish (ie, prospectively Italian)" that was far too extensive to be admissible. Accordingly, British officials—believing they had "no reason . . . to modify the views which they [had] hitherto held respecting Egyptian territory"—steeled themselves for an impending fight with the Italian government.[137]

It was not long, however, before the British embraced the eventuality of an Italian victory over the Ottomans. Soon after the initial shock of the Italian blockade had worn off, some Foreign Office officials began considering the idea of ceding Jaghbub to the Italians. One official noted that "the actual value of Jaghbub" to Egypt is doubtful, and that any power attempting to control it would lead to a "collision with Senussism."[138] Kitchener agreed with the assessment that Egypt had little use for Jaghbub, especially since, according to some British officials, it had "never been administered by the Egyptian Government" to begin with (despite their past reluctance to admit this).[139] This is apparently the moment when Kitchener—envisaging a new geopolitical reality without the Ottomans in the picture—started to consider new possibilities for pursuing Egypt's strategic interests in the borderland. In a memo to Foreign Secretary Grey, he argued that it "would not be desirable to withdraw from this position unless we got something in return," suggesting that they should only "abandon Egypt's claim to Jaghbub in return for an adequate quid pro quo."[140] It was only a month or so later that he traveled to Sollum and sketched the infamous "Kitchener lines" on a new proposed boundary map.

The Ottoman evacuation of Sollum at the end of December seemed to confirm the emerging sensibility among the engaged state powers that a new era was dawning in the borderland. By the end of January 1912, the British were coming to grips with the fact that they had "ultimately to deal with Italy and not with Turkey"[141] in thinking through their border policy. The Italians, for their part—treating their victory over the Ottomans as a fait accompli—asked the British not to "allude to the 1907 correspondence" any more, since that "would show that they already had designs on Tripoli" well before the actual occupation.[142]

The Ottomans, too, were forced to adjust to the new geopolitical reality in the borderland. On one hand, the government's official line once the war broke out was that the Egyptian takeover of Sollum was only provisional, and that the Ottoman military would reassume its post after the war ended. On the other hand, there is evidence that the Ottomans, too, were preparing for the eventuality of their defeat and subsequent loss of the Libyan provinces. In March 1912, the Ottoman Cabinet met to discuss the significance of Kitchener's "Line A"—the one that began twenty-five miles west of Sollum and thus represented the Egyptian government's maximalist territorial claim. Although the Cabinet strongly disapproved of this aggressive proposal, which would remove Jaghbub from Ottoman territory and threaten to extend Britain's sphere of influence far into the Benghazi interior, the Cabinet decided that it was crucial to put off any discussions about the boundary line until *after* the war.

The subtext of the Cabinet decision seems to be that, in the event of an Ottoman defeat, it would be preferable for Egypt, rather than Italy, to have control of the borderland. The Ottoman Cabinet was thus making one last-ditch effort to use ambiguity as a strategic tool. By avoiding a delimitation treaty at this juncture, the Ottomans hoped they could wait for the war's outcome before adopting a clear territorial policy in the borderland. If, in the event of an Ottoman defeat, the borderland could some-how remain under the sovereignty of Egypt—still technically an Ottoman province—then there might be some wiggle room for the Ottomans to reassert a modicum of control. It was a risky policy, as the Ottomans were well aware; but in light of the new reality on the ground, it was the best chance they had.[143]

The Ottoman-Italian War marked the end of a highly fluid and conten-tious period of border formation that never evolved beyond a tentative initial "allocation" phase. Although it would be another decade and a half before an actual border was delimited and demarcated, the remov-al of the Ottomans from the picture compelled the British to abandon their long-standing policy of border hedging, and prepare instead for an eventual diplomatic settlement with Italy—a rival colonial occupier that posed a different sort of threat to British interests than the Ottomans ever had.

Throughout the decade before 1911, the British and Ottoman governments deliberately avoided drawing an official border, fearing an uncomfortable diplomatic confrontation that would unearth deep unre-solved tensions within the Ottoman-Egyptian legal-political relationship. Only the Italians—seeking to enlarge the scope of their prospective colo-nial domains—consistently pressed for clear-cut territorial definition in the borderland. This Italian insistence on formally demarcated territorial-ity clashed with the multivalent, relational modes of territorial sovereignty that had been previously exercised in the region by both the Egyptian and Ottoman authorities.

By examining the dynamics of borderland formation *before* delimita-tion, we observe how an abstract sense of bounded political space became sharper despite the lack of a borderline. Once again, local actors' lived experiences of territoriality propelled events forward. Although it is un-clear if the region's bedouin tribes ever truly saw themselves as "Egyptian" or "Ottoman" during this period, they acted with a heightened awareness of their Eastern Saharan homeland as a contested borderland—a point of convergence between two distinct political spheres, bearing disparate sov-ereign capabilities and thus offering different advantages in terms of pro-tection and justice. At the same time, it was the constant mobility of these tribes across the invisible border—as well as their increasing tendency to articulate their claims in terms of bordered political identities—that compelled the state powers to think ever more seriously about the contours of political membership in the region.

In this climate of intensified inter-imperial contestation, there were clear winners and losers. It was in this pivotal decade that the Egyptian state's sovereign capabilities gained ascendance in the borderland. Most centrally, the Egyptian Coast Guard evolved to become the paramount arm of the Egyptian government in the region, more firmly integrated into the machinery of the state. This steady rise of Egyptian sovereign authority in the borderland caused the Ottomans great consternation. In response, from their new home base in Sollum, the local Ottoman authorities adopted a more aggressive approach to regional governance. Only in this way could the Ottomans mask, or attempt to reverse, the fundamental limitations of their own sovereignty in the Eastern Sahara—limitations that Egypt's recent assertiveness in the region had only exacerbated.

The stakes were perceived to be extremely high. This much Darna's *kaymakam* had made perfectly clear with his impassioned response to the disastrous bedouin summit of 1909, which he felt so palpably demonstrated Ottoman weakness vis-à-vis the Egyptians. As he sat idly in Sollum for a week, humiliated by the Ottomans' inability to keep up their end of the bargain, the *kaymakam* had a front-row view of his empire's ebbing sovereign grip over Egypt—an erstwhile autonomous province now starting to flex its muscles as a nascent independent nation-state.

# Conclusion
## Unsettling the Egyptian-Libyan Border

In hindsight, the Ottoman *kaymakam* of Darna had good reason to lament his empire's slipping grasp over Egypt. Whatever room for maneuver the Ottomans had hoped to retain in the borderland after their loss of the Libyan provinces to Italy in 1912 was foreclosed during World War I.[1]

In December 1914, the British formally severed Ottoman suzerainty over Egypt by declaring it a British protectorate, so that the British military could "adopt all measures necessary for the defence of Egypt and the protection of its inhabitants and interests."[2] The British also deposed 'Abbas Hilmi II and replaced him with his uncle, Husayn Kamil, now decorated with the title of "sultan." Over the course of the war, the Ottomans mounted a series of challenges to British rule in Egypt: in January 1915, Ottoman forces crossed the Sinai Peninsula and staged a fierce raid on the Suez Canal, in what would be the first skirmish in an ongoing Sinai campaign; and the Ottomans also encouraged Sanusi resistance in key locales across the Egyptian Western Desert. But these efforts proved unsuccessful. By February 1917, Ottoman forces (and their Sanusi proxies) had been decisively defeated on both the eastern and western fronts in Egypt, and the British campaign against the Ottomans headed north into Palestine.

The aftermath of the war witnessed the renewal of a protracted diplomatic struggle between the British and Italian governments over the western border of Egypt. This time around, however, with the removal of the Ottomans from the equation, the British were no longer under any illusions that they could temporize and avoid a formal delimitation agreement. Among the first points of tension to arise was the question of the

nationality of those "Libyans"—presumably many bedouin tribesmen—
who had been living in Egypt upon the outbreak of hostilities in 1914.

In April 1913, following its victory over the Ottomans, the Italian
government issued a proclamation stipulating that all "Libyans"—meaning
those born in the territories recently annexed from the Ottomans—would
henceforth become Italian subjects. The Egyptian government was not
inclined to agree, however. According to Egypt's foreign minister, "The
Egyptian Government never admitted that the change in the political status of Libya, an old Ottoman province, would have a retroactive effect on
Libyans already settled in Egypt. And it only consented, first and foremost,
to recognize as Italian subjects those Libyans who migrated to Egypt *after*
the annexation." This did not stop the Italians from reaching out to the
so-called "Libyan migrants" in Egypt. As the Egyptian foreign minister
observed, "a considerable number of Libyans residing in Egypt allowed
themselves to be registered in Italian consulates," and also received "the
most formal support on the part of these consular authorities." The situation escalated into an "acute conflict" that lasted until 1917, when—after a
"long and rather bitter correspondence with the Italian government"—the
Egyptian government agreed to cede those "Libyans" who had migrated
*before* the annexation, "provided they had arrived in Egypt at a relatively
recent date and maintained their ties with their country of origin."[3]

The matter of defining the two governments' respective spheres of
territorial sovereignty in the borderland was to prove even more troublesome. During World War I, the Italians had occupied the port town of al-
Bardiya (about twenty miles north of Sollum), in hopes of increasing their
diplomatic leverage with the British after the war. The location of a possible border was discussed briefly at the Paris Peace Conference of 1919, but
the two governments reached an impasse over control of Sollum, as well as
the question of whether the oasis of Jaghbub, the erstwhile headquarters of
the Sanusiyya Brotherhood, would ultimately be "Egyptian" or "Libyan."[4]
At the center of the debate were the two "Kitchener lines" from 1911—the
more territorially maximalist "Line A," which departed from the Mediterranean coast to the west of Sollum (from a point known as Ras al-Milha);
and "Line B," which departed from Beacon Point and thus yielded control
of al-Bardiya, as well as the strategic mountains around Sollum, to the
Italians. Both lines, however, established beyond any doubt that Jaghbub
would remain firmly within Egyptian territory.

In the years following the Paris talks, the Egyptian and Italian governments repeatedly clashed over their respective territorial claims vis-à-vis the Egyptian-Libyan border. The British remained particularly stubborn when it came to the Jaghbub question. According to a memo from the Egyptian financial counsellor, the British "had constantly maintained, in all its diplomatic correspondence, that Jaghbub was located in Egypt, and that this claim found its justification in all the old maps that could be consulted."[5] It was convenient for the British, of course, that the one map that mattered more than all the others—the Ottoman map appended to the 1841 firman—was nowhere to be found at this time. Moreover, according to the financial counsellor, the possession of Jaghbub, "where the tomb of the Grand Sanusi was located, was advantageous for Egypt as a point of protection against any attacks directed towards the Oasis of Siwa." But the Italians were adamant that Jaghbub must be annexed to their new Libyan colonies. In their view, the Sanusi connection was crucial: given that "Sanusis were much more numerous in Tripoli than in Egypt," it was only logical that a Sanusi stronghold such as Jaghbub should be under Italian sovereignty.[6]

Matters took an interesting turn in 1921, with the convening of an Egyptian "military commission" under the presidency of Mahmud 'Azmi Pasha, the former Siwan ma'mur and key player in the 1909 murder case, now a military general (liwa). Under 'Azmi's direction, the commission investigated all the borders of Egypt, adopting some now-familiar nationalist positions on Egypt's territorial integrity (for instance, that the Sudan "forms an undivided part of Egypt"). When it came to the western border, however, the members of 'Azmi's commission were somewhat more flexible. Of paramount importance, in their view, was the issue of military defense: 'Azmi claimed it "was necessary that the frontier between Egypt and Tripoli should be such as would allow Egypt to defend itself whenever attacked. Such defense could not be easily effected unless the frontier were to begin West of the Port of Bardia." Accordingly, the commission arrived at the firm conclusion that Kitchener's "Line A" should be considered the most suitable boundary line for the defense of Egypt"; only in this way would "Sollum and all the surrounding mountains . . . be in the possession of the Egyptian government."[7] Control of Sollum and its environs was doubly important "on account of the fact that there [were] no other points that could be used for defense purposes between Sollum and Matruh."

At the same time, however, the military commission was prepared to make a major concession in order to safeguard the military defense of

Sollum. According to military engineer ʿAbd al-Qawi Effendi Ahmad, "it is therefore necessary that this line [Line A] be adopted even if Egypt were to sacrifice part of its territory near Jaghbub and give the Oasis of Jaghbub to Italy," especially since the oasis was "regarded by Italy as essential for her because of the fact that it is the headquarters of the Sanusis, whom she wishes to have under her authority."[8] Considerations of this particular compromise would continue to underlie Egyptian strategic thinking throughout the border negotiations.

A year later—against the backdrop of Egypt's qualified independence, which it gained from Britain on February 22, 1922—the Egyptian government took another important step toward achieving a final resolution to the western border conflict. In July 1922, the Council of Ministers appointed an "Egyptian commission of military experts" to survey the western borderland and undertake the necessary inspection work in advance of an ultimate diplomatic settlement with Italy. The commission was led by Ibrahim Fathi—Egyptian minister of war and the navy—and included ʿAzmi as well as two other officers; they also tapped several officials from the Frontier Districts Administration to serve as their guides.[9] On August 23, 1922, the commission left Alexandria for Marsa Matruh and traveled throughout the region for nearly two weeks (including stops in Sollum, Siwa, and al-Bardiya).[10]

Upon its return to Cairo, the commission issued a formal report to the Council of Ministers regarding the desired location of the border. Similar to what ʿAzmi's military commission had determined a year prior, Fathi and his men recommended drawing a boundary that roughly followed Kitchener's "Line A," departing from the Mediterranean coast at a point ten kilometers north of Sollum. Fathi's commission did not necessarily agree that Jaghbub should be sacrificed, however. As they put it in their report, Jaghbub "is an Egyptian possession as indicated by a French map from 1827 as well as a German map. It is very close to Siwa, which makes it part of the Kingdom of Egypt. The inhabitants of the two oases are linked by all sorts of relations. Many inhabitants of Cyrenaica . . . are Sanusis. It is possible they will threaten the security of this border, as took place during the Great War."[11] Yet Fathi (like ʿAbd al-Qawi Effendi Ahmad before him) was resigned to the possibility that Jaghbub would ultimately have to be sacrificed. In a private memo to the Council of Ministers, he proposed an even more territorially maximalist line as "compensation for the loss of Jaghbub"—one that would "encompass within Egyptian territory a band of terrain on the Mediterranean coast extending from Wadi al-Ramla until a point 10 kilometers to the north of Bardiya, or 30 kilometers to the north of Sollum."[12]

Even with Fathi's commission's recommendations in hand, the Egyptian government refrained from adopting any official policy decision at this time.[13] Consequently, negotiations over the border stalled for another couple of years, even as the Italians consistently pressed for a resolution. The situation reached a fever pitch in the summer of 1924. The Italians—desperate to curb the flow of arms from Egypt into Cyrenaica, where 'Umar Mukhtar's anti-colonial insurgency was well underway—augmented their military presence in several locales around Sollum. By September 1924, Italian garrisons in the area comprised over seven hundred men, along with "30–40 Fiat cars, 26 Ford Cars, and 2 aeroplanes."[14]

The Egyptian government also learned at this time that the Italians intended to occupy the disputed oasis of Jaghbub. This news created quite a stir among members of the Egyptian Council of Ministers, even though they seemed strikingly uninformed on the particulars of the Jaghbub question. In its session on August 3, 1924, for instance, the Council puzzled over the existence of two seemingly discrete oases in all the extant documentation on the western borderland: "Jaghbub" and "Jarabub."[15] Two days later, in a letter to an Italian envoy, Egyptian Foreign Minister Ahmad Ziwar argued stridently that Egypt would insist on its "undisputed and inalienable rights over 'Jaghbub' and 'Jarabub.'" This prompted a swift response from the Italian envoy, gently admonishing Ziwar that "Jaghbub" and "Jarabub" were in fact one and the same: "the oasis that contains the tomb of the founder of the Sanusi Brotherhood."[16]

This standoff between Egyptian and Italian forces in the summer of 1924 set in motion an intense year-long process that would culminate, at long last, with the signing of an official border treaty. According to A. W. Green, commandant of the Sollum District of the FDA's Western Desert Province, Italian officials were now adamant that the international border must be settled, since "Egypt had no right to attempt to impose on Italy a line which would limit the latter's activities in attempting to prevent arms, supplies, etc. reaching the rebels in Cyrenaica." Green concluded by underscoring how this new round of Italian escalation made a final border resolution imminent: "Egypt therefore may in all probability in the extremely near future find herself called upon to either accept the conditions laid down by Italy . . . which will involve the entire loss of the very considerable trade Egypt now enjoys with the West in addition to her loss of her prestige among the Arab peoples; or to be prepared to abide by the consequences that a refusal to comply with the Italian demands may entail."[17]

Once Egyptian officials in Cairo ascertained the facts on the ground, it appears that the fluidity of identity among the borderland's bedouins again figured decisively in the government's thinking. Egyptian officials were reluctant to become involved with Italy's struggle against Mukhtar and the Cyrenaican rebels, out of fear of alienating Egypt's own bedouin population. As General Parker Pasha, the director-general of the FDA, put it:

It is neither the duty nor the wish of the Egyptian Government to involve itself in the Italian struggle with the Arabs. These Arabs over a large area of both the Italian and the Egyptian spheres of influence are indivisibly one in sympathy and feeling; and this in fact makes it impossible for Egypt to take measures against tribes, even though recognized as living within the Italian sphere, without alienating Arabs of the Western Desert, who have hitherto, since the War, been friendly and obedient to the Egyptian government.[18]

In the ensuing months, the Egyptian Council of Ministers weighed its fierce commitment to securing Jaghbub within Egyptian territory against its profound anxiety about being drawn into a wider conflict with Italy, particularly once Italian special forces intensified their counterinsurgency operations around Jabal al-Akhdar late in 1924.

In April 1925, after months of deliberations, the Council of Ministers authorized the Ministry of War to dispatch another fact-finding western border commission. This time it was to be led by the recently appointed director-general of the Frontier Districts Administration, Ahmad Shafiq, who, as we saw in Chapter 4, was formerly a close confidant of the Khedive 'Abbas Hilmi II and had served as public director of the *Diwan al-Awqaf* under him.[19] Shafiq's commission was tasked with two main objectives: addressing the question of Egypt's "strategic defense" in the region (yet again); and determining the possible repercussions of an "eventual abandonment of Jaghbub to Italy" from both a political and commercial point of view.[20] Following in the footsteps of Fathi's commission three years prior, Shafiq and his men departed from the port of Alexandria on April 5, 1925; they, too, would undertake a comprehensive two-week-long tour of inspection across the western borderland.

In their report back to the government, the members of Shafiq's commission held fast to a territorially maximalist position vis-à-vis Italian claims. First, they defended the proposed boundary line that Fathi's commission had recommended back in 1922. On the basis of their own survey work, as well as a careful perusal of different border maps from over the years (including Kitchener's), they claimed that this line—departing from the seacoast at a point approximately ten kilometers northwest of Sollum—was the only acceptable solution from the standpoint of military defense. Additionally, they argued strongly against the cession of Jaghbub to Italy. They feared that such a move would "provoke all the Arabs established on Egyptian territory for several reasons, the principal one being of a religious nature." After all, they continued, "Jaghbub is considered by the Arabs to be the Mecca of the Desert, and the tomb of the Grand Sanusi is like the Ka'ba. . . . They have their students there from all the tribes to learn the Qur'an." The commission thus affirmed that "the trust of the Arabs of Egypt would be completely shaken with regard to this country if they learned that Egypt had ceded Jaghbub to a foreign power."[21]

On the other hand, the commission also offered an economic rationale for holding onto Jaghbub. Customs revenues on imports and exports to Sollum and Siwa had "reached around 19,000 Egyptian pounds in 1924, according to official statistics," and consequently "the cession of Jaghbub would divert these revenues to the profit of Italy." Moreover, even though they acknowledged that this sum was "relatively small when compared with the international difficulties" that might arise, the commission officials argued that the moral as well as material cost would be high when the Jaghbub issue was considered from "the point of view of commercial and political exchange among the Arabs of the two countries, related to each other by kinship ties." Ultimately, the harm caused by the loss of Jaghbub "would be great, especially since commerce is in a state of continuous development and would, in the absence of the troubles of recent years and the difficulties between the Arabs and Italians, reach double the amount cited above."[22]

The Egyptian government was not entirely persuaded by the commission's report, however. Shortly afterward, in May 1925, the Ministry of Foreign Affairs ordered its ambassador in Turkey to search for the elusive 1841 map in the Ottoman archives in Istanbul.[23] Officials in Cairo apparently sought even more evidence upon which to build their case against Italy, though the 1841 map would not actually arrive back in Cairo until a week after the official western border treaty was signed. Ultimately, the

Egyptian government opted for the diplomatic compromise that Shafiq's commission had argued so stridently against: Jaghbub would be ceded to the Italians, in exchange for a border that would place the strategic heights around Sollum firmly within Egyptian territory. To address their concern about the potentially destabilizing effect of this settlement on the borderland's bedouin population, the Egyptian foreign minister, Ahmad Ziwar, made a special plea to his Italian counterpart, imploring the Italian authorities to "respect the religious freedom of the people" as well as to protect the tomb of the Grand Sanusi.[24]

The border agreement signed by the Italian and Egyptian governments on December 6, 1925, marked the official close of the long, drawnout process of borderland territorialization that has been the focus of this book. After applying constant pressure for over two decades, the Italians finally succeeded in securing the Egyptian government's consent for an official delimitation of the western border. The broad swath of the Eastern Sahara that had emerged gradually, over the second half of the nineteenth century, as a contested borderland was now transformed into two politically distinct "bordered lands."[25] Article 1 of the treaty carefully outlined the southward trajectory of the border: departing from a point along the Mediterranean coast ten kilometers northwest of Sollum, as the Egyptians had urged, the line took an irregular, sinuous path until it reached the twenty-ninth parallel north. At this point the border adopted a linear course, precisely tracing the twenty-fifth meridian east until it reached the twenty-second parallel north (the dividing line between Egypt and Sudan).[26] Delimited in this way, the borderline would pass about twenty-two miles east of Jaghbub, thereby placing the oasis firmly within Libyan territory.

But the western border agreement of 1925 actually left quite a bit unsettled. Article 4 acknowledged the continuation of the "free passage of caravans" between (Egyptian) Sollum and (Libyan) Jaghbub; at the same time, these caravans would be exempt from paying any taxes or duties. Article 5 gave permission to Egyptian subjects to cross into Libya from Sollum to obtain potable water from the wells at Ramla. Finally, articles 3 and 8 provided for the establishment of a "mixed commission" to consider a series of questions that could not be settled prior to the signing of the treaty. Most centrally, there was the lingering issue of whether inhabitants of the region within the ten-kilometer radius north of Sollum, as well as the area around Jaghbub, might be granted the "right to choose" their nationality.

But the mixed commission was also tasked with determining "pasturage, watering, and seeding rights" for the nomadic populations that regularly crossed the border, as well as establishing an equitable customs regime, and settling outstanding judicial questions for those "individuals living in a state of nomadism" in the vicinity of the border.[27] For a treaty designed to define the territorial limits of Egypt and (Italian) Libya once and for all, it is striking how much both governments labored to accommodate the continuous mobility of the borderland denizens, who now found themselves living astride a bona fide international border for the first time.

The relative slackness of the new border was underscored in a second Egyptian-Italian treaty signed nearly a year later, on November 9, 1926, following months of deliberations by the mixed Italian-Egyptian commission that had been convened in accordance with the provisions of the December 1925 settlement.[28] Although the new treaty redressed some lingering ambiguities in the *delimitation* of the northern part of the border,[29] by providing a more precise description of the line's southward trajectory up until it merged with the twenty-fifth meridian east, the treaty's provisions for the border's *demarcation* were still fairly lax. In fact, the commission did not mandate the placement of any signs or cairns south of the twenty-ninth parallel north (about seventy-five miles south of Sollum).[30]

The mixed commission's decision to demarcate only the northernmost stretch of the new border left the treaty vulnerable to ongoing political contestation. In 1932, British and Italian authorities resumed their feud—this time over the southernmost portion of the border, in the region known as the Sarra Triangle, lying at the intersection of Egypt, Libya, and the Sudan.[31] Oddly enough, the fateful 1841 map of Egypt once again lay at the center of the dispute. The British doubted the authenticity of the map the Egyptian ambassador to Turkey had produced in 1925, and consequently appealed to their own ambassador to conduct another search in the Ottoman archives. In March 1934, he discovered a different version of the 1841 map—one printed on silk and deemed by Foreign Office experts to be the original.[32] Ironically, however, this second map proved useless to the British,[33] and ultimately wound up buried in the British Foreign Office archives, only to be rediscovered several decades later by Gideon Biger, an Israeli researcher investigating the historical geography of the Sinai Peninsula.[34]

Questions over the indeterminacy of the western border's location resurfaced a few years later, when, at the request of the FDA, the Egyptian

Survey Department authorized another joint Egyptian-Italian demarcation commission. In April 1938, this commission erected twenty new "special beacons" to replace the provisional markers that had been laid down in 1926–27. Even then, all the commission's work extended only as far south as the twenty-ninth parallel north; most of the border therefore remained wide open, as ever. This failure to demarcate much of the border with precision gave rise to another dispute in the years following World War II, when Egypt began to reassert its claims over key borderland locations such as al-Bardiya and Jaghbub. Even as late as 1966, the boundary had been demarcated for only 206 out of its approximately 693 miles.[35] Things came to a head yet again in July 1977, with the outbreak of a four-day border war between Egypt and Libya, following Egyptian accusations that Qaddafi's government was plotting to seize the oasis of Siwa.[36] In the aftermath of the fighting, which left one hundred Egyptians and four hundred Libyans dead or wounded, the two governments once again scrambled to reach a decisive agreement that would prevent any further border disputes.[37]

If the Egyptian-Italian agreements of 1925–26 thus left the border's location open to several more decades of intermittent political contestation, they also failed to resolve the vexing question of nationality for the local borderland population. In the case of the territory within ten kilometers to the north of Sollum, the mixed commission determined that "there are no true 'inhabitants,'" since "the individuals who stay in this zone from time to time, and have the rights to use the wells and gardens found there, belong to some well-known 'bayt' families." Accordingly, it was not necessary to impose any nationality law in that area.[38]

Matters were far more complicated when it came to Jaghbub, however. In that case, the mixed commission was hamstrung by its inability even to "agree on the definition of the term 'inhabitants'" as it had been rendered in the December 1925 treaty. While the Italian and Egyptian delegations agreed that the right to choose between Egyptian and Italian nationality would be offered to those who could rightfully claim to be "inhabitants" of Jaghbub, the situation was moot if it could not be determined who was an inhabitant to begin with. The crux of the dispute was how to establish residency—whether, as the Egyptians argued, "Jaghbubians" were necessarily those who had been born in the oasis or established a "fixed residence" there for a period of, say, ten years; or else, as the Italians retorted, whether it was sufficient for an individual to have made Jaghbub his "ordinary residence" at some point during the period between the end of the Ottoman-Italian War in 1912 and the December 1925 treaty. Unable to agree on a set of fixed criteria to determine permanent residency in this historic Eastern Saharan crossroads, where mobility across the "border" was the norm, the mixed commission ultimately punted the matter to the two governments in hopes that further diplomatic negotiations might settle the question of borderland nationality once and for all.[39] It is unclear whether such negotiations ever took place.

Peter Sahlins has argued that "the zonal character of the frontier persists after the delimitation of a boundary line," despite what nationalist ideologues or national maps might attest.[40] In light of the foregoing analysis, there is no doubt that Sahlins's point holds true for the Egyptian-Libyan borderland after the delimitation agreements of 1925–26. But the case of the Egyptian-Libyan borderland—partly due to the way the border treaties officially inscribed the malleable "zonal" character of the local population's political identity—raises yet more profound questions about the limitations of the Egyptian state's sovereign claims in its western periphery, even after the border was drawn. The ongoing elusiveness of Egyptian territorial sovereignty in the West, and the shortcomings of the government's efforts to circumscribe a distinctively Egyptian body politic in this predominantly bedouin region, were in fact thrown into high relief during one suggestive episode from World War II.

On November 25, 1940, a few months after the North African Campaign was underway, a group of bedouins from the Egyptian Western Desert sent a long petition to Egypt's Ministry of Defense.[41] These bedouins had recently been arrested and thrown into a prison for foreigners, and their families were suffering gravely in their absence; they thus demanded an explanation for why they were being victimized as if they weren't really Egyptians. As they put it in the petition: "We are your subjects [naḥnu ri'āyakum], and if the government does not want us to be its subjects, we implore you to let us know the name of a state that we can join in order to request compensation for our families for the duration of the time we are in prison." The rest of the petition, interlaced with similar moments of sarcasm, constituted a scathing indictment of the government's treatment of the bedouins as if they were strangers in their native land. As they concluded, "We truly believe that we do not belong to the Egyptian government; for, if we did belong to it, adhering to its laws, it would not subject us to treatment as foreigners."[42]

That the Egyptian government seemed to regard its Western Desert bedouin population with such suspicion and contempt at this critical juncture raises questions about its very faith in the mechanisms through which Egyptian territorial sovereignty arrived in the country's borderlands. A decade and a half after independence, and the subsequent delimitation of the western border, Egypt was still a state bereft of a cohesive nation. The Egyptian state had not managed to forge a unified sense of nationhood across its newly delineated territorial domain, so that when war erupted once again onto Egyptian soil, the bedouins of the Western Desert were automatically viewed as a dangerous fifth column.

Historian David Ludden has described spatial history in Asia over the *longue durée* as an ongoing series of "contested transactions between mobility and territorialism." According to this view, forces of mobility and territorialism are not intrinsically antagonistic, but rather coexist symbiotically—they "need one another and live together, however roughly, because mobile forms of social life intersect settled environs and escape control by settled authority." Indeed, "territorial forms always include mobile spaces that overlap, transect, perforate, inform, enrich, and challenge territorial order."[43]

At the same time, however, the overarching spatial logic of modernity has been to conceal this symbiotic relationship between territorialism and mobility—to "habitually bury mobility inside territorial order," as Ludden puts it, so that territorial states emerge as the ostensibly natural container, indeed the telos, of a given region's history. With the aid of scientific mapping and border demarcation as its paramount spatial technologies, "modernity consigned human mobility to the dusty dark corners of archives that document the hegemonic space of national territorialism. As a result, we imagine that mobility is border crossing, as though borders came first, and mobility, second."[44] But the truth is more complex. Even as national maps unyieldingly strive to "conceal the pervasive importance of mobility in the ever present past of boundary making," the fact remains that "most if not all human societies emerge inside mobile geographies, where attachments to territory always change with the times."[45] Accordingly, national border formation can never truly compartmentalize a region's history; on the contrary, it is precisely the ongoing transactions between mobility and territorialism that regularly "make and remake boundaries."[46]

This has been the case for Egypt as much as it has for the South Asian milieu that Ludden describes. Moreover, the dynamic interplay between the forces of mobility and nation-state territoriality that I have documented throughout this book did not suddenly cease with the demarcation of an international boundary with Libya in 1925–26, as the case of the Western bedouins' plight during World War II attests. Instead, Egypt's western borderland remained the site of ongoing contestation between the Egyptian state's territorial ideal of bounded, uniform, centralized national sovereignty, and lived experiences of territoriality that were ever shifting, dynamic, overlapping, and mobile.

The bounds of Egypt's national territoriality in the western borderland are still being actively negotiated in the present day. On one hand, the Egyptian government refuses to give up on its long-standing dream of making the Western Desert bloom. President 'Abd al-Fattah al-Sisi—following in the footsteps of 'Abbas Hilmi II, that great early pioneer of Western Desert development—has recently launched a series of initiatives to increase Egypt's cultivable territory while, it is hoped, encouraging the settlement of millions of Egyptians beyond the confines of the Nile Valley. The "1.5 Million Feddans project," for instance, will involve the drilling of thirteen hundred wells, and the construction of several new towns throughout the vast, empty West. At the same time, al-Sisi has revived a notorious Mubarak-era agricultural expansion project known as Toshka, located in the southern zone of the Western Desert, alongside the Sudanese border. Toshka cost the Mubarak government an estimated 44 million Egyptian pounds, all for naught, but this did not deter al-Sisi from allocating another 992 feddans (approximately 4 million square meters) to the project. This was despite vociferous criticism from countless experts who have pointed out the futility and wastefulness of all agricultural "megaprojects" that have been undertaken in the Western Desert since World War II, owing to the lack of water and other environmental factors.[47]

On the other hand, the ideal of robust territorial development in the Egyptian West has been hamstrung by renascent forms of unregulated mobility in the Eastern Sahara—particularly the infiltration of Islamic State affiliates across the border from Libya. This has led to a handful of attacks on Egyptian security forces, at least since the notorious "Farafra massacre" of July 2014, which saw the murder of twenty-two Egyptian border guards at a remote outpost.[48] It was, in fact, in response to the increasing threat of ISIL operatives in the Western Desert that al-Sisi visited military sites throughout the western borderland—making him the first Egyptian leader to travel to the region since King Fu'ad in the 1920s.[49] The most dramatic example of the Egyptian government's renewed fixation on mobility as a threat to national security in the Western Desert was its botched anti-terror operation outside the oasis of Bahariya in September 2015. Claiming to be targeting a convoy of Islamist extremists who had crossed into Egypt from Libya, Egyptian security forces launched an aerial assault on what turned out to be a caravan of Mexican tourists on a desert safari, killing twelve and wounding numerous others.[50]

Egypt is a desert country—at least if the mapped geo-body of today's Egypt is anything to go by. Yet Egyptian history has typically been crafted over the centuries as the ebb and flow of a sedentary civilization that has flourished along the miraculous Nile—that oasis of fertility amid a sea of barren wastes. This book has argued for an alternate conception of Egypt's constitution as a modern territorial nation-state. Territorial Egypt emerged within, and in dialogue with, the mobile social geographies of its broader Eastern Saharan milieu, for which Egypt's western borderland always served as a sort of gateway. The delimitation of an international boundary in 1925–26 might have irrevocably altered the spatial dynamics of the borderland, but contested transactions between mobility and territorialism in the region persist to this day. What it means to be Egyptian in the western borderland is still an open question, as Egyptian history still struggles to catch up to the bounds of its own expansive territory.

# Notes

## Introduction

1. Geographer Gideon Biger coined this term for the 1841 map. See Biger, "The First Map of Modern Egypt"; Biger, "The First Political Map of Egypt."

2. Enclosed with Başbakanlık Osmanlı Arşivi (BOA): İ.MTZ(05) 34/2004 (Jan. 6, 1906 / 30 Zilkade 1323). The text at the bottom reads as follows: "This is a copy of the sealed map, drawn up in the office of the Imperial School of Military Engineers, that was graciously sent when the Province of Egypt was granted to the late Mehmed 'Ali Pasha with the privilege of inheritance in 1256 [A.H.; 1841 A.D.]." The map appears to be a modification of the well-regarded Jacotin map, drawn by surveyors during the French occupation of Egypt from 1798–1801 and published in 1816. Biger, "First Political Map," 88.

3. The standoff began when the Egyptian army occupied Ottoman Syria and Palestine in 1831. At one point, Mehmed 'Ali's forces advanced within approximately sixty miles of Istanbul. It was only British military intervention that thwarted the Pasha's designs and compelled him to reach a compromise with the Ottoman government. See Fahmy, *Mehmed Ali*.

4. Hatt-ı Şerif of Feb. 13, 1841 (21 Zilhicce 1256). A second firman, issued that same day, addressed Egypt's possessions in the Sudan by offering a slightly different formulation: Mehmed 'Ali would now control Nubia, Darfur, Kordofan, and Sennar, in addition to "the Governorship of Egypt, comprised within its known limits." See Association Égyptienne de Paris, *Documents diplomatiques concernant l'Égypte.*

5. The map indicates Ras al-Kana'is as the precise point along the coastline where the borderline begins (Marsa Matruh, which only grew to become a town of any consequence in the mid-twentieth century, was not labeled).

6. Winichakul, *Siam Mapped,* 16–18; 129–40.

7. Brownlie, "Arab Republic of Egypt-Libya," 103–4.

8. According to Egyptian historian Fatima 'Alam al-Din 'Abd al-Wahid, the map was

lost or concealed deliberately. 'Abd al-Wahid, *Ḥudūd Misr al-gharbiyya*, 11–12. See, also, Biger, "First Political Map," 83–84.

9. BOA: Y.A.HUS 256/51.

10. BOA: İ.MTZ(05) 34/2004 (Jan. 6, 1906 / 30 Zilkade 1323).

11. Archivio Storico Diplomatico del Ministero degli Affari Esteri (MAE): Ambasciata d'Italia in Egitto (AIE) 117 (Cromer memo, June 14, 1907).

12. Royal Geographic Society, Foyle Reading Room (RGS): *La Frontière Occidentale de l'Égypte*, doc. 1.

13. For two influential examples of the new critical cartography, see Harley, *New Nature of Maps*; Wood, *Power of Maps*.

14. Wood, "How Maps Work," 66.

15. Winichakul argues that "mapping created a new Siam—a new entity whose geobody had never existed before." Benjamin Fortna has shown how modern classroom maps that collated the totality of the Ottoman Empire's domains within one image were vital instruments for producing a new generation of loyal Ottoman subjects. Firoozeh Kashani-Sabet, in her seminal study of territoriality in modern Iranian national discourse, shrewdly argues that "the mapping of 'Iran' reinforced the sense that something concrete sustained the idea"—in short, that the emergence of modern nationalism was contingent upon the ability of Iranians to *see* the nation. Winichakul, *Siam Mapped*, 130; Fortna, *Imperial Classroom*, ch. 5; Kashani-Sabet, *Frontier Fictions*, 17.

16. As Winichakul puts it, for the case of Thailand: "The geo-body of a nation is merely an effect of modern geographical discourse whose prime technology is a map. To a considerable extent, the knowledge about the Siamese nationhood has been created by our conception of Siam-on-the-map, emerging from maps and existing nowhere apart from the map." Winichakul, *Siam Mapped*, 17.

17. As Timothy Mitchell has suggested, political life in modern territorial nation-states requires that people "reduce the significance of those interconnections, exchanges, genealogies, hegemonies, moral systems, and migrations that defined a social landscape whose horizons reached beyond what became the boundaries of the nation." Mitchell, *Rule of Experts*, 180. At the same time, however, national maps always fall short of their ultimate objective: they never completely circumscribe the contours of the imagined nation. As Peter Perdue has pointed out in his study of Qing China's westward expansion, an "ironic gap between the surveyors' claims to universal, standardized abstract space and the local particularities of place" inevitably threatened to unsettle the territorial imperatives of modernizing states. Perdue, *China Marches West*, 460.

18. Winichakul, *Siam Mapped*; Edney, *Mapping a Nation*; Kashani-Sabet, *Frontier Fictions*; Craib, *Cartographic Mexico*; Burnett, *Masters of All They Surveyed*; Carter, *Road to Botany Bay*. Benedict Anderson also addressed the importance of national maps as discursive tools in the second edition of *Imagined Communities*.

19. This was a significant improvement on the state's past attempts at cadastral mapping, particularly given that trigonometrical survey methods were being used for the first time. Mitchell, *Rule of Experts*, 9; 85–94. As Aaron Jakes has recently pointed out, another striking feature of Egypt's trigonometrical survey project—even more historically conse-

quential than the creation of a panoptic "great land map"—was the production of tens of thousands of smaller cadastral maps that circulated widely. See Jakes, "State of the Field," introduction.

20. British colonial officer Claude Jarvis would later claim that the cadastral map of 1907 remained "surrounded by a huge white space of untouched paper" until well after World War I; before then, "everything outside the cultivation of the Nile was an unknown quantity as far as real survey work was concerned." Jarvis, *Three Deserts*, 105–6 (quoted in Fletcher, *British Imperialism and the "Tribal Question,"* 85).

21. This language is a deliberate nod to Raymond Craib's *Cartographic Mexico*. For Craib, in contrast to the Egyptian case, national mapping was one of the main "spatial fixations," or top-down territorial imperatives, of the nineteenth-century Mexican state. Craib goes on to suggest that these state fixations were constantly thwarted by "fugitive landscapes—"intensely local settings" that were "created and recreated through the prisms of memory, practical wisdom, use, and collective decision making." Craib, *Cartographic Mexico*, 8–12.

22. This was an interesting paradox: leaving aside the seemingly more obvious question of how to conceive the territorial bounds of Egypt proper, these intellectuals posited instead a complex definition of territorial Egyptianness that hinged on their country's putative inseparability from the Sudan. This dynamic is treated in depth in Eve Troutt Powell's pathbreaking *Different Shade of Colonialism*. Omnia El Shakry has called this discursive move an "ideological bid for territorial integrity based on ethnographic and geographic claims." El Shakry notes that this discourse gained currency in the 1890s, against the backdrop of Great Britain's reassertion of military control in the Sudan, which culminated in the signing of the Condominium agreement in 1899. El Shakry, *Great Social Laboratory*, 74–83.

23. This idea that Egypt consistently sought to distinguish itself from the rest of Africa through its own colonial projects in the Sudan and further south is another salient theme of Troutt Powell's work.

24. Quoted in Donald Reid, "The Egyptian Geographical Society," 541. The quote is taken from one of Schweinfurth's texts published in the *Bulletin de la Société Khédiviale de Géographie de l'Égypte*, series 1 (1875–76).

25. Di-Capua, *Gatekeepers of the Arab Past*, 48–49. Di-Capua argues that Fikri's work broke from the time-honored Ottoman-Egyptian *khitat* tradition, which approached geography through the lens of city-hinterland relationships, and is exemplified most famously by 'Ali Mubarak's *al-Khitat al-Tawfiqiyya al-jadida li-Misr al-Qahira wa-muduniha wa-bilādiha al-qadīma wa-l-shahīra*.

26. The full first line of the text is as follows: "Egypt is a great state in the Northeast of Africa. Its natural boundary to the north is the Mediterranean Sea; to the east it is the Gulf of Suez and the Red Sea; to the west it is the Libyan Desert; and to the south it is the lands of Nubia." Fikri, *Jughrāfiyat Misr*, 1.

27. Boinet, ed., *Dictionnaire géographique de l'Égypte*.

28. By contrast, territoriality has been richly theorized in the social sciences—particularly by geographers. Robert Sack, *Human Territoriality*, remains a key touchstone for this literature.

29. See also Goswami, "From Swadeshi to Swaraj"; Osterhammel, *Transformation of the World*, 107–13.

30. Maier, "Consigning the Twentieth Century to History," 808.

31. Maier, *Once Within Borders*, 9–12; emphasis in original. See also Maier, "Transformations in Territoriality."

32. Maier, *Once Within Borders*, 194.

33. Ibid., 231. This analysis of the mechanisms of nineteenth-century state centralization (particularly railroads and schools) is reminiscent of Eugen Weber's classic work on French state-building under the Third Republic, *Peasants into Frenchmen*.

34. Maier, *Once Within Borders*, 5.

35. Ibid., 228.

36. Hanley, *Identifying with Nationality*, 8–9. See also Goswami, "Rethinking the Modular Nation Form."

37. Ismael Vaccaro, Allan Charles Dawson, and Laura Zanotti suggest that territoriality connotes multiple "processes involved in the social translation of space as an abstract category into territory as a socially meaningful quotidian reality." It entails ongoing negotiation, as "physical differences in space are made social through the communication of boundaries, markers, borders, patterns of usage, and histories of settlement." What is particularly appealing about this framework is the scope it opens up for exploring the intersection between multiple layers and meanings of territoriality, and the "social processes triggered when different forms of territoriality are pushed by history to share the same space." At the same time, however, this framework—by presenting territoriality as a universal feature of how humans interact as they move through space—loses sight of territoriality as a historical product, taking shape through the confluence of particular conditions at different key moments. Vaccaro, Dawson, and Zanotti, "Negotiating Territoriality," 1–2.

38. Again, this conception of territoriality parallels Hanley's analysis of how prevailing understandings of "nationality" evolved and spread in the same period. As Hanley puts it: "It is clear that top-down reform projects suggested communitarian frames for populations, and individuals and groups responded in the same idiom by adopting those frames. By the late nineteenth century, communitarian frames were an accepted rubric for political organization and social identification." Hanley, *Identifying with Nationality*, 3.

39. In this vein, I am following in the footsteps of pathbreaking borderland historians such as Peter Sahlins, Michiel Baud, Willem van Schendel, Samuel Truett, and Elliott Young. The body of work these scholars have produced exemplifies how borderland histories allow us to glimpse broader aspects of state formation that are otherwise distorted or obscured by the center's own perspective. As Baud and van Schendel have suggested, borderland historians "should ask which social and political impulses originated in borderlands and what effect they had . . . particularly in relation to state building on both sides of the border. The crucial question is what borderlands can teach us about ways of conceptualizing social space and local identity, and the roles these have played in promoting or thwarting the development of modern states." Similarly, Truett and Young have argued that "struggles to delimit and define national and ethnic identities in the borderlands exposed the incoherency of the imagined bounded space of the nation." Baud and van Schendel,

"Toward a Comparative History of Borderlands," 241; Truett and Young, "Making Transnational History," 2.

40. As numerous scholars have shown, the major ideological thrust of Egyptian national discourse formation in this period was not the defense of the nation's territorial integrity, strictly speaking, but rather the assertion of a robust anti-colonial identity, articulated most typically through the language of modernity. See: Gershoni and Jankowski, *Egypt, Islam, and the Arabs*; Lockman, "Imagining the Working Class"; Russell, *Creating the New Egyptian Woman*; Pollard, *Nurturing the Nation*; Baron, *Egypt as a Woman*; El Shakry, *Great Social Laboratory*; Gasper, *Power of Representation*; Jacob, *Working Out Egypt*; Gitre, "Performing Modernity"; Fahmy, *Ordinary Egyptians;* Ryzova, *Age of the Efendiyya.*

41. It is as though a generation of scholarship on Egyptian nation-statehood has simply taken the 1841 firman—with its vague gesture towards the "ancient" and "known" territorial bounds of Egypt—at its word. Examples abound, but we see this tendency in scholarship both old and new. Charles Wendell argued decades ago that the "geographical or territorial factor"—that "Egypt is determinable with unusual ease and little or no dispute"—greatly facilitated the rise of Egyptian national consciousness. Similarly, Ziad Fahmy has suggested that "the topography of Egypt . . . with most of its inhabitants living in an easily accessible thin strip of land stretching from Aswan to the Mediterranean, has historically facilitated centralization efforts." Wendell, *Evolution of the Egyptian National Image*, 123–24; Fahmy, *Ordinary Egyptians*, 21.

42. See also: Hamdan, *Ṣafaḥāt min awrāqihi al-khāṣṣa*; ʿAbd al-Wahid, *Ḥudūd Miṣr al-gharbiyya*; Fawda, *Ḥudūd Miṣr al-dawliyya*; Khashshab, *Tārīkh taṭawwur ḥudūd Miṣr*; Muhammad Safi al-Din et al., *Dirāsāt fī jughrāfiyat Miṣr*; Quhayba, *Dirāsāt fī jughrāfiyat Miṣr al-tārīkhiyya.*

43. For Alexandria: Reimer, *Colonial Bridgehead*; Hanley, *Identifying with Nationality*; Hanley, "Papers for Going, Papers for Staying"; Minkin, "In Life as in Death"; Minkin, "Documenting Death." For Upper Egypt: Abul-Magd, *Imagined Empires*; Reynolds, "Building the Past"; Rieker, "The Saʿid and the City"; Derr, "Cultivating the State." For the Delta: Jakes, "State of the Field"; Jakes, "The Scales of Public Utility"; Boyle, "Sickness, Scoundrels, and Saints." For the Suez Canal and Red Sea region: Wick, *Red Sea*; Belli, *Incurable Past.*

44. The recent work of the "Dakhleh Oasis Project" is one laudable exception. See Peters, *Wathāʾiq madīnat al-Qasr bi-l-wāḥāt al-Dakhla.* Additionally, Alan Mikhail's *Nature and Empire in Ottoman Egypt* includes historical analysis of the oasis of Fayyum (sixty-two miles southwest of Cairo), though for the early modern period.

45. Not least in international law. See Genell, "Empire by Law," for an extended analysis of the status of Ottoman Egypt within international law, as well as Istanbul's ongoing diplomatic struggles with the British to retain a modicum of sovereignty over Egypt.

46. Although Mehmed ʿAli and his descendants adopted the title of "khedive" (instead of *wali*) early on, it was not officially recognized by Istanbul until 1867, when Sultan Abdülaziz issued a firman that sanctioned its use by Ismaʿil and his successors.

47. While I agree with Maier's formulation of sovereignty and territoriality as "twinned

concepts," my analysis here diverges from his framework, which stipulates that sovereignty within a territorial state is indivisible. Maier, *Once Within Borders*, 9, 72–81.

48. Sheehan, "The Problem of Sovereignty," 3.

49. This framework is reminiscent of early modern legal theorist Jean Bodin's analysis of sovereignty. For Bodin, different political actors achieve ascendancy in a given domain by extending what he referred to as sovereign "marks" across space. See Benton, *Search for Sovereignty*, 131–37, 288–90. For a provocative analysis of sovereign capabilities through the lens of Bodin's "marks of sovereignty," see Lombard, "Raiding Sovereignty in Central African Borderlands," introduction.

50. In emphasizing the continued salience of the Ottoman imperial context for modern state-building in Egypt, I am influenced by Khaled Fahmy's historiographical intervention in *All the Pasha's Men*.

51. Sahlins, *Boundaries*, 23.

## Chapter 1

1. Dumreicher, *Trackers and Smugglers*, ix.

2. Dumreicher overstates his case. The coast guard did not assert a strong presence in the Western Desert until the first decade of the twentieth century, when it responded to an eruption of bedouin conflicts in the region (see Chapter 6).

3. Fakhry, *Siwa Oasis*, 7.

4. Belgrave, *Siwa*, 7.

5. See, for instance, Cassandra Vivian, *Western Desert of Egypt*.

6. The scholars associated with the "Dakhleh Oasis Project" have pursued this line of inquiry. See Peters, *Wathāʾiq madīnat al-Qasr bi-l-wāḥāt al-Dakhla*; Peters, "Body and Spirit of Islamic Law."

7. Jarvis, *Three Deserts*, 2.

8. See Ramzi, *al-Qāmūs al-jughrāfī*, vol. 2, pt. 4, 13.

9. Ramzi's geographical dictionary, though an invaluable resource, contains some errors regarding the timing of each oasis's annexation by the Egyptian government. Ramzi claims, for example, that Siwa was incorporated into Buhayra governorate only in 1898, whereas several documents, discussed below, suggest that Siwa's incorporation occurred earlier.

10. For a useful overview of the foundation and expansion of the FDA, see Fletcher, *British Imperialism and the "Tribal Question,"* 85–96. Fletcher argues that the British created the FDA in response to their profound "ignorance" in the face of the Sanusi rebellion, which had caught them by surprise.

11. Jarvis, *Three Deserts*, 2.

12. Benton, *Search for Sovereignty*, 30. Of course, Benton's claims are reserved for legal enclaves inside empires—such as the Indian Raj's princely states or hill stations—and not nation-states. But I believe her analysis is also apt for conceptualizing the emergence of legal enclaves within modern territorializing nation-states in the nineteenth century. As this chapter demonstrates, vast and uneven geographies were not exclusively imperial qualities.

13. Hohler contends that most Siwans did learn Arabic in the period between around 1860 and his visit in 1900, but other travelers—such as Grunau and Steindorf (who visited

the oasis in 1899 and 1904, respectively)—wrote that most did not. See Hohler, *Report on the Oasis of Siva*, 22; Cline, *Notes on the People of Siwah*, 8.

14. Gawhari, *Jannat al-Sahra*, 1.

15. Ibid., 6.

16. In Egypt, the title of *ma'mur* was given to the local government official in charge of either a *markaz* or *qism*, both provincial subdivisions that can be roughly translated as "district." A *markaz* was a subdivision of a *mudiriyya*, whereas a *qism* was a subdivision of a *muhafaza*. The character of 'Abd al-Zahir was loosely based on real-life Siwan *ma'mur* Mahmud 'Azmi, who served in that post in the late-1890s. Taher was right to point out that, at the time of his writing, "no published historical information" concerning 'Azmi was extant. Fortunately, I have been able to uncover more about 'Azmi's career after his tenure as Siwan *ma'mur* (see Chapter 3 for an analysis of his role in resolving a murder case in the oasis).

17. Taher, *Sunset Oasis*, 50.

18. Ibid., 18.

19. Ibid., 303; emphasis added. In the postscript, Taher also acknowledges his debt to Ahmed Fakhry, whose study *Siwa Oasis* was his "point of entry" into the period. This was in some ways an unfortunate choice: as I show in this and the following chapter, Fakhry gets some important historical details wrong.

20. The scant historiography of modern Siwa suffers from its reliance on a flimsy source base. Some authors refer to a great "Siwan Manuscript" or "great written record," which was said to be in the possession of a local shaykh named 'Umar Musallam over a century ago; former FDA officer Charles Dalrymple Belgrave purportedly had access to this written chronicle for his study of the oasis, as did military officer Rif'at Gawhari. If this written record is still extant, however, it has remained inaccessible to scholars for some time.

Given the dearth or inaccessibility of written documents for Siwa's history, several authors have uncritically accepted and repeated many of the same dubious claims. In some cases, passages are lifted and reprinted wholesale (for example, the historical section in Gawhari's *Jannat al-Sahra* matches T. B. Hohler's Interior Ministry report almost verbatim). In other works, authors have distorted the passages they borrowed, such that Siwan historiography has ended up full of internal contradictions.

Throughout this and the following chapter, I privilege Hohler's report for two main reasons. First, it seems to reflect the best available information at the time—gathered from fieldwork conducted in 1900 by P. W. Machell, an advisor to the Ministry of the Interior, and "supplemented by such information as could be obtained by careful enquiry, or extracted from reports of present or past Egyptian Officials who have represented the Government in that district." Also, Hohler's report appears to be the touchstone for several subsequent texts. The key sources on Siwan history in the modern period are: Hohler, *Report on the Oasis of Siva*; Stanley, "The Oasis of Siwa"; Belgrave, *Siwa*; Gawhari, *Jannat al-Sahra*; Rifa'i, *Wāḥat Siwa*; Fakhry, *Siwa Oasis*; Fu'ad, *Wāḥāt Misr al-shahira*.

21. Stanley, "The Oasis of Siwa," 321–22; Cline, *Notes on the People of Siwah*, 11–12; Belgrave, *Siwa*, 98–99. Belgrave says this occurred around 1700; the other authors claim it was around 1807.

22. Belgrave, *Siwa*, 95.

23. According to a count of Siwa's adult male population undertaken in 1888, there were 415 Westerners (all Sanusi brethren) and 755 Easterners (of whom 330 were Sanusi; many others followed the rival Madani order). Hohler, *Report on the Oasis of Siva*, 17. It is impossible to corroborate the accuracy of this tabulation, however, or to determine whether it accords with data from the 1897 Egyptian census, which put the official population of Siwa at fifty-two hundred.

24. Hohler, *Report on the Oasis of Siva*, 23; Rifaʻi, *Wāḥat Siwa*, 23–25; Belgrave, *Siwa*, 102–3. Some basic discrepancies persist in the available accounts of this expedition. According to Rifaʻi, the 1820 campaign was yet another development in Siwa's factional conflict—it was actually the Westerners who had provoked the Egyptian government to intervene, and thus the Easterners had resisted them. Rifaʻi and Belgrave claim that Shamashurghi's campaign comprised thirteen hundred troops; Fuʼad says it was two thousand; but Hohler puts the number at a thousand to thirteen hundred.

25. According to Hohler, the tribute was a thousand "dollars"; Rifaʻi says it was worth ten thousand "*riyals*."

26. Rifaʻi, *Wāḥat Siwa*, 24–25. He adds that this campaign included a section of bedouin troops from the Hijaz. Fakhry, for his part, claims that the campaign took place in 1829 with two hundred fewer troops. Fakhry, *Siwa Oasis*, 106.

27. Hohler, *Report on the Oasis of Siva*, 23–24; Rifaʻi, *Wāḥat Siwa*, 24–25.

28. Rifaʻi, *Wāḥat Siwa*, 24–25; Hohler, *Report on the Oasis of Siva*, 24.

29. Hohler, *Report on the Oasis of Siva*, 24. According to Fakhry, when British traveler Bayle St. John arrived in the oasis in 1847, he reported that there was "neither a Maʼmur nor ʻUmda in Siwa." Fakhry, *Siwa Oasis*, 107.

30. The government also allegedly embarked on a short-lived experiment to co-opt local notables by simultaneously appointing two *ʻumda*s—one Easterner, one Westerner. Hohler, *Report on the Oasis of Siva*, 24. Rifaʻi, for his part, suggests that the new post of *maʼmur* was intended to replace the *ʻumda* system once and for all. Rifaʻi, *Wāḥat Siwa*, 25–26.

31. Hohler, *Report on the Oasis of Siva*, 24. Belgrave's work contains a similar passage. Belgrave, *Siwa*, 109.

32. Durham University Library (DUL): Wingate Papers, Box 131/2 (Sheets 1–48: "Statement of Muhammad Makki, late Qadi of Siwa, on the Oasis of Siwa," translation in original).

33. For this story, see Fakhry, *Siwa Oasis*, 109–10; Rifaʻi, *Wāḥat Siwa*, 25–27.

34. For a basic account of the Stack murder, see Badrawi, *Political Violence in Egypt*, 203–7. The British residency harnessed the event as a pretext to achieve several political objectives all at once, including the withdrawal of all Egyptian military officers from the Sudan. The British also pressured Prime Minister Saʻad Zaghlul to resign, leading to the fall of the popular *Wafd* government.

35. Beginning in 1899, the Egyptian Khedive ʻAbbas Hilmi II financed the construction of a railway that would run along the Mediterranean coastline, as far as the area around Marsa Matruh (see Chapter 4).

36. Middle East Centre Archive, St. Antony's College (MEC), Thomas Russell Papers (doc. 1/6: "Report of the Cairo Special Branch").

37. Ibid. See also MEC: Russell Papers (1/14/7–8: letter to Sir Francis Moore).

38. MEC: Russell Papers (doc. 1/6: "Report of the Cairo Special Branch").

39. See Fletcher, *British Imperialism and the "Tribal Question,"* 89–96. According to Fletcher, the FDA's "overlapping and confused jurisdictions" would lead to enduring tensions throughout the interwar period.

40. Khanka is a town in al-Qalyubiyya province, about eighteen miles northeast of Cairo.

41. For an account of this period of legal reform in Egypt, see Wood, *Islamic Legal Revival*; Brown, *Rule of Law in the Arab World*; Hanley, *Identifying with Nationality*.

42. Brown, *Rule of Law*, 29–33. The Native Courts continue to serve as the cornerstone of Egypt's contemporary justice system.

43. See Dār al-Wathā'iq al-Qawmiyya (DWQ): *Majlis al-Nuẓẓār wa-l-Wuzarā'* (MNW) 0075–042390 for mention of this original 1871 law (#94 of *Dhu'l-Qa'da* 1287 A.H.). Unfortunately I could not locate the original version of this decree; I relied instead on short summaries cited as precedent in later legislation.

44. See *Bulletin des lois et decrets*. Also, DWQ: MNW 0075–042390; 0075–003444. All of Buhayra was placed under the jurisdiction of this court.

45. Indeed, the 1871 law confirming *Majlis Siwa* is explicitly invoked twice in the text of the decree. See DWQ: MNW 0075–042390 (*Amr 'Ali* of Sept. 9, 1884).

46. DWQ: MNW 0075–003444. It is curious that the Egyptian officials referred to Siwans as bedouin Arabs (*'urbān*), given that the Siwans' Berber lineage and language, as well as their historically sedentary, agricultural lifestyle, rendered them distinct from Egypt's bedouin population.

47. The governor invoked the aforementioned Law #94 of *Dhu'l-qa'da* 1287 A.H.

48. DWQ: MNW 0075–003444.

49. Ibid.

50. Ibid.

51. I have not been able to determine the location of al-Wajh, though I have chosen to include this document regardless, given the clear language suggesting that its remoteness from the Nile Valley made it a parallel case to Siwa. One intriguing possibility is that the document refers to the coastal town of al-Wajh in the Hijaz, in present-day Saudi Arabia, which is the only "al-Wajh" I could locate on the contemporary maps I consulted.

52. DWQ: MNW 0075–042391.

53. Shafiq, *Mudhakkirāt 'an wāḥāt Misr*, 10.

54. Ibid., 11.

55. Ibid., 12.

56. It appears from the text of one document that it was the initial law passed on June 14, 1883 that altered the jurisdiction of Kharga and Dakhla, and not the December law that ultimately affected Siwa. See DWQ: MNW 0075–041460.

57. Shafiq, *Mudhakkirāt 'an wāḥāt Misr*, 12–13. In this regard, he was placed on equal footing with the qadi, *'umda*, and shaykhs of the oasis.

58. Ibid., 12–13.

59. Shafiq says that the law was passed on Feb. 22, but according to the document contained in DWQ: MNW 0075–041460, the correct date is Feb. 20, 1890.

60. See Decree (*Amr 'Ali*) #93 and #95 of 1888 (accessed through the *Tashri'at* database at the AUC library).

61. DWQ: MNW 0075–041460 (*Amr 'Ali* #10 of 1890).

62. Shafiq, *Mudhakkirāt 'an wāḥāt Miṣr*, 13; See, also: *Amr 'Ali* #75 of 1891 (accessed through the *Tashri'at* database).

63. See Decree of June 29, 1900 (accessed through the *Tashri'at* database). Some of the text of this decree is provided in Lamba's legal manual. While the local oasis courts were granted these renewed authorities, it remained the case—similar to events in Siwa—that all appeals continued to be handled in the district centers—Beni Suef for Bahariya, and Asyut for Dakhla and Kharga.

64. Lamba, ed., *Droit public et administratif.*

65. Shafiq, *Mudhakkirāt 'an wāḥāt Miṣr*, 13.

66. For comprehensive studies of Egypt's bedouins in the long-nineteenth century, see Aharoni, *Pasha's Bedouin*; and 'Amir, *al-'Urbān wa dawruhum*. Other important sources for Egypt's bedouin tribes in the Ottoman period and long-nineteenth century include: Baer, *Studies in the Social History*; Winter, *Egyptian Society Under Ottoman Rule*, ch. 3; Obermeyer, *Structure and Authority*; Cole and Altorki, *Bedouin, Settlers, and Holiday-Makers*; Murray, *Sons of Ishmael*; Kennett, *Bedouin Justice*.

67. Winter, *Egyptian Society Under Ottoman Rule*, ch. 3.

68. Aharoni, *Pasha's Bedouin*, 22; Murray, *Sons of Ishmael*, 30–31, 276–77; Obermeyer, *Structure and Authority*, 8. Since the last decades of the eighteenth century, the Awlad 'Ali had been moving steadily eastward into Egypt from their long-standing homeland in Cyrenaica's Jabal Akhdar region.

69. Obermeyer, *Structure and Authority*, 8–9.

70. According to Aharoni, some fifteen thousand bedouins saw action in the Hijaz. Murray mentions that a large cavalry of Western bedouins, accompanied by some seven hundred 'Ababda on dromedaries, were instrumental in the Sudan expedition. Aharoni, *Pasha's Bedouin*, 190–91, 195–201; Murray, *Sons of Ishmael*, 31. To this day, the Awlad 'Ali understand this long-standing tradition of military exemption, initially welcomed by their forebears, to have done their tribe a major disservice by fostering the "marginalization of the Bedouin from Egypt's modernizing political economy." Cole and Altorki, *Bedouin, Settlers, and Holiday-Makers*, 71–72.

71. This move has been read by Cole and Altorki as an "assertion by Mehmed 'Ali that these territories fell within his domain of formal authority": the land was his alone to give and thus belonged to the emergent Egyptian state, not to the bedouins. Cole and Altorki, *Bedouin, Settlers, and Holiday-Makers*, 72.

72. Cole and Altorki, *Bedouin, Settlers, and Holiday-Makers*, 73. Obermeyer, for his part, suggests that the tribes' tax-free usufruct rights were so central to their identity that "the term 'Bedouin,' as it was defined by the government of Egypt, came to mean one who did not legally own land and hence was not subject to forced labor or military service." Obermeyer, *Structure and Authority*, 9–10.

73. According to Gabriel Baer, this strategic move disrupted the traditional social fabric of bedouin tribes by engendering a new sort of class consciousness among these elite land-owning shaykhs, thereby alienating them from their tribesmen. Baer, *Studies in the Social History*, 6–12. Cole and Altorki describe how Awlad ʿAli tribesmen today consider their ʿumdas and shaykhs to have been both a "blessing and curse to the tribe"—seen as "government men, not ours." This was due to their accumulation of wealth and property, and their long periods of absence from the tribal domains once they adopted a sedentary life in the Nile Valley. Cole and Altorki, *Bedouin, Settlers, and Holiday-Makers*, 70–71.

74. Baer, *Studies in the Social History*, 5–6.

75. The responsibilities of these newly appointed ʿumdas included assisting "the state in regional administration, the maintenance of law and order in the desert, and the guarding of Egypt's western border." Cole and Altorki, *Bedouin, Settlers, and Holiday-Makers*, 69.

76. For the Awlad ʿAli, at least, that role historically belonged to the ʿaqila. Obermeyer, *Structure and Authority*, 14–15. The invention of the tribal ʿumda under Mehmed ʿAli re-calls Mahmoud Mamdani's discussion of indirect rule in colonial Africa as "decentralized despotism." Mamdani, *Citizen and Subject*, chs. 2–4.

77. Mohsen, *Quest for Order*, 25–26.

78. Aharoni, *Pasha's Bedouin*, 5–6.

79. Ibid., 5–6, 174, 213–14.

80. Ibid., 159–60.

81. ʿAmir, *al-ʿUrbān wa dawruhum*, 33–34.

82. Murray, *Sons of Ishmael*, 1.

83. ʿAmir, *al-ʿUrbān wa dawruhum*, 8.

84. For an attempt to classify the different types of bedouins and outline the extent to which different tribes embraced agricultural life in the Delta and Nile Valley, see ʿAmir, *al-ʿUrbān wa dawruhum*, 33–46. To this day, many denizens of Egypt's rural areas continue to identify as ʿurbān, thereby signaling their divergent origins from their fellahin neighbors.

85. DWQ: MNW 0075–027157.

86. DWQ: MNW 0075–029853. The qadi also petitioned the Council of Ministers not to force him into retirement.

87. DWQ: MNW 0075–031195. They would be sent either to the Mediterranean or to Fazoghli.

88. Ibid.

89. ʿAmir, *al-ʿUrbān wa dawruhum*, 10; Cole and Altorki, *Bedouin, Settlers, and Holiday-Makers*, 26. The limited evidence I have seen, however, emphasizes this role for the bedouin tribes of the Eastern Desert (as opposed to the Western Desert), given the Sinai's historical importance as a strategic crossroads between Egypt and the Mashriq, and its place along the pilgrimage route to Mecca.

90. DWQ: MNW 0075–003447.

91. Ibid.

92. Egypt. No. 1 (1896), *Report on the Finances, Administration, and Condition of Egypt, and the Progress of Reforms*; Jakes, "State of the Field," ch. 2.

93. "Ḥawādīth al-ʿurbān al-jadīda," *al-Muʾayyad* (July 22, 1896).

94. Ibid.

95. "Body politic" is a liberal translation of *silk abnā' al-bilād*. One could also translate this as "body of national citizens," or even just "political community."

96. "Ḥawādīth al-'urbān al-jadīda," *al-Mu'ayyad* (July 22, 1896).

97. Ibid.

98. Ibid.

99. Baer, *Studies in the Social History*, ch. 1.

100. According to Cromer's Annual Report for 1898, there had been 247,000 bedouins counted in the 1882 census, and a "somewhat remarkable" figure of 574,000 counted in the 1897 census. Cromer concluded that "during the last fifteen years large numbers of Bedouins have been absorbed into the settled inhabitants of the Nile Valley." Egypt. No. 1 (1898), *Report by Her Majesty's Agent and Consul-General on the Finances, Administration, and Condition of Egypt and the Soudan in 1898*.

As G. W. Murray put it, the artificially high number of bedouins "terribly complicates the task of the recruiting authorities." Indeed, a special census was undertaken by the military recruiting authorities in 1904, which yielded the "following inflated totals of different 'Bedouin' tribes": 290,095 settled and living in their own farm colonies; 240,880 living among the fellahin; and 70,472 "real Bedouins or nomads." This put the grand total at 601,447 bedouins (nearly 400,000 lower than the figure of one million given in the *Mu'ayyad* article cited above). Murray, *Sons of Ishmael*, 31.

101. Falls, *Three Years in the Libyan Desert*.

102. MEC: Jennings-Bramly papers (File 2/2: "Western Badawins," 7).

103. Ibid.

104. The idea that "legibility" is a primary goal of modern centralizing states is famously developed by James C. Scott in *Seeing Like a State*. Incidentally, Scott begins his analysis by focusing on the sedentarization of nomadic populations.

105. As transcribed in Lamba, ed., *Droit public et administratif*.

106. DWQ: MNW 0075–003562. For a full French translation of the 1905 law, see Wathelet and Brunton, eds., *Codes égyptiens et lois usuelles en vigueur en Égypte*, 97–100.

107. Aaron Jakes suggests that these reforms transformed *'umda*s and shaykhs into "the petty bureaucrats of colonial designs." Jakes, "State of the Field," 176.

108. DWQ: MNW 0075–003562.

109. Law #6 of 1908, printed in full in Wathelet and Brunton, eds., *Codes égyptiens et lois usuelles en vigueur en Égypte*, 100–102. For drafts and deliberations, see DWQ: MNW 0075–014962, 0075–016044, 0075–014961.

110. DWQ: MNW 0075–014961 (memo from minister of war to Council of Ministers, Feb. 25, 1908). I was unable to find any more information on the earlier bedouin census to which the Minister refers.

111. DWQ: MNW 0075–014962.

112. Ibid.

113. DWQ: MNW 0075–016044.

114. Weber, *Peasants into Frenchmen*. For more recent works that engage with Weber's

model, see, for example, Dunlop, *Cartophilia*; Judson, *Guardians of the Nation*; Applegate, *Nation of Provincials*.

115. Weber, *Peasants into Frenchmen*, 9. The answer was to deploy key centralizing mechanisms—compulsory national schooling, military conscription, the expansion of roads and railroads, and the consolidation of nation-wide markets—in what was a "determined assault against provincialism (334). See chs. 17–18 for an extended discussion of the military and schools as key sites of national assimilation.

116. For example, both Omnia El Shakry and Timothy Mitchell provide close readings of various state projects to study, measure, and civilize Egypt's "backwards" populations in the mid-twentieth century (though their works pay particular attention to the rural fellahin, not the bedouins). El Shakry, *Great Social Laboratory*; Mitchell, *Rule of Experts*.

## Chapter 2

1. For a complete account of the episode, see Blunt, *My Diaries*, 241–76. From his entries on Siwa, it appears that the primary objective of the trip was to penetrate deep into Sanusi territory, to gather as much information as possible about the Brotherhood. Blunt also harbored certain Orientalist fantasies about the Sanusiyya: "I had, too, at the back of my mind, the thought that perhaps I might find among the Senussis something of the better tradition of Islam I had been so often disappointed of in the more civilized Mohammedan lands, and possibly that true desert hermitage I had so often dreamed of" (247–48). It is thus quite ironic that he returned from Siwa with such a vitriolic hatred of the Sanusiyya.

2. National Archives (NA): FO 78/4956 (Blunt to Cromer, Mar. 3, 1898).

3. Ibid.

4. NA: FO 78/4956 (Cromer to Blunt, Mar. 7, 1898).

5. NA: FO 78/4956 (Blunt to Cromer, Mar. 16, 1898).

6. NA: FO 78/4956 (Cromer to Blunt, Mar. 7, 1898).

7. Cromer was by no means the only colonial official to refer to the Sanusiyya pejoratively as "fanatical." Sanusi "fanaticism" was a recurrent trope in European discourse ever since the very first French studies of the Brotherhood were published, beginning with Henri Duveyrier's *La confrerie musulmane de Sidi Mohammed Ben ʿAli Es-Senousi et son domaine géographique*. For an analysis of how the label of "fanaticism" was reproduced in colonial discourse, see Le Gall, "The Ottoman Government and the Sanusiyya," 91–93.

8. See Jakes, "State of the Field," ch. 2.

9. Baud and van Schendel, "Toward a Comparative History of Borderlands," 241.

10. Belgrave, *Siwa*, 110. Belgrave would go on to serve as an advisor to the rulers of Bahrain for over three decades.

11. The Sanusiyya have typically been interpreted strictly as a Libyan movement in the relevant scholarly literature. The Brotherhood is in fact most familiar to scholars for its key role spearheading the opposition to the Italian occupying forces throughout the 1920s, and for the short-lived Sanusi monarchy that was established in Libya after World War II. See Evans-Pritchard, *Sanusi of Cyrenaica*; Gazzini, "Jihad in Exile"; Dajani, *al-Ḥaraka al-Sanusiyya*; Ziadeh, *Sanusiyah*.

12. For a recent examination of the origins and spread of the Sanusiyya, as well as

their relationship with the Ottoman state in the last decades of the nineteenth century, see Minawi, *Ottoman Scramble for Africa*, 29–39.

13. The reasons for this move are not entirely clear. The conventional European narrative stresses al-Sanusi's political differences with the established authorities and *'ulama* in Mecca, suggesting his need to flee. Knut Vikør posits instead that al-Sanusi actively sought a particular new environment, such as he would find in the Sahara, to implement new organizational ideas for his brotherhood. Vikør, *Sufi and Scholar*.

14. According to some sources, al-Sanusi founded the first *zawiya* in North Africa at Siwa. For example, see Hassanein, *Lost Oases*, 59.

15. In 1895, Muhammad al-Mahdi al-Sanusi moved the headquarters of the brotherhood to Kufra. Interpretations of Muhammad al-Mahdi's motives typically stress either his desire to move farther from encroaching European power, or from the increasingly bothersome presence of Ottoman authorities in the province of Benghazi.

16. Hassanein, *Lost Oases*, 57–58; Vikør, *Sufi and Scholar*, 189–90.

17. Vikør, *Sufi and Scholar*, 198.

18. Ibid., 184.

19. Evans-Pritchard, *Sanusi of Cyrenaica*, 24–25, 72.

20. White, *From Sphinx to Oracle*, 122.

21. Hassanein, *Lost Oases*, 63.

22. NA: FO 78/5240 ("Notes on the History of Senussism and its Relation to the African Possessions of Foreign Powers").

23. White, *From Sphinx to Oracle*, 128.

24. Evans-Pritchard, *Sanusi of Cyrenaica*, 82.

25. Ibid., 73.

26. Vikør, *Sufi and Scholar*, 150.

27. Evans-Pritchard, *Sanusi of Cyrenaica*, 15–16; Vikør, *Sufi and Scholar*, 179.

28. Vikør, *Sufi and Scholar*, 197–98.

29. DUL: Wingate Papers, Box 131/2 (Sheets 51–71: "Qadi's Visit to Jaghbub," translation in original).

30. DUL: Wingate Papers, Box 131/2 (Sheets 73–81: Wingate intelligence report, June 1889).

31. Cordell, "Eastern Libya, Wadai, and the Sanusiya," 21.

32. Hohler, *Report on the Oasis of Siva*, 18.

33. Ibid., 25.

34. This was likely part of the general restructuring of the Interior Ministry that had been underway since the previous year. See Egypt, No. 1 (1896), *Report on the Finances, Administration, and Condition of Egypt, and the Progress of Reforms*.

35. Hohler, *Report on the Oasis of Siva*, 25.

36. Gawhari, *Jannat al-Sahra*, 100.

37. Jennings-Bramly, who would later serve in the Frontier Districts Administration, founded the settlement of Burg al-'Arab in the Maryut region. See Fakhry, *Siwa Oasis*, 11 n. 1.

38. MEC: Jennings-Bramly papers (File 2/2: "Western Badawins," 7).

39. Jennings-Bramly, "A Journey to Siwa," 599–600.

40. Ibid., 600.

41. Ibid., 603.

42. Ibid. Although Jennings-Bramly's visit to Siwa gave Maher's mission a much-needed boost, it was otherwise a bust. Jennings-Bramly never felt welcomed by the Siwans, who insisted on speaking only in "Berber" among themselves. He was also forbidden from entering Shali, which had been one of the primary objectives of his voyage. Tired of feeling under suspicion at every turn and getting harassed by "constant questionings," he decided to leave Siwa the next morning after his arrival (606).

43. Hohler, *Report on the Oasis of Siwa*, 26; Gawhari, *Jannat al-Sahra*, 100–101.

44. Hohler, *Report on the Oasis of Siwa*, 26.

45. Article 1 of 1896 Criminal Law (transcribed in Gawhari, *Jannat al-Sahra*, 122).

46. Article 33 of 1896 Criminal Law (transcribed in Gawhari, *Jannat al-Sahra*, 131).

47. Hohler, *Report on the Oasis of Siwa*, 26.

48. Ibid., 27; Gawhari, *Jannat al-Sahra*, 101; Belgrave, *Siwa*, 111.

49. Hohler, *Report on the Oasis of Siwa*, 27.

50. DUL: Wingate Papers, Box 131/2 (Sheets 51–71: "Qadi's Visit to Jaghbub").

51. White, *From Sphinx to Oracle*, 13, 173–74.

52. Ibid., 179.

53. Ibid., 193.

54. The extant sources disagree on the date of this tree census. Hohler's report says it was 1871, but other evidence suggests it took place in 1869.

55. Stanley, *Report on the Oasis of Siwa*, 44. See, also, Rifaʿi, *Wāḥat Siwa*, ch. 5; Hohler, *Report on the Oasis of Siwa*, 33. Hohler's report suggests that Maher made his own rough estimate of date and olive trees in 1896, but this is not reflected anywhere in the ensuing tax legislation.

56. DWQ: MNW 0075–011307.

57. DUL: Wingate Papers, Box 131/2 (Sheets 51–71: "Qadi's Visit to Jaghbub").

58. Hohler, *Report on the Oasis of Siwa*, 36.

59. Twenty pounds would come from the Oasis of Qara, which was attached to the *markaz* of Siwa. Qara, also known as "Umm al-Saghir," is located approximately eighty miles northeast of Siwa.

60. Gawhari, *Jannat al-Sahra*, 138–39; Hohler, *Report on the Oasis of Siwa*, 35.

61. Every shaykh was entitled to 2 percent of the tax revenue he helped collect. In addition, every shaykh serving on the council of notables received two Egyptian pounds annually. Hohler, *Report on the Oasis of Siwa*, 36; Gawhari, *Jannat al-Sahra*, 138.

62. Gawhari, *Jannat al-Sahra*, 139. Taxation in Siwa would continue to vex the Egyptian government for decades to come, even despite these modest reforms. In April 1921, the Egyptian Finance Committee considered abolishing the date-palm tax in Siwa altogether, considering the oasis's exemptions from all other property and land taxes. In 1922 and again in 1925, the government significantly reduced the tax burden on Siwans in light of the oasis's financial hardships; and in 1929, the government granted a reprieve for two years of taxes. DWQ: MNW 0075–022582 ("Note from the Finance Committee to the Council of Ministers," Apr. 30, 1921); Rifaʿi, *Wāḥat Siwa*, 80–81.

63. See, for example, Gawhari, *Jannat al-Sahra*.

64. The legislation Gawhari refers to as the "1897 Law" seems, from the texts he included in the 1946 edition of *Jannat al-Sahra*, to comprise three separate laws from that
year: one dealing specifically with the jurisdiction and protocol of *Majlis Siwa*, passed on
May 25; one outlining the special privileges and rights of Siwan shaykhs, approved by an
assembly of Siwan notables on February 13; and, finally, the new tax law for Siwa, passed
on April 20. The contents of these laws are far too extensive to cover fully; instead, it must
suffice to list those provisions of these laws that are most illustrative of Siwa's persistence as
an enclave of legal exceptionalism.

65. Lamba, ed., *Droit public et administratif*.

66. Gawhari, *Jannat al-Sahra*, 108.

67. Ibid., 110.

68. Ibid., 108.

69. There was some precedent for this decision. One law from August 1893 underscores
the Egyptian government's reluctance to tinker with legal custom in the oasis. The decree,
passed after the return of a special commission that the Khedive ʿAbbas Hilmi II had dispatched to investigate the Siwan court's handling of a recent murder case, allowed *Majlis
Siwa* to continue serving as the court of first instance for civil, commercial, and criminal
cases, whereas all *appeals* cases would now revert to the Alexandria Native Court. At the
same time, the new law mandated that *Majlis Siwa* must apply the "civil, commercial, and
penal codes in use among the Native Courts" in all its judgments, though with the caveat
that these same judgments must "take into account the established usages" in Siwa and
avoid being "contrary to public order and morality." DWQ: MNW 0075–040666.

70. Gawhari, *Jannat al-Sahra*, 108–9.

71. Ibid., 114

72. Ibid., 117.

73. Ibid., 115.

74. Ibid., 112–21.

75. Ibid., 115.

76. Sahlins, *Boundaries*, 9.

77. See Ranger, "The Invention of Tradition in Colonial Africa." Mamdani's ground-
breaking *Citizen and Subject* brought the tools of postcolonial theory to bear on this earlier
literature on indirect rule.

78. See, for instance, Scott, *Art of Not Being Governed*.

79. Hohler, *Report on the Oasis of Siva*, 11. The mail was delivered twice a month, via
Marsa Matruh.

80. Ibid., 30. It appears that the Siwan *maʾmur* was assisted by a police force of twenty
to thirty officers.

81. According to this census, Siwa's population was 5,200 in 1897.

82. Hohler, *Report on the Oasis of Siva*, 29.

83. White, *From Sphinx to Oracle*, 150, 199. White was apparently the first European to
successfully visit Shali (Siwa's sacred inner town).

84. Ibid., 155.

85. Ibid., 152.

86. Ibid., 158.

87. Ibid., 191.

88. Hohler, *Report on the Oasis of Siva*, 22.

89. Gawhari, *Jannat al-Sahra*, 102.

90. Fakhry, *Siwa Oasis*, 112.

91. The numbers vary according to the account. Stanley, citing the oral history of 'Umar Musallam, says that seven shaykhs including Mansur were killed, along with 180 rank and file. Hohler also mentions that seven shaykhs were killed in the tumult, though his casualty figure is on the low end of the spectrum (around ninety). Stanley, "The Oasis of Siwa," 315; Hohler, *Report on the Oasis of Siva*, 28.

92. For an account of the "Widow's War," see Belgrave, *Siwa*, 111–15. Belgrave's version includes some internal contradictions, however. See, also, Hohler, *Report on the Oasis of Siva*, 27–28; Gawhari, *Jannat al-Sahra*, 100–101; Fakhry, *Siwa Oasis*, 111–12; White, *From Sphinx to Oracle*, 150–51.

93. White, *From Sphinx to Oracle*, 150–51. See also Belgrave, *Siwa*, 114; Fakhry, *Siwa Oasis*, 112.

94. Hohler, *Report on the Oasis of Siva*, 28.

95. Fakhry, *Siwa Oasis*, 112; Belgrave, *Siwa*, 114. The unique *siyaha* festival celebrated annually in Siwa is said to commemorate the reconciliation between Easterners and Westerners fostered by the Sanusiyya at this time.

96. Hohler, *Report on the Oasis of Siva*, 18.

97. Ibid., 29–30.

98. NA: FO 78/4956 (Blunt to Cromer, Mar. 3, 1898).

99. Ibid.

100. Blunt, *My Diaries*, 268–69.

101. Ibid., 271–72.

102. Ibid., 252.

103. Muhammad Sa'id, a follower of the Madani sect, had long been involved in intrigue against the Sanusi leadership in Siwa. At one point, he traveled to Cairo to plead his case for becoming *'umda*. Later on, he successfully persuaded the government to remove a *ma'mur* who had been sympathetic to the Sanusiyya. See Hohler, *Report on the Oasis of Siva*, 24–25.

104. Blunt, *My Diaries*, 271.

105. Ibid.

106. NA: FO 78/4956 (Blunt to Cromer, Mar. 7, 1898).

107. Blunt, *My Diaries*, 271.

108. Ibid., 272.

109. Ibid., 271–72.

110. NA: FO 78/4956 (Blunt to Cromer, Mar. 3, 1898).

111. NA: FO 78/4956 (Blunt to Cromer, Mar. 16, 1898).

112. Ibid.

113. Ibid.

## Chapter 3

1. This document, like a few others examined in this chapter, refers to a prominent Siwan notable known as "Shaykh Saʿudi" (not Saʿud). From the context of this set of documents, however, I believe the referent to be none other than Shaykh Saʿud Muhammad Saʿud Tawiya, the local representative (*wakil*) of the Khedive's *Daʾira Khassa* in Siwa. While it is possible there was another shaykh by the name of Saʿudi at this time, I do not think it likely. I did not find any mention of a Shaykh Saʿudi in the few documents I perused that compile lists of Siwan notables from this period. Moreover, in all the letters and reports I read from the *Daʾira Khassa* files, I repeatedly saw the signature of Shaykh Saʿud Muhammad Saʿud Tawiya, but never one by a shaykh Saʿudi. For the sake of consistency, then, I assume that any mention of "Saʿudi" is really a reference to Shaykh Saʿud.

2. DUL: Abbas Hilmi II Papers (AHII) File 165/578–80 (Husayn Effendi Fahmi to Ahmad Sadiq, Aug. 5, 1907).

3. Ibid.

4. Before the 1840s, there was no single administrative unit for the vast estates Mehmed ʿAli had accumulated during the previous decade (as distinct from both the "domain lands" he granted to his family members or government officials, and the *miri* lands that became state property). See Hunter, *Egypt Under the Khedives,* 63–65.

5. Esmeir, *Juridical Humanity,* 209–10.

6. Ibid., 211–14. Esmeir notes, for example, that 450,000 acres of *Daʾira Saniyya* land was sold between 1900 and 1906.

7. Goldschmidt, "The Egyptian Nationalist Party," 310; Jakes, "State of the Field," 171.

8. ʿAbbas Hilmi II, *Last Khedive of Egypt,* 77–79.

9. The Khedive's partnership with the nationalists would start to sour after around 1904, and his close relationship with Sir Eldon Gorst, Cromer's replacement as consul-general in 1907, made him particularly anathema to the nationalists for several years. But the political sands shifted again in 1911, when Gorst was succeeded by ʿAbbas Hilmi's long-time adversary, Lord Kitchener: for the remaining three years of his reign, the Khedive would be firmly back in the embrace of the National Party (now led by Muhammad Farid). See Goldschmidt, "Egyptian Nationalist Party," 312–33.

10. Ibid., 310–20.

11. Jakes, "State of the Field," 170–74.

12. Ibid.

13. Ibid., 177–79.

14. The Khedivial spy network operated throughout the Egyptian countryside in its effort to document the fallout of the British Interior Ministry reforms of 1896. See Jakes, "State of the Field," ch. 2.

15. The core analysis of this chapter draws from a set of ninety *Daʾira Khassa* documents, located within the vast collection of ʿAbbas Hilmi's private papers (which contain five massive files on the *Daʾira Khassa* alone). What makes these ninety documents particularly noteworthy is the unique lens they offer into local Siwan politics (and the Khedive's involvement in it) before World War I.

16. Like much else in Siwan history, the narrative of the Khedivial expedition remains

shrouded in some mystery. It is not even entirely clear when this seminal event took place. According to German Egyptologist J. C. Ewald Falls, the Khedive's esteemed travel companion, the main leg of the journey commenced in early February 1906. The *Egyptian Gazette* seems to corroborate that a major Khedivial voyage took place in February 1906, though—confusing matters somewhat—the newspaper also published translated excerpts of Falls's account of the expedition only in early 1907.

On the other hand, according to Ahmad Shafiq—a key member of the Khedive's entourage, and a participant in some of the Siwan land deals that will be discussed below—the Siwan expedition took place in February 1907. Egyptian archaeologist Ahmed Fakhry, for his part, suggests there were two separate visits—one in 1904, the other in 1907. It is conceivable that there were in fact multiple Khedivial visits to Siwa, which have become conflated in the relevant sources. Having weighed all the evidence, however, I believe we can establish that one important Khedivial visit to Siwa indeed occurred in February 1906. See Falls, *Three Years in the Libyan Desert*; Fakhry, *Siwa Oasis*; Shafiq, *Mudhakkirāt 'an wāḥāt Misr*.

17. The desert route from Marsa Matruh to Siwa was known alternately as *Masrab al-Istabl* (The Stable Road) or *Sikkat al-Sultan* (The Sultan's Path), so called because it is purportedly the route that Alexander the Great followed.

18. Falls, *Three Years in the Libyan Desert*, 271–72.

19. "Translation from Ewald Falls," *Egyptian Gazette*, Feb. 27, 1907.

20. Falls was apparently one of only four Europeans in the caravan; the Khedive's personal physician, Dr. Kausky Bey, was another. The rest were all "Egyptians and Arabs," including two *Da'ira Khassa* officials: Mahmud Effendi Nagati, chief engineer, and Ahmad Sadiq, the aforementioned senior agent of the *Da'ira Khassa*. See Falls, *Three Years in the Libyan Desert*, 264; Shafiq, *Mudhakkirāt 'an wāḥāt Misr*, 83; *Egyptian Gazette*, Feb. 9, 1906.

21. MAE: AIE 108 (Guicciardini memo to MAE, Mar. 18, 1906).

22. BOA: DH.MKT 1072/57 (*Dahiliye* memo, Apr. 22, 1906).

23. MAE: AIE 108 (memo from MAE to Salvago Raggi, May 28, 1906).

24. MAE: AIE 108 (memo from Salvago Raggi to MAE, Mar. 18, 1906; MAE to Conte Manzoni, Sept. 10, 1906). I have loosely translated *mettere in valore* here as "reclaim," to capture the sense of developing previously idle lands and rendering them profitable. I will explore this theme in more depth in Chapter 4.

25. Falls notes that the caravan first stopped at what he believed to be a Sanusi mosque resembling a "fortress." Falls, *Three Years in the Libyan Desert*, 274.

26. Ibid.; Fakhry, *Siwa Oasis*, 114.

27. Falls, *Three Years in the Libyan Desert*, 274–75.

28. Shafiq, *Mudhakkirāt 'an wāḥāt Misr*, 83. Sidi Sulayman was a prominent Siwan shaykh and judge from the medieval era. Venerated for his purported miracles and association with bountiful harvests, Sidi Sulayman is considered akin to Siwa's "patron saint." See Fakhry, *Siwa Oasis*, 63–65; Rifa'i, *Wāḥat Siwa*, 23–24.

29. Shafiq, *Mudhakkirāt 'an wāḥāt Misr*, 83–84.

30. Ibid., 84. According to a survey undertaken in the 1960s, there was a total of 281 known natural springs in and around Siwa.

31. Ibid.

32. It should be noted that one countervailing account of the Khedive's acquisition of 'Ayn Qurayshat exists. According to Ahmed Fakhry, Siwan notables actually gave this spring (and all the land surrounding it—some two thousand acres) to the Khedive as a gift in honor of his son, the Crown Prince 'Abd al-Mun'im. Shafiq's testimony that this land was purchased by the Khedive and then registered in the Crown Prince's name seems more trustworthy, however. Fakhry, *Siwa Oasis*, 36, 113–14; Shafiq, *Mudhakkirātī fī niṣf al-qarn*, 134.

33. DUL: AHII 165/591–96 (Khalil Hafiz to Muhammad 'Uthman, July 22, 1906).

34. Ibid.

35. Shafiq, in one of his memoirs, offers an account of how the Khedive managed to snatch up lands that he had forced members of his own entourage (Shafiq included) to relinquish, after receiving angry petitions from Siwans. According to Shafiq, the Khedive was quick to act, lest the episode "open up the eyes and ears" of the British and compel them to "intervene in Siwan affairs." Shafiq, *Mudhakkirātī fī niṣf al-qarn*, 133–34.

36. Musallam, mentioned in Chapter 2, was the Easterner shaykh who served as the custodian of Siwa's great written record.

37. DUL: AHII 165/574–75.

38. Hamid was paid a salary starting at two Egyptian pounds. In his letter, Fahmi also offered a detailed financial report for 'Ayn Qurayshat, including a list of *Da'ira Khassa* expenditures. DUL: AHII 165/565–6 (Husayn Fahmi to Ahmad Sadiq, Apr. 24, 1908).

39. DUL: AHII 165/559–60 (report from Shaykh Sa'ud, undated but must be after July 27, 1913).

40. This idea is supported by Fakhry, who notes that the Khedive "encouraged the Siwans to work for him by raising their wages from one piaster to three piasters per day." Fakhry, *Siwa Oasis*, 115.

41. DUL: AHII 165/588 (Shaykh Sa'ud to Khedive, June 2, 1909).

42. DUL: AHII 165/601–2 (Mitwalli Effendi Hilmi to Ahmad Sadiq, May 10, 1909).

43. DUL: AHII 165/551–54 (*Ma'mur Siwa* to Khedive, Oct. 1, 1912). This document even contains a diagram of the agricultural lands located at 'Ayn Qurayshat.

44. Shafiq, *Mudhakkirāt 'an wāḥāt Misr*, 66.

45. Belgrave, *Siwa*, 139.

46. DUL: AHII 165/582–83 (expense reports of Jan. 2 and 22, 1909). For example, from Dec. 19–31, 1908, the *Da'ira Khassa* paid 11 Egyptian pounds and 660 *miliem*s toward the mosque.

47. DUL: AHII 165/584 (Shawqi to the Khedive, Jan. 10, 1909).

48. DUL: AHII 165/635 (Shawqi to the Khedive, Apr. 27, 1910).

49. DUL: AHII 165/586 (Shawqi to Sadiq, Mar. 21, 1909).

50. Ibid.

51. Ibid.

52. See DWQ: MNW 0075–007493. In a report to the governor of Buhayra, Sayyid Effendi Muhammad suggests that it might have been taken by a worker, or even a child.

53. DWQ: MNW 0075–007494. The ministry also revoked Sayyid Effendi Muham-

mad's right to the standard vacation due to all officials upon completion of their tour of duty in Siwa.

54. DWQ: MNW 0075–007493 (Sayyid Effendi Muhammad to *Mudir* Buhayra, May 6, 1909).

55. Ibid. At the end of his report, Sayyid Effendi Muhammad offered a couple of possible reasons why Shawqi would have spread such vicious rumors about him: at the beginning of March, he had prevented Shawqi from intervening in some administrative projects, including one involving a land purchase. Shawqi had also recently become entangled in a quarrel with several state officials (including the qadi, the town doctor, and the police sergeant).

56. DWQ: MNW 0075–007494 (doc. 2).

57. Ibid.

58. DWQ: MNW 0075–007498 (*Mudir* Buhayra to Interior Ministry, undated). Shaykh Sa'ud was also dealing with an accusation involving misconduct toward one of his servants. In addition, the investigators pointed out that some animosity might have arisen between Shawqi and Sayyid Effendi Muhammad when the former attempted to interfere in the matter of the land rights of a merchant named 'Abd al-'Aziz Karam (who will be discussed below).

59. In fact, some of the most fascinating documents from the *Da'ira Khassa* collection for Siwa are written by Shaykh Sa'ud either directly to the Khedive, or else to one of the Khedive's *Da'ira Khassa* agents in Cairo. Shaykh Sa'ud's importance as a key node in the network connecting the most prominent notables to the Khedive is underscored further when we recall that he was related through marriage to 'Uthman Habun (Siwa's most powerful notable, and a local Sanusi agent). Shaykh Sa'ud grew so close to 'Abbas Hilmi that he would stay in the Khedivial palace when visiting him in Alexandria. See "The Oasis of Siwa," *Egyptian Gazette*, Oct. 14, 1909.

60. NA: FO 371/664 (Gorst to Grey, Nov. 26, 1909). See also Dumreicher, *Trackers and Smugglers*, 33–34. In one letter Shaykh Sa'ud claims that the Interior Ministry actually ordered Hilmi to make the arrest. DUL: AHII 165/604–5 (Shaykh Sa'ud to Khedive, Oct. 2, 1909). The *Egyptian Gazette*, for its part, reported two different version of the events, the second of which—focusing on Habun's role in a recent bedouin raid (of which more below)—seems to confirm Shaykh Sa'ud's claim that the order to arrest Habun came from Cairo. See "The Oasis of Siwa," *Egyptian Gazette*, Oct. 22, 1909; and "The Oasis Tragedy," *Egyptian Gazette*, Nov. 27, 1909.

61. DUL: AHII 6/249–54 (report from Muhammad Kamil Muhammad, Oct. 16, 1909). I have based my account of the murder incident on this report by Kamil Muhammad, Mitwalli Hilmi's second-in-command, since he was one of the first responders and was actively involved in spearheading the investigation. Other narratives of the case will be mentioned if they diverge in suggestive ways.

62. DUL: AHII 6/249–54 (report from Muhammad Kamil Muhammad, Oct. 16, 1909).

63. By staging the siege after midnight, Hilmi was violating restrictions against nighttime police raids. Dumreicher, *Trackers and Smugglers*, 34.

64. DUL: AHII 6/249–54 (report from Muhammad Kamil Muhammad, Oct. 16, 1909). Another version of events maintains that Hamadu first struggled with the *ma'mur* and stripped him of his revolver, which then became the murder weapon. The accuracy of this account is dubious, however, given that the author of this document claims that Hamadu committed all three murders, whereas the formal investigation concluded that he was guilty of murdering only Mitwalli Hilmi. See MAE: AIE 117 (copy of letter from Sidi Ibrahim al-Ma'aruf to Muhammad 'Ali Bey, Nov. 4, 1909).

65. DUL: AHII 165/616–7 ('Azmi to *Mudir* Buhayra, Nov. 7, 1909).

66. DUL: AHII 165/597–600 (Shaykh Sa'ud to Khedive, Oct. 28, 1909). This testimony, along with Kamil Muhammad's account, reveals a factional dimension to the murder case that has been overlooked in the few published accounts of the incident.

67. DUL: AHII 6/249–54 (report from Muhammad Kamil Muhammad, Oct. 16, 1909).

68. Ibid. See also DUL: AHII 165/597–600 (Shaykh Sa'ud to Khedive, Oct. 28, 1909). It is unclear if this marks the second time (at least!) that Habun made a narrow escape dressed in women's clothing, or if the other noteworthy incident—during the so-called "Widow's War," mentioned in Chapter 2—has been wrongly conflated with the 1909 murder case in some scholarship.

69. NA: FO 371/664 (Gorst to Grey, Nov. 26, 1909).

70. DUL: AHII 6/249–54; 165/597–600.

71. DUL: AHII 165/604–5 (Shaykh Sa'ud's testimony differs on this point. In one letter to the Khedive, he writes that Hamadu came to the *markaz* on his own).

72. DUL: AHII 6/249–54. Shaykh Sa'ud recalls the wording of the proclamation slightly differently: "The obedient man stays in the East; the rebel stays in the West." DUL: AHII 165/597–600. Yet in a different document, he reports that the town crier actually said, "The obedient man goes to the East, to the *zāwiya* of the *ustādh* al-Sanusi." DUL: AHII 165/604–5.

73. DUL: AHII 6/249–54; 165/597–600.

74. DUL: AHII 165/604–5.

75. DUL: AHII 6/249–54; 165/597–600; 165/604–5. 'Azmi found the following weapons in the Habun compound: fifty Remington bullets, eight revolvers, gunpowder, swords, knives, and "Arab bullets." See MAE: AIE 117 (Sidi Ibrahim al-Ma'aruf to Prince Muhammad 'Ali, Nov. 9, 1909).

76. NA: FO 371/664 (Graham to Hardinge, Oct. 13, 1909). It is surprising that this official could be so ignorant of Habun's Sanusi affiliation given that other British officials, including Cromer, were aware of this connection for over a decade.

77. NA: FO 371/664 (Gorst to Grey, Nov. 26, 1909).

78. MAE: AIE 117 (report from Dec. 13, 1909).

79. "The Oasis of Siwa," *Egyptian Gazette*, Oct. 14, 1909. The alleged Sanusi threat evidently struck a chord with a French diplomat named Ribot, who suspected that "it would be dangerous and inopportune to carry out hostile acts towards the Sanusiyya in Siwa, precisely while the French have a serious discord with that Sect over their advance in Wadai." MAE: AIE 117 (Martino to Tittoni, Italian minister of foreign affairs, Nov. 17, 1909).

80. NA: FO 371/664 (Gorst to Grey, Nov. 26, 1909). This is another instance of erroneously labeling Siwans as "bedouins."

81. DUL: AHII 6/249–54.

82. It is unclear who in the government actually appointed 'Azmi—a question that takes on further significance as the case played out, as I suggest below. Some evidence indicates that the British took credit for the appointment. Yet by 'Azmi's own account, the expedition was personally commissioned by the Khedive. See NA: FO 371/664 (Graham to Hardinge, Oct. 13, 1909).

83. NA: FO 371/664 (Graham to Hardinge, Oct. 13, 1909).

84. The officers were recruited from the police forces of Minya, Asyut, Maryut, and Aswan. According to the *Egyptian Gazette*, 'Azmi and his men were armed to the hilt: they were carrying "a hundred rounds of ball ammunition," and "the equipment of the force shows that the serious state of affairs revealed by the murder of the Mamour [*sic*] of the Oasis is fully appreciated." See "The Oasis of Siwa," *Egyptian Gazette*, Oct. 14, 1909; "The Oasis of Siwa," *Egyptian Gazette*, Oct. 16, 1909; "The Oasis of Siwa—Interesting Scene at Wardian," *Egyptian Gazette*, Oct. 18, 1909.

85. DUL: AHII 165/627–30 ('Azmi to *Mudir* Buhayra, Oct. 28, 1909).

86. 'Azmi found the people of Qara to be "in a state of dread from what had happened in Siwa." 'Azmi summoned the shaykhs of the oasis to give them assurances of the Khedive's good will, and then proceeded to visit many shaykhs in their homes. According to 'Azmi, the residents of the oasis all paid tribute to the government and extolled the Khedive.

87. DUL: AHII 165/627–30 ('Azmi to *Mudir* Buhayra, Oct. 28, 1909).

88. DUL: AHII 165/597–600 (Sa'ud to Khedive, Oct. 28, 1909).

89. DUL: AHII 165/616–7 ('Azmi to *Mudir* Buhayra, Nov. 7, 1909).

90. Ibid.

91. Eleven suspects were given ten years; four were given three years; and one was sentenced to one year. A full list of the thirty-one suspects and their respective sentences was included with a report that 'Azmi sent to Ahmad Sadiq. DUL: AHII 165/625–6. See also NA: FO 371/664 (Gorst to Grey).

92. DUL: AHII 165/608 ('Azmi to *Mudir* Buhayra, Nov. 1909).

93. His power derived from many different sources. Foremost among these was his prestige as the main Sanusi agent in the oasis. He had also amassed great wealth as a merchant and smuggler. Dumreicher called him "the only prosperous inhabitant" of Siwa. Additionally, Habun was also in charge of Siwa's *waqf* properties, which he guarded closely. See Dumreicher, *Trackers and Smugglers*, 31; DUL: AHII 165/572 (Undated letter from al-Madani ibn Mustafa); 165/590.

94. DUL: AHII 165/585 (Karam to the Khedive).

95. MAE: AIE 117 (memo from Cairo Embassy to minister of foreign affairs, Nov. 12, 1909).

96. Dumreicher, *Trackers and Smugglers*, 31.

97. Ibid., 33.

98. "The Oasis Tragedy," *Egyptian Gazette*, Nov. 27, 1909. The episode actually began a year before the raid against the Hassuna tribesmen, when a coast guard unit intercepted

a caravan of Hassuna hashish smugglers. Seven tribesmen died in the scuffle that ensued, after which the Hassuna retaliated by crossing over into Egypt and pillaging the Awlad 'Ali (the event that became the fateful catalyst for the Siwan conspiracy).

99. NA: FO 371/664 (Graham to Hardinge, Oct. 13, 1909); MAE: AIE 117 (memo from Cairo Embassy to minister of foreign affairs, Nov. 12, 1909).

100. DUL: AHII 165/610-11 ('Azmi to *Mudir* Buhayra, Dec. 8, 1909).

101. Ibid.

102. DUL: AHII 165/585 (Karam to the Khedive).

103. DUL: AHII 165/625–26.

104. DUL: AHII 165/585.

105. Ibid.

106. Ibid.

107. NA: FO 371/664 (Graham to Hardinge, Oct. 13, 1909).

108. We know from the paper trail 'Azmi left behind that he was writing regularly to administrators of the *Da'ira Khassa*, not just to state officials in Cairo or Damanhur (the provincial capital of Buhayra). 'Azmi's decision to punish two of the Siwan shaykhs who had allegedly set Habun up, and who had refused to play by 'Azmi's rules after the alleged bribe he took from Habun's wife, can also be explained by a possible collusion with the Khedive. It seems plausible that it was the Khedive who had in fact pushed for 'Azmi to head the Siwa campaign.

109. NA: FO 371/664 (Gorst to Grey, Nov. 26, 1909).

110. Dumreicher tells the story of Habun's execution. Apparently Habun was told that he would not be hanged, and that "it would only be a sort of little ceremony or joke they had to go through, to prove that the Government, when it wished, was strong enough to carry out the sentence in the midst of his relations." And so Habun was duped into ascending to the gallows to say his prayers, when the hangman pushed him down to his death. If this account is true, then the Habun era in Siwa ended with a remarkable act of deceit. Dumreicher, *Trackers and Smugglers*, 34–35.

111. NA: FO 371/664 (Gorst to Grey, Dec. 16, 1909).

112. Hamadu and the other two murder suspects were officially pardoned by King Fu'ad in 1928, on the occasion of his visit to Siwa. Dumreicher, *Trackers and Smugglers*, 35.

113. DUL: AHII 165/597–600 (Shaykh Sa'ud to the Khedive, Oct. 28, 1909).

114. Ibid.

115. Ibid.

116. MAE: AIE 117 (memo from Cairo Embassy to minister of foreign affairs, Nov. 12, 1909).

117. There is evidence that the Khedive returned to Siwa at least one more time after 1906. According to what I could ascertain from the *Egyptian Gazette*, which regularly covered the Khedive's movements around the country, the Khedive traveled as far west as Sollum in January 1912, and also traveled to Siwa on another Western Desert excursion in January 1914.

118. Falls, *Three Years in the Libyan Desert*, 268–69; emphasis added.

119. Ibid., 270–71.

## Chapter 4

1. Cole and Altorki, *Bedouin, Settlers, and Holiday-Makers*, 80.

2. Sidi 'Awam was a revered local religious figure whose tomb was a pilgrimage site for the region's bedouins. Dumreicher, *Trackers and Smugglers*, 12.

3. *Iftitāḥ Masjid Marsa Matruh*.

4. See Skovgaard-Petersen, *Defining Islam for the Egyptian State*, 133–40.

5. *Iftitāḥ Masjid Marsa Matruh*.

6. In the afternoon, in additional to more ceremonial events, Shafiq oversaw the distribution of large amounts of food to the local poor.

7. Quoted in Cole and Altorki, *Bedouin, Settlers, and Holiday-Makers*, 77–78.

8. Conklin, *Mission to Civilize*, 40–43. See also Goswami, *Producing India*, ch. 1.

9. Worsfold, *Redemption of Egypt*, 1–3.

10. "A Modern Joseph: The Plan of an American to Make Egypt Bloom Again," *The Sun* (undated). See also Cope Whitehouse, *Raiyān Moeris*.

11. Quoted in Falls, *Three Years in the Libyan Desert*, 334. Around the same time, the Archaeological Society of Alexandria began to undertake some explorations of the Maryut region, even though the stretch of coastline comprising ancient Marmarica was still "the least-known region of all of Egypt." See "*La Marmarique et les Aoulad-Aly,*" *Bulletin de la Société Khédiviale de Géographie*, series 6 (Mar. 17, 1906).

12. De Cosson, *Mareotis*, 59–60. De Cosson was the brother-in-law of Wilfred Jennings-Bramly, whom we met in Chapters 1–2. Jennings-Bramly launched his own *mise en valeur* projects around Burg al-'Arab, a settlement he established in 1915.

13. Davis, *Resurrecting the Granary of Rome*, 3. As Davis argues, the deep irony of the French narrative is that their own colonial development projects—which reached their height between 1880 and 1930—ultimately led to the most deforestation and active degradation of the North African environment.

14. The "conquest of wasteland" (*kibush ha-shemamah*) was a popular formulation among settlers of the Second Aliyah in Palestine. See Boaz Neumann, *Land and Desire in Early Zionism*.

15. Between the efforts of Beadnell and his colleague, John Ball (whose expertise was in the Sinai and Egypt's Eastern Desert), the Egyptian Geological Survey published numerous scholarly works on the geology and topography of Egypt's deserts and oases. See Beadnell, *Recent Geological Discoveries*; Beadnell, *Farafra Oasis*; Beadnell, *Dakhla Oasis*; Beadnell and Ball, *Baharia Oasis*; Beadnell, *Topography and Geology of Fayum Province*; Beadnell, *An Egyptian Oasis*.

16. "Novel Transport Experiments in the Desert," *Egyptian Gazette*, Feb. 23, 1904.

17. "Corporation of Western Egypt," *Egyptian Gazette*, Jan. 30, 1906.

18. Ibid.

19. Quoted in "The Corporation of Western Egypt, Ltd." (official notice), *The Statist: A Journal of Practical Finance and Trade* 59 (Jan. 12, 1907): ii.

20. *Mining Journal, Railway, and Commercial Gazette* 78 (Dec. 16, 1905): 670.

21. Beadnell, *An Egyptian Oasis*, vii; "Retirement of Mr. Hugh J. Llewellyn Beadnell, F.G.S.," *Geological Magazine* 2 (Jan.–Dec. 1905): 527–28.

22. Beadnell, *An Egyptian Oasis*, 9.

23. *Mining Journal, Railway, and Commercial Gazette* 78 (Dec. 16, 1905): 670.

24. "Corporation of Western Egypt," *Egyptian Gazette*, Feb. 23, 1906.

25. *Mining Journal, Railway, and Commercial Gazette* 78 (Dec. 16, 1905): 670.

26. In January 1907, the Corporation issued another 235,143 capital shares to expedite the light rail construction project. See MAE: AIE 117 (report of Jan. 9, 1907); "The Corporation of Western Egypt, Ltd." (official notice), *The Statist: A Journal of Practical Finance and Trade* 59 (Jan. 12, 1907): ii.

27. "Corporation of Western Egypt, Limited," *The Economist*, Apr. 11, 1908, 799.

28. Jakes, "State of the Field," 53–59.

29. Ibid., 53–56.

30. "The Corporation of Western Egypt, Ltd." (official notice), *The Statist: A Journal of Practical Finance and Trade* 59 (Jan. 12, 1907): ii.

31. Ibid.

32. *Mining Journal, Railway, and Commercial Gazette* 78 (Dec. 16, 1905): 670.

33. Ludden, "India's Development Regime."

34. *Mining Journal, Railway, and Commercial Gazette* 78 (Dec. 16, 1905): 670.

35. Ibid.

36. Article [title unknown] from *Progrès*, Mar. 10, 1906.

37. The phrase used here was "*mettere in valore*," which is the Italian equivalent to *mise en valeur*. See MAE: ASMAI, vol. II 103/2 (letter to minister of foreign affairs, Il Conto Guicciardini, May 11, 1906).

38. MAE: ASMAI, vol. II 101/1/2 (memo on "Italian Society of Commercial Exploration," undated). It was the government's hope that this company would secure a train concession in Benghazi from the Ottoman government, in order to facilitate the expansion of "agricultural colonies, similar to those that the Sublime Porte has even granted to the German government in Syria and Palestine."

39. MAE: ASMAI, vol. II 103/3/18 (memo to Ministro degli Affari Esteri, Dec. 17, 1906).

40. MAE: AIE 108 (report from Cairo Embassy, March 1907).

41. Remarks of chairman of the Corporation of Western Egypt, E. Manville, "Corporation of Western Egypt, Limited," *The Economist*, April 11, 1908, 799. Although it went unmentioned in the chairman's remarks, it seems almost certain that the onset of a protracted financial crisis in Egypt in 1907 would have had an adverse impact on the Corporation's fortunes. See Jakes, "State of the Field," ch. 4.

42. Remarks of Chairman of the Corporation of Western Egypt, E. Manville, "Corporation of Western Egypt, Limited," *The Economist*, April 11, 1908, 799. According to the minutes of the meeting, one Sir Charles Cameron tried to raise suspicions about some shady dealings between the Corporation and the Oases Syndicate—which had passed on the concession to the Corporation back in 1904—but a motion was passed to keep him from speaking further.

43. "Corporation of Western Egypt," *Egyptian Gazette*, May 6, 1909.

44. Baedeker, *Egypt and the Sudan*, 380–81.

45. Hobbs, "A Pilgrimage in Northeastern Africa," 346.

46. Quoted in Pallini and Scaccabarozzi, "British Planning Schemes for Alexandria," 191–92.

47. Falls, *Three Years in the Libyan Desert*, 339–40.

48. See, for example, the case of one Faltuos Bey. DWQ: MNW 0075–022509 (memo from Ministry of Finance to Council of Ministers, Sept. 19, 1903).

49. Falls, *Three Years in the Libyan Desert*, 341–42.

50. DWQ: MNW 0075–058015 (report from Commander W. F. Caborne—Captain of the Khedive's Coast Guard Service, Feb. 14, 1895).

51. Ibid.

52. DWQ: MNW 0075–008640 (finance minister memo to Council of Ministers, Nov. 22, 1904); 0075–008639 (finance minister memo to Council of Ministers, June 6, 1905). These documents were nearly identical, save for the name of the firm and the allotment of feddans to each one, respectively.

53. Ludden, "India's Development Regime."

54. Mazlum's phrase here is *mise à profit*, which I've chosen to take as a loose synonym of *mise en valeur*, to connote "reclamation" of land in the sense of rendering it profitable or productive.

55. DWQ: MNW 0075–008640 (finance minister memo to Council of Ministers, Nov. 22, 1904); 0075–008639 (finance minister memo to Council of Ministers, June 6, 1905). The challenges of securing a water supply never abated. In 1907, when Falls visited Marsa Matruh (over a decade after Caborne's survey expedition), he noted that the water supply was still "the great question for the future of Marsa Matruh." See Falls, *Three Years in the Libyan Desert*, 218.

56. MAE: ASMAI, vol. II 101/2/24 (letter from Arrivabene, in Cairo, to Ministero degli Affari Esteri, Sept. 13, 1905).

57. Dumreicher, *Trackers and Smugglers*, 8. The *Abdel Moneim*—named for the Khedive's son (the crown prince)—was one of three large cruisers that the Egyptian Coast Guard Administration operated. MAE: ASMAI, vol. II 103/3/21 (unsigned report from Nov. 16, 1907).

58. MAE: ASMAI, vol. II 103/3/21 (unsigned report from Nov. 16, 1907). Telegraph stations were built along the way at 'Amriyya, al-'Umayyid, and al-Dab'a. See also "Mariout Development: The Khedive's Railway," *Egyptian Gazette*, July 11, 1907.

59. It also ran up to, but did not encompass, the oasis of Siwa. DWQ: MNW 0075–003226; 0075–058015 (doc. 2).

60. *Journel Officiel*, May 9, 1906. Al-'Umayyid (or "El-Omayed") is now a touristic nature preserve in Egypt.

61. DWQ: MNW 0075–003226; 0075–058015 (doc. 2).

62. By the end of the decade, the coast guard had stations at several locations along the western coastline: Sidi Barrani (twelve men); Bagbag (six men); Dhalla (twelve men); Gara (eighteen men); Bahrayn (twenty-two men); and Siwa (three men). MAE: ASMAI, vol. II 103/3/21 (unsigned report from Nov. 16, 1907).

63. Dumreicher, *Trackers and Smugglers*, 8–9, 13.

64. MAE: ASMAI, vol. II 101/2/24 (letter to minister of foreign affairs from Cairo, July 3, 1904).

65. DWQ: MNW 0075–008640 (finance minister memo to Council of Ministers, Nov. 22, 1904); 0075–008639 (finance minister memo to Council of Ministers, June 6, 1905); emphasis added.

66. See Omar, "Rule of Strangers." Omar argues that the Khedive's budgetary control over the *Diwan al-Awqaf* enabled him to dispatch a network of loyal agents to mosques around the country.

67. "The Question of Maher Pasha," *Egyptian Gazette*, Oct. 25, 1909.

68. Cromer, *Abbas II*, 69–70.

69. Falls, *Three Years in the Libyan Desert*, 217.

70. Quoted in Guerville, *New Egypt*, 112–13.

71. Ibid., 121.

72. *Egyptian Gazette*, Mar. 28, 1907.

73. Guerville, *New Egypt*, 116.

74. In 1904, for instance, the Khedive seems to have spent much of the winter exploring various sites along the coastline while residing at his villa in Maryut. See, for instance, the *Egyptian Gazette* (articles from Jan. 26, 1904 and Mar. 2, 1904). The Khedive's frequent trips to the northwest are borne out in numerous sources, including the memoirs by Falls and Guerville.

75. Quoted in Guerville, *New Egypt*, 113.

76. *Railway Age* 58 (1915); Guerville, *New Egypt*, 114.

77. NA: FO 371/1636 (Garstin to *Da'ira Khassa*, July 4, 1899).

78. The Ministry of Public Works accepted the proposal only after it had first been approved by Ministry of Finances, which dealt with any issues of "crossing of state land," as well as the Ministry of War. NA: FO 371/1636 (translation of Arabic letter from the *Da'ira Khassa* to the Ministry of Finances, Mar. 14, 1903; letter from Ministry of Public Works to the *Da'ira Khassa*, Oct. 21, 1903; letter from H. Fakhry, agent of the Ministry of Public Works, to the *Da'ira Khassa*, Nov. 3, 1903; letter from the Ministry of Finances to the *Da'ira Khassa*, Nov. 17, 1903).

79. Falls, *Three Years in the Libyan Desert*, 205.

80. Shafiq, *Mudhakkirātī fi nisf al-qarn*, 325. See, also, NA: FO 371/1636 (Kitchener to Grey, Mar. 16, 1913).

81. NA: FO 371/1636 ("Working Agreement between Egyptian State Railways and Maryut Railway for exchange of traffic to and from Maryut line," signed by Macauley and Ali Siddiq, Nov. 12, 1906).

82. Falls, *Three Years in the Libyan Desert*, 204–6.

83. The railway's property included "27 large engines, five saloon and first class carriages, four second class saloons, and seventeen third class," in addition to eleven brake and luggage vans, twenty-five covered trucks, fifty-six goods wagons, twenty-five ballast wagons, and eleven cattle trucks. "The Khedive's Railway (Part 2): Mariout Development," *Egyptian Gazette*, July 20, 1907.

84. Guerville, *New Egypt*, 129.

85. DUL: AHII 172/49 ("Daira Khassa du Kédive: Ligne de Mariout, Service des Trains a partir du 1er Mai 1909").

86. MAE: ASMAI, vol. II 103/3/21 (memo from Nov. 16, 1907).

87. Falls, *Three Years in the Libyan Desert*, 204–5.

88. NA: FO 371/1636 (Kitchener to Grey, Mar. 16, 1913).

89. MAE: ASMAI, vol. II 101/2/24 (memo to Ministero degli Affari Esteri, July 3, 1904).

90. Quoted in Guerville, *New Egypt*, 113.

91. *Egyptian Gazette*, July 20, 1907.

92. DUL: AHII 169/522–23 (report to the [*Da'ira*] *Khassa* on inspection work in Hammam from May 29 to June 6, 1905).

93. DUL: AHII 169/206 (report from officer at Ikingi Maryut, through June 30, 1902).

94. "Mariout Development—The Khedive's Railway," *Egyptian Gazette*, July 11, 1907.

95. "The Khedive's Railway," *Egyptian Gazette*, July 17, 1907.

96. "The Khedive's Railway—Mariout Development," *Egyptian Gazette*, July 20, 1907.

97. Ibid.

98. Guerville, *New Egypt*, 129–30.

99. "Mariout District: Progress and Development," *Egyptian Gazette*, Mar. 28, 1907.

100. MAE: ASMAI, vol. II 103/3/21 (Nov. 16, 1907). This claim is substantiated by Falls, who also mentioned that the Khedive often prayed in the Sanusi mosque in Sidi ʿAbd al-Rahman. Falls, *Three Years in the Libyan Desert*, 213.

101. MAE: ASMAI, vol. II 103/3/21 (Nov. 16, 1907). The Italian author of this report also mentioned the existence of *zawaya* in Sidi Barrani, Siwa (where there were two), Fayyum, Kharga, Dakhla, and Farafra.

102. "Mariout District: Progress and Development," *Egyptian Gazette*, March 28, 1907.

103. BOA: Y.PRK.UM 78/97 (memo from *mutasarrif* of Benghazi to Yıldız Palace, 28 Safer 1324).

104. Falls, *Three Years in the Libyan Desert*, 159.

105. Ibid., 231–33.

106. Guerville, *New Egypt*, 130–31.

107. Evidence from British sources suggests that the Khedive took the decision to sell the Maryut Railway only begrudgingly, in order to pay off his spiraling debts.

108. NA: FO 371/1637 (Rodd to Grey, Mar. 23, 1913).

109. Ibid. This syndicate—which counted among its ranks key agents of the Bank of Rome—was established on May 16, 1910. The Italian government had actively encouraged its formation at that time to help facilitate the construction of a coastal railroad in Cyrenaica, and even brought the Khedive into the syndicate to allay potential Ottoman concerns about the project. No real progress had been made on a Cyrenaican railway, however, when the Ottoman-Italian War broke out in September 1911.

Additionally, according to Rodd, the Bank of Rome had become the primary financial backer for Italian projects in Tripoli and Cyrenaica. See NA: FO 371/1637 (Rodd to Grey, Mar. 23, 1913).

110. NA: FO 371/1636 (Kitchener to Grey, Jan. 19, 1913).

111. NA: FO 371/1636 (Foreign Office memo, Mar. 13, 1913).

112. NA: FO 371/1636 (Kitchener to Grey, Mar. 15, 1913).

113. NA: FO 371/1636 (Grey to Rodd, Mar. 19, 1913).

114. NA: FO 371/1636 (Kitchener to Grey, Mar. 16, 1913).

115. Shafiq, *Mudhakkirātī fī nisf al-qarn*, 325.

116. NA: FO 371/1636 (Grey to Kitchener, Mar. 19, 1913).

117. NA: FO 371/1636 (memo by Lord Cecil, enclosed with Kitchener report of Mar. 16, 1913).

118. NA: FO 371/1637 (note from Rodd to Grey, Mar. 25, 1913).

119. The crisis got consistently more dire between 1907 and 1910, when the Agricultural Bank reported that forty thousand of its loans were in default. For an analysis of the 1907 financial crisis in the broader context of Anglo-Egyptian economism, see Jakes, "State of the Field," ch. 4.

120. Briggs, *Through Egypt in War-Time*, 118.

121. NA: FO 371/1636 (Grey to Kitchener, Mar. 27, 1913).

122. Telegram from Grey to the Khedive. Quoted in 'Abbas Hilmi II, *Last Khedive of Egypt*, 119.

123. NA: FO 371/1637 (Kitchener to Grey, Apr. 3, 1913).

124. NA: FO 141/635/3 (letter from Shafiq, director-general of the Maryut Railway, to the minister of public works, Mar. 23, 1913).

125. In a letter to the *Da'ira Khassa*, a British official had written that, as a result of the Ottoman-Italian War, "Egypt is thus found to have as a neighboring power not the Suzerain power any longer, but rather Italy. The question of the railroad connecting at the border changes its aspect completely and takes on a major importance." See NA: FO 371/1637 (draft letter from Egyptian government to the *Da'ira Khassa*).

126. NA: FO 141/635/3 (letter from Shafiq, director-general of the Maryut Railway, to the minister of public works, Mar. 23, 1913).

127. NA: FO 371/1637 (Rodd to Grey, Mar. 23, 1913).

128. See, for example, NA: FO 371/1637 (Rodd to Grey, Mar. 23, 1913).

129. NA: FO 371/1637 (Grey to Rodd, Mar. 24, 1913).

130. NA: FO 371/1966 (Kitchener to Grey, Feb. 6, 1914). Shafiq puts the sum at 390,000 Egyptian Pounds. Shafiq, *Mudhakkirātī fī nisf al-qarn*, 325.

131. NA: FO 371/1966 (Kitchener to Grey, Feb. 6, 1914).

132. NA: FO 371/1637 (Kitchener to Grey, May 11, 1913).

133. 'Abbas Hilmi II, *Last Khedive of Egypt*, 113.

134. Ibid., 114.

135. Ibid., 115.

136. Jakes, "State of the Field," 60–62, 84–85.

137. Cromer, *Abbas II*, 83–84.

138. At the same time, the Khedive employed a civilizing discourse towards the bedouins of the Egyptian West. In a photobook that the *Diwan al-Awqaf* published to commemorate the opening of the Sidi 'Awam Mosque in Marsa Matruh, the author of a short introduc-

tory essay noted that it was hoped that the mosque might provide the local bedouin Arabs with "civilization and instruction in obedience to God." See *Iftitāḥ Masjid Marsa Matruh.*

139. De Cosson, *Mareotis,* 189.

140. Cole and Altorki, *Bedouin, Settlers, and Holiday-Makers,* 30–31.

## Chapter 5

1. NA: FO 78/5490 (Findlay to Lansdowne, July 18, 1902); 78/5227 (Findlay to Lansdowne, July 20, 1902).

2. NA: FO 78/5490 (Oakes memo, July 19, 1902).

3. NA: FO 78/5490 (Major Hills memo, July 21, 1902).

4. NA: FO 101/92 (Alvarez memo, May 28, 1902).

5. NA: FO 101/92 (Alvarez memo, June 26, 1902).

6. NA: FO 101/94 (Alvarez memo, June 28, 1902).

7. Egypt was one of a handful of autonomous provinces. For a complete list of autonomous provinces, see Genell, "Empire by Law."

8. Adelman and Aron, "From Borderlands to Borders."

9. The implicit teleology of this part of the analysis—the notion that borderland territorialization must inevitably yield ossified "bordered lands"—has come under some criticism. See, for example, Truett and Young, "Making Transnational History," 16.

10. In more conventional scholarship on Ottoman frontiers and borderlands, historians have tended to prioritize the paradigm of imperial centralization and decentralization, thereby reducing the borderland to being a site for investigating center-periphery dynamics across imperial history. As such, the "frontier" is typically represented as a straightforward proxy for the Ottoman "periphery" and thus can only be meaningfully analyzed vis-à-vis its fluctuating relationship with Istanbul. See, for example: Karpat and Zens, introduction to *Ottoman Borderlands*; A. C. S. Peacock, introduction to *Frontiers of the Ottoman World.* For a thorough critique of the Ottoman borderlands historiography, see my review essay, "Over the Borderline?" For some notable newer approaches to Ottoman borderlands, see: Klein, *Margins of Empire*; Ateş, *Ottoman-Iranian Borderlands*; Blumi, "Thwarting the Ottoman Empire"; Blumi, "The Frontier as a Measure of Modern Power."

11. This rhetorical strategy reflected Istanbul's broader diplomatic effort to insist upon its formal sovereignty over Egypt, which meant engaging the British in a ceaseless debate over the country's status in international law throughout the period of the veiled protectorate. See Genell, "Empire by Law," intro. and ch. 2. The Ottomans adopted a similar approach to its formal definitions of territory in the Yemeni borderlands. See Blumi, "Frontier as a Measure of Modern Power"; Kuehn, *Empire, Islam, and Politics of Difference.*

12. Genell, "Empire by Law," intro. and ch. 2.

13. Anscombe, *Ottoman Gulf*; Rogan, *Frontiers of the State*; Deringil, *Well-Protected Domains*; Messick, *Calligraphic State*; Blumi, *Rethinking the Late Ottoman Empire*; Klein, *Margins of Empire*; Kasaba, *Moveable Empire*; Kuehn, *Empire, Islam, and Politics of Difference.*

14. The major scholarly works on late-Ottoman Libya are: Anderson, "Nineteenth-Century Reform in Ottoman Libya"; Anderson, *State and Social Transformation*; Le Gall, "Pashas, Bedouins, and Notables"; Ahmida, *Making of Modern Libya*; Akarli, "The Defence

of the Libyan Provinces"; Deringil, "'They Live in a State of Nomadism and Savagery'";
Minawi, *Ottoman Scramble for Africa*.

15. See, for example: Anderson, *State and Social Transformation*, cf. Le Gall, "Pashas,
Bedouins, and Notables."

16. Le Gall, "Pashas, Bedouins, and Notables," 253–54.

17. Le Gall, "Ottoman Reaction to the European 'Scramble for Africa,'" 135, cf. Minawi,
*Ottoman Scramble for Africa*, 4; Deringil, "Les Ottomans et le Partage de l'Afrique."

18. Le Gall, "Pashas, Bedouins, and Notables," 57–59. British proconsuls stationed in
Benghazi, for their part, seemed to consider their posts a particularly cruel form of torture.
See, for example, the passionate appeal of proconsul Hutton Dufaues to be transferred.
NA: FO 101/68 (Dufaues memo, Apr. 7, 1880).

19. Anderson, "Nineteenth-Century Reform in Ottoman Libya," 328; Le Gall, "Pashas,
Bedouins, and Notables," 184; Ahmida, *Making of Modern Libya*, 15, 75.

20. Ahmida, *Making of Modern Libya*, 15. In the estimate of an Italian ethnographer,
in 1922 Benghazi had 10,000 inhabitants whereas Darna had around 9,700 and Marj had
1,540. De Agostini, *Le popolazioni della Cirenaica*.

21. In 1881, the Ottomans had only two regular infantry battalions stationed in Benghazi, totaling eleven hundred troops; this was one tenth the size of the standing army in
Tripoli. By 1890, there were still only five battalions (thirty-five hundred troops). Since
there was no conscription in the Libyan provinces throughout the nineteenth century,
the Ottomans sometimes formed irregular units, though this was not common practice in
Benghazi during the 1880s; more typically, reserve troops would be brought in from Tripoli
when needed. Le Gall, "Pashas, Bedouins, and Notables," 185–86.

22. Le Gall, "Pashas, Bedouins, and Notables," 57–59; NA: FO 195/2160 (Alvarez
memo, June 21, 1904).

23. NA: FO 195/1082 (Hutton Dufaues to Layard, March 1, 1879). According to Le
Gall, the public works environment never improved. Even at the start of the twentieth century, the Ottoman government had "completed only a few public works projects and most
of them, including the building of new schools in the town of Benghazi, would not have
been completed had the imperial treasury not supplied loans and aid." Le Gall, "Pashas,
Bedouins, and Notables," 253.

24. See Anscombe, *Ottoman Gulf,* for an apt comparison with Benghazi's fiscal travails.

25. Le Gall, "Pashas, Bedouins, and Notables," 71–73.

26. This experiment in independence—which marked a fundamental change from the
province's erstwhile status as a *sancak* of Tripoli—lasted only ten years. In 1888 Benghazi
was downgraded to a *mutasarrıflık*, though this meant its governor still reported directly to
the Interior Ministry in Istanbul, not to the governor of Tripoli. Le Gall, "Pashas, Bedouins, and Notables," 186–87.

27. Le Gall, "Pashas, Bedouins, and Notables," 206.

28. The nature of the Ottoman-Sanusi relationship in the era of state re-centralization
has been the subject of unyielding debate within the historiography of modern Libya. The
debate revolves around three key questions: first, the alleged Sanusi exemption from state
taxes; second, the extent to which the Ottomans saw the Sanusiyya as both allies and civi-

lizers of the tribal Eastern Sahara; and third, the degree to which the Sanusiyya supported Ottoman re-centralization in the Libyan provinces, and—by extension—their campaign to claim sovereignty in Central Africa (particularly the Lake Chad Basin). Michel Le Gall, pursuing these questions in the 1980s and early-1990s, sought to overturn the prevailing literature, which he found to be rooted in colonial-era paranoia regarding Islamic "fanaticism." In his view, while the Ottomans did occasionally seek Sanusi assistance in Libya and Central Africa, they ultimately found the Sanusiyya wholly unreliable—either unable or unwilling to do much for them. Mostafa Minawi takes a diametrically opposed stance, highlighting what he calls the Ottoman-Sanusi "strategic partnership." As he puts it, "I argue not only that the Ottoman state's policy and the Sanusi philosophy of administration were ideologically synchronistic but also that their work on the ground was complementary, cooperative, and at times even synergetic" (36). Le Gall, "Ottoman Government and the Sanusiyya"; Minawi, *Ottoman Scramble for Africa*, 34–39, 50–60, 81–95.

My take on the Ottoman-Sanusi relationship lies somewhere in between these views. I suggest that Ottoman policy toward the Sanusiyya in the last decades of the nineteenth century was ever evolving, never entirely consistent, and almost always rooted in the particular exigencies of the moment. On one hand, I do not believe the Ottomans ever trusted the Sanusiyya nearly enough to form a long-standing "strategic partnership," and it is clear from the tax campaigns against the bedouins—most of them Sanusi followers—that the Ottomans were willing to jeopardize their standing with the Sanusi leadership. On the other hand, the Ottomans were loath to antagonize the Sanusiyya completely, and they kowtowed to the Brotherhood at moments when they felt their rule to be particularly vulnerable in the Libyan provinces. In 1905, for example, the Sanusiyya successfully lobbied the Ottoman government to remove a *mutasarrıf* of Benghazi, named Zühdü Paşa. See BOA: DH.MKT 1004/43, docs. 4, 6 (memos from Zühdü Paşa to the Interior Ministry and to the Grand Vezir, respectively).

29. Le Gall mentions that a "partial" land survey had been started around 1860 but was never completed. Le Gall, "Pashas, Bedouins, and Notables," 216.

30. Rogan, *Frontiers of the State*, ch. 3.

31. Le Gall, "Pashas, Bedouins, and Notables," 207.

32. For the latter campaign, see Rogan, *Frontiers of the State*, 49–52.

33. For a detailed examination of the three tax campaigns, see Le Gall, "Pashas, Bedouins, and Notables," 205–24. See, also, Le Gall, "Ottoman Government and the Sanusiyya," 99–101.

34. NA: FO 101/72 (Wood to Granville, May 1, 1883).

35. NA: FO 101/72 (Wood to Granville, July 11, 1883, and Dec. 24, 1883).

36. Le Gall, "Ottoman Government and the Sanusiyya," 100.

37. Le Gall, "Pashas, Bedouins, and Notables," 211.

38. Ibid., 216.

39. Ibid., 217–19.

40. Ibid., 222, 251, 253.

41. See, for instance, Benghazi governor Zühdü Paşa's appeals to Istanbul. BOA: DH.MKT 1004/43.

42. Throughout this section, I use the term *border* only inasmuch as the Ottoman state and bedouin tribes alike consistently seemed to invoke one, even though its referent—an indeterminate *hatt-ı fasl*—was never clearly defined at this time.

43. BOA: A.MKT 8/67 (Jan. 28, 1844/7 Muharrem 1260). This document indicates that the Ottomans deemed the matter extremely important, passing it up through the official channels of authority. Amin Efendi sent the shaykhs' letters to the *mutasarrıf* of Benghazi, who in turn forwarded them to the governor of Tripoli.

44. In this respect, the evidence I've found for the Ottoman Libyan provinces fits seamlessly with Reşat Kasaba's account of the Ottomans' shifting tribal policy across the empire. According to Kasaba, the mid-nineteenth century witnessed a marked expansion of the Ottomans' system of intelligence gathering on nomadic bedouins, all for the purposes of security and taxation. Kasaba, *Moveable Empire*, 105–7.

45. In one document, the verb used to describe their crossing over is from *savuşmak* (to "flee" or "abscond"). BOA: A.MKT.UM 231/84.

46. BOA: A.MKT.UM 231/84; A.MKT.MVL 80/95.

47. BOA: A.MKT.MVL 80/95.

48. BOA: A.MKT.UM 231/84; A.MKT.MVL 80/95.

49. BOA: A.MKT.MVL 80/95.

50. Ibid.

51. BOA: A.MKT.MHM 292/86 (doc. 1).

52. BOA: A.MKT.MHM 292/86 (doc. 2). It is unclear whether the request was implemented. Regardless, the document is noteworthy for its specific instructions concerning how these notables should appear, and be treated, upon their arrival in Istanbul. For an extensive treatment of Ottoman ceremonial as a means to cultivate the allegiance of provincial tribes, see Deringil, *Well-Protected Domains*.

53. One *keyse* was worth five hundred piasters. See Redhouse, *Turkish and English Lexicon*, 1612; Blackburn, "Collapse of Ottoman Authority in Yemen."

54. BOA: A.MKT.UM 371/57; A.MKT.UM 384/54.

55. BOA: A.MKT.UM 371/57. This document clearly reflects the civilizing language that emerged as a common feature of the Ottoman state's discourse vis-à-vis Tripoli's and Benghazi's nomadic tribes. See Deringil, "'They Live in a State of Nomadism and Savagery,'" 317–24.

56. BOA: A.MKT.UM 371/57.

57. Ibid.

58. Ibid.

59. Ibid.

60. The document describing this case points out that the Awlad ʿAli were originally from Benghazi but had long since settled in Egypt (specifically in Buhayra and Aqaba). See BOA: İ.MTZ(05) 18/668 (docs. 6, 7).

61. BOA: İ.MTZ(05) 18/668 (docs. 6, 8).

62. BOA: İ.MTZ(05) 18/668 (doc. 6).

63. BOA: İ.MTZ(05) 18/668 (doc. 8).

64. The mere existence of the *İrade* file wherein this case is described indicates that the

decree was in fact issued; at the same time, the lack of any ensuing paper trail makes it difficult to know if Sa'id followed through on his Sultanic obligation.

65. BOA: İ.MTZ(05) 18/668 (doc. 7).

66. BOA: DH.MKT 1524/92.

67. BOA: DH.TMIK.S 14/4 (doc. 4).

68. BOA: DH.TMIK.S 14/4 (doc. 3). It is unclear if the document's author is referring solely to Bomba and Tobruk, the *kaza* of Darna, or else a wider stretch of tribal Benghazi.

69. BOA: DH.TMIK.S 14/4 (doc. 4).

70. Aside from more indirect forms of taxation such as toll taxes, the Ottoman government generally collected four types of taxes from its population in Tripoli and Benghazi: the state or *mîrî* tax, collected on the basis of income; the tithe (paid in kind); the livestock tax; and (when applicable) a building or property tax (*emlâk*). From this document, it seems officials were conceding that the unsettled tribesmen had only typically been responsible for the livestock tax, though this, too, went largely unpaid (which explains the introduction of the livestock toll). See De Agostini, *Popolazioni della Cirenaica*, 10–11.

71. BOA: DH.TMIK.S 14/4 (doc. 4).

72. BOA: DH.TMIK.S 14/4 (doc. 3).

73. NA: FO 195/2054 (Alvarez memo, Mar. 9, 1899).

74. NA: FO 195/2054 (Alvarez memo, Feb. 27, 1899).

75. NA: FO 195/2054 (Alvarez memo, Apr. 24, 1899).

76. BOA: DH.MKT 489/56 (doc. 22).

77. Ibid.

78. Though it is difficult to locate Defne on contemporary maps of Libya, it seems to have been located in the vicinity of Tobruk, close to the area known today as Zawiyat Zanzur.

79. NA: FO 101/92 (Alvarez to Lansdowne, Mar. 3, 1902).

80. BOA: DH.MKT 489/56, (doc. 3: Foreign Ministry to Interior Ministry, Apr. 16, 1902 / 7 Muharrem 1320).

81. This route from Benghazi to Egypt, along the coast, constitutes one of the two major caravan routes in the borderland (the other was the north-south route from Wadai to the town of Benghazi). According to Ahmida, the tribal population in Benghazi had long seen various locales in western Egypt, as well as Alexandria, as the natural markets for their goods. In 1891, for instance, tribes from Benghazi exported 920 camels, 248 horses, and 53,131 sheep (worth a total of 51,600 pounds) to Egypt. In 1900, 160,000 sheep were exported to Egypt and Malta; this number increased to 200,000 in 1901 and 300,000 in 1902. Ahmida, *Making of Modern Libya,* 81.

82. NA: FO 195/1446 (Wood report, Mar. 18, 1883).

83. Ibid.

84. NA: FO 101/92 (Alvarez to Lansdowne, Mar. 3, 1902; Foreign Office note, Mar. 3, 1902).

85. NA: FO 101/92 (Alvarez to Lansdowne, Mar. 3, 1902).

86. NA: FO 101/92 (Foreign Office note, Mar. 3, 1902).

87. NA: FO 101/92 (Alvarez memo, Apr. 28, 1902).

88. The introduction of similar internal tolls or excise taxes in the Hasa region of Arabia—against reformer Midhat Paşa's will, and in violation of his promises to the local population—was a major source of revenue in that cash-strapped province. See Anscombe, *Ottoman Gulf*, 58, 63, 168.

89. NA: FO 101/92 (Alvarez to Lansdowne, Mar. 3, 1902).

90. Ibid.

91. NA: FO 101/92 (Alvarez memo, Nov. 19, 1902). The primary quarantine site was Malta.

92. BOA: DH.MKT 489/56 (doc. 3).

93. NA: FO 101/92 (Alvarez to Lansdowne, Mar. 3, 1902).

94. NA: FO 101/92 (Alvarez memo, Apr. 3, 1902).

95. NA: FO 101/92 (Statement of Mr. Joseph Abuharoun, May 19, 1902).

96. Ibid.

97. NA: FO 101/92 (Alvarez to Lansdowne, Mar. 3, 1902).

98. NA: FO 101/92 (Alvarez memo, July 21, 1902).

99. This analysis of the *Derbend-i Defne* tax echoes early modern legal theorist Hugo Grotius's concept of *jurisdictional* sovereignty, which he contrasted with the idea of territorial "dominion," or ownership, of space. Jurisdiction primarily implied the ability of sovereign agents to police and control the movement of *people* and their goods through spaces (such as oceans) that they did not (or could not) own. See Benton, *Search for Sovereignty*, 131–37.

100. This was apparently in response to news that the Ottoman government was proceeding with plans to construct new military bases nearby at Port Sulayman and Tobruk. It is possible, however, that this news was apocryphal. Egyptian Coast Guard officials consistently maintained that they never established a permanent presence any further west than Sidi Barrani, a small settlement some fifty miles east of Sollum. See, for example, DWQ: MNW 0075–011200 (Purvis to Egyptian Ministry of the Interior, May 13, 1907); and NA: FO 101/94 (memo from Aug. 10, 1903).

101. BOA: MV 102/28 (Cabinet minutes from May 14, 1901 / 25 Muharrem 1319).

102. BOA: MV 103/67 (Cabinet minutes from Feb. 26, 1902 / 18 Zilkade 1319).

103. BOA: MV 104/13 (Cabinet minutes from May 4, 1902 / 25 Muharrem 1320).

104. NA: FO 78/5227 (Findlay to Lansdowne, July 12, 1902).

105. NA: FO 78/5227 (Findlay to Lansdowne, July 20, 1902).

106. NA: FO 78/5490 (cover sheet to Intelligence Division memos, July 21, 1902).

107. NA: FO 78/5490 (Findlay memo, July 25, 1902).

108. NA: FO 78/5490 (Hogg report, July 23, 1902).

109. NA: FO 78/5490 (Shalabi Mustafa report, Oct. 6, 1904).

110. NA: FO 78/5490 (Dumreicher to Purvis, Oct. 7, 1904).

111. NA: FO 78/5490 (Purvis memo, Oct. 11, 1904).

112. NA: FO 78/5490 (undated memo from the director of intelligence of the Sudan government).

113. NA: FO 78/5490 (Cromer memo, Dec. 15, 1904).

114. NA: FO 78/5367 (Coast Guard memo, Oct. 25, 1904; undated Sheehan memo; Cromer to Lansdowne, Oct. 29, 1904).

115. BOA: Y.MTV 268/166 (*Dahiliye* memo, Dec. 1, 1904 / 23 Ramazan 1322).

116. The Grand Vezir pointed out that the Egyptian Khedive would be able to confirm the presence of an Ottoman garrison at Sollum, since he had visited the port "not so very long ago."

117. NA: FO 78/5490 (Townley to Lansdowne, Nov. 29, 1904).

118. NA: FO 78/5490 (Townley to Lansdowne, Nov. 22, 1904).

119. NA: FO 78/5490 (Townley to Tewfik Pasha, Feb. 14, 1905; Townley to Lansdowne, Feb. 14, 1905).

120. NA: FO 78/5490 (Cromer to Lansdowne, Feb. 28, 1905).

121. Historian Fatima 'Alam al-Din 'Abd al-Wahid suggests that—whereas the Ottoman government did not give any weight whatsoever to the British diplomatic memos of November and February spelling out the Egyptian government's position on the western border—the British "considered the [Ottomans' subsequent] silence as a sign of the Ottoman state's acceptance" of the claim. 'Abd al-Wahid, *Ḥudūd Miṣr al-gharbiyya*, 27–28. As I will discuss in the following chapter, the British did in fact periodically revisit the Townley declarations of 1904–5, particularly when arguing their position to the Italians.

122. Kasaba, *Moveable Empire*, 8.

## Chapter 6

1. NA: FO 141/634/1 (memo from Egyptian Coast Guard station at Sidi Barrani, Oct. 12, 1911).

2. NA: FO 141/634/1 (memo from Hunter, Nov. 12, 1911).

3. NA: FO 141/634/1 (memo from Hunter, Nov. 6, 1911).

4. See BOA: MV 162/87 (Ottoman Cabinet minutes of Mar. 16, 1912); and NA: FO 141/634/1 (British Foreign Office Aide-Memoire of Jan. 9, 1912).

5. NA: WO 106/218 (Fitzgerald memo, Jan. 1, 1912).

6. Ibid.

7. The Survey Department was established in June 1898. Under the direction of British Geologist H. G. Lyons, it united several older institutions: the Revenue Survey, the Hydrographical Survey, the Geological Survey, and the Map Drawing Office of the Ministry of Public Works. Two years later, the Survey Department added the Astronomical and Meteorological Observatory at 'Abbasiyya. Until 1905, the Survey Department was under the auspices of the Egyptian government's Ministry of Public Works, at which point it became subject instead to the Ministry of Finance. The Survey Department was responsible for the "first systematic survey of a large desert area in Egypt," which took place in the Northern Sinai between 1908–14. No comparable surveying project was undertaken in the Western Desert prior to the First World War. See Murray, *Survey of Egypt*, 1–3.

8. NA: WO 106/218 (Fitzgerald memo, Jan. 1, 1912).

9. The war provided the Ottomans with a small window of opportunity to regain the Libyan provinces from Italy. While the British were preoccupied with their campaign against the Ottomans in the Sinai, Ottoman officers such as Enver Bey worked with the Sanusiyya and bedouin chiefs in eastern Benghazi to provoke a short-lived rebellion against the British throughout the Egyptian West. See McGuirk, *Sanusi's Little War*.

10. For a classic example, see Prescott, *Political Frontiers and Boundaries*.

11. Ibid., 72.

12. Ibid., ch. 3.

13. See Donnan and Wilson, *Borders: Frontiers of Identity, Nation and State*; Donnan and Wilson, eds., *Border Approaches*; Brandell, ed., *State Frontiers*; Anderson, *Frontiers*; Rumley and Minghi, eds., *Geography of Border Landscapes*; Migdal, ed., *Boundaries and Belonging*; Blake and Schofield, eds., *Boundaries and State Territory*; Wilson and Donnan, eds., *Border Identities*.

14. For key examples of the former, see Sahlins, *Boundaries*; Ateş, *Ottoman-Iranian Borderlands*; Winichakul, *Siam Mapped*. For the latter, see Burnett, *Masters of All They Surveyed*; Edney, *Mapping an Empire*; Carter, *Road to Botany Bay*; Ryan, *Cartographic Eye*.

15. Prescott, *Political Frontiers and Boundaries*, 72.

16. NA: FO 101/94 (Currie memo, Jan. 10, 1902).

17. NA: FO 101/94 (Lansdowne to Currie, Jan. 31, 1902).

18. NA: FO 101/94 (Cromer memo, Jan. 14, 1902). The term "frontier" was used interchangeably with "border" and "boundary" in many British documents and publications of the period.

19. NA: FO 101/94 (Cromer memo, Feb. 20, 1902).

20. NA: FO 101/94 Cromer memo, Feb. 21, 1902).

21. NA: FO 101/94 (Intelligence Division memo, Feb. 26, 1902).

22. NA: FO 101/94 (Lansdowne to Currie, Jan. 31, 1902; Currie to Lansdowne, Mar. 15, 1902).

23. NA: FO 101/94 (Alvarez memo, Feb. 12, 1902).

24. NA: FO 101/92 (Alvarez memo, May 31, 1902).

25. NA: FO 101/92 (Alvarez memo, August 6, 1902).

26. See, for instance, NA: FO 101/94 (Findlay to Lansdowne, Sept. 14, 1902).

27. See NA: FO 101/94 (Alvarez memo, June 7, 1902).

28. NA: FO 101/94 (Alvarez to Lansdowne, Aug. 20, 1902).

29. It is unknown what came of this annexation movement. The Egyptian War Office reported a year later that the "agitation is still more or less alive, and that the Khedive is interested in it." NA: FO 101/94 (Gleichen memo, Cairo Intelligence News, May 31, 1903).

30. 'Abd al-Wahid's historical study of the western border is the only work I have encountered that addresses this conflict, but the analysis is hamstrung by its limited source base, as well as the author's tendency to reify the distinction between Ottoman and Egyptian territorial realms before it is historically accurate to do so. 'Abd al-Wahid, *Ḥudūd Miṣr al-gharbiyya*, ch. 2.

31. NA: FO 78/5490 (Shalabi Mustafa to Officer Commanding of the Coast Guard Administration's Western District, enclosed with Cromer memo, Feb. 28, 1905).

32. BOA: DH.MKT 914/6 (doc. 3: Benghazi *mutasarrıf* to *Dahiliye Nezareti*, Sept. 21, 1904 / 11 Receb 1322).

33. NA: FO 78/5490 (Shalabi Mustafa to Officer Commanding of the Coast Guard Administration's Western District, enclosed with Cromer memo, Feb. 28, 1905). An ardeb is an Egyptian unit of capacity equivalent to 5.619 U.S. bushels.

34. Dumreicher, *Trackers and Smugglers*, 48.

35. NA: FO 78/5490 (Shalabi Mustafa to Officer Commanding of the Coast Guard Administration's Western District, enclosed with Cromer memo, Feb. 28, 1905).

36. BOA: DH.MKT 914/6 (doc. 6: Egyptian Interior Ministry memo to Ottoman Interior Ministry, Feb. 7, 1905 / 2 Zilhicce 1322).

37. NA: FO 78/5490 (petition from "Kateefa group" of the Awlad 'Ali bedouins to Shalabi Mustafa, enclosed with Cromer memo, Feb. 28, 1905; Shalabi Mustafa memo).

38. NA: FO 78/5490 (Shalabi Mustafa to Officer Commanding of the Coast Guard Administration's Western District, enclosed with Cromer memo, Feb. 28, 1905; Cromer to Lansdowne, Feb. 28, 1905).

39. NA: FO 78/5490 (Cromer to Lansdowne, Feb. 6, 1905; petition from bedouin Shaykhs of Marsa Matruh to Shalabi Mustafa, enclosed with Cromer memo, Feb. 28, 1905).

40. BOA: DH.MKT 914/6 (doc. 6: Egyptian Interior Ministry memo to Ottoman Interior Ministry, Feb. 7, 1905 / 2 Zilhicce 1322); NA: FO 78/5490 (Cromer to Lansdowne, Feb. 6, 1905).

41. NA: FO 78/5490 (petition from "Kateefa group" of Awlad 'Ali bedouins to Shalabi Mustafa, enclosed with Cromer memo, Feb. 28, 1905).

42. NA: FO 78/5490 (petition from bedouin shaykhs of Marsa Matruh and environs to Shalabi Mustafa, enclosed with Cromer memo, Feb. 28, 1905); emphasis added.

43. NA: FO 78/5490 (Shalabi Mustafa to Officer Commanding of the Coast Guard Administration's Western District, enclosed with Cromer memo, Feb. 28, 1905). Dumreicher, for his part, heaps praise on Shalabi Mustafa for his savvy handling of Egypt's Western bedouins. Dumreicher, *Trackers and Smugglers*, 6, 48.

44. NA: FO 78/5490 (Shalabi Mustafa to Officer Commanding of the Coast Guard Administration's Western District, enclosed with Cromer memo, Feb. 28, 1905).

45. Ibid.

46. NA: FO 78/5490 (Cromer to Lansdowne, Feb. 28, 1905). Alvarez, for his part, described the Awlad 'Ali as "Egyptian subjects." See NA: FO 101/96 (Alvarez memo, Mar. 1, 1905).

47. NA: FO 78/5490 (two memos from Cromer to Lansdowne, Feb. 28, 1905).

48. NA: FO 78/5490 (Cromer to Lansdowne, Feb. 6, 1905; Townley to Lansdowne, Feb. 14, 1905; Cromer to Lansdowne, Feb. 28, 1905).

49. NA: FO 78/5490 (Cromer to Lansdowne, Feb. 28, 1905).

50. NA: FO 101/96 (Alvarez memo, Mar. 1, 1905).

51. NA: FO 78/5490 (Cromer to Lansdowne, Feb. 28, 1905).

52. NA: FO 101/96 (Alvarez memo, Mar. 19, 1905); NA: FO 78/5490 (O'Conor to Lansdowne, Mar. 21, 1905).

53. NA: FO 78/5490 (O'Conor to Lansdowne, Mar. 21, 1905).

54. NA: FO 78/5490 (Cromer to Lansdowne, Feb. 25, 1905).

55. NA: FO 101/96 (Alvarez memo, Mar. 19, 1905).

56. NA: FO 101/96 (Alvarez memo, Apr. 7, 1905).

57. Dumreicher, *Trackers and Smugglers*, 49.

58. BOA: DH.MKT 914/6 (doc. 7: Undated memo from Benghazi *Mutasarrıf* Zühdü Paşa to *Dahiliye Nezareti*).

59. MAE: ASMAI, vol. II 103/3/16 (report from July 13, 1906).

60. MAE: AIE 108 (vice-consul in Benghazi to vice-consul in Tripoli, Apr. 26, 1906; MAE to Italian embassy in Cairo, May 28, 1906).

61. MAE: AIE 108 (vice-consul in Benghazi to vice-consul in Tripoli, Apr. 26, 1906; MAE to Italian embassy in Cairo, May 28, 1906).

62. This toponym should not be confused with Bomba, a port town located between Darna and Tobruk in Benghazi. The Ottomans and Egyptians sometimes conflated the two, however. See DWQ: MNW 0075–011200 (Purvis memo, May 13, 1907).

63. BOA: Y.A.RES 132/17 (doc. 2: *Dahiliye* minister to the Grand Vezir, Apr. 5, 1905 / 29 Muharrem 1323).

64. BOA: MV 111/31 (Cabinet minutes of May 4, 1905 / 28 Safer 1323).

65. BOA: Y.A.RES 132/17 (doc. 2: *Dahiliye* minister to the Grand Vezir, Apr. 5, 1905 / 29 Muharrem 1323).

66. BOA: MV 112/58 (Cabinet minutes of Dec. 11, 1905 / 13 Şevval 1323).

67. DWQ: MNW 0075–011210 (Egyptian Interior Ministry to Grand Vezir, Jan. 15, 1906).

68. Ibid.

69. NA: FO 371/346 (letter from Egyptian minister of the interior to *mutasarrıf* of Benghazi, Feb. 4, 1907 / 20 Zilhicce 1324).

70. NA: FO 141/634/1 ("Note upon Present Situation Western Frontier," May 15, 1907).

71. NA: FO 371/247 ("Translation of memo sent by Yuzbashi Ahmed Effendi Fahmy, Ma'mur of Marsa Matruh to the Governorate of Alexandria," Mar. 1907).

72. MAE: ASMAI, vol. II 101/2/33–4 (Tritonj to Italian Consul at Tripoli, Jan. 2, 1907).

73. Ibid.

74. MAE: ASMAI, vol. II 101/2/33–4 (MAE to Italian ambassador in London, Jan. 23, 1907; MAE to consul-general in Tripoli, Feb. 9, 1907).

75. NA: FO 371/247 (Cromer to Grey, Feb. 1, 1907).

76. NA: FO 371/346 (letter from Egyptian minister of the interior to *mutasarrıf* of Benghazi, Feb. 4, 1907 / 20 Zilhicce 1324).

77. Ibid.

78. NA: FO 371/346 (Fontana memo, Feb. 23, 1907).

79. NA: FO 371/247 (memo from Egyptian Interior Ministry to Cromer, Mar. 18, 1907; Cromer to Grey, Mar. 20, 1907).

80. Ibid.

81. NA: FO 371/247 (Procès-Verbal of Mar. 18, 1907; "Report by Yuzbashi Ahmed Effendi Fahmy, Ma'mur of Marsa Matruh to the Governorate of Alexandria," Mar. 1907).

82. According to Dumreicher, the Bara'sa were threatening to raise a force of "1,500 men armed with good modern rifles," while the Awlad 'Ali were steeling themselves for

further retaliatory incursions into "Turkish territory." Dumreicher, *Trackers and Smugglers*, 45–47.

83. NA: FO 371/247 (Cromer to Grey, Mar. 20, 1907).

84. NA: FO 371/247 (Cromer to Grey, Mar. 7, 1907).

85. NA: FO 371/247 (Cromer to Grey, Mar. 20, 1907).

86. NA: FO 371/247 (Cromer to Grey, Mar. 21, 1907).

87. NA: FO 371/247 (O'Conor to Grey, Mar. 23, 1907).

88. DWQ: MNW 0075–011200 (Grand Vezir to Khedive, Apr. 4, 1907).

89. NA: FO 371/247 ("Report by Yuzbashi Ahmed Effendi Fahmy, Ma'mur of Marsa Matruh to the Governorate of Alexandria," Mar. 1907).

90. NA: FO 371/247 (Cromer to Grey, Apr. 5, 1907). A month later, though, the Ottomans reported that they played a key role in helping resolve the Bara'sa-Awlad 'Ali feud. In turn, a group of Awlad 'Ali shaykhs in Egypt sent the Benghazi governor a telegraph "thanking him for settling the matter so satisfactorily." NA: FO 371/245 (Fontana to O'Conor, May 26, 1907).

91. NA: FO 371/245 (Grey to O'Conor, Mar. 25, 1907).

92. NA: FO 371/247 (Cromer to Grey, Mar. 23, 1907).

93. NA: FO 371/246 (memo from Italian Embassy, Feb. 25, 1907).

94. NA: FO 371/246 (Cromer memo, Mar. 4, 1907).

95. NA: FO 371/247 (Grey to Egerton, May 28, 1907).

96. NA: FO 371/247 (Italian ambassador to Grey, June 12, 1907). The ambassador attached a map to his communiqué that clearly delineated the proposed boundary.

97. MAE: ASMAI, vol. II 101/2/33–4 (consul-general of Tripoli to MAE).

98. NA: FO 371/247 (Foreign Office notes enclosed with memo from Italian ambassador to Grey, June 12, 1907).

99. NA: FO 371/247 (Grey to Gorst, June 7, 1907).

100. NA: FO 371/247 (Grey to Des Graz, July 18, 1907).

101. NA: FO 371/247 (Grey to Marquis di San Giuliano, Aug. 20, 1907; Grey to Des Graz, July 18, 1907).

102. NA: FO 371/247 (Grey to Des Graz, Aug. 27, 1907; Grey to Gorst, Dec. 16, 1907).

103. NA: FO 371/247 (Grey to Marquis di San Giuliano, Dec. 24, 1907).

104. The rumor was true. MNW: DWQ 0075–004339 (Marshall to Mustafa Pasha); 0075–011200 (Egyptian Interior Ministry to Muhafazat Iskandriyya, June 3, 1907); NA: FO 371/248 (Gorst to Grey, June 8, 1907). Ironically, the coast guard's motives had been discovered even despite strict orders "to avoid all contact with the Turkish Government" by fixing the western limit of their patrols to be approximately ten to fourteen miles from Sollum. See DWQ: MNW 0075–011200 (Purvis to Interior Ministry, May 13, 1907).

105. NA: FO 141/634/1 (report from 'Ali Shahin, June 1, 1907).

106. NA: FO 141/634/1 (Dumreicher to director-general of the coast guard, June 8, 1907).

107. DWQ: MNW 0075–011200 (Khedive 'Abbas Hilmi II to the Ottoman sultan, June 9, 1907).

108. NA: FO 371/248 (translation of undated report from Ahmad Abu Shadi, officer commanding at Marsa Matruh).

109. NA: FO 371/248 (Graham to Grey, Aug. 3, 1907).

110. BOA: İ.MTZ(05) 32/1866 (*Serasker* memo, Aug. 12, 1907 / 3 Receb 1324).

111. NA: FO 371/248 (O'Conor to Grey, Aug. 27, 1907).

112. NA: FO 371/247 (Graham to Grey, Aug. 26, 1907; Graham to Grey, Sept. 1, 1907).

113. NA: FO 371/247 (Graham to Grey, Sept. 1, 1907).

114. NA: FO 141/634/1 (note to Cecil, Aug. 27, 1907).

115. NA: FO 141/634/1 (undated note to Cecil; Cecil to Graham, Sept. 7, 1907); NA: FO 371/247 (Graham to Grey, Sept. 15, 1907).

116. NA: FO 371/247 (Graham to Grey, Sept. 1, 1907).

117. NA: FO 371/247 (Graham to Grey, Sept. 15, 1907; Sept. 22, 1907; Sept. 23, 1907).

118. NA: FO 141/634/1 (note to Cecil, Aug. 27, 1907), emphasis in original.

119. NA: FO 371/247 (Purvis to Ministry of Finance, Aug. 27, 1907).

120. In Benghazi, the bank took over the building formerly held by the local chapter of the Dante Alighieri Club. See NA: FO 371/346 (Alvarez memo, Mar. 1, 1907).

121. NA: FO 371/539 (Fontana memo, Feb. 21, 1908).

122. NA: FO 371/535 (Alvarez memo, Jan. 18, 1908).

123. NA: FO 371/552 (Graham to Grey, Aug. 31, 1908).

124. DWQ: MNW 0075–003230 (letter from Ahmad Muhammad Sawan to Shalabi Mustafa, May 4, 1908 / 2 Rebiülahir 1326).

125. BOA: Y.EE 128/93 (memo from Apr. 27, 1909 / 6 Rabiülahir 1327).

126. Suakin (in present-day Sudan) and Massawa (in present-day Eritrea) were two Red Sea port towns that had been under loose Ottoman control since 1517. In 1865, the Ottoman sultan granted ruling authority over the two colonies to the Egyptian Khedive Ismaʻil; the Egyptians controlled the ports until the Sudanese Mahdist revolt in 1881. After Kitchener's victory over the Mahdists in 1898, the colonies fell under British control. See Talhami, *Suakin and Massawa Under Egyptian Rule*; Jeppie, "Constructing a Colony on the Nile."

127. BOA: Y.EE 128/93 (memo from Apr. 27, 1909 / 6 Rabiülahir 1327).

128. Ibid.

129. Ibid.

130. This mention of other conflicts in tandem with the ʻAwaqir-Shihabat episode may help explain an ostensible discrepancy between two different archives. Whereas the Ottoman documents explain that the intention of the bedouin summit was a decisive resolution to the ʻAwaqir/Shihabat feud, British sources mention a deputation of four shaykhs that similarly "proceeded to the Tripoli frontier and waited there a week"—but in this case, the objective was to resolve a dispute between the Awlad ʻAli and the Hassuna. See: NA: FO 371/664 (Graham to Grey, Oct. 8, 1909; Dumreicher memo, Sept. 29, 1909).

131. BOA: DH.MKT 2896/74 (doc. 1: *Kaymakam* of Darna to *mutasarrıf* of Benghazi, June 16, 1909 / 27 Cemaziülevvel 1327). The *kaymakam*, fearing he would be singled out

and punished for leading such a spectacularly botched diplomatic mission, wrote directly to the Grand Vezir, making the case that he "should not be held responsible" for this failure. This was an extremely rare move for a *kaymakam*, since it bypassed several links in the chain of command. See: BOA: DH.MKT 2896/74 (doc. 3: *Kaymakam* of Darna to Grand Vezir, June 20, 1909 / 27 Cemaziülevvel 1327).

132. BOA: DH.MKT 2896/74 (doc. 1: *Kaymakam* of Darna to *mutasarrıf* of Benghazi, June 16, 1909 / 1 Cemaziyülahir 1327).

133. BOA: DH.MKT 2896/74 (doc. 5: *Mutasarrıf* of Benghazi to *Dahiliye Nezareti*, July 15, 1909 / 26 Cemaziyülahir 1327).

134. BOA: DH.MKT 2896/74 (doc. 6: cover sheet from *Mektûbî Kalemi*, Aug. 11, 1909 / 24 Receb 1327). It is unclear from both Ottoman and British documents how this situation was resolved. One *Meclis-i Vükelâ* document suggests that new, more aggressive tactics would be adopted by the Benghazi government, to prevent the recurrence of raiding. See BOA: MV 137/74 (Cabinet minutes of Mar. 4, 1910 / 21 Safer 1328).

135. NA: FO 371/1110 (Foreign Office minute, enclosed with Cheetham memo of July 5, 1911).

136. Ibid.; NA: FO 371/1110 (Grey to Marling, July 11, 1911).

137. NA: FO 371/1110 (Grey to Kitchener, Oct. 18, 1911).

138. NA: FO 371/1110 (Foreign Office memo, Oct. 12, 1911).

139. As late as August 1911 the British consistently asserted that their government had always "claimed Jaghbub as Egyptian territory, and that the Italian Government should be aware of this claim" from the Townley memo of November 1904. But the Italians still inquired about Jaghbub and Kufra on five separate occasions over the course of 1907. NA: FO 371/1110 (Grey to Cheetham, Aug. 25, 1911; Foreign Office memo, Oct. 12, 1911).

140. NA: FO 371/1110 (Kitchener to Grey, Nov. 4, 1911).

141. NA: FO 371/1361 (Foreign Office minute enclosed with Grey to Lowther, Jan. 23, 1912).

142. NA: FO 371/1361 (Foreign Office minute, undated).

143. BOA: MV 162/87 (Cabinet Minutes of Mar. 16, 1912 / 27 Rebiülevvel 1330).

## Conclusion

1. With the signing of the Treaty of Ouchy, on October 15, 1912, the Ottoman Empire formally relinquished its Libyan provinces. The treaty did not define the boundaries of Italian-occupied Libya, however.

2. See "Egypt a British Protectorate," *American Journal of International Law* 9:1 (Jan. 1915): 202.

3. DWQ: MNW 0075–018655 (undated memo from minister of foreign affairs to president of the Council of Ministers); emphasis added.

4. DWQ: MNW 0075–050751 ("Note on the Question of the Western Frontier, from the beginning up until 30 April 1925").

5. DWQ: MNW 0075–050646.

6. DWQ: MNW 0075–050751 ("Note on the Question of the Western Frontier, from the beginning up until 30 April 1925").

7. DWQ: MNW 0075–050648 (doc. 2: "Minutes of the Meeting of the Military Committee, signed by Mahmud 'Azmi, July 23, 1921).

8. DWQ: MNW 0075–050646 (docs. 4, 8: undated "Memorandum on the Western Frontier" from 'Abd al-Qawi Effendi Ahmad, Secretary of Military Committee).

9. DWQ: MNW 0075–050646 (docs. 11, 12: minutes from Council of Ministers session).

10. DWQ: MNW 0075–050646 (doc. 14: "Journey of the commission authorized to inspect the Western border of Egypt").

11. DWQ: MNW 0075–050751 (summary of report from Fathi commission to Council of Ministers—Sept. 16, 1922).

12. DWQ: MNW 0075–050646 (doc. 15: "Personal opinion of Fathi Pasha on the subject of the frontier line between the Kingdom of Egypt and the Kingdom of Italy," Sept. 6, 1922).

13. DWQ: MNW 0075–050751 ("Note on the Question of the Western Frontier, from the beginning up until 30 April 1925").

14. DWQ: MNW 0075–050647 ("Report on the Current Situation Regarding the Western Frontier of Egypt," by A. W. Green, commandant of the Sollum District of the Frontier Districts Administration, Western Desert Province).

15. DWQ: MNW 0075–050647 (minutes from meeting of the Egyptian Council of Ministers, Aug. 3, 1924).

16. DWQ: MNW 0075–050647 (letter from Ahmad Ziwar to Comte Caccia Dominioni, Aug. 5, 1924; letter from Caccia Dominioni to Ziwar Pasha, Aug. 5, 1924).

17. DWQ: MNW 0075–050647 ("Report on the Current Situation Regarding the Western Frontier of Egypt," by A. W. Green).

18. DWQ: MNW 0075–050647 (memo from Parker Pasha to the minister of war, Sept. 28, 1924).

19. Shafiq would later write a noteworthy memoir about his service for the FDA in the Western Desert (see Chapter 1). Shafiq, Mudhakkirāt 'an wāḥāt Miṣr.

20. DWQ: MNW 0075–050751 ("Report of the Egyptian Western Frontier Commission, constituted by the decision of the Council of Ministers on April 2, 1925").

21. Ibid.

22. Ibid.

23. Biger, "The First Political Map of Egypt," 84.

24. DWQ: MNW 0075–050651 (letter from minister of foreign affairs to secretary-general of the Council of Ministers, Feb. 11, 1926).

25. See Adelman and Aron, "From Borderlands to Borders."

26. "Accord entre l'Egypte et l'Italie au sujet de la délimitation de la frontière égyptienne de l'Ouest, portant la date du 6 Décembre 1925." La frontière occidentale de l'Égypte.

27. Ibid.

28. The November 1926 treaty was published in Cairo the following year, along with the recently re-discovered 1841 map. Shafiq was appointed by the Italian and Egyptian delegations to serve as president of the mixed commission.

29. For instance, based on the survey work of "topographical experts" attached to the

mixed commission, the treaty stipulated that "the center of the arc of a circle with a radius of 10 kilometers around Sollum shall be placed in the spot marked on the maps as Beacon Point and on the terrain by a cairn placed on the cape that closes the Bay of Sollum." The treaty also specified that a truck route passing through "the arc of the circle in question" would henceforth be considered Egyptian territory.

30. *La frontière occidentale de l'Égypte*, ch. 1.

31. This remote desert region, which includes the oasis of 'Uwaynat as well as the plateau known as the Gilf Kebir, was immortalized as the setting of Michael Ondaatje's novel *The English Patient*.

32. See Biger, "The First Political Map of Egypt," 83–87.

33. The British ended up ceding 'Uwaynat and the Sarra Triangle to the Italians in 1934.

34. Biger, "The First Map of Modern Egypt," 325.

35. Brownlie, "Arab Republic of Egypt-Libya," 108–9. The long linear segment along the twenty-fifth meridian east was largely undemarcated, due to the onerous survey work necessary to fix geometrical lines on the ground.

36. Diplomatic tensions between the two nations had actually been festering for years, ever since Egyptian President Sadat negotiated a peace deal with Israel following the 1973 War. In 1974, the Egyptian government chafed at Libya's frequent deportations of Egyptian migrant workers. Things heated up again in 1976, following the purported Egyptian discovery of a Libyan plot to assassinate Sadat; when Egypt started to pursue possible retaliatory measures, Libya threatened to break off diplomatic relations. A couple of weeks later, Egyptian authorities pinned a bombing in a government office near Tahrir Square on Libyan agents. Both governments accused one another of operating networks of spies and saboteurs in their respective countries.

37. Brownlie, "Arab Republic of Egypt-Libya," 109.

38. RGS: "Explanatory Memorandum," in *Western Frontier of Egypt: Egyptian-Italian Treaty of Nov. 9, 1926 (In Execution of the Treaty of Dec. 6, 1925)*.

39. Ibid.

40. Sahlins, *Boundaries*, 4.

41. They also sent a copy of the petition to Ahmed Hassanein Pasha—the celebrated Western Desert explorer and author of *The Lost Oases*—who now was serving as the president of King Fu'ad's royal *diwan*.

42. DWQ: MNW 0075–014965 (petition to the Egyptian Department of Defense, Nov. 25, 1940).

43. David Ludden, "Presidential Address: Maps in the Mind and the Mobility of Asia," 1062.

44. Ibid., 1061–62.

45. Ibid., 1069.

46. Ibid., 1064.

47. See, for example: "Egypt Allocates Additional Land to Toshka Project," *Mada Masr* (Aug. 12, 2016); Peter Schwartzstein, "Farming the Sahara," *Takepart* (Jan. 8, 2016); "Thinking Big," *The Economist* (Mar. 19, 2015).

48. Although attacks on Egyptian security forces have been rarer in the Western Desert than in the Sinai Peninsula, they continue to occur. The most recent incident, at the time of this writing, took place in January 2017: at least eight Egyptian police officers were killed (and three wounded) at a security checkpoint in Egypt's New Valley province in the Western Desert. "Police officers die in attack in Egypt's Western Desert," *Al-Jazeera.com*, Jan. 16, 2017.

49. See: Erica Wenig, "Egypt's Security and the Libyan Civil War," *Fikra Forum* (Washington Institute for Near East Policy), www.washingtoninstitute.org/fikraforum/view/egypts-security-and-the-libyan-civil-war (accessed Aug. 29, 2017).

50. "Egyptian Forces Kill 12 in Tourist Convoy," *Al-Jazeera.com*, Sept. 14, 2015.

# Bibliography

## Archival Sources

*Egypt*
Dār al-Wathā'iq al-Qawmiyya (DWQ), Egyptian National Archives, Cairo.
　*Diwān al-Dākhiliyya* (DD).
　*Majlis al-Nuẓẓār wa-l-Wuzarā'* (MNW).

*Italy*
Archivio Storico Diplomatico del Ministero degli Affari Esteri (MAE), Historical-Diplomatic
Archive of the Ministry of Foreign Affairs, Rome.
　*Ambasciata d'Italia in Egitto, 1864–1940* (AIE).
　*Archivio Storico del Ex-Ministero dell'Africa Italiana*, vol. II, *Libia, 1859–1945* (ASMAI).

*Turkey*
Başbakanlık Osmanlı Arşivi (BOA), Prime Ministry's Ottoman Archives, Istanbul.
　*Dahiliye Nezareti Mektûbî Kalemi* (DH.MKT).
　*Dahiliye Nezareti Tesr-i Muamelât ve Islahat Komisyonu* (DH.TMIK.S).
　*Hariciye Nezareti Hukuk Müşavirliği İstişare Odası Evrakı* (HR.HMŞ.İŞO).
　*Hariciye Nezareti Mektûbî Kalemi Evrakı* (HR.MKT).
　*İrade Eyalet-i Mümtaze Mısır* (İ.MTZ[05]).
　*Meclis-i Vâlâ Evrakı* (MVL).
　*Meclis-i Vükelâ Mazbataları* (MV).
　*Sadaret Mektûbî Kalemi Evrakı* (A.MKT).
　*Sadaret Mektûbî Kalemi Meclis-i Vâlâ Evrakı* (A.MKT.MVL).
　*Sadaret Mektûbî Mühimme Kalemi Evrakı* (A.MKT.MHM).
　*Sadaret Mektûbî Umum Vilâyat Evrakı* (A.MKT.UM).
　*Yıldız Esas Evrakı* (Y.EE).
　*Yıldız Mütenevvi Mâruzat* (Y.MTV).

*Yıldız Sadaret Hususî Mâruzat Evrakı* (Y.A.HUS).
*Yıldız Sadaret Resmi Mâruzat Evrakı* (Y.A.RES).

**United Kingdom**
Durham University Library (DUL), Special Collections, Durham.
    Abbas Hilmi II Papers.
    G. G. Hunter Collection.
    General Sir Reginald Wingate Papers.
Middle East Centre Archive (MEC), University of Oxford, St. Antony's College, Oxford.
    Sir Thomas Wentworth Russell Collection.
    Wilfred Jennings-Bramly Collection.
National Archives (NA), Kew Gardens, London.
    Foreign Office (FO).
    War Office (WO).
Royal Geographic Society (RGS), Foyle Reading Room, London.
    Manuscript Archive.
    Maps and Atlases.

**United States**
Hoover Institution Library, Stanford, California.

## Printed Government Documents, Reference Works, and Published Compilations

*Actes diplomatiques et firmans imperiaux relatifs à l'Égypte.* Cairo: Imprimerie Nationale, 1886.

Artin, Yacoub, ed. *al-Aḥkām al-marʿiyya fī shaʾn al-arāḍī al-Misriyya.* Bulaq Misr, Egypt: al-Maṭbaʿa al-Kubrā al-Amīriyya, 1888.

Association Égyptienne de Paris. *Documents diplomatiques concernant l'Égypte: De Mehemet-Ali jusqu'en 1920.* Paris: E. Leroux, 1920.

Baedeker, Karl. *Egypt and the Sudan: Handbook for Travelers.* London: T. Fisher Unwin, 1914.

———. *Egypt: Handbook for Travellers.* Leipsic: K. Baedeker, 1878.

Boinet, Albert, ed. *Dictionnaire géographique de l'Égypte.* Cairo: Imprimerie Nationale, 1899.

Brownlie, Ian. "Arab Republic of Egypt-Libya." In *African Boundaries: A Legal and Diplomatic Encyclopaedia.* London: C. Hurst, 1979.

Budge, E. A. Wallis. *Cook's Handbook for Egypt and the Egyptian Sudan.* London: T. Cook & Son, 1906.

*Bulletin des lois et decrets.* Port Said, Egypt: Imprimerie Française, 1883.

Dağdelen, İrfan, ed. *İstanbul Büyükşehir Belediyesi Atatürk Kitaplığı haritalar kataloğu.* İstanbul: İstanbul Büyükşehir Belediye Başkanlığı, Kütüphane ve Müzeler Müdürlüğü, 2002.

Dajani, Ahmad Sidqi, and 'Abd al-Salam Adham, eds. *Wathā'iq tārīkh Libiya al-ḥadīth: al-wathā'iq al-'Uthmāniyya, 1881–1911.* Benghazi, Libya: Jamī'at Benghazi, 1974.

Egypt. *La frontière occidentale de l'Égypte. Accord italo-égyptien du 9 novembre 1926 en execution de l'accord du 6 décembre 1925.* Cairo: Imprimerie Nationale, 1927.

———. No. 1 (1896). *Report on the Finances, Administration, and Condition of Egypt, and the Progress of Reforms.* London: Harrison and Sons, 1896.

———. No. 1 (1898). *Report by Her Majesty's Agent and Consul-General on the Finances, Administration, and Condition of Egypt and the Soudan in 1898.* London: Harrison and Sons, 1898.

Gélat, Philippe, ed. *Répertoire général annoté de la législation et de l'administration égyptiennes.* Alexandria, Egypt: Imprimerie J. C. Lagoudakis, 1906.

Groom, N. St. J. *A Dictionary of Arabic Topography and Placenames: A Transliterated Arabic-English Dictionary, with an Arabic Glossary of Topographical Words and Placenames.* Beirut: Librairie du Liban, 1983.

Hariciye Nezareti. *Mısır meselesi.* Istanbul: Matbaa-yı Amire, 1918.

Hertslet, Edward, ed. *The Map of Africa by Treaty.* London: Cass, 1967.

*Iftitāḥ Masjid Marsa Matruh.* Cairo: Diwān 'Umūm al-Awqāf, 1910.

Lamba, Henri, ed. *Droit public et administratif de l'Égypte: Lois organiques du khédivat, administration, finances, justice.* Cairo: Imprimerie Nationale, 1909.

Lorin, Henri. *Bibliographie géographique de l'Égypte.* Cairo: Société Royale de Géographie d'Égypte, 1929.

Lowis, C. C., ed. *The Census of Egypt Taken in 1907.* Cairo: Government Press, 1909.

Nahum, Hayyim, ed. *Recueil de firmans impériaux Ottomans adressés aux Valis et aux Khédives d'Égypte 1006 H.-1322 H. (1597 J.-C.–1904 J.-C.) Réunis sur l'ordre de Sa Majesté Fouad Ier, Roi d'Égypte.* Cairo: Imprimerie de l'Institut Français d'Archéologie Orientale du Caire, 1934.

Ramzi, Muhammad. *al-Qāmūs al-jughrāfī li-l-bilād al-Misriyya, min 'ahd qudamā' al-Misriyyin ila sanat 1945.* Cairo: Maṭba'at Dār al-Kutub al-Misriyya, 1953.

Redhouse, James W. *A Turkish and English Lexicon.* Istanbul: A. H. Boyajian, 1890.

St. John, Ronald Bruce. *Historical Dictionary of Libya.* Lanham, Md.: Scarecrow Press, 2006.

Vilar, Juan. *Mapas, planos y fortificaciones hispánicos de Libia [1510–1911]. Hispanic Maps, Plans and Fortifications of Libya [1510–1911].* Madrid: Cultura Hispánica, 1998.

Wahba, Malak, and Amr Fangary, eds. *Egypt in the Cartographic Heritage, 1595–1840 a.d.: The Cartographic Collection of the National Library of Egypt.* Cairo: Dār al-Kutub wa-l-Wathā'iq al-Qawmiyya, 2008.

Wathelet, J., and R. G. Brunton, eds. *Codes égyptiens et lois usuelles en vigueur en Égypte.* Brussels: Veuve F. Larcier, 1919.

## Other Published Works

'Abbas Hilmi II, *The Last Khedive of Egypt: Memoirs of Abbas Hilmi II.* Translated and edited by Amira Sonbol. Cairo: American University in Cairo Press, 2006.

'Abd al-Wahid, Fatima 'Alam al-Din. *Ḥudūd Miṣr al-gharbiyya: dirāsa wathā'iqiyya.* Cairo: al-Hay'a al-Misriyya al-'Āmma li-l-Kitāb, 1994.

Abul-Magd, Zeinab. *Imagined Empires: A History of Revolt in Egypt.* Berkeley: University of California Press, 2013.

Adelman, Jeremy, and Stephen Aron. "From Borderlands to Borders: Empires, Nation-States, and the Peoples in Between in North American History." *American Historical Review* 104:3 (1999): 814–41.

Ágoston, Gabor. "A Flexible Empire: Authority and Its Limits on the Ottoman Frontiers." In *Ottoman Borderlands: Issues, Personalities, and Political Changes,* edited by Kemal H. Karpat and Robert Zens, 15–30. Madison: University of Wisconsin Press, 2003.

Aharoni, Re'uven. *The Pasha's Bedouin: Tribes and State in the Egypt of Mehemet Ali, 1805–1848.* London: Routledge, 2010.

Ahmida, Ali Abdullatif. *The Making of Modern Libya: State Formation, Colonization, and Resistance, 1830–1932.* Albany: State University of New York Press, 2009.

Akarli, Engin. "The Defence of the Libyan Provinces (1882–1908)." In *Studies on Ottoman Diplomatic History: Ottomans in Africa,* edited by S. Deringil and S. Kuneralp, 75–85. Istanbul: Isis Press, 1991.

Alexander, Frances Gordon (Paddock). *Wayfarers in the Libyan Desert.* New York: G. P. Putnam's Sons, 1912.

'Amir, Iman Muhammad 'Abd al-Mun'im. *al-'Urbān wa dawruhum fī al-mujtamaʻ al-Misri fī al-nisf al-awwal min al-qarn al-tāsiʻ 'ashar.* Cairo: al-Hay'a al-Misriyya al-'Āmma li-l-Kitāb, 1997.

Anderson, Benedict. *Imagined Communities: Reflections on the Origins and Spread of Nationalism.* Rev. ed. London: Verso, 1991.

Anderson, Ewan. "Geopolitics: International Boundaries as Fighting Places." *Journal of Strategic Studies* 22:2 (1999): 125–36.

Anderson, James, and Liam O'Dowd. "Borders, Border Regions, and Territoriality: Contradictory Meanings, Changing Significance." *Regional Studies* 33:7 (1999): 593–604.

Anderson, Lisa. "Nineteenth-Century Reform in Ottoman Libya." *International Journal of Middle East Studies* 16:3 (1984): 325–48.

———. *The State and Social Transformation in Tunisia and Libya, 1830–1980.* Princeton, N.J.: Princeton University Press, 1986.

Anderson, Malcolm. *Frontiers: Territory and State Formation in the Modern World.* Cambridge: Polity Press, 1996.

Anscombe, Frederick. *The Ottoman Gulf: The Creation of Kuwait, Saudi Arabia, and Qatar, 1870–1914.* New York: Columbia University Press, 1997.

Applegate, Celia. *A Nation of Provincials: The German Idea of Heimat.* Berkeley: University of California Press, 1990.

Ateş, Sabri. "Bones of Contention: Corpse Traffic and Ottoman-Iranian Rivalry in Nineteenth-Century Iraq." *Comparative Studies of South Asia, Africa and the Middle East* 30:3 (2010): 512–32.

———. *Ottoman-Iranian Borderlands: Making a Boundary, 1843–1914.* Cambridge: Cambridge University Press, 2013.

Austen, Ralph A. *Trans-Saharan Africa in World History*. New York: Oxford University Press, 2010.

Azimzade, Sadık el-Müeyyed. *Afrika Sahrâ-yı Kebîri'nde seyahat: bir Osmanlı zâbitinin büyük Sahra'da seyahati*. Edited by İdrıs Bostan. Istanbul: Çamlica, 2010.

Badrawi, Malak. *Political Violence in Egypt, 1910–1924: Secret Societies, Plots, and Assassinations*. Richmond, England: Curzon, 2000.

Baer, Gabriel. *Studies in the Social History of Modern Egypt*. Chicago: University of Chicago Press, 1969.

Baldinetti, Anna. *Orientalismo e colonialismo: La ricerca di consenso in Egitto per l'impresa di Libia*. Roma: Istituto per l'Oriente C. A. Nallino, 1997.

———. *The Origins of the Libyan Nation: Colonial Legacy, Exile and the Emergence of a New Nation-State*. London: Routledge, 2010.

Ball, John. *Contributions to the Geography of Egypt*. Cairo: Government Press, 1939.

———. *Egypt in the Classical Geographers*. Cairo: Government Press, 1942.

Barfield, Thomas J. *The Nomadic Alternative*. Englewood Cliffs, N.J.: Prentice Hall, 1993.

Baron, Beth. *Egypt as a Woman: Nationalism, Gender, and Politics*. Berkeley: University of California Press, 2007.

Baud, Michiel, and Willem van Schendel. "Toward a Comparative History of Borderlands." *Journal of World History* 8:2 (1997): 211–42.

Bayle, St. John. *Adventures in the Libyan Desert and the Oasis of Jupiter Ammon*. New York: G. P. Putnam, 1849.

Beadnell, H. J. Llewellyn. *Dakhla Oasis: Its Topography and Geology*. Cairo: National Printing Department, 1901.

———. *An Egyptian Oasis: An Account of the Oasis of Kharga in the Libyan Desert, with Special Reference to Its History, Physical Geography, and Water-supply*. London: J. Murray, 1909.

———. *Farafra Oasis: Its Topography and Geology*. Cairo: National Printing Department, 1901.

———. *Recent Geological Discoveries in the Nile Valley and Libyan Desert*. Hertford, England: Stephen Austin & Sons, 1900.

———. *The Topography and Geology of Fayum Province of Egypt*. Cairo: National Printing Department, 1905.

Beadnell, H. J. Llewellyn, and John Ball. *Baharia Oasis: Its Topography and Geology*. Cairo: National Printing Department, 1903.

Belgrave, Charles Dalrymple. *Siwa: The Oasis of Jupiter Ammon*. London: John Lane, 1923.

Belli, Mériam. *An Incurable Past: Nasser's Egypt Then and Now*. Gainesville: University Press of Florida, 2013.

Bender, Barbara, and Margot Winer, eds. *Contested Landscapes: Movement, Exile, and Place*. Oxford: Berg, 2001.

Ben-Ghiat, Ruth, and Mia Fuller, eds. *Italian Colonialism*. New York: Palgrave Macmillan, 2008.

Benton, Lauren A. *A Search for Sovereignty: Law and Geography in European Empires, 1400–1900*. New York: Cambridge University Press, 2010.

Benvenisti, Meron. *Sacred Landscape: The Buried History of the Holy Land Since 1948.* Berkeley: University of California Press, 2002.

Berque, Jacques. *Egypt: Imperialism and Revolution.* New York: Praeger, 1972.

Biger, Gideon. "The First Map of Modern Egypt: Mohammed Ali's Firman and the Map of 1841." *Middle Eastern Studies* 14:3 (1978): 323–25.

———. "The First Political Map of Egypt." *Cartographica: The International Journal for Geographic Information and Geovisualization* 19:3 (1982): 83–89.

Blackburn, J. Richard. "The Collapse of Ottoman Authority in Yemen, 968/1560–976/1568." *Die Welt des Islams* 19:1 (1979): 119–76.

Blake, Gerald H., and Richard Schofield, eds. *Boundaries and State Territory in the Middle East and North Africa.* The Cottons, Cambridgeshire, England: Middle East & North African Studies Press, 1987.

Blumi, Isa. "The Frontier as a Measure of Modern Power: Local Limits to Empire in Yemen, 1872–1914." In *The Frontiers of the Ottoman World,* edited by A. C. S. Peacock, 289–304. Oxford: Oxford University Press, 2009.

———. "Illicit Trade and the Emergence of Albania and Yemen." In *Understanding Life in the Borderlands: Boundaries in Depth and in Motion,* edited by Ira William Zartman, 58–84. Athens: University of Georgia Press, 2010.

———. *Reinstating the Ottomans: Alternative Balkan Modernities, 1800–1912.* New York: Palgrave Macmillan, 2011.

———. *Rethinking the Late Ottoman Empire: A Comparative Social and Political History of Albania and Yemen, 1878–1918.* Istanbul: Isis Press, 2010.

———. "Thwarting the Ottoman Empire: Smuggling through the Empire's New Frontiers in Yemen and Albania, 1878–1910." *International Journal of Turkish Studies* 9:1 (2003): 251–70.

Blunt, Wilfred Scawen. *My Diaries: Being a Personal Narrative of Events, 1888–1914.* New York: Alfred A. Knopf, 1932.

Bonola, Federico. *L'Égypte et la géographie: sommaire historique des travaux géographiques exécutés . . . sous la dynastie de Mohammed Aly.* Cairo: Société de Géographie d'Égypte, 1889.

Boyle, Stephanie. "Sickness, Scoundrels, and Saints: The World in Tanta and Tanta in the World, 1854–1907." Ph.D. diss., Northeastern University, 2012.

Brandell, Inga, ed. *State Frontiers: Borders and Boundaries in the Middle East.* London: I. B. Tauris, 2006.

Brauer, Ralph W. *Boundaries and Frontiers in Medieval Muslim Geography.* Philadelphia: American Philosophical Society, 1995.

Breccia, Evaristo. *With King Fuad to the Oasis of Ammon.* Milan: Bestetti & Tumminelli, 1929.

Brenner, Neil. "Beyond State-Centrism? Space, Territoriality, and Geographical Scale in Globalization Studies." *Theory and Society* 28:1 (1999): 39–78.

Brenner, Neil, and Stuart Elden. "Henri Lefebvre on State, Space, Territory." *International Political Sociology* 3 (2009): 353–77.

Briggs, Martin Shaw. *Through Egypt in War-Time.* London: T. Fisher Unwin, 1918.

Brower, Benjamin. *A Desert Named Peace: The Violence of France's Empire in the Algerian Sahara, 1844–1902*. New York: Columbia University Press, 2009.

Brown, Kate. *A Biography of No Place: From Ethnic Borderland to Soviet Heartland*. Cambridge: Harvard University Press, 2003.

Brown, Keith. *The Past in Question: Modern Macedonia and the Uncertainties of Nation*. Princeton, N.J.: Princeton University Press, 2003.

Brown, Nathan J. *The Rule of Law in the Arab World: Courts in Egypt and the Gulf*. Cambridge: Cambridge University Press, 1997.

Burnett, D. Graham. *Masters of All They Surveyed: Exploration, Geography, and a British El Dorado*. Chicago: University of Chicago Press, 2000.

Carter, Paul. *The Road to Botany Bay: An Essay in Spatial History*. London: Faber and Faber, 1987.

Chatterjee, Partha. *The Nation and Its Fragments: Colonial and Postcolonial Histories*. Princeton, N.J.: Princeton University Press, 1993.

Ciammaichella, Glauco. *Libyens et français au Tchad, 1897–1914: La confrérie Senoussie et le commerce transsaharien*. Paris: Éditions du Centre National de la Recherche Scientifique, 1987.

Clancy-Smith, Julia. "The Maghrib and the Mediterranean World in the Nineteenth Century: Illicit Exchanges, Migrants, and Social Marginals." In *The Maghrib in Question: Essays in History and Historiography*, edited by Michel Le Gall and Kenneth J. Perkins, 222–49. Austin: University of Texas Press, 1997.

———. *Mediterraneans: North Africa and Europe in an Age of Migration, c. 1800–1900*. Berkeley: University of California Press, 2011.

Clapham, Christopher. "Sovereignty and the Third World State." *Political Studies* 47:3 (2002): 522–37.

Cline, Walter Buchanan. *Notes on the People of Siwah and El Garah in the Libyan Desert*. Menasha, Wisc.: George Banta, 1936.

Cole, Donald, and Soraya Altorki. *Bedouin, Settlers, and Holiday-Makers: Egypt's Changing Northwest Coast*. Cairo: American University in Cairo Press, 1998.

Conker, Mehmet Nuri. *Trablusgarp*. Istanbul: Tercüman-ı Hakikat Matbaası, 1914.

Conklin, Alice. *A Mission to Civilize: The Republican Idea of Empire in France and West Africa, 1895–1930*. Stanford, Calif.: Stanford University Press, 1997.

Cordell, Dennis D. "Eastern Libya, Wadai, and the Sanusiya: A Tariqa and a Trade Route." *Journal of African History* 18:1 (1977): 21–36.

Craib, Raymond. *Cartographic Mexico: A History of State Fixations and Fugitive Landscapes*. Durham, N.C.: Duke University Press, 2004.

Cromer, Evelyn Baring. *Abbas II*. London: Macmillan, 1915.

Curzon, George Nathaniel. *Frontiers*. Oxford: Clarendon Press, 1907.

Dajani, Ahmad. *al-Ḥaraka al-Sanusiyya, nash'atuha wa-namū'uha fi al-qarn al-tāsi' 'ashar*. Beirut: Dār Lubnan, 1967.

Daly, M. W., ed. *Modern Egypt, from 1517 to the End of the Twentieth Century*. Vol. 2 of *The Cambridge History of Egypt*. Cambridge: Cambridge University Press, 1998.

Davis, Diana. *Resurrecting the Granary of Rome: Environmental History and French Colonial Expansion in North Africa.* Athens: Ohio University Press, 2007.

Dawson, Allan Charles, Laura Zanotti, and Ismael Vaccaro, eds. *Negotiating Territoriality: Spatial Dialogues Between State and Tradition.* New York: Routledge, 2014.

De Agostini, Enrico. *Le popolazioni della Cirenaica: Notizie etniche e storiche.* Benghazi, Libya: Azienda Tipo-Litografica della Scuola d'Arti e Mestieri, 1923.

De Cosson, Anthony. *Mareotis: Being a Short Account of the History and Ancient Monuments of the North-western Desert of Egypt and of Lake Mareotis.* London: Country Life, 1935.

Del Boca, Angelo. *Gli italiani in Libia.* Rome: Laterza, 1986.

Della Cella, Paolo. *Viaggio da Tripoli di Barberia alle frontiere occidentali dell'Egitto fatto nel 1817.* Naples: R. Marotta e Vanspandoch, 1830.

Deringil, Selim. "Les Ottomans et le partage de l'Afrique, 1880–1900." In *Studies on Ottoman Diplomatic History: Ottomans in Africa,* edited by S. Deringil and S. Kuneralp, 121–33. Istanbul: Isis Press, 1991.

———. "'They Live in a State of Nomadism and Savagery': The Late Ottoman Empire and the Post-Colonial Debate." *Comparative Studies in Society and History* 45:2 (2003): 311–42.

———. *The Well-Protected Domains: Ideology and the Legitimation of Power in the Ottoman Empire, 1876–1909.* London: I. B. Tauris, 1998.

Derr, Jennifer. "Cultivating the State: Cash Crop Agriculture, Irrigation, and the Geography of Authority in Colonial Southern Egypt, 1868–1931." Ph.D. diss., Stanford University, 2009.

Di-Capua, Yoav. *Gatekeepers of the Arab Past: Historians and History Writing in Twentieth-Century Egypt.* Berkeley: University of California Press, 2009.

Diener, Alexander and Joshua Hagen, eds. *Borderlines and Borderlands: Political Oddities at the Edge of the Nation-State.* Lanham, Md.: Rowman & Littlefield, 2010.

Donnan, Hastings, and Thomas M. Wilson. *Borders: Frontiers of Identity, Nation, and State.* Oxford: Berg, 1999.

———, eds. *Border Approaches: Anthropological Perspectives on Frontiers.* Lanham, Md.: University Press of America, 1994.

———, eds. *Border Identities: Nation and State at International Frontiers.* Cambridge: Cambridge University Press, 1998.

Doumani, Beshara. *Rediscovering Palestine: Merchants and Peasants in Jabal Nablus, 1700–1900.* Berkeley: University of California Press, 1995.

Dumreicher, André von. *Trackers and Smugglers in the Deserts of Egypt.* New York: Dial Press, 1931.

Dun, T. I. *From Cairo to Siwa: Across the Libyan Desert with Armoured Cars.* Cairo: E. & R. Schindler, 1933.

Dunlop, Catherine. *Cartophilia: Maps and the Search for Identity in the French-German Borderland.* Chicago: University of Chicago Press, 2016.

Duveyrier, Henri. *La confrerie musulmane de Sidi Mohammed Ben 'Ali Es-Senousi et son domaine géographique.* Paris: Société de Géographie, 1886.

Edney, Matthew H. *Mapping an Empire: The Geographical Construction of British India, 1765–1843.* Chicago: University of Chicago Press, 1997.

Elden, Stuart. *The Birth of Territory.* Chicago: University of Chicago Press, 2013.

Ellis, Matthew H. "Anomalous Egypt? Rethinking Egyptian Sovereignty at the Western Periphery." In *The Long 1890s in Egypt: Colonial Quiescence, Subterranean Resistance,* edited by Marilyn Booth and Anthony Gorman, 169–94. Edinburgh: Edinburgh University Press, 2014.

———. "Over the Borderline? Rethinking Territoriality at the Margins of Empire and Nation in the Modern Middle East (Parts I and II)." *History Compass* 13:8 (2015): 411–34.

El Shakry, Omnia. *The Great Social Laboratory: Subjects of Knowledge in Colonial and Postcolonial Egypt.* Stanford, Calif.: Stanford University Press, 2007.

Esherick, Joseph, Hasan Kayali, and Eric Van Young, eds. *Empire to Nation: Historical Perspectives on the Making of the Modern World.* Lanham, Md.: Rowman & Littlefield, 2006.

Esmeir, Samera. *Juridical Humanity: A Colonial History.* Stanford, Calif.: Stanford University Press, 2012.

Evans-Pritchard, E. E. *The Sanusi of Cyrenaica.* Oxford: Clarendon Press, 1949.

Fahmy, Khaled. *All the Pasha's Men: Mehmed Ali, His Army, and the Making of Modern Egypt.* Cambridge: Cambridge University Press, 1997.

———. *Mehmed Ali: From Ottoman Governor to Ruler of Egypt.* Oxford: Oneworld, 2009.

Fahmy, Ziad. *Ordinary Egyptians: Creating the Modern Nation Through Popular Culture.* Stanford, Calif.: Stanford University Press, 2011.

Fakhry, Ahmed. *Recent Explorations in the Oases of the Western Desert.* Cairo: Press of the French Institute of Oriental Archaeology, 1942.

———. *Siwa Oasis.* Cairo: American University in Cairo Press, 1990.

Falls, J. C. Ewald. *Three Years in the Libyan Desert, Travels, Discoveries, and Excavations of the Menas Expedition (Kaufmann Expedition).* London: T. F. Unwin, 1913.

Fawda, ʿIzz. *Ḥudūd Miṣr al-dawliyya.* Cairo: Markaz al-Buḥūth wa-l-Dirāsāt al-Siyāsiyya, 1993.

Febvre, Lucien. "Frontière: The Word and the Concept." In *A New Kind of History: From the Writings of Lucien Febvre,* edited by Peter Burke, 208–18. New York: Harper Torchbooks, 1973.

Fikri, Muhammad Amin. *Jughrāfiyat Miṣr.* Cairo: Maṭbaʿat Wadi al-Nil, 1879.

Fletcher, Robert. *British Imperialism and the "Tribal Question."* Oxford: Oxford University Press, 2015.

Fortes, Meyer, and E. E. Evans-Pritchard, eds. *African Political Systems.* London: Published for the International African Institute by Oxford University Press, 1970.

Fortna, Benjamin. *Imperial Classroom: Islam, the State, and Education in the Late Ottoman Empire.* Oxford: Oxford University Press, 2002.

*Frontières: Problèmes de frontières dans le Tiers-monde: Journée d'études des 20 et 21 Mars 1981.* Paris: L'Harmattan, 1982.

Fuʾad, Muhammad. *Wāḥāt Miṣr al-shahīra: murshid li-l-mudarrisīn.* Egypt: [n.p.], [n.d.].

Furlong, Charles W. *The Gateway to the Sahara: Observations and Experiences in Tripoli.* New York: C. Scribner's Sons, 1909.

Gasper, Michael. *The Power of Representation: Publics, Peasants, and Islam in Egypt.* Stanford, Calif.: Stanford University Press, 2009.

Gawhari, Rifʿat. *Jannat al-Sahra: Siwa aw wāḥat Amūn.* Cairo: al-Dār al-Qawmiyya li-l-Ṭibāʿa wa-l-Nashr, 1962.

Gazzini, Claudia A. "Jihad in Exile: Ahmad al-Sharif al-Sanusi, 1918–33." M.A. thesis, Princeton University, 2004.

Genell, Aimee. "Empire by Law: Ottoman Sovereignty and the British Occupation of Egypt, 1882–1923." Ph.D. diss., Columbia University, 2013.

Gerber, Haim. *Ottoman Rule in Jerusalem, 1890–1914.* Berlin: K. Schwarz, 1985.

Gershoni, Israel, and James Jankowski. *Egypt, Islam, and the Arabs: The Search for Egyptian Nationhood, 1900–30.* New York: Oxford University Press, 1986.

Gershoni, Israel, Meir Hatina, and Hagai Erlikh, eds. *Narrating the Nile: Politics, Cultures, Identities.* Boulder, Colo.: Lynne Rienner, 2008.

Gitre, Carmen M. K. "Performing Modernity: Theater and Political Culture in Egypt, 1869–1923." Ph.D. diss., Rutgers University, 2011.

Godlewska, Anne. "Map, Text, and Image: The Mentality of Enlightened Conquerors; A New Look at the Description de l'Égypte." *Transactions of the Institute of British Geographers* 20:1 (1995): 5–28.

Goldschmidt, Arthur, Jr. "The Egyptian Nationalist Party, 1892–1919." In *Political and Social Change in Modern Egypt,* edited by P. M. Holt, 308–33. London: Oxford University Press, 1968.

Gordon, John W. *The Other Desert War: British Special Forces in North Africa, 1940–1943.* New York: Greenwood Press, 1987.

Goswami, Manu. "From Swadeshi to Swaraj: Nation, Economy, Territory in Colonial South Asia, 1870 to 1907." *Comparative Studies in Society and History* 40:4 (Oct. 1998): 609–36.

———. *Producing India: From Colonial Economy to National Space.* Chicago: University of Chicago Press, 2004.

———. "Rethinking the Modular Nation Form: Toward a Sociohistorical Conception." *Comparative Studies in Society and History* 44:4 (2002): 770–99.

Gregory, Derek. *Geographical Imaginations.* Cambridge, Mass.: Blackwell, 1994.

Gregory, Derek, Ron Martin, and Graham Smith, eds. *Human Geography: Society, Space, and Social Science.* Minneapolis: University of Minnesota Press, 1994.

Guerville, Amédée Baillot de. *New Egypt.* London: William Heinemann, 1906.

Gwatkin-Williams, R. S. *Prisoners of the Red Desert: Being a Full and True History of the Men of the "Tara."* New York: E. P. Dutton, 1923.

Haag, Michael. *Alexandria: City of Memory.* New Haven, Conn.: Yale University Press, 2004.

———. Introduction to *The Lost Oases,* by Ahmed Hassanein, v–xiii. Cairo: American University in Cairo Press, 2006.

Hajjaji, Salem. *The New Libya: A Geographical, Social, Economic and Political Study.* Tripoli, Libya: Government Printing Press, 1967.

Hakim, Sami. *Jaghbub, al-wāḥa al-Misriyya al-mughtaṣiba.* Cairo: Markaz al-Dirāsāt al-Ṣuḥufiyya bi-Muʾassasat Dār al-Taʿāwun, 1978.

Hämäläinen, Pekka and Samuel Truett. "On Borderlands." *Journal of American History* 98:2 (2011): 338–61.

Hamdan, Gamal. *Ṣafaḥāt min awrāqihi al-khāṣṣa: mudhakkirāt fī al-jughrāfiyā al-siyāsiyya.* Cairo: Dār al-Ghad al-ʿArabi, 1996.

———. *Shakhṣiyat Misr: dirāsa fī ʿabqariyat al-makān.* Cairo: ʿAlam al-Kutub, 1984.

Hamilton, James. *Wanderings in North Africa.* London: J. Murray, 1856.

Hanley, Will. *Identifying with Nationality: Europeans, Ottomans, and Egyptians in Alexandria.* New York: Columbia University Press, 2017.

———. "Papers for Going, Papers for Staying: Identification and Subject Formation in the Eastern Mediterranean." In *A Global Middle East: Mobility, Materiality, and Culture in the Modern Age, 1880–1940,* edited by Liat Kozma, Avner Wishnitzer, and Cyrus Schayegh, 177–200. London: I. B. Tauris, 2015.

Hanotaux, Gabriel. *Histoire de la nation égyptienne.* Paris: Société de l'Histoire Nationale, 1931.

Harley, J. B. *The New Nature of Maps: Essays in the History of Cartography.* Baltimore: Johns Hopkins University Press, 2001.

Harvey, David. "Between Space and Time: Reflections on the Geographical Imagination." *Annals of the Association of American Geographers* 80:3 (1990): 418–34.

———. "Space as a Keyword." In *David Harvey: A Critical Reader,* edited by Noel Castree and Derek Gregory, 270–93. Oxford: Blackwell, 2006.

Hashaʾishi, Muhammad. *Voyage au pays des Senoussia à travers la Tripolitaine et les pays Touareg.* Paris: Challamel, 1903.

Hassanein, Ahmed. *The Lost Oases.* Edited by Michael Haag. Cairo: American University in Cairo Press, 2006 [1925].

Hilmi, Ahmed, and Ismail Cömert. *Senûsîler ve Sultan Abdülhamid: asr-ı Hamîdî'de âlem-i İslâm ve Senûsîler.* Istanbul: Ses Yayınları, 1992.

Hobbs, William H. "A Pilgrimage in Northeastern Africa, with Studies of Desert Conditions." *Geographical Review* 3:5 (1917): 346.

Hohler, T. B. *Report on the Oasis of Siva.* Cairo: n.p., 1900.

Hoskins, G. A. *Visit to the Great Oasis of the Libyan Desert; with an Account, Ancient and Modern, of the Oasis of Amun, and the Other Oases Now Under the Dominion of the Pasha of Egypt.* London: Longman, Rees, Orme, Brown, Green & Longman, 1837.

Hrdlička, Aleš. *The Natives of Kharga Oasis, Egypt.* Washington, D.C.: Smithsonian Institution, 1912.

Hubbard, Phil, Rob Kitchin, and Gill Valentine, eds. *Key Thinkers on Space and Place.* London: Sage Publications, 2004.

Hunter, Robert F. *Egypt Under the Khedives, 1805–1879: From Household Government to Modern Bureaucracy.* Cairo, Egypt: American University in Cairo Press, 1984.

Hurşîd, Mehmed. *Seyâhatnâme-i hudûd.* Istanbul: Simurg Kitapçılık ve Yayıncılık, 1997.

Jackson, Robert H. *Quasi-States: Sovereignty, International Relations, and the Third World.* Cambridge: Cambridge University Press, 1990.

Jacob, Wilson Chacko. *Working Out Egypt: Effendi Masculinity and Subject Formation in Colonial Modernity, 1870–1940.* Durham, N.C.: Duke University Press, 2011.

Jakes, Aaron G. "The Scales of Public Utility: Agricultural Roads and State Space in the Era of the British Occupation." In *The Long 1890s in Egypt: Colonial Quiescence, Subterranean Resistance,* edited by Marilyn Booth and Anthony Gorman, 57–86. Edinburgh: Edinburgh University Press, 2013.

———. "State of the Field: Agrarian Transformation, Colonial Rule, and the Politics of Material Wealth in Egypt, 1882–1914." Ph.D. diss., New York University, 2015.

Jarvis, C. S. *Desert and Delta.* London: J. Murray, 1938.

———. *Three Deserts.* New York: E. P. Dutton, 1937.

Jennings-Bramly, Wilfred. "A Journey from Farafra to Siwa, 1898." *Geographical Journal* 19:1 (1902): 73–75.

———. "A Journey to Siwa in September and October, 1896." *Geographical Journal* 10:6 (1897): 597–608.

Jeppie, Shamil. "Constructing a Colony on the Nile, circa 1820–1870." Ph.D. diss., Princeton University, 1996.

Jobbins, Jenny and Mary Megalli. *Alexandria and the Egyptian Mediterranean: A Traveler's Guide.* Cairo: American University in Cairo Press, 2006.

Judson, Pieter M. *Guardians of the Nation: Activists on the Language Frontiers of Imperial Austria.* Cambridge, Mass.: Harvard University Press, 2007.

Kafadar, Cemal. *Between Two Worlds: The Construction of the Ottoman State.* Berkeley: University of California Press, 1996.

Karasapan, Celal Tevfik. *Libya: Trablusgarp, Bingazi ve Fizan.* Ankara: Resimli Posta Matbaasi, 1960.

Karpat, Kemal H., and Robert Zens, eds. *Ottoman Borderlands: Issues, Personalities, and Political Changes.* Madison: University of Wisconsin Press, 2003.

Kasaba, Reşat. "Dreams of Empire, Dreams of Nations." In *Empire to Nation: Historical Perspectives on the Making of the Modern World,* edited by Joseph Esherick, Hasan Kayali and Eric Van Young, 198–225. Lanham, Md.: Rowman & Littlefield, 2006.

———. *A Moveable Empire: Ottoman Nomads, Migrants, and Refugees.* Seattle: University of Washington Press, 2009.

Kashani-Sabet, Firoozeh. *Frontier Fictions: Shaping the Iranian Nation, 1804–1946.* Princeton, N.J.: Princeton University Press, 1999.

Kaufman, Asher. *Contested Frontiers in the Syria-Lebanon-Israel Region: Cartography, Sovereignty, and Conflict.* Washington, D.C.: Woodrow Wilson Center Press, 2014.

Keene, Edward. *Beyond the Anarchical Society: Grotius, Colonialism, and Order in World Politics.* Cambridge: Cambridge University Press, 2002.

Kennett, Austin. *Bedouin Justice: Laws and Customs Among the Egyptian Bedouin.* Cambridge: Cambridge University Press, 1925.

Kezer, Zeynep, "Spatializing Difference: The Making of an Internal Border in Early Republican Elazığ (Turkey*).*" *Journal of the Society of Architectural Historians* 73:4 (2014): 507–27.

Khashshab, Ulfat. *Tārīkh taṭawwur ḥudūd Miṣr: wa-ta'thīruhu 'alā al-amn al-qawmī al-Miṣri, 1892–1988*. Cairo: Dār al-Shurūq, 2008.

Khoury, Dina Rizk. *State and Provincial Society in the Ottoman Empire: Mosul, 1540–1834.* Cambridge: Cambridge University Press, 1997.

Khoury, Philip S., and Joseph Kostiner, eds. *Tribes and State Formation in the Middle East.* Berkeley: University of California Press, 1990.

King, William Joseph Harding. *Mysteries of the Libyan Desert: A Record of Three Years of Exploration.* London: Seeley, Service, and Co., 1925.

Klein, Janet. *The Margins of Empire: Kurdish Militias in the Ottoman Tribal Zone.* Stanford, Calif.: Stanford University Press, 2011.

Klippel, Ernst. *Études sur le folklore bédouin de l'Égypte.* Cairo: Imprimerie Nationale, 1911.

Kuehn, Thomas. *Empire, Islam, and Politics of Difference: Ottoman Rule in Yemen, 1849–1919.* Leiden: Brill, 2011.

Labanca, Nicola. *Oltremare: Storia dell'espansione coloniale italiana.* Bologna: Società Editrice il Mulino, 2002.

Laoust, Emile. *Siwa.* Paris: E. Leroux, 1931.

Leclant, Jean. *Oasis: Histoire d'un mot.* Paris: Guethner, 1993.

Lefebvre, Henri. *The Production of Space.* Oxford: Blackwell, 1991.

Le Gall, Michel. "The Ottoman Government and the Sanusiyya: A Reappraisal." *International Journal of Middle East Studies* 21:1 (1989): 91–106.

———. "Ottoman Reaction to the European 'Scramble for Africa': The Defense of the Hinterland of Tripolitania and Cyrenaica." *Asian and African Studies* 24 (1990): 109–35.

———. "Pashas, Bedouins, and Notables: Ottoman Administration in Tripoli and Benghazi, 1881–1902." Ph.D. diss., Princeton University, 1986.

Le Gall, Michel, and Kenneth Perkins, eds. *The Maghrib in Question: Essays in History and Historiography.* Austin: University of Texas Press, 1997.

Lockman, Zachary, "Imagining the Working Class: Culture, Nationalism, and Class Formation in Egypt, 1899–1914." *Poetics Today* 15:2 (1994): 157–90.

Lombard, Louisa. "Raiding Sovereignty in Central African Borderlands." Ph.D. diss., Duke University, 2012.

Lovell, Nadia, ed. *Locality and Belonging.* London: Routledge, 1998.

Lowry, Heath. *The Nature of the Early Ottoman State.* Albany: State University of New York Press, 2003.

Ludden, David. "India's Development Regime." In *Colonialism and Culture*, edited by Nicholas Dirks, 247–87. Ann Arbor: University of Michigan Press, 1992.

———. "Presidential Address: Maps in the Mind and the Mobility of Asia." *Journal of Asian Studies* 62:4 (2003): 1057–78.

Lugard, F. D. *The Dual Mandate in British Tropical Africa.* Edinburgh: W. Blackwood and Sons, 1922.

Lydon, Ghislaine. *On Trans-Saharan Trails: Islamic Law, Trade Networks, and Cross-Cultural*

*Exchange in Nineteenth-Century Western Africa.* Cambridge: Cambridge University Press, 2009.

Lyons, H. G. *The Cadastral Survey of Egypt, 1892–1907.* Cairo: National Printing Department, 1908.

———. *The History of Surveying and Land-Measurement in Egypt.* Cairo: National Printing Department, 1907.

Mahmud, Mohammad. *Siwan Customs.* Cambridge, Mass.: Harvard University Press, 1917.

Maier, Charles S. "Consigning the Twentieth Century to History: Alternative Narratives for the Modern Era." *American Historical Review* 105:3 (2000): 807–31.

———. *Leviathan 2.0: Inventing Modern Statehood.* Cambridge, Mass.: The Belknap Press of Harvard University Press, 2012.

———. *Once Within Borders: Territories of Power, Wealth, and Belonging Since 1500.* Cambridge, Mass.: The Belknap Press of Harvard University Press, 2016.

———. "Transformations in Territoriality, 1600–2000." In *Transnationale Geschichte: Themen, Tendenzen und Theorien,* edited by Gunilla Budde, Sebastian Conrad, and Oliver Janz, 32–55. Göttingen, Germany: Vandenhoeck & Ruprecht, 2006.

Makdisi, Ussama. *The Culture of Sectarianism: Community, History, and Violence in Nineteenth-Century Ottoman Lebanon.* Berkeley: University of California Press, 2000.

———. "Ottoman Orientalism." *American Historical Review* 107:3 (2002): 768–96.

Mamdani, Mahmood. *Citizen and Subject: Contemporary Africa and the Legacy of Late Colonialism.* Princeton, N.J.: Princeton University Press, 1996.

Martin, B. G. *Muslim Brotherhoods in Nineteenth-Century Africa.* Cambridge: Cambridge University Press, 1976.

McDougall, James. "Frontiers, Borderlands, and Saharan/World History." In *Saharan Frontiers: Space and Mobility in Northwest Africa,* edited by James McDougall and Judith Scheele, 73–90. Bloomington: Indiana University Press, 2012.

McGuirk, Russell. *The Sanusi's Little War: The Amazing Story of a Forgotten Conflict in the Western Desert, 1915–1917.* London: Arabian Publications, 2007.

Messick, Brinkley. *The Calligraphic State: Textual Domination and History in a Muslim Society.* Berkeley: University of California Press, 1996.

Migdal, Joel, ed. *Boundaries and Belonging: States and Societies in the Struggle to Shape Identities and Local Practices.* Cambridge: Cambridge University Press, 2004.

Mikhail, Alan. *Nature and Empire in Ottoman Egypt: An Environmental History.* Cambridge: Cambridge University Press, 2011.

Milad, Salwa. *Wathā'iq al-wāḥāt al-Misriyya: dirāsa wa-nashr wa-taḥqīq.* Cairo: Maṭba'at Dār al-Kutub wa-l-Wathā'iq al-Qawmiyya bi-l-Qahira, 2003.

Minawi, Mostafa. *The Ottoman Scramble for Africa: Empire and Diplomacy in the Sahara and the Hijaz.* Stanford, Calif.: Stanford University Press, 2016.

Minkin, Shane. "Documenting Death: Inquests, Governance, and Belonging in 1890s Alexandria." In *The Long 1890s in Egypt: Colonial Quiescence, Subterranean Resistance,* edited by Marilyn Booth and Anthony Gorman, 31–56. Edinburgh: Edinburgh University Press, 2014.

———. "In Life as in Death: The Port, Foreign Charities, Hospitals, and Cemeteries in Alexandria, Egypt, 1865–1914." Ph.D. diss., New York University, 2009.

Mitchell, Timothy. *Colonising Egypt*. Cambridge: Cambridge University Press, 1988.

———. "The Limits of the State: Beyond Statist Approaches and Their Critics." *American Political Science Review* 85:1 (1991): 77–96.

———. *Rule of Experts: Egypt, Techno-Politics, Modernity*. Berkeley: University of California Press, 2002.

Mohsen, Safia Kassem. *Conflict and Law Among Awlad 'Ali of the Western Desert*. Cairo: National Center for Social and Criminological Research, 1975.

———. *Quest for Order Among Awlad Ali of the Western Desert of Egypt*. Ann Arbor: University of Microfilms International, 1983.

Mubarak, 'Ali. *al-Khiṭaṭ al-Tawfiqiyya al-jadīda li-Misr al-Qahira wa-muduniha wa-bilādiha al-qadīma wa-l-shahīra*. Cairo: al-Maṭbaʿa al-Kubrā al-Amīriyya, 1886–88.

Muhsin, Muhammet. *Afrika Delili*. Cairo: el-Fellah Ceridesi Matbaası, 1896.

Munier, Henri. *La Société Royale de Géographie d'Égypte: Guide du visiteur*. Cairo: E. & R. Schindler, 1934.

Murray, G. W. *Dare Me to the Desert*. London: Allen & Unwin, 1967.

———. *The Egyptian Desert and its Antiquity*. Cairo: Survey of Egypt, 1950.

———. *Sons of Ishmael: A Study of the Egyptian Bedouin*. London: G. Routledge & Sons, 1935.

———. *The Survey of Egypt, 1898–1948*. Cairo: Ministry of Finance and Survey of Egypt, 1950.

Neep, Daniel. "State-Space Beyond Territory: Wormholes, Gravitational Fields, and Entanglement." *Journal of Historical Sociology* (2016).

Neumann, Boaz. *Land and Desire in Early Zionism*. Waltham, Mass.: Brandeis University Press, 2011.

Novak, Paolo. "The Flexible Territoriality of Borders," *Geopolitics* 16 (2011): 741–67.

Obermeyer, Gerald Joseph. *Structure and Authority in a Bedouin Tribe: The 'Aishaibat of the Western Desert of Egypt*. New Haven, Conn.: Human Relations Area Files, 1969.

Omar, Hussein. "The Rule of Strangers: Political Ideas in Khedival Egypt, 1869–1914." Ph.D. diss., University of Oxford, 1914.

O'Shea, Maria T. "The Demarcation of the Turco/Persian Border." In *The Boundaries of Modern Iran*, edited by K. McLachlan, 47–57. New York: St. Martin's Press, 1994.

Osterhammel, Jürgen. *The Transformation of the World: A Global History of the Nineteenth Century*. Princeton, N.J.: Princeton University Press, 2014.

Owen, Roger. *State, Power, and Politics in the Making of the Modern Middle East*. London: Routledge, 1992.

Pacho, J. R. *Relation d'un voyage dans la Marmarique, la Cyrénique, et les Oasis d'Audjelah et de Maradéh*. Paris: Firmin Didot, 1827.

Pallini, Cristina, and Annalisa Riccarda Scaccabarozzi. "British Planning Schemes for Alexandria and Its Region, 1834–1958." In *Urban Planning in North Africa*, edited by Carlos Nunez Silva, 187–204. New York: Ashgate, 2016.

Peacock, A. C. S., ed. *The Frontiers of the Ottoman World*. Oxford: Oxford University Press, 2009.

Pellow, Deborah, ed. *Setting Boundaries: The Anthropology of Spatial and Social Organization*. Westport, Conn.: Bergin & Garvey, 1996.

Perdue, Peter. *China Marches West: The Qing Conquest of Central Eurasia*. Cambridge, Mass.: Harvard University Press, 2005.

Peters, Rudolph. "Body and Spirit of Islamic Law: *Madhhab* Diversity in Ottoman Documents from Dakhla Oasis, Egypt." In *Islamic Law in Theory: Studies on Jurisprudence in Honor of Bernard Weiss*, edited by A. Kevin Reinhart and Robert Gleave, 317–30. Leiden: Brill, 2014.

————. *Wathāʾiq madīnat al-Qasr bi-l-wāḥāt al-Dakhla maṣdaran li-tārīkh Misr fī al-ʿaṣr al-ʿUthmāni*. Cairo: Dār al-Kutub wa-l-Wathāʾiq al-Qawmiyya, 2011.

Pollard, Lisa. *Nurturing the Nation: The Family Politics of Modernizing, Colonizing, and Liberating Egypt (1805–1923)*. Berkeley: University of California Press, 2005.

Powell, Eve Troutt. *A Different Shade of Colonialism: Egypt, Great Britain, and the Mastery of the Sudan*. Berkeley: University of California Press, 2003.

Prescott, J. R. V. *The Geography of Frontiers and Boundaries*. Chicago: Aldine Publishing, 1965.

————. *Political Frontiers and Boundaries*. London: Allen & Unwin, 1987.

Quhayba, ʿAbd al-Fattah Muhammad. *Dirāsāt fī jughrāfiyat Misr al-tārīkhiyya*. Alexandria, Egypt: Muʾassasat al-Thaqāfa al-Jāmiʿiyya, 1962.

Ranger, Terence. "The Invention of Tradition in Colonial Africa." In *The Invention of Tradition*, edited by E. J. Hobsbawm and T. O. Ranger, 211–62. Cambridge: Cambridge University Press, 1983.

Reid, Donald. "The Egyptian Geographical Society: From Foreign Laymen's Society to Indigenous Professional Associaton." *Poetics Today* 14:3 (1993): 539–72.

Reimer, Michael. *Colonial Bridgehead: Government and Society in Alexandria, 1807–1882*. Boulder, Colo.: Westview Press, 1997.

Reynolds, Nancy. "Building the Past: Rockscapes and the Aswan High Dam in Egypt." In *Water on Sand: Environmental Histories of the Middle East and North Africa*, edited by Alan Mikhail, 181–206. New York: Oxford University Press, 2013.

Rieker, Martina. "The Saʿid and the City: Subaltern Spaces in the Making of Modern Egyptian History." Ph.D. diss., Temple University, 1997.

Rifaʿi, Husayn ʿAli. *Wāḥat Siwa min al-nawāḥi al-tārīkhiyya wa-l-jughrāfiyya wa-l-ijtimāʿiyya wa-l-iqtiṣādiyya*. Cairo: al-Maṭbaʿa al-Amīriyya, 1932.

Rodoslu, Ebülmuzaffer. *Trablusgarp ahvali: yeni dünya*. Istanbul: Ahmet İhsan ve Sürekâsı Matbaacılık Osmanlı Şirketi, 1911.

Rogan, Eugene. "Aşiret Mektebi: Abdülhamid II's School for Tribes (1892–1907)." *International Journal of Middle East Studies* 28:1 (1996): 83–107.

————. *Frontiers of the State in the Late Ottoman Empire: Transjordan, 1850–1921*. Cambridge: Cambridge University Press, 1999.

Rumley, Dennis, and Julian V. Minghi, eds. *The Geography of Border Landscapes*. London: Routledge, 1991.

Rusch, Walter, and Lothar Stein, eds. *Siwa und die Aulad Ali: Darstellung und Analyse der sozialökonomischen, politische und ethnischen Entwicklung der Bevölkerung der westlichen Wüste Ägyptens und des Prozesses ihrer Integration in den Ägyptischen Staat von Beginn des 19. Jahrhunderts bis 1976*. Berlin: Akademie, 1988.

Russell, Mona. *Creating the New Egyptian Woman: Consumerism, Education, and National Identity, 1863–1922*. New York: Palgrave Macmillan, 2004.

Russell, Thomas Wentworth. *Egyptian Service, 1902–1946*. London: J. Murray, 1949.

Ryan, Simon. *The Cartographic Eye: How Explorers Saw Australia*. Cambridge: Cambridge University Press, 1996.

Ryzova, Lucie. *The Age of the Efendiyya: Passages to Modernity in National-Colonial Egypt*. Oxford: Oxford University Press, 2014.

Sack, Robert. *Human Territoriality: Its Theory and History*. Cambridge: Cambridge University Press, 1986.

Safi al-Din, Muhammad, Ahmad Salih Zahid, and Muhammad Mahmud Sayyad. *Dirāsāt fī jughrāfiyat Misr*. Cairo: Maktabat Misr, 1957.

Sahlins, Peter. *Boundaries: The Making of France and Spain in the Pyrenees*. Berkeley: University of California Press, 1989.

Salzmann, Ariel. *Tocqueville in the Ottoman Empire: Rival Paths to the Modern State*. Leiden: Brill, 2004.

Sandes, E. W. C. *The Royal Engineers in Egypt and the Sudan*. Chatham, England: Institution of Royal Engineers, 1937.

Sayyid-Marsot, Afaf Lutfi. *Egypt and Cromer: A Study in Anglo-Egyptian Relations*. New York: Praeger, 1969.

Schama, Simon. *Landscape and Memory*. New York: Alfred A. Knopf, 1995.

Schayegh, Cyrus. "The Many Worlds of 'Abud Yasin; or, What Narcotics Trafficking in the Interwar Middle East Can Tell Us About Territorialization." *American Historical Review* 116:2 (2011): 273–306.

Schilcher, Linda S. "Violence in Rural Syria in the 1880s and 1890s." In *Peasants and Politics in the Modern Middle East*, edited by Farhad Kazemi and John Waterbury. Miami: Florida International University Press, 1991.

Schofield, Clive, and Richard Schofield, eds. *The Middle East and North Africa: World Boundaries Volume 2*. London: Routledge, 1994.

Scholz, J. Martin Augustin. *Travels in the Countries Between Alexandria and Paraetonium: The Lybian Desert, Siwa, Egypt, Palestine, and Syria, in 1821*. London: R. Phillips, 1822.

Scott, James C. *The Art of Not Being Governed: An Anarchist History of Upland Southeast Asia*. New Haven, Conn.: Yale University Press, 2009.

———. *Seeing Like a State: How Certain Schemes to Improve the Human Condition Have Failed*. New Haven, Conn.: Yale University Press, 1998.

Shafiq, Ahmad. *Mudhakkirāt 'an wāḥāt Misr wa-l-Sahra al-Gharbiyya*. Cairo: al-Maṭbaʿa al-Amīriyya, 1929.

———. *Mudhakkirātī fī nisf al-qarn*. Cairo: Maṭbaʿat Misr, 1934.

Shechter, Relli. *Smoking, Culture, and Economy in the Middle East: The Egyptian Tobacco Market, 1850–2000*. London: I. B. Tauris, 2006.

Sheehan, James J. "The Problem of Sovereignty." *American Historical Review* 111:1 (2006): 1–15.

Simon, Rachel. *Libya Between Ottomanism and Nationalism: The Ottoman Involvement in Libya During the War with Italy (1911–1919).* Berlin: K. Schwarz, 1987.

Simpson, G. E. *The Heart of Libya: The Siwa Oasis, Its People, Customs and Sport.* London: H. F. & G. Witherby, 1929.

Skovgaard-Petersen, Jakob. *Defining Islam for the Egyptian State: Muftis and Fatwas of the Dār al-Iftā.* Leiden: Brill, 1997.

Stanley, C. V. B. "The Oasis of Siwa." *Journal of the Royal African Society* 11:43 (1912): 290–324.

———. *A Report on the Oasis of Siwa.* Cairo: Government Press, 1912.

Stein, Mark. *Guarding the Frontier: Ottoman Border Forts and Garrisons in Europe.* London: Tauris Academic Studies, 2007.

Steele, Diana, and Laura Zanotti. "Contested Border Crossings: Territorialities in the Brazilian and Peruvian Amazon." In *Negotiating Territoriality: Spatial Dialogues Between State and Tradition,* edited by Allan C. Dawson, Laura Zanotti and Ismael Vaccaro, 99–113. New York: Routledge, 2014.

Stewart, Frank. *Bedouin Boundaries in Central Sinai and the Southern Negev: A Document from the Ahaywat Tribe.* Wiesbaden, Germany: O. Harrassowitz, 1986.

Taher, Baha'a. *Sunset Oasis (Wāḥat al-ghurūb).* Translated by Humphrey Davies. London: Sceptre, 2010.

Talhami, Ghada Hashem. *Suakin and Massawa Under Egyptian Rule, 1865–1885.* Washington, D.C.: University Press of America, 1979.

Tapper, Richard. *Frontier Nomads of Iran: A Political and Social History of the Shahsevan.* Cambridge: Cambridge University Press, 1997.

Tegani, Ulderico. *Bengàsi: Studio coloniale.* Milan: Casa Editrice Sonzogno, 1922.

Tezcan, Baki. *The Second Ottoman Empire: Political and Social Transformation in the Early Modern World.* New York: Cambridge University Press, 2010.

Toledano, Ehud. *State and Society in Mid-Nineteenth-Century Egypt.* Cambridge: Cambridge University Press, 1990.

Toussoun, Omar. *La géographie de l'Égypte à l'époque arabe.* Cairo: L'Imprimerie de l'Institut Français d'Archéologie Orientale pour la Société Royale de Géographie d'Égypte, 1926.

Truett, Samuel, and Elliot Young. "Making Transnational History: Nations, Regions, and Borderlands." In *Continental Crossroads: Remapping US-Mexico Borderlands History,* edited by Samuel Truett and Elliott Young, 1–32. Durham, N.C.: Duke University Press, 2004.

Vaccaro, Ismael, Allan Charles Dawson, and Laura Zanotti. "Negotiating Territoriality: Spatial Dialogues Between State and Tradition." In *Negotiating Territoriality: Spatial Dialogues Between State and Tradition,* edited by Allan C. Dawson, Laura Zanotti and Ismael Vaccaro, 1–17. New York: Routledge, 2014.

Vandewalle, Dirk J. *A History of Modern Libya.* Cambridge: Cambridge University Press, 2006.

Vikør, Knut. *Sufi and Scholar on the Desert Edge: Muhammad b. ʿAli al-Sanūsī and His Brotherhood*. London: Hurst, 1995.

Vivian, Cassandra. *The Western Desert of Egypt: An Explorer's Handbook*. Cairo: American University in Cairo Press, 2008.

Wakid, ʿAbd al-Latif. *Wāḥāt Misr: juzur al-raḥma wa-jannat al-Sahra*. Cairo: Maktabat al-Anjlū al-Misriyya, 1957.

Walker, W. Seymour. "An Outline of Modern Exploration in the Oasis of Siwa." *Geographical Journal* 57:1 (1921): 29–34.

Warf, Barney, and Santa Arias, eds. *The Spatial Turn: Interdisciplinary Perspectives*. London: Routledge, 2009.

Weber, Eugen. *Peasants into Frenchmen: The Modernization of Rural France, 1870–1914*. Stanford, Calif.: Stanford University Press, 1976.

Wendell, Charles. *The Evolution of the Egyptian National Image: From Its Origins to Ahmad Lutfi al-Sayyid*. Berkeley: University of California Press, 1972.

White, Arthur Silva. *From Sphinx to Oracle; Through the Libyan Desert to the Oasis of Jupiter Ammon*. London: Hurst and Blackett, 1899.

Whitehouse, Frederick Cope. *The Raiyān Moeris*. New York: Press of Clark and Zugalla, 1890.

Wick, Alexis. *The Red Sea: In Search of Lost Space*. Berkeley: University of California Press, 2016.

Winichakul, Thongchai. *Siam Mapped: A History of the Geo-Body of a Nation*. Honolulu: University of Hawaii Press, 1994.

Winlock, Herbert. *Ed Dakhleh Oasis: Journal of a Camel Trip Made in 1908*. New York: Metropolitan Museum of Art, 1936.

Winter, Michael. *Egyptian Society Under Ottoman Rule, 1517–1798*. London: Routledge, 1992.

Wood, Denis. "How Maps Work." *Cartographica* 29:3–4 (1992): 66–74.

———. *The Power of Maps*. New York: Guilford Press, 1992.

Wood, Leonard. *Islamic Legal Revival: Reception of European Law and Transformations in Islamic Legal Thought in Egypt, 1875–1952*. Oxford: Oxford University Press, 2016.

Worsfold, Basil W. *The Redemption of Egypt*. London: George Allen, 1899.

Yerasimos, Stephane. "Comment furent tracées les frontières actuelles au Proche-Orient." *Herodote* 41:2 (1986): 123–61.

Yosmaoğlu, Ipek. "Constructing National Identity in Ottoman Macedonia." In *Understanding Life in the Borderlands: Boundaries in Depth and in Motion*, edited by Ira William Zartman, 160–88. Athens: University of Georgia Press, 2010.

Zartman, Ira Z., ed. *Understanding Life in the Borderlands: Boundaries in Depth and in Motion*. Athens: University of Georgia Press, 2010.

Ziadeh, Nicola. *Sanusiyah: A Study of a Revivalist Movement in Islam*. Leiden: Brill, 1958.

# Index

Printed and bound by CPI Group (UK) Ltd, Croydon, CR0 4YY

09/06/2025

14685866-0001